Michael Rodegang Drescher
Poets of Protest

American Culture Studies | Volume 18

In Liebe und Dankbarkeit Lucy und Christian gewidmet.

Michael R. Drescher (Dr.) teaches American literature at the University of Heidelberg. His research interests include democracy and aesthetics, cognition, consciousness, and genre theory.

Michael Rodegang Drescher

Poets of Protest

Mythological Resignification in American Antebellum and German Vormärz Literature

[transcript]

So we beat on, boats against the current, borne back ceaselessly into the past
(Fitzgerald/The Great Gatsby).

Bibliographic information published by the Deutsche Nationalbibliothek
The Deutsche Nationalbibliothek lists this publication in the Deutsche Nationalbibliografie; detailed bibliographic data are available in the Internet at http://dnb.d-nb.de

© 2017 transcript Verlag, Bielefeld

All rights reserved. No part of this book may be reprinted or reproduced or utilized in any form or by any electronic, mechanical, or other means, now known or hereafter invented, including photocopying and recording, or in any information storage or retrieval system, without permission in writing from the publisher.

Cover layout: Kordula Röckenhaus, Bielefeld
Printed in Germany
Print-ISBN 978-3-8376-3745-8
PDF-ISBN 978-3-8394-3745-2

Table of Contents

Acknowledgements | 7

1. Introduction:
The Nature of Myth and Mythological Resignification | 9

THE PUSHING OF HORIZONS

2. Nathaniel Hawthorne's *The Scarlet Letter*
and the Opening of Fences | 33

2.1 From Crime to Heresy: The New England Witch as Transgressor | 34
2.2 Puritan Fathers and the Treatment of Dissent | 42
2.3 The Order of Roses | 62
2.4 The Recuperation of Mercy and the 3Foundations of Civil Society | 81

3. Karl Gutzkow's *Wally, die Zweiflerin*
and the Despair of Artificiality | 105

3.1 Germanic Myths and the Aesthetics of *Das Junge Deutschland* | 106
3.2 The Abandoned Lovers and the Wails of *Weltschmerz* | 114
3.3 The Skeptical Maiden and the Rules of the Game | 131
3.4 The Signue Myth and Alternative Paths to Salvation | 141
3.5 Cäsar and the Conquest of Individuality | 162

THE TREADING OF PATHWAYS

4. William Wells Brown's *Clotel*
and the Puritan Voyage Reversed | 173

4.1 Establishing Individuality and the Roads towards Freedom | 174
4.2 The Puritan Voyage Reversed | 181
4.3 The Revolutionary Emigrant and Europa the Free | 200
4.4 The Naturalization of National Identity | 212

**5. Heinrich Heine's *Wintermärchen*
and the Laughter of the Age** | 219

5.1 A New Song and the Silencing of Death-Knells | 220
5.2 Dreaming Freedom and the Dethroning of Saints | 238
5.3 The Sleeping Kaiser and the Sealing of Graves | 253
5.4 The Song of Joy and Germany's Future | 266

**6. Conclusion:
The Rewriting of Foundations** | 283

Works Cited | 303

Acknowledgements

The present study, a doctoral dissertation completed at the University of Heidelberg, is not only the result of my own exertions. It has been made possible by a number of people and institutions that have guided, supported, and inspired me along the way. My gratefulness to my family and their unwavering faith in my endeavors needs no elaboration. The most heartfelt gratitude goes to my supervisor Günter Leypoldt for his exemplary, warm, and unfailing support of my work. Also, to the Heidelberg Center of American Studies, especially to Dietmar Schloss, Martin Thunert, and Tobias Endler for their ongoing and much needed support and counsel, my sincerest gratitude.

I further wish to thank the German National Academic Foundation for making me part of an inspiring community and for their financial and academic support throughout this entire project. Also, I thank the Heidelberg Graduate Academy for a stipend which has enabled me to complete this study without last-minute worries. Moreover, I would like to express my gratitude to Harvard's English Department, especially to Werner Sollors for his welcoming supervision during my time in Cambridge, Massachusetts. In addition, a warm and sincere thank you to Harvard's Institute for Folklore and Mythology for taking me in with open arms, especially to Stephen Mitchell, whose guidance and input are and remain much appreciated.

For graciously undertaking the enormous task of proofreading, I wish to thank Wiebke Beushausen and Lennart Keding. And finally, to a legion of loved ones, friends, and colleagues, all of which have inspired, aided, criticized, and borne with me for the last years: You must go unmentioned but shall ever be deeply, truly appreciated.

1. Introduction
The Nature of Myth and Mythological Resignification

> Every story gives an Achilles' heel to sheer power.
> BLUMENBERG/WORK ON MYTH

In 1833, Rufus Choate called upon the inhabitants of Salem, Massachusetts. Choate, a lawyer and politician, was touring the country so as to inspire in his fellow citizens a sense of urgency. Like many of his contemporaries, he felt that the nation was slipping. He was aware of the fact that national unity was slowly giving way to the pressures and divisions of the Antebellum period. In this age of societal unrest, political controversy, and cultural insecurity, he urged his audiences to stand against the problems that threatened the union. Interestingly, he did not elaborate on political or legal factors but invoked a cultural force: the power of literature.

Choate claimed that the "significant American romance" had not yet been written and lamented the fact that the U.S. lacked a literary work which would speak directly to the "affections and imagination of the whole people" (in Boudreau 338). A romance, he argued, would have the power to unify the nation. Such a romance would have to be historical: It would have to look to the past, thereby "taking the people closer to the source of their common experiences." This, Choate hoped, would help "to heal the wounds caused by diversity" and "recreate one people" (Boudreau 339). In sum, he called for a national literature: Literary works that would unify the nation by giving the people a sense of their origins, their common values, and their shared destiny. He was, in fact, calling for myth. Mythological literature was to excavate, reflect, and *create* national identity. In this context, he drew an interesting comparison: Choate regarded the national myths of the Greeks as "great Waverley Novels" (11). The time had come, he claimed, for the American "Iliad and Odyssey" (12).

As topic of such a national myth, Choate envisioned a specific literary material: the Puritan character.[1] The novelist should return to this "heroic age" and highlight Puritanism's *"human* influences" (Choate 2, 22). These secular notions might be relied upon to guide the nation through the crisis (Boudreau 339). Thus, by remembering the Puritan fathers, modern, more secular Americans would be reminded of their origin, their mission, and their common patriotic duty. Such a novel's focus was to lie on the "infant people" of the Unites States (Choate 22, 17). The "founders of the race", however, were to stand side by side with the Revolutionary fathers, those who "walked hand in hand together through the valley of Death in the War of Independence" (24, 37). An American romance, Choate hoped, would effect the changes in the national mindset to "perpetuate the Union itself." It would constitute an "ancestral recollection," a "fountain for the healing of the nations" that could render the union indivisible: "Reminded of our fathers, we should remember that we are all brethren" (36f).

In the following decades, many an author would answer Choate's call, but they would not merely reflect a historical past. In their writing, novelists included the demands of the future and thus rewrote the present. This was, however, not restricted to America. A similar development occurred on the other side of the Atlantic.

Also in 1833, a young writer and scholar returned to his alma mater in Kiel to lecture on aesthetics. Indeed, it would be his first and last engagement as lecturer. But Ludolf Wienbarg would continue to work as a publisher, writer, and journalist, although his efforts increasingly attracted statist persecution. The famous Bundestag prohibition of 1835 against the Young Germans would seriously dampen his creative endeavors. Nevertheless, the literary movement which the 1835 prohibition sought to crush takes its name from Wienbarg's lectures at the University of Kiel. *Aesthetische Feldzüge* [Aesthetic Crusades], published 1834 in Hamburg, is devoted to the vision of a united, free, and democratic Germany. On the title page, he dedicates the book to "the young Germany"[2] (Wienbarg i). The loosely connected literary group, which included Heine and Gutzkow, would henceforth be referred to as *Junges Deutschland* [Young Germany].

Like Choate, Wienbarg invokes the power of literature to transform the nation. In his dedication, he calls upon all German authors to make a choice: to either write for the old or for the new Germany. He goes on to programmatically define what

---

1   It should be noted that Choate elaborates on a second topic for the writing of a national romance, namely the fate of Native Americans during King Philip's war. Aware that modern Americans built "houses upon their graves," he calls to "preserve their history" (25). Thus, Choate offers a second, colonial subject for the writing of a national American novel.

2   [Dem jungen Deutschland gewidmet].

that choice must entail. Calling oneself liberal, for instance, is insufficient, for many who write for the nobility or for academia designate themselves as liberals (Wienbarg v). So as to write for a young and modern Germany, three steps are necessary. First, one must occupy a clear anti-feudal position and abjure the "old German nobility."[3] Second, one needs to reject an "overcome scholarliness"[4] and ban it to the "grave"[5] where it belongs. Third, one has to oppose all forms of "old German philistinism." Wienbarg's literary program rests on the elaboration of a historically informed dialectic: the old, bigoted, and decadent Germany vs. the young, free, and contemporary Germany. Like Choate, Wienbarg calls for literary endeavors so as to influence the state of the nation. He envisions a "better and more beautiful life for the people"[6] as a result (vi).

This call to literary arms seems necessary to Wienbarg, because the academic institutions, once the cultural "levers of change,"[7] have grown decadent and teach slavery instead of freedom (vi, viii). Literature, on the other hand, is deemed to possess the power to raise its voice for the establishment of something new and thus hail a cultural spring which will end the long inertia of German politics (x). Wienbarg does not prescribe a specific topic like Choate, nor does he advise looking to the past. Indeed, he rather urges his audience to look forward. But he insists on the marriage between literature and politics so as to influence history and establish a better future for the German nation.

The call for political literature is what unites Wienbarg and Choate's speeches. Both invest in literature as a vehicle for political change. At the same time, Choate explicitly calls for an archaic strategy, i.e. for the use of the past to make sense of the present. Wienbarg, in contrast, rejects all past institutions and calls for a focus on the now. Whether they excavate or reject historical narratives, Wienbarg and Choate make narratives of the past a paramount factor in the consolidation of their respective nations. The literary and political work on those narratives, more precisely described as mythologies, will occupy the study at hand.

Mythological Resignification

I am interested in how authors used mythologies for their own purposes. Traditional myths experienced a phase of conscious political rewriting in the early 19th century, and I wish to inquire as to the exact nature of that transformative semiological pro-

---

3   [altdeutschem Adel].
4   [todte Gelehrsamkeit].
5   [Grabgewölbe].
6   [besseren und schönerem Volksleben].
7   [Hebel des Umschwungs].

cess. Indeed, I hold that some authors employed a specific strategy to effect the transformation of older narratives, a transformation which resulted in myths that would be applicable to their contemporary situation. They resignified myths so as to invest them with democratic qualities, thereby furthering the dissemination of their own political ideas in the process of national identity building. This study examines the literary strategy which guided their rewriting process.

This strategy is best described as *mythological resignification*. Barthes notes that myth is related to *form* rather than to content; it is "a mode of signification" defined not by the "object of its message, but by the way it utters this message" (109). I am interested in the exact manner in which these systems of signification are transformed in order to redefine the inherent message. For the signification *is* the myth, it is the only aspect that is "consumed in actual fact." Here, Barthes relies on Saussure to parallel mythological signification and linguistic sign. The signification presents the "associative total" of myth's meaning-making process, a semiological entity which "points out" and "notifies," which makes "us understand something and imposes it on us" (113, 117). In this context, it is crucial to understand that myth, in order to function, distorts history: Its *form* is emptied of previous meaning (history, morality, geography, biography etc.) and then enriched again with a new *concept*. The concept is "at once historical and intentional," it "reconstitutes a chain of causes and effect, motives and intentions" and thus implants new meaning and knowledge in the signification (117-120).

This distortion, however, is not "obliteration." Meaning that has been distorted is "deprived of memory" but "not of existence:" Meaning can be recuperated (Barthes 122). There is always a "halo of virtualities" in the final signification of myth, a space "where other possible meanings are floating." It is in these "remains" of meaning, I argue, that *re*signification comes into play (132). By returning to lost or distorted meaning (i.e. through historical critique), old meanings can be refuted and new meanings can be installed to inform a myth. If myth is indeed speech "stolen and restored," then this act of semiological theft can be repeated (125). Thus, mythological resignification entails acts of *appropriation, transformation,* and *reinstallation* of meaning in the process of myth-making.

Relying on Barthes, I define mythological resignification as a politically informed method of writing characterized by the appropriation, transformation, and reinstallation of a mythology.[8] Mythological resignification uses a traditional civic

---

8   A number of similar approaches need to be contextualized at this point. The first is *usable past*. Tuleja notes that usable past originates with Brook's critique of commercial traditions in America (16) and shows how traditional practices can be revived and appropriated in order to suit contemporary concerns (1). Texts in this study use the past, but the semiological processes at play here are not covered by this terminology. Usable past is con-

myth, distills its core meaning (*mytheme*), and transforms or adds to that meaning so as to produce a variant myth. This variant is designed to be applicable to the contemporary situation and (like all civic myth) negotiates a national identity. Importantly, I deem mythological resignification to be a conscious political strategy to reinterpret the foundational values of a community; these acts of semiological transformation represent the pushing of a value-system by means of literature.[9]

Myths were paramount for the negotiations of nationality before the American Civil War and the German March Revolution. Some texts used mythological references for the sake of argument, imagery, or ornament (*referential treatment*). Others made use of myths in order to either confirm (*affirmative treatment*) or refute them (*critical treatment*). But there are some texts that transcend referentiality, af-

---

cerned with invention rather than evolutionary transformation; the term does not entail the transformative element that resignification insists upon. The latter is not concerned with the excavation of past material to be used in the present but with presently existent material which is transformed. Usable past, for my purposes, is too broad a term. Further, Fludernik's idea of *narrativization* describes the cognitive-constructivist notion that readers "narrativize texts as they read." In other words, they transform any given discourse into a narrative. Thus, narrativity is "projected" onto or "recognized" in the text by the reader (109). Narrativization is useful for processes that construct a narrative from pictorial/performative representations of myth. But it does not apply in the case of resignification, which illustrates the conscious transformation of an already existent narrative into a variant. Lastly, a term to which mythological resignification is highly indebted is Blumenberg's *work on myth*. Work on myth explains how Western thought has relied on transforming myths so as to explain history and communities. Blumenberg claims that "the stock of myth that has come down to us is the product, not of a reverent handing down [...], but of an unsparing process of 'natural selection.'" Myths have been "optimized," especially by storytellers, in order to adequately explain the world (Work xx). Mythological resignification is work on myth: It attempts a refinement of Blumenberg's broader argument of evolutionary transformation. While Blumenberg concerns himself largely with the anthropological function and historical-evolutionary nature of myth, mythological resignification seeks to grasp the exact narratological and semiological processes of the rewriting process.

9 Blumenberg notes that a myth may be historically given but must not present an a priori nucleus from which variants evolve. It rather presents one variant (usually the most successful variant) that has survived the test of time and societal appreciation. Thus, mythological resignification is governed by a "Darwinism of verbosity." Just as ancient myths are the result of an evolutionary process, modern myths are the result of a process of textual and oral evolution (Work 176).

firmation, and/or critique. This latter group used myth to produce new civic mythologies which were attuned to modern democratic demands.

So as to illuminate this issue, I chose four literary works for my analysis: Nathaniel Hawthorne's *The Scarlet Letter* (1851), William Wells Brown's *Clotel* (1853), Karl Gutzkow's *Wally, die Zweiflerin* (1835) and Heinrich Heine's *Deutschland. Ein Wintermärchen* (1844). Their analysis has produced the chart below. Indeed, the following is but a theorization of the strategies given in the texts and particular deviations will be discussed later. But in its essence, mythological resignification adheres to the following:

I. Work on Basic Myth:	a. Preparation
	b. Exposition
	c. Denaturalization
II. Work on Variant Myth	a. Preparation
	b. Mythemic Elaboration
	c. Naturalization

Mythological resignification begins with the basic myth (I). Here, the resignification is achieved in three steps: the preparation of the basic myth (Ia), its exposition (Ib), and its denaturalization (Ic).

In the *preparation* phase, authors recur to mythological references or design images that foreshadow the basic myth. This prepares the reader for the second step, the *exposition* of the basic myth, where the actual mythological narrative is presented. As the basic myth is given, a process of *denaturalization* begins: Historical critique is employed to reveal the mythology as mythology. Thus, the basic myth's capacity to present itself as historical is rendered mute, and the myth is revealed as either the present's nostalgic (mis)interpretation of the past or as the expression of a past overcome by the present. The main function of denaturalization is the revelation of the basic myth's incompatibility with contemporary reality and/or the revelation of the present's deviation from traditional values. Indeed, a denaturalized basic myth is no longer able to claim influence on society and a new myth needs to be constructed to fill that void. This denaturalization focuses on the basic myth's mytheme, i.e. its core meaning, which is exposed in the process.

As the basic myth is denaturalized, the variant myth is constructed (II). This construction process can also entail a preparation phase (Ia), followed by a mythemic elaboration (IIb), and a subsequent naturalization of the variant (IIc).

The *preparation* of the variant takes place at different points, sometimes after the work on the basic myth, sometimes parallel to it. In a second step, new material and meaning are infused in the making of the myth. As mentioned, the basic myth's denaturalization distills its core meaning, its mytheme. This mytheme is now unfolded, transformed, or expanded, a process best described as *mythemic elaboration*. Mythemic elaboration offers the possibility to construct a variant and results in the *naturalization* of the same. The variant is developed into a myth proper, once more blurring the lines between fiction and fact.

The process of mythological resignification as given here cannot be more than a theoretical and simplified summary of the processes evident in the texts. But the study of myth demands a precise scientific terminology. So, in order to secure a terminological clarity throughout, I will refer to the specific stages of mythological resignification using the given terms and abbreviations (e.g. exposition of basic myth [Ib], naturalization of variant myth [IIc]).

Myth is a highly complex field. At the same time, it is perhaps one of the most important and underestimated cultural forces in our societies – despite (and because of) the alleged victory of *logos* over *mythos*. Indeed, Antebellum and Vormärz authors used archaic strategies and recurred to witches, heroes, gods, and kings to further democracy. However, they rewrote myths not so much to describe the past but to affect the present. In order to do so, they constructed new, civic mythologies which are also inhabited by witches, heroes, gods, and kings but of a different, modern kind.

Myth and National Identity

So as to discuss the use of mythology to further democratization and to produce a national identity in the United States and Germany, I generally define *myth* as a narrative system of meaning which unites a chain of interlocked concepts and produces a collective and cultural identity (Barthes in O'Brien 62).[10] In defining national identity, I rely on Anderson and hold that a *nation* is an "imagined political community," a "limited" and "sovereign" communal construct. It imagines a societal "communion" and a "character" which sets it apart from other nations (6f). But

---

10 Two aspects need to be highlighted here. First, myth is a narrative system of meaning; it is permeable and subject to transformation. Second, myth produces identity, and the resignification of myth as discussed in this study aims at the construction of an American and German national identity.

while the "dawn of the nation" can be allocated in the 18th century, negotiations of what it meant to be American or German continue into the 19th and beyond (11).

Indeed, for Germany, which regarded itself as a nation without a nation-state, negotiations of national identity were paramount. Wehler notes that in the early 1800s, German elites began to develop a nationalism based on the ideas of liberalism and unity (Dynastien 167). The idea of the nation was originally carried by a bourgeois reform movement, and intellectuals and writers tried to excavate German characteristics by investigating the origin of Germans as a people. This early idea of the nation was still influenced by humanist values of freedom and equality (Scheuer 13). However, the qualities of this "Emanzipationsideologie" [ideology of emancipation] would be transformed in the course of the century, continuing the establishment of a nationality which was of such crucial concern to Vormärz culture (Eke 24, 26).

National identity was also an issue in America. Boyer notes that the U.S. – albeit a consolidated nation-state at the time – was threatened by dissent and dissolution and likewise had to negotiate a cohesive identity. Like in Germany, intellectuals and writers discussed the characteristics of what it meant to be American. But immigration, calls for cultural independence, the conflict between federal and state levels of government, and the issue of slavery fractured the young nation. The resulting threat of disunion was answered by a developing nationalism which still needed to articulate itself both politically and culturally (537). Again, national identity was central to these negotiations.[11]

Both German and American approaches to national identity rely on Hegelian ideas. While the state is imagined as the institutionalized "organization" of a community, the nation becomes synonymous with the people (*Volk*). Nationality was held to exist in peoples that are aware of themselves and of their particular "nature" (Perperzak 513). As such, the nation presents a primarily "spiritual principle," although being part of a people may also have natural (read ethnic) aspects. Nationality is believed to be a "natural phenomenon," perhaps the most basic phenomenon of human existence (514). In this context, a people is invested with a spirit (*Geist*) which has a "typical way of life and work, including intellectual and ethical abilities and customs." The nation, subsequently, presents the "incarnation of the universal spirit [*Weltgeist*], which differentiates itself in materially and psychically different configurations." The spirit of an individual nation (*Volksgeist*), then, is the expres-

---

11 Bercovitch has written on the relevance of the Puritan myth for national identity building, and my analysis of American texts is indebted to his research. His work on the Puritan myth is extensive. For more see Bercovitch: *The Office of the Scarlet Letter* (1991); *The Rites of Assent* (1993); *The Puritan Imagination* (1974); *The Puritan Origins of the American Self* (1975); *The American Jeremiad* (1978).

sion of the *Weltgeist* in a historical moment and in a specific people. While the term nation derives from Latin *nasci* (to be born) and suggests a "natural genesis," the principle that rules a people's culture and history is "spiritual:" The *Volksgeist* constitutes "the spirit of a people, which makes itself known in the national self-consciousness" (516).

Nationalism and national identity are complex and controversial terms and almost impossible to define.[12] For this study, I shall use Anderson for the term nation and rely on his concept in defining *national identity* as a set of constructed notions and characteristics which describe origin and inherent qualities of a people. National identity allows for the definition of membership in the community and thereby enables belonging and rejection. It further defines general characteristics of the people that form the nation. National identity is dynamic and governed by a complex process of societal negotiations which attach meaning to its constructed categories.

Anderson notes that the idea of a nation produces categories infused with cultural meaning (12). I shall return to this issue, for authors diverge on their understanding of nation. Still, a general adherence to Anderson's conceptualization should be born in mind throughout this study. The nation in the 19th century presents a *community*, and this community is believed to possess a *character*. Its members have specific characteristics, a common genesis, a *Volksgeist*, and importantly, a future destiny. How the texts position these identities in the flow of history, where they allocate their origin, and how they imagine their community's future will occupy the analysis. What they all do, however, is employ an archaic strategy: They look back to the past so as to determine the origins of their communities and thus deduct aboriginal (read mythological) characteristics.

Mythologies often deal with the foundation of worlds, communities, and nations. But they also touch upon the individual, their nature and place in reality. In this context, American and German authors employed myth so as to employ literature politically. Their assumption of political control through myth is a crucial point for the texts in this study. The mythologies that will be analyzed in the following are found in texts of authors who seek to *rewrite* the most fundamental values of

---

12 For more on the rise of nationalism in Germany, see Winkler: *Der lange Weg nach Westen*, Vol.1. (2001), especially chapters 1, 3, and 5; Michalski: *Der Gang des deutschen Denkens* (2010); Berger: *The Past as History* (2015); Poole: *Nation and Identity* (1999). For a history of American national identity, see Cananau: *Constituting Americanness* (2015); Hacker (ed.): *The Early Republic and the Rise of National Identity* (2014); Pollard: *The Literary Quest for an American National Character* (2009); Citrin: *American Identity and the Politics of Multiculturalism* (2014); Taylor: *Thinking America* (2010); Kermes: *Creating an American Identity* (2008).

their respective polities. They do so to open up the confinements of national identity and allow for a broader, more democratic approach to nationality, unity, and belonging. Rewriting mythology means the rewriting of the world itself, and these stories' ambition is nothing less.

I am interested in the method with which authors endeavored to influence politics through literature. This interest includes questions pertaining to the mythological material that is used in order to effect said influence. As I will use and compare American and German texts, I will also ask about methodological and material similarities and differences. Which myths are significant for American and German identity? How are they rewritten and why? Which images, metaphors, and plot structures are used to effect the rewriting? Which values are worked on and to what end? And finally: What do American and German narratives share and what makes them differ? These are the questions that inform this study.

The answers given will illuminate the concept of mythological resignification, elaborate on processes of national identity making, and comment on the nature of political literature. They will further inform on the transnational character of mythological resignification as a literary method. However, the concept of mythological resignification is indebted to a number of scholarly approaches. Thus, a few comments must be made regarding this study's methodological foundations.

Myth as Narrative Emancipation

Myth is a mode of narration which may occur orally and is later preserved in written form. It may also present itself pictorially in the case of images, acoustically in music, or in rites, customs, and performances. In short, it is impossible to give a satisfactory definition of myth that achieves absolute accuracy: "No single theory of myth can cover all kinds of myth. The variety of traditional tales is matched by their variety of origins and significance; as a result, no monolithic theory can succeed in achieving universal applicability" (Morford and Lenardon 3). In order to develop the notion of myth, I will offer a more complex definition relying on mythologists Morford and Lenardon:

> Myth is a many-faceted personal and cultural phenomenon created to provide a reality and a unity to what is transitory and fragmented in the world we experience—[it] provides us with absolutes in the place of ephemeral values and with a comforting perception of the world that is necessary to make insecurity and terror of existence bearable. (4)

This definition points to three crucial aspects. First, myth is both personal and cultural. It applies to the individual as well as to the community. Second, myth produces a social reality. It creates unity and cohesion in an otherwise fragmented world. Third, myth creates and carries values and ideas which bear didactical and therapeutic functions. It dispenses insecurity and allows for agency while simultaneously alleviating the terror of existence.

This study will elaborate especially on *foundational myths* which explicate a nation's past and origin. In this context, myth satisfies the societal yearning for "fundamental orientation." Indeed, this desire was at its most intense in ages of cultural insecurity like the Antebellum and the Vormärz. Mythologies appease this desire by relating "events surrounding the beginnings and origins of things" and thus construct a fixed point of societal reference (Morford and Lenardon 5).

Civic myth is another term for this type of myth and goes back to Roger Smith. Civic myths describe "'compelling stories' that explain 'why persons form a people, usually indicating how a political community originated, who is eligible for membership, who is not and why, and what the community's values and aims are'" (in Thomas 184). I shall use *civic* and *foundational* myth as synonyms, as they both describe narratives that focus on national genesis and transport social values. Here are stories that derive the explication of the present (and the future) form an imagined aboriginal state of nature. Blumenberg notes that such a *status naturalis* is always prevalent in mythology. Stories of beginnings are found in the Hebrew bible, the Norse Edda, and in Greek and Roman myths. Foundational myths, indeed, are among the most common stories in the mythological repertoire (Arbeit 53).

I am highly indebted to Hans Blumenberg and his elaboration on the nature and function of myth. In his study *Arbeit am Mythos* [*Work on Myth*] (1979), Blumenberg explains how and why myth was used in imagining societal beginnings. He notes that myth exists to fulfill a very specific function: human empowerment and the prevention of anxiety (Work 15). Mythological empowerment opposes "archaic anxiety," a feeling caused by the overwhelming "absolutism of reality." This emotion is not appeased or dissolved by myth but rather "avoided:" Anxiety is prevented by giving form and materiality to those conditions of life which are formless and immaterial (9).

Blumenberg holds that this obviation of anxiety is of Adamic character; it presents an act of name-giving and the subsequent assumption of control (Arbeit 10). It is rooted in humanity's comprehension that objective reality lies outside their dominion: "What [reality's absolutism] means is that man came close to not having control of the conditions of his existence and, what is more important, believed that he simply lacked control of them" (Work 4f). The *overcoming* of reality's absolutism is one of the central functions of myth (Arbeit 10). Primordial "*Angst*" [anxiety] is rationalized into "*Furcht*" [fear]. Here is a rationalization based on the "supposition of familiarity," the explanation for the inexplicable, and the nominalization of the unnamable (Work 5f). The method to achieve this transformation is not just nominalization but rather its expanded form: the "Kunstgriff" [trick of art] of *fictionality* (Arbeit 10).

What has become identifiable by means of a name is raised out of its unfamiliarity by means of metaphor and is made accessible, in terms of its significance, by telling stories. Panic and paralysis [...] are dissolved by the appearance of calculable magnitudes to deal with and regulated ways of dealing with them. (Work 6)

For Blumenberg, myth becomes "Lebenskunst" [life's art], a capacity that functions towards the possession of the world and a wresting of control from the powers that be (Arbeit 13). Art – in this case fiction – becomes the weapon that wrests power from reality and transfers it into human hands: "To have a world is always the result of an art" (Work 7).

This form of mythological empowerment always begins in an aboriginal state of nature: The first step from absolute human submission to a free (but adverse) reality on Earth occurs in this *Naturzustand*. Adversity aside, this newly created reality is *man's domain*, a sphere in which humanity is empowered to act out freedom. These states of nature tend to be free of time and space but are not restricted to the unknowable past. Modernity, for instance, looks to the medieval ages and finds its own "Dark Age" from which a supposedly more powerful (because enlightened) human race emerges (Arbeit 16). Similarly, Vormärz and Antebellum negotiations of origins need not look to a timeless past but find their national geneses in historical time.

Every new beginning, be it primordial or historical, offers material for myth. This is especially true if those who write these myths seek to overcome absolute powers that need to be checked by a soon-to-be empowered humanity; this is the case in ages when humanity seeks, as Heine puts it, "the re-installment of man in his divine privileges" (in Work 13). Blumenberg claims that if a community is faced with absolute powers, the writing of myth presents an attempt at overcoming. This is true for the Genesis or the Prometheus myth. But it also holds for the beginnings of nations: Every text in this study entails a proactive democratic dissent, a refusal to bow to the respective powers that be – may they be monarchy or slavery – so as to wrest power from those who hold it and transfer it to those who seek it.

Blumenberg states that, when facing gods, it is helpful to know their weaknesses. Indeed, these weaknesses, the floors in the divine armor, are *written*. When Paris faced Achilles during the sack of Troy, he aimed for his heel, the only spot where the demi-god was vulnerable. I hold that mythological resignification does the same. By rewriting stories, it rewrites the powers themselves: "every story gives an Achilles' heel to sheer power" (Work 16). This is what the authors in the following chapters endeavored to do. This is what mythological resignification seeks to accomplish: the writing of Achillean heels.

Work on Myth and Basic Mythologies

The mythological explication of reality to dispense powerlessness points towards a crucial yet fallible distinction: *mythos* vs. *logos*. Blumenberg notes that in contrast to Enlightenment views, which derogate myth as the stuff of irrationality, myth is an intricate part of the human drive for knowledge (Arbeit 37). Myth, according to its critics, only found the objects for which philosophy offered the adequate (i.e. rational) method of explanation. However, myth is not a "precursor" to science or philosophy but a dynamic part of their processes: "The boundary lines between myth and logos is imaginary and does not obviate the need to inquire about the logos of myth in the process of working free of the absolutism of reality. Myth itself is a piece of high-carat 'work of logos'" (Work 12).

Myth and logos are not opposites but rather interwoven approaches to reality. Blumenberg reminds us that myth is not primarily interested in explanation but in agency: It centers on the connecting to, positioning in, and influencing of reality. It goes beyond the epistemological character of logos although it partakes in the human need to explain (Arbeit 19). Myth, therefore, produces an "anthropomorphic relaxation" in the face of material power. It soothes the bitter "seriousness of life" and, by means of its empowerment, feels for the frontiers of human possibility (Work 23). It pushes the limits of what may seem possible; a crucial ability for human progress, and of course, political literature.

If myth pushes the preconceived borders of the possible, how does the rewriting of myths work to effect political change? For the term *mytheme*, I rely on Lévi-Strauss' elaborations in *The Structural Study of Myth* (1955). Mythological resignification is concerned with this structural element which presents myth's "gross constituent units," i.e. the central topoi or motifs of a mythology (Lévi-Strauss 431). In this context, Blumenberg gives numerous examples of reworked mythologies (Arbeit 89, 129, 166, 438). The writing of variants seeks to give myth a new form while staying true to its inherent mythemes. Variants adhere to mythemes, they present a variation of meaning and interpretation. They may parodize or negate them, but they nevertheless keep faith with the very nucleus of representation (Arbeit 40, 165). The latter claim, we shall see in the following analysis, is not without its issues. Indeed, a mytheme can and sometimes must be transformed (but not rejected) to successfully achieve a transformation in meaning.

Further, Blumenberg differentiates between *Grundmythos* and *Variationsmythos*. The "*basic myth*"[13] is a full blown narrative (e.g. the Prometheus myth) encap-

---

13 In translating *Grundmythos* and *Variationsmythos* as basic and variant myth, I dissent from Wallace's translation (fundamental myth and art myths) (Work 174). Blumenberg

sulating an inherent mytheme (e.g. *Fire-is-Culture*). The "*variant myth,*" in contrast, presents the transformation of the basic myth (Work 192). Blumenberg holds that variants are myths of the given time, variations of the basic myth's timelessness poured into the here and now of history, and a direct result of the ongoing work on myth (Arbeit 192).[14] Be that as it may, I will not endeavor a genealogy of myth in this study but focus on the *use* of specific existent myths, on the process of rewriting and adapting myths for political purposes within Antebellum and Vormärz cultures.[15]

Blumenberg is correct when he states that myths, regardless of age, are continuously dynamic; the process of working on them is ever ongoing. Myths seem to concern the past, while they in fact concern the present:

The [basic myth] occupies, if one may put it this way, a special position. It is located precisely on the axis of symmetry between where we come from and where we are going, between what comes to be and what ought to be, between fall and ascent. (Work 188)

This fixation on the present may comfort our ignorance regarding the exact genesis of myth. Blumenberg notes that theories about the source of myth are redundant, because we do not and cannot know them: "Is that bad? No, since we don't know anything about the 'origins' in other cases either" (45).

---

understands *Kunstmythos* and *Variationsmythos* as synonyms; I have chosen *Variationsmythos* as the term is better suited for this analysis.

14 Blumenberg complicates this clear cut distinction because it suggests a normative hierarchy or genealogical chronology of myth. The notion of basic myth, he states, is very often confounded with what may be called an original myth. Yet the basic myth, no matter how ancient, should not be regarded as the beginning of myth (Arbeit 192). The conception of a basic myth as original is an illusion, a kind of imagined mythological *status naturalis*. The basic myth is rather the *visible form* of mythology: It "is not what was pre-given, but rather what remains visible in the end, what was able to satisfy the receptions and expectations" (Work 74). Therefore, basic and variant myths do not exist in a clear cut hierarchy or chronology; they rather exist next to each other.

15 Again, one needs to be aware of the fallacy of assuming a clear cut genealogy of myth. The ancient visible forms of myths are not the sires of the newer visible forms; they are *all* variants of stories that at one time or another became visible in written form. They are interconnected and related yet present but *one* moment in the evolution of myth. This certainly is frustrating; but the prerequisite of scientifically investigating mythologies is to allow for a certain degree of chaos. It lies in the very nature of myth to resist institutionalization, to be pluralistic, and partially ineffable (Arbeit 203).

Variant Mythologies

The partial ineffability of myth demands an even more precise scientific treatment of the matter. In order to bring order to the chaotic realm of myth, the following table may be helpful.

Mythology:	Narrative system of meaning
Mytheme:	Inherent core motif or topos of a myth
Basic Myth:	Textual myth acting as referent
Variant Myth:	Textual myth resulting from resignifying a basic myth
Civic Myth:	Textual myth transporting societal origin, values, and aims

The development of variant myths is constituted by the elaboration on a mytheme: It is never "pure imagination that is at work, but rather the elaboration of fundamental patterns" that constructs the variant (Work 176) By means of this elaboration, the variants are successful in presenting that which is already inherent in the basic myth itself. This process distills and excavates mythemes by working on them.

Blumenberg exemplifies this by recurring to Plato's *Allegory of the Cave*. He describes this narrative as a variant of myths that imagine human beings emerging from the earth. There are numerous examples for this basic myth: In Genesis, the creator forms Adam from the "dust of the ground" (KJV Genesis 2:7); Greek gods fashion mankind from the metals found in the depths of the planet (Hamilton 85); Zeus forms woman out of earth (Hesiod 121). Plato's variant is able to distill these stories' mytheme. *Leaving-the-Cave* is inherent to all these mythologies: the emergence from darkness to light (Arbeit 84).

Indeed, mythological elements are formable and encourage transformation. Myth – an ever dynamic product – eludes the rigid categorizations of chronology. As mentioned above, one cannot regard myth in a clear cut line of cause and effect but needs to be aware that the processes of transformation present the constituting elements of the mythological condition itself. We never see a last, complete, and perfect myth: All we see is myth at work. And while I follow Blumenberg's concept of work on myth, I need to rely on another approach for the details of the actual reworking process. How is resignification effected in narratological, aesthetic, and imaginary terms? So as to elucidate the exact mechanizations of mythological resignification, I must return to Roland Barthes.

Mythological Naturalization

Barthes approaches mythology differently from Blumenberg. His study *Mythology* (1957) centers on the linguistic explication of modern myths, encompassing wrestling, haute cuisine, and striptease. Barthes finds myth in everyday life, a visible and yet invisible (because *naturalized*) cultural force. He focuses on the linguistics and aesthetics of myth, i.e. on the semiotic construction and the pictorial representation of myths as value-transmitting narratives.

His approach, like Blumenberg's, is of great importance to the present study, as it is the use of imagery, metaphor, and plot that will guide and inform the textual analysis. Barthes' notions allow for insights into the machinations of myths, especially how they function as text and image and how they generate reader impact. While Blumenberg provides the cultural nature and function of myth, I rely on Barthes to elaborate on the more intricate processes that govern the resignifying practice. Also, his notions are telling in answering one of the fundamental questions of this study: Can literature change societal values?

Mythology in a Barthesian sense presents a linguistic-narrative system of interlocked concepts, a "system of communication" "made of material which has already been worked on" (109f). For myth to function it must already exist in the cultural mind: It presupposes a "signifying consciousness." In this manner, myth, whether represented in a text, a film, or in the images of an advertisement, can function "at one stroke" (110).

If we, for instance, consider a painting of mythological significance such as Raphael's *The Sistine Madonna* (1512), a professional or academic understanding of the history of art or of the painting's inherent theology is not necessary to know what it represents. The signifying consciousness that stores the cultural materials of myth quickly decodes the image. Simultaneously, an observer who is out of touch with Western and Christian culture will not be able to access its meaning.

Raphael's masterpiece in mind, we may recur to Hugues Merle's painting entitled *The Scarlet Letter* (1861) and thus illustrate a further point: Myth is "speech stolen and restored" (Barthes 125). The imagery of the Virgin mythology presented in its basic form in Raphael's work is used for the depiction of a variant in Merle's. Here is a representation of an adulteress (Hester Prynne) cradling her illegitimate daughter in her arms – a posture mirroring the infant Christ cradled by his virgin mother Mary. Indeed, Hawthorne's *The Scarlet Letter* is in itself a rewriting of myth, and I will revisit the novel in Chapter 2. For now, let it suffice to say that the image of the variant functions mythologically due to the fact that the basic myth is resignified in the same yet remains recognizable. A clear referential relationship can thereby be established by the viewer. Herein lies the potential for the transformation and reinterpretation of the basic myth: Myth is "speech stolen and restored. Only speech which is restored is no longer quite that which was stolen: when it was brought back, it was not put back exactly in its place" (ibid.).

The change that occurs in the process of resignifying mythology allows for the transmission of previously unconsidered material. Thus, resignifying myth means newly interpreting on the grounds of core meanings: The variant needs to stand in an organic relationship to the basic myth's mytheme, even if it transforms or adds to it. This is what occurs in this comparison: The mytheme of the Virgin myth (*Birth-out-of-Purity*) is not violated but cited and restored in a way that a new, albeit darker meaning is achieved. Here is an opportunity for the reevaluation, reinterpretation, and reinstallation of meaning (and values) in the process of resignification. When considering mythologies which define societal values and norms, working on such myths offers the potential for societal change. Democratic dissent, therefore, finds an ally in mythology. Myth was (and is) used as political vehicle.

However, myth transcends referentiality. It transforms "history" into "nature." The imagined is presented and received as if it were *real*: As if it were history, not fiction. Barthes explains that this, the process of *naturalization*, is one the most crucial principles of myth. Mythology tends to be either too obscure or too obvious to allow for ambiguity (129). The reader sees it "not as a semiological system, but as an inductive one." But semiological systems (i.e. signifying systems) are *value* systems, and the reader "takes [their] signification for a system of facts" (131).

Myth has power to transport, negotiate, and reform societal values, but it does not automatically encourage *reflection*. Literature can alleviate this by creating ambiguity or following a rational argumentation. But myth's force of impact can be dangerous, especially in the realm of imagery, where impact and consumption are by nature more inductive than in reading. Further, myth can create a degree of ideological clarity which can be disastrous if applied to a complex social reality. The same characteristics that make myth a ready ally for democratic dissent also offer their services to every other kind of ideologically charged *politicum*. This study will focus on the democratic side of things. One should, however, be aware of the fact that the results of mythological resignification depend on the hand that wields the pen. Fortunately, it is not enough to rewrite a myth to induce societal change. The question remains how dissent through myth functions in the realm of society, and in which way literature can constitute politics.

Myth as Political Dissent

Political literature and society stand in a specific relationship. The fields of art and society are not separate but find themselves in a relational condition constituted by cooperation and influence. Regarding the following analyses, I will focus on texts and their authors, not on reader reception; and in order to situate literary dissent in the broader societal picture, I rely on Jean Cohen and Andrew Arato and their study *Civil Society and Political Theory* (1992). Their approaches to the civic realm will be of crucial importance, as they illuminate the conditions that govern literature's influence on politics.

Cohen and Arato imagine a political community in three categories: a civil, political, and economic society (ix). It is with the first and second that this study is concerned, especially with their reciprocal influence. Civil society is a "sphere of social interaction between economy and the state, composed of the intimate sphere (especially the family), the sphere of associations (especially voluntary associations), social movements, and forms of public communications" (ibid). Political literature is situated in the last and presents a form of public communication: It partakes in the complex dialogue between authors, readers, publishers, critics, and more. The intermingling of private and public concern and the discussion of values takes place inside this sphere.

Indeed, civil society – in a democratic system – enjoys a privileged (because foundational) position. It is "locus of both democratic legitimacy and rights, composed of private but also of public concern [which] act in concert in order to influence political society and, indirectly, decision making" (Cohen and Arato 564). Civil society is both source and primary sphere of the political process, i.e. the articulation of interest, the holding of debate, and the generation of consent and public will (Schmidt 625). This sphere, Cohen and Arato note, is the center of "normative integration," a space for the reevaluation and legitimization of values and norms (ix). Here, democratic dissent[16] finds its locus: The ability of a polity – i.e. the entirety of political institutions (Schmidt 627) – to allow and respect dissent as a citizen activity is, as Rawls put it, the "crucial test case" for a mature democracy (in Cohen and Arato 568).

Habermas holds that in a democracy, dissent presents a normalized because necessary "component of the political culture" (in Cohen and Arato 567). Dissent for the sake of democratization (especially in a non-democratic polity) is even more crucial. Here, dissent is not only a necessary but a *constituting* element. For polities that are yet to be transformed into a democracy (e.g. the German Confederation) and for democratic polities which need to expand their democratic character (e.g. the Antebellum U.S.), dissent is the fundamental driving force, the "motor" of de-

---

16 I rely on Schmidt and define dissent as the differently-minded and diverging position which stands in relation and opposition to a majority or dominant position (192). I shall use the term protest if I wish to highlight the verbal character of dissent (650). Further, democratic dissent is understood as the position-taking for and the furthering of democratic principles against an un-democratic or less democratic dominant opinion. Finally, literary dissent is the expression of dissent by literary means.

mocratization (Cohen and Arato 567). Democratization is, indeed, both: the process of *establishing* a democracy and the *furthering* of the democratic principle in a given polity (Schmidt 167).

This illuminates the central role of dissent for the establishment, defense, and improvement of democracy. A democracy, after all, is the political system whose forms of state and government organizations emanate from the people (Schmidt 164). Dissent is what establishes, defends, and rejuvenates democratic rule (650). The analysis of literary dissent in the given 19th century texts will elaborate on the democratic idea but will also show how literature sought to establish and improve democratic governance.

Indeed, I hold literary dissent to be a clear act of *politics*, i.e. the conscious action of pushing a specific policy (Schmidt 601). This means that I will work under the presumption that authors enacting literary dissent influence the political, not *vice versa*. Rather than reflecting social reality and the myths that inform it, their texts rewrite, retranslate, and reinterpret social reality in the literary (Speller 68). They do so in order to disseminate democratic ideas and effect desired changes. How authors effected their dissent and which policies where supported are questions that will be answered in the textual analysis. For now, let it suffice to say that acts of dissent constitute crucial instances for the change and development of democratic polities:

[L]iving in a democracy means dissenting. In short, democracy is nothing more than the institutionalization of a culture that cherishes public dissent; public dissent is nothing more than the cultural process of celebrating democracy. It is a paradox, but it works. (Hartnett 176)

If one wishes to understand how dissent creates order, it is essential to keep the paradoxical relation between dissent and consent in mind. Acts of dissent, literary or otherwise, establish, protect, and further the democratic principle in civil society, a sphere which constitutes the very foundation of liberal democracy (Thomas 202). The question is how literary dissent negotiated these foundations in the U.S. and Germany.

Comparing Antebellum and Vormärz Literature

The comparison of Antebellum and Vormärz literature renders fascinating insights. If we regard the transformative developments in the 19th century, a transatlantic comparison of democratic authors and their writing strategies can illuminate our understanding of cultural and literary connectivity. At the same time, we may further our knowledge of the way in which national identities were negotiated and to which degree these negotiations concurred or differed. Lastly, we may better comprehend the role literature played in the political and cultural transformations of the time.[17]

At a first glance, the Antebellum U.S. and Vormärz Germany present two completely different polities: the first, a young, democratic federal state, the other a loose confederation of monarchies. However, both found themselves in an age of transformation. While the polities may be different, the forces that molded them were the same: industrialization, urbanization, economic reform, advances in communication and transportation, literary democratization, rise of political dissent, and, importantly, the constant struggle to keep the polity together. Blumenberg notes that times of historical and systemic transition evidence a heightened need for myth (Arbeit 41). And indeed, regional and statist diversity in both countries resulted in the same societal reaction: the desire for a cohesive national identity through myth. American and German societies were in the midst of intense identity negotiations, negotiations which were orientated towards national consolidation by means of the imagination of a national past, present, and future. This, however, was a cultural task. On both sides of the Atlantic, literature was paramount to these processes.

Regarding American national identity, exceptionalism continues to inform the academic debate. Scholars like Bercovitch and Lipset allocate the U.S. outside and in contrast to the historical developments that governed European trajectories.[18] The U.S. thus becomes the *first new nation* (Lipset) and develops a uniquely American ideology. Indeed, while Germany's identity negotiations were conditioned by its feudal past and other distinctive factors, the U.S., seemingly, was free of such restrictions and able to develop a radically different, liberal, and individualistic identity based on the dissent of its first settlers. Following Lipset, this "American Creed" constitutes the basic values which would form the nation's identity: liberty, egalitarianism, individualism, populism, and laissez-faire (19). In contrast, German national identity was informed by liberal as well as royalist, conservative, and socialist ideas, all of which competed in the framework of a feudal-monarchic past and the imagination of linguistic and historical genealogy.

---

17 For an authoritative account of the Antebellum, see Howe: *What Has God Wrought* (2007); Boyer (ed.): *The Oxford Companion to United States History* (2001). For the Vormärz, see Winkler: *Der lange Weg nach Westen*, Vol.1 (2001); Nipperdey: *Deutsche Geschichte 1800-1866* (1998).

18 For more on American exceptionalism see Lipset: *The First New Nation* (1963) and *American Exceptionalism* (1997); Bercovitch: *The Rites of Assent* (1981); Lockhart: *The Roots of American Exceptionalism* (2003); Hodgson: *The Myth of American Exceptionalism* (2009); Ludwig: *Die besondere Nation* (2011).

Indeed, the alleged difference between America and Europe, which Bercovitch termed "transatlantic contrast," resurfaces in Hawthorne and Brown's texts (Office 35). But nations on the other side of the Atlantic are not only represented as ideological other: Europe is also a space of origin, inspiration, and return. While Hawthorne and Brown affirm a specific American exceptionalism, they also question and contextualize it, especially with regard to their perspectives on the Old Continent.

It is crucial to remember that American exceptionalism, elaborated for the first time in Tocqueville's *Democracy in America* (1835), has always been indebted to a comparative, transnational perspective focusing on Europe (Lipset 17). Exceptionalism does not automatically include a claim of superiority but offers the simple assertion of divergence: The U.S. was regarded as a cultural "outlier" with "qualitative differences" (18). But claims of differences, and similarities for that matter, cannot result from a narrow perspective; a broad, in this case transnational approach is constitutive to the elaboration of national qualities.

For national characteristics are themselves negotiated constructions of the time and need to be considered in the context of transatlantic relationality: There are no "autonomous cultures" free of influence (Jay 3). The fact that Boston, home to both Hawthorne and Brown's literary productions, constituted one of the major transfer sites of transatlantic connectivity, and that Hegelian notions of history, nationhood, and identity influenced American and German authors alike necessitates a transnational perspective.[19] Americans were not only highly aware of European struggles for freedom and identity; Germans, too, were caught up in an ideological force field that championed liberty and individuality across the Atlantic. I will not join Bourne in arguing that there is no "distinct American culture" – or no distinct German culture, for that matter (in Fluck et al. 59). I am also not interested in reciprocal influence on an intratextual, material, or personal level. But I will be paying attention to the *manner* in which national identities are negotiated in literature, and to what degree we need to relocate the borders of national literature if we consider 19th century literary work on identity-making values. Barthes notes that mythologists study "ideas-in-form" (112). The question, indeed, is whether or not American and German mythological forms share similar ideas.

---

19 For more on transnationalism and the transnational turn in American Studies see Manning and Taylor (eds): *Transatlantic Literary Studies* (2007); Jay: *Global Matters* (2010); Edwards and Gaonkar: *Globalizing American Studies* (2010); Fluck et al: *Re-Framing the Transnational Turn in American Studies* (2011) and *Transnational American Studies* (2007); Hebel (ed.): *Transnational American Studies* (2012); Christ et al: *American Studies/Shifting Gears* (2010).

For Americans are not alone in their belief in exceptionality. Germany claims, in fact, its very own historical exceptionalism, albeit a pessimistic one.[20] Scholars like Winkler, Wehler, and Plessner insist on the distinct otherness of Germany's democratic development when compared to other Western nations. Its hegemonic role in the Holy Roman Empire, its "Reichsmythos" [myth of empire] and traditional federalism, its philosophical and religious currents, and its insistence on culture over civilization are often invoked to explain German history (Winkler 2, 40). These aspects are meant to elucidate on how Germans became the "belated"[21] members in the family of Western democracies (Plessner 11). Wehler's controversial idea of a specifically German path towards democracy (*Deutscher Sonderweg*) seeks to explain the country's fall from civilization in the 20th century but also its historical struggle with liberal and democratic ideologies (Kaiserreich 11). In this context, national identity is imagined as being restricted to an ethno-historical genealogy. German-ness, so to speak, is not an ideology like in the U.S. – and thus subject to individual assent – but an aboriginal, organic, and historical category (Plessner 48). This claim, indeed, is highly contestable for the Vormärz and will find its critical elaboration in Heine's and Gutzkow's texts. But a scholarly assessment of German exceptionalism, indeed, cannot rest solely on the analysis of German works. It needs a transnational perspective.

A transnational comparison of American and German literature can broaden the preconceptions of our field regarding transatlantic relationality in the 19th century. Such an approach will contextualize and challenge the primacy of national literatures and their "insular concerns" (Jay 2). Indeed, national identity is always negotiated in a way that results in some form exceptionalism. The goal of all identity negotiations is to render one's own national character unique, legitimized, and cohesive and thus contrastive to that of others. That, however, does not mean that the construction process is not an open one, allowing and requiring influence, inspiration, and communication. To argue that a national identity is exceptional because its negotiators aimed at exceptionalism is a blatant tautology which must be avoided if we really want to understand the processes of national identity building through myth.

The Antebellum was one of the most dynamic periods in American history, and the Vormärz does not fall short in comparison. I am interested in the role literature

---

20 For more on German exceptionalism see Winkler: Der lange Weg nach Westen (2000); Wehler: Das deutsche Kaiserreich (1973); Plessner: Die verspätete Nation (1934); Elsässer: Der deutsche Sonderweg (2003); Raulet (ed): Historismus, Sonderweg und dritte Wege (2001); Gretz: Die deutsche Bewegung (2007); Grebing: Der deutsche Sonderweg in Europa (1986).

21 [die Zuspätgekommenen].

played in these tumultuous times. We know that it had a decisive role in cultural and political processes, but the *manner* in which literature negotiated these issues still requires our attention. Did American and German authors approach dissent differently; are their methods of creating national identities similar? Indeed, we should not easily assume divergence on the grounds of national difference, for nationality is a construction: Literature produces nationality rather than *vice versa*. Thus, this study will ask *how* German and American authors created civic myths and whether or not their methods were based on what Fluck calls transculturation (1).

Further, a comparison will help to better define the nature of political literature itself. When does a text become political, and how can we legitimate the use of art for political purposes? When does literature cross the boundaries of aesthetics, when does it become agitation or propaganda, and to what degree does the autonomy of art enter such considerations? Can authors ensure reflection and agency in literature that carries a vested interest? These questions can be answered best by comparing two literary cultures. Such an approach will render differences and similarities and thus help to more comprehensively elaborate the tenets of political literature in the 19th century.

For despite the efforts and sacrifices of German democratic authors, one must conclude that their literary endeavors failed in one respect: Political literature may have furthered the revolutionary effort, but it was not able to stir the revolution in a direction which would have resulted in democracy. Similarly, American authors failed in their attempts to peacefully consolidate the nation by means of identity making. Despite their best intentions, the pressures of the age were finally resolved in civil war. It is this literary-historical parallel which further motivates a comparison. Yes, it would be naïve to suggest that literature alone could have prevented the mid-century events. But it must be asked whether and how it could have done its part.

Today, the U.S. remains a deeply divided nation.[22] Highly divergent political, ethnic, and cultural issues dominate the national discourse, and political institutions seem to be unable to effectively overcome these problems. Similarly, the European Union is in the midst of political and economic crises which threaten the foundations of European peace and integration. Europe is in the process of negotiating a cohesive identity, and we must ask whether cultural, intellectual, and political elites can learn from 19th century history. Can a new European myth aid the construction of a nation state? Can a redefinition of the American Way placate modern divisions? Who and/or what is to effect an improved democratic integration? A comparison between Antebellum and Vormärz approaches towards unity and identity can

---

22 For a recent transatlantic perspective on this issue see: Grabowski and Kosàk (eds): The U.S. as a Divided Nation (2014).

only further our understanding in this context, and, in the best case scenario, effect a "reciprocal process of Transcultural learning" (Hornung in Fluck et al. 2).

Today, the U.S. and Germany are among the most powerful and influential democracies in the West. But it was the early 19th century which began to define their national identities. The analysis and comparison of Antebellum and Vormärz literature offers important insights into the national geneses of these countries. In the transformative 19th century, America and Germany found themselves at a point where people like Choate and Wienbarg called upon literature to make sense of a chaotic world and give their nation a past, a present, and a democratic future.

Poets of Protest is constituted by two parts. In Part I, *The Pushing of Horizons*, I will analyze novels which use and focus on one central basic myth, seeking to redefine societal values and construct a new outlook on national identity. These texts feel for the frontiers of individual sovereignty and hope to open societal fences. Here, characters change their communities by means of an proactive dissent and thus strive to develop and democratize their societal surroundings. I will discuss Hawthorne's *The Scarlet Letter* in Chapter 2 and analyze this novel's resignification of the Puritan myth. In Chapter 3, I will turn to Gutzkow's *Wally, die Zweiflerin* and present the construction of a variant based on the Sigune myth.

Part II, *The Treading of Pathways*, will be devoted to texts which employ more than one basic myth and whose mythopoetic logic differs from the novels discussed in the preceding chapters. Here, the given texts deal with subjective journeys and employ a more focalized and personalized mythological resignification. Their work revolves around the fact that the character's fates are intricately interwoven with the nation itself. These texts imagine a society shaped by the lives (and deaths) of its individual members; rather than seeking to accommodate the subject inside the societal framework, these works reveal the nation in the character's trajectories. Chapter 4 will elaborate on Brown's *Clotel* and discuss the resignification of the Puritan and Revolution myth. Chapter 5, devoted to Heine's *Deutschland. Ein Wintermärchen*, elucidates on the resignification of the Three Magi and the Barbarossa myth.

Lastly, a brief conclusion will discuss the consequences of mythological resignification for national identity building in the U.S. and Germany and bring this study to a close by elaborating on the nature of political literature in the 19th century.

2. Nathaniel Hawthorne's *The Scarlet Letter* and the Opening of Fences

> In the beginning there was the fence.
> TRIER/ZAUN UND MANNRING

Myth is full of chaos, violence, and struggle. It is out of such struggle that an ordered and peaceful domain for humanity emerges. But with time, even the darkest civic myth can be changed. Blumenberg notes that due to the overcoming of its more violent aspects, myth may be brightened by means of a more aesthetic imagery (Arbeit 45, 412). Frank L. Baum, author of *The Wonderful Wizard of Oz*, admits to this endeavor. He presents his story as a "modernized fairytale, in which the wonderment and joy are retained and the heart-aches and nightmares left out" (xx). Witchcraft, for instance, is appropriated and remolded in his novel. Dorothy Gale crosses from one world to another, becomes a sorceress herself, and is confronted with good and evil witches in the Land of Oz. Her border-crossing illuminates something that is crucial to another witch-like character in the history of American literature. Like Dorothy, Nathaniel Hawthorne's Hester Prynne is a woman who dares to cross fences.

Understanding *The Scarlet Letter* as an effort at mythological resignification means to understand this novel as a rewriting of a civic myth. Hawthorne writes and rewrites American national identity based on the history and identity of New England Puritans. At the same time, *The Scarlet Letter* is the story of a woman at odds with the rules and regulations of Puritan Boston. In this chapter, I will elaborate on Hester Prynne's political significance and analyze Hawthorne's mythological resignification. Hester, as several of her fellow characters, is in many ways like Baum's Dorothy Gale: She crosses borders, transgresses social norms, and journeys outside the commonplace.

This novel's mythological resignification taps into the basic Puritan myth to open it up for more democratic possibilities. It achieves this by saturating its characters with an imagery that dominates much of Hawthorne's oeuvre: witchcraft. The text presents its heroine as someone who opens Puritan fences: Hester Prynne becomes a hedgerider. As hedgerider, she pushes the social and ideological horizons of theocratic Boston and is able to open up a coercive society to new, more sympathetic, and civic possibilities.

2.1 FROM CRIME TO HERESY: THE NEW ENGLAND WITCH AS TRANSGRESSOR

In order to understand the mythological resignification in *The Scarlet Letter* one needs to comprehend witchcraft's cultural conception. New England's witchcraft beliefs are the result of the historical evolution of witchcraft and magic. That evolution begins with the remnants of Pagan rites in Northern Europe, followed by magical practices in the Middle Ages, and their subsequent absorption into 16th century penal codes. It ends with the concept's transplantation to America by the Puritans, who gave it a socio-theological turn. Witchcraft developed from a cultural practice to crime, and in the Puritan context, to heresy and treason. It is the Puritan perspective that will clarify how the use of witchcraft imagery in Hawthorne's novel elaborates on one of the basic political problems of both Puritan and Antebellum America: the question of how to deal with dissent, heterodoxy, and separatism.

Commenting on the development of law, Carl Schmitt refers to linguist Jost Trier and his famous dictum "In the beginning was the fence" (in Schmitt 74). "[L]aw and peace," he writes, "originally rested on *enclosures in the spatial sense*," i.e. the world is given order and law by erecting fences. The symbolism of the fence is literally clear-cut: It is an object that separates. It makes possible distinction (and discrimination) and creates categories, identities, and finally law. Law as a social construct to control human behavior relies on the act of fencing, i.e. on constructing borders that must not be crossed. The fence creates the social realities humans live in; it is the line that separates the town from the forest, the civilized from the wild, the lawful from the criminal. As such, Schmitt notes that words like "fence" and "forest" describe spaces that are *orientational* in character (74). The fence becomes crucial to the imagery of witchcraft, because it is witches who cross the lines between the town's *nominal* space and the forest, a realm "never subjugated by human law" (SL 130).[1]

Hawthorne uses witchcraft as a foil for several reasons. Hester's association with Mistress Hibbins and the Black Man, for instance, function as a marker of her proximity to radical evil (Weinauer 380). Scholars like Michael J. Colacurcio further emphasize the analogy between Hester and Ann Hutchinson, the latter of which was presented as a witch giving "monstrous births" to Antinomian heresies (305, 317). While I generally agree that witchcraft characters are used to position the protagonist in the tensions between good and evil, I disagree in restricting its significance to that particular notion.

The significance of witchcraft functions on a deeply mythological level in Barthes' sense. Witchcraft presents material the reader is familiar with and which – if worked on – experiences a denaturalization (and subsequent naturalization) of what it can signify. I hold that the use of witchcraft in Hawthorne's novel serves to write about an alternative to traditional Puritan perspectives. In the novel, the demonization of witchcraft does not remain absolute. In associating Hester and other characters with it, the significance of witchcraft is changed. As we will see, witches are nothing else but transgressors of given law. The mythological resignification in play here opens the possibility for the acceptance and toleration of dissenting individuals. For this is what *witch* ultimately means: transgressor.[2]

---

1   For quotation purposes I use the Norton Critical Edition edited by Person (ed.): *Nathaniel Hawthorne: The Scarlet Letter, and Other Writings* (2005). Quotations will be given as (SL) throughout. Other primary sources will be abbreviated in the same manner.

2   The English term *witch* derives from Old English *wicca* (female *wicce*) and means a person who possesses magical powers (OED 2327). German *Hexe* or Dutch *Heks* are more telling regarding the significance of the concept. The first derives from *Hagazussa*, the latter from *Haghetesse*, both of which mean hedgerider, or soul on the fence. The Old English *Haegtesse* resounds in the modern day hag and hedge, while *Hexe* and *Hecke*, German for witch and hedge, are still almost homophonic (Vries 11). Guerber notes that the concept of the witch describes individuals who transgress boundaries others abide to. The underworld, the Germanic Hel, and later the fires of Christian hell, are the spheres into which such a hedgerider ventures. Here are persons who travel from one reality to another. The idea of hell as an evil sphere, however, is of rather recent date. In Germanic mythology, the underworld was the sphere of the dead ruled by Loki's daughter Hel. In contrast to Odin's Hall (*Valhalla*), were the god-father feasts heroes, Hel is the realm for the rest of humankind, who receive their due in the after-life (94). Crossing the fence between these worlds had specific goals. Vries comments that it was undertaken to gain wisdom, to broaden the horizons of those who dwell in Middle-Earth by means of com-

Throughout history, witches had a predominantly negative reputation. This was not so much given to the nature of the magical art *per se* but rather because it was seen as un*just*. The transgression of law for personal reasons condemned the hedgeriders. But what happened if a transgression resulted in good or was motivated by noble reasons? If that was the case, the witch could fulfill the mythological definition of the hero. There is a difference between selfish and social quests, and the true hero takes the latter road. According to Campbell, heroes cross the fence so as to return wiser and better suited to serve the community: "The courage to face the trials and to bring a whole new body of possibilities into the field of experience for other people to experience – that is the hero's deed" (49).

The hedgerider is a concept that allows us to recapture a more neutral signification of the witch. It describes individuals who perform border-crossing acts. These transgressions can touch the essence of civic myth if they affect the community at large: They can partake of the negotiations between reality's absolutism and the human effort to stand against powers that dwell behind the horizon. By crossing fences, the transgressor can create spaces in which humans have partial sovereignty. Pushing the horizon does not mean total victory over reality. But it can mean a land gain. Of course, if one wishes the community to be closed and fenced in, those who cross borders are everything but welcome.

Witchcraft in Puritan New England

In the 17th century, European and American communities perceived witchcraft as a threatening reality, and Massachusetts Bay would not see the century end before staging its own reenactment of European witch crazes. Despite their efforts to begin anew, Puritan settlers proved to be Europeans at heart. Weinauer notes that witchcraft was a capital crime in England and Massachusetts (373). While New England Puritans partook of the witch mythology of their European contemporaries, the fear of such otherworldly agents was heightened by their Colonial situation. It is worthwhile to dwell on the Puritan conception of witchcraft so as to understand how and why *The Scarlet Letter* is saturated with references to the supposed handmaidens of Satan.

The general perception of the witch and their primary realm – magic – derives from Northern Europe after its conversion to Christianity. Kieckhefer comments that while the veneration of Germanic gods was forbidden, other Pagan aspects were accommodated in the process of conversion, e.g. the endowment of traditional festivals with Christian meaning (44f). Traditionally, magic and religion were in-

---

munication with the dead (13). The English term *witch* attained the meaning of devil worshipper later; originally, it simply meant a female magician (OED 2327).

clusive parts of the Pagan perspective. Odin himself was a magician, who went through immense trouble to gain mastery in the art (Guerber 21). Christian missionaries, however, equated Paganism with demon-worship. Gods like Odin and Frigga became demons, and magic was linked to this redefinition of Germanic religion as a demonic cult (Kieckhefer 45). Still, magical practices survived the conversion without establishing a survival of Pagan religiosity. The veneration of Pagan gods was separated from practical magic; this allowed the continuity of magic and witchcraft as performance (51f).

Yet throughout Germanic mythology, the witch carries negative connotations. Kieckhefer notes that this is rooted in the perception of magic as trickery. Magic was not seen as unnatural or demonic, nor was the witch excluded from society or believed to be anything but a human being. Witchcraft was perceived as *crime*, an un*just* means of achieving one's goal. One may "find magic reprehensible not because it is violent, but because it is unfair" (50). The fact that witches were ultimately linked to demon-worship is the result of the Christian conflation of two separate categories: religiosity and performance (52).

The practice of magic was so commonplace that scholars speak of a common European tradition. If we consider the practice of magic in the Middle Ages,

we find various types of people involved in diverse magical activities: monks, parish priests, physicians, surgeon-barbers, midwives, folk healers and diviners with no formal training, and even ordinary women and men who, without claiming special knowledge and competence, used whatever magic they happened to know. (Kieckhefer 56)

Especially medicine was saturated with magical practices, including midwives and lay practitioners commonly referred to as leeches (58). Midwives and lay healers in particular will occupy the Puritan perception of witchcraft.

The perception of witchcraft as performance is reflected in its inclusion into European penal codes. Witchcraft was a legal issue, its persecution a prerogative of courts of law. Puritan emigrants brought this legal perception with them as they crossed the Atlantic. However, a mixture of theological fervor and colonial circumstance molded the original perspective and rendered a new conceptualization. Witchcraft was transformed from crime to theological heresy and ultimately, I argue, to political treason.

New England's witchcraft imagery was a branch of English perceptions on the matter.[3] However, the colonists' "special conditions of life" in New England "led

---

3   Karlsen notes that "New England witchcraft has its roots in the villages and towns of England. It was so much part of the culture the settlers transported from the old world to the new that the continuities rather than the differences stand out. The colonists shared

them gradually to alter some of their ideas on witchcraft," especially notions regarding the witch's socio-economic status (2).[4] For New England Puritans, the witch was a human person, usually a woman, with supernatural powers. Their main ability lay in the performance of magical acts motivated by malice (*maleficium*). The harm they could bestow upon fellow settlers knew numerous forms.[5] The abilities of New England witches were no different from their European counterparts, and it was generally believed that they acquired these powers through a pact with Satan. This pact included the signing of their name in a book and sexual intercourse with the devil. Those who signed the pact carried a mark where the devil touched them. Also identical with European conceptions is the notion of the Witches' Sabbath, i.e. regular congregation of witches and demons characterized by drinking, feasting, and general merriment. It was also here were new recruits would be initiated (Karlsen 10, 12).

Karlsen is correct in claiming that the idea that witches sought to recruit others brings us closer to the fundamental difference between European and New England witches. Witches would recruit new members, again mostly young women, by either promise or torture. If the potential resisted, she was possessed by the witch (or the devil) and suffered fits and other physical pains. These potential witches played a crucial part in the Salem witch trials, because they were thought to possess a spe-

---

with their counterparts in England many assumptions about what kinds of people witches were, what kinds of practices they engaged in, and where and how they attained their supernatural power. They also knew how to detect witches and how to rid their communities of the threat that witches posed. Indeed, belief in the existence and danger of witches was so widespread, at all levels of society, that disbelief was itself suspect" (2f).

4   While Europe found its witches in the intersection of female and poor, New England tended to blur these categories. Mistress Hibbins, the bad tempered "witch-lady" in Hawthorne's novel, was executed in 1656 (SL 79). Her wealth and position would have probably spared her in England, but in Massachusetts "economic status was becoming irrelevant to the identity of the witch" (Karlsen 28).

5   Puritans believed that a witch could inflict physical harm on persons. They damaged farms, crops, and livestock; they could control the weather, sink vessels, and destroy harvests. Other misdeeds included the spoiling of beer and the drying of cows. Importantly, they were able to obstruct reproductive processes; they had the ability to cause impotence in men and miscarriages in women and were responsible for childbirth fatalities, abortion, infanticide, and monstrous births. The witch could also send animal familiars such as cats and dogs to do their bidding. They could assume the shape of an animal or turn others into animals. *Malefici* were performed by look, touch, or verbal curse. Preternatural knowledge, e.g. divination, was also part of their repertoire. Finally, they were able to fly, become invisible, and conjure spirits from the beyond (Karlsen 6ff).

cial power: the *spectral sight*. The spectral sight constituted the ability to see (and therefore denounce) Satan's agents in the colony (12). Thus, they were able to assuage a very Puritan anxiety, one which Europeans did not share to that extend: The fear of being undermined by minions of Satan.

The devil's pact was central to the Puritan conception of the witch, as it presented a *counter-covenant*. Whereas Europeans feared a witch's misdeeds, New England witches became active satanic agents to bring down God's state. In

[e]xchanging their natural subjection to God for a diabolical subjection to Satan [...] they were not merely threats to their neighbors' physical and economic well-being, but heretics. Witches were enemies not only of society, but of God. When confronted with witches in New England, ministers in particular worried about the Devil's success in recruiting people to help destroy Puritan churches. (Karlsen 4)

The Puritan covenant had both legal and theological implications. Likewise, the witch's counter-covenant carried a legal import (crime) and a new, distinctly Puritan dimension: witchcraft as *heresy*. Indeed, this shift towards heresy was the result of magisterial and clerical meditations and had but small influence on the popular perception of witchcraft (19). But "the clergy's own insistence on the primacy of the witch's relationship with Satan was contributing to [a] redefinition in ways the clergy never intended" (28f). Especially during the Salem craze, the clerical view dominated, causing the possessed to identify witches in all social strata (39).

Karlsen discusses the shift from crime to heresy predominantly in theological and gender-related terms. But the shift does not stop there. If witches were seen as agents of a counter-covenanted community, the threat was also *political*. I argue that the development of the witch in New England ranges from crime to heresy to *treason*. While Karlsen sees the treatment of dissenters like Ann Hutchinson as motivated by their disturbance of social and gender hierarchy, I will focus on the political aspect of witches as outside agents who challenge the unity and sovereignty of Puritan theocracy. The anxiety to be undermined by transgressors is caused by the colony's extreme cohesion and inability to deal with dissent. It is of little importance if a person is a Quaker, a Catholic, a Tolerationist, or an Antinomian. As soon as they are not Puritan, they are tinged with the imagery of witchcraft.[6]

This Puritan either/or ideology makes witchcraft a ready imagery for the branding of dissenters. Bercovitch notes that it is precisely this either/or ideology which Hawthorne seeks to replace with a both/and perspective (Office 9). In order to achieve this transformation, he uses imagery that designated the ultimate enemy and

---

6   Karlsen offers a detailed analysis of how Anne Hutchinson and her fellow Antinomians were linked to witchcraft. See Karlsen: *The Devil in the Shape of a Woman* (1998).

in the course of the novel separates what was once wrongfully conflated: devil-worship and acts of transgression. With Puritan Boston and witchcraft as stage, Hawthorne answers a question that plagued Antebellum America: How may one secure unity in the face of obvious diversity?

Witchcraft and the Quest for Alternatives

In *Young Goodman Brown* (1835), Hawthorne tells the story of a Witches' Sabbath and the initiation of young Puritan witches. In his sketch *Mrs. Hutchinson* (1830), he links womanhood and dissent in the context of the Antinomian controversy and again uses witchcraft to make his point. Indeed, Hawthorne's oeuvre often recurs to witchcraft. But no other work presents so many allusions to witchcraft like *The Scarlet Letter*.

A few examples may be due to clarify my point. Roger Chillingworth is repeatedly cast as a malefic leech, a healer who works evil on his unsuspecting victim. His laboratory is illuminated by hellfire (SL 86); he collects herbs and roots which he uses as medicine (80); a "ghastly fire" (86) gleams in his eyes; he is, ultimately, the "black man" (90) and a "tempter" of souls (159). Similarly, Arthur Dimmesdale is also associated with witchcraft. Reminiscent of Goodman Brown, Arthur is transformed after his forest meeting with Hester and experiences malefic impulses. He appears as one possessed: A person that is not yet a witch, but who finds himself in the process of being tempted. As a witch-potential, he possesses the spectral sight and is enticed to do what witches do: *malefici*. As he returns from the forest, he finds that once "familiar objects" have changed in his perception (138). And it is made clear that it was the "enemy of souls" who caused these changes in the reverend (139).

Dimmesdale is very aware of his transformation. As a true representative of Puritanism, he immediately recognizes the nature of his predicament: "Did I make a contract with [the devil] in the forest, and sign it with my blood?" (SL 140). Unsure, he recreates himself with representatives of Puritan Others, e.g. Spanish (read Catholic) sailors. I shall discuss the significance of the recurring images of Catholicism later. For now let it suffice to say that if Arthur was still in doubts as to his situation, Mistress Hibbins reassures him of their shared status:

'So, reverend sir, you have made a visit into the forest,' observed the witch-lady, nodding her high head-dress at him. 'The next time I pray you to allow me only a fair warning, and I shall be proud to bear you company. Without taking overmuch upon myself, my good word will go far towards gaining any strange gentleman a fair reception from yonder potentate you wot of.' (141)

Arthur denies a pact, but the narrator confirms that, motivated by the temptation of happiness, he "had made a bargain very like it" (ibid.). A discussion of Hester and Arthur's forest meeting must wait for now. However, Arthur is clearly associated with witchcraft and "the world of perverted spirits" (142).

Despite their presentation through witchcraft imagery, Hawthorne's characters remain human and nothing more than – for lack of a better word – civilians. The only real witch in the novel is Mistress Hibbins; and even her nature is questioned. Here, Hawthorne employs a writing strategy which may be called *myth-then-ratio*. This technique entails the exposition of mythological material and its complication by an immediately following rational counter-explanation. Myth-then-ratio forms part of the author's celebrated use of ambiguity, and Bercovitch notes that this usage has aesthetic and political dimensions: By insisting on ambiguity, the author is able to "sustain certain ideas *and* deny the immediate claims." Thus, he demands a perspective indebted to a "faith in ambiguity," which allows for gradualism, consensus, and a fundamental hope for the future (Office 17). Semiologically, this technique presents an "avenue to multiple meanings" and allows for different interpretations. Bercovitch describes this use of ambiguity as a "technique of multiple-choice." The political dimension of such ambiguity, however, is a celebration of pluralism (18). The whole novel presents itself as an "interpreter's guide into perplexity" (19); a literary nightmare for those who, like the Puritans, sought for the unity of meaning. But myth-then-ratio helps the text to suggest the reality of witchcraft to an Antebellum reader. It rejects the imperative of unilateral meaning and produces interpretative possibilities that shift the focus from one truth to the possibility of many.

The encounter between Arthur and Hibbins may serve as example. Directly following the dialogue between the minister and the witch-lady – a dialogue in which Hibbins is presented as a real witch (the myth) – the narrator calls the whole event into question and offers a logical explanation (the ratio) for what is now presented as mere metaphor: "And his encounter with old Mistress Hibbins, if it were a real incident, did but show its sympathy and fellowship with wicked mortals" (SL 142).[7] Who is to decide if Hibbins was a real witch? The myth-then-ratio technique thus

---

[7] Another example for this technique can be found in Hawthorne's *Young Goodman Brown*. When Brown encounters the devil, the reader is given mythological imagery as proof of the stranger's diabolical nature: "But the only thing about him that could be fixed upon as remarkable was his staff, which bore the likeness of a great black snake, so curiously wrought that it might almost be seen to twist and wriggle itself like a living serpent." The image is barely given time to work when the narrator counters it with a rational explication. The whole impression, he argues, "must have been an ocular deception, assisted by the uncertain light" (YGB 179).

forces a process of reflection and the balancing of interpretative alternatives. Ultimately, decision making lies with the reader, which is the whole (democratic) point of this technique.

What I wish to elucidate is the way in which mythological resignification functions in *The Scarlet Letter*. As both an aesthetic and political technique, mythological resignification works on the imagery of witchcraft to first denaturalize (Ic) the basic Puritan myth and later naturalize a variant (IIc) based on the basic myth's mytheme. The resignification seeks to democratize the Puritan myth so as to make it applicable to the Antebellum situation. For Puritan Boston was a theocracy in which transgression in the religious realm was analogous to political transgression; any heterodox element that threatened religious orthodoxy constituted political threat. Therefore, political as well as theological undesirables are treated as witches. The diversity of dissent is conflated, because all dissent is *treason* to the covenant. For Hawthorne's America, a civic myth based on such single-minded notions would not do to resolve the nation's issues; indeed, theocratic policies are unfit, even contra-productive, to a democratic polity. Therefore, the novel seeks to create alternatives and produce a national identity that rejects the Puritan either/or rhetoric and embraces a new, more inclusive perspective based on the principles of debate and consensus: a politics of both/and (Office 9).

In order to do so, Hawthorne uses the notion of witches as transgressors. He is able to create new spaces for identities that do not conform to the Puritan mindset, civic spaces of sympathy that lay the foundations for the development of civil society. At the same time, he does not completely reject the Puritan legacy and excavates notions that allow for mercy, ambiguity, and the accommodation of pluralistic social realities. Thereby, *The Scarlet Letter* dissents from and consents to the fundamental civic myth of Antebellum America.

2.2 PURITAN FATHERS AND THE TREATMENT OF DISSENT

In order to construct a national identity, Antebellum America relied on two distinctive mythologies: the Puritan and the Revolution myth. It is with the first that *The Scarlet Letter* concerns itself. Bercovitch notes that the novel forms part of a body of literature that was written so as to work on the "idea of America;" and it takes the Puritan myth as the basis on which to effect its rewriting. Indeed, the "legends of the founding fathers" were transformed; this transformation, however, presented a "process of revision, not replacement" (Assent 36). Hawthorne's novel works on this basic myth and produces a variant: a rewriting and extending of "the meaning of Puritan migration" (27).

Legends of migration abound in Christian theology, and the myths of Exodus and the search for the Promised Land certainly form the biblical basis for the Puritan myth. Yet the idea of salvation and conversion through voyage also harks back to younger texts. *The Pilgrim's Progress* (1678) by John Bunyan is an apt example.[8] Bunyan's allegory describes the journey of Christian, who sets out from "the City of Destruction" to search for the "Celestial City." On his way, he meets powers that contest to guide and misguide him, among them characters like "Hopeful," "Faithful," "Ignorance," and "Despair" (Bunyan x). Bunyan's allegory was immensely popular, producing numerous editions during his lifetime and retaining its popularity till today. Cynthia Wall notes that one of the "most astonishingly successful reworkings" of Bunyan's narrative is Hawthorne's *The Celestial Rail-Road* (1843), which is –despite its ironic undertones – faithful to the idea of the Puritan voyage (xiii). Similarly, Pooley notes that it is the notion of migration (the "journey motif") which constitutes the very core of Bunyan's narrative (89). Bunyan's story thus recaptured older narratives and made them accessible to Puritan congregations: *Progress* disseminated the tenets of the Pilgrim's journey to "the Celestial City" and thereby exemplifies the foundations of the Puritan myth (x).

Bercovitch famously notes that the Puritan myth offered a "cultural genealogy" for Antebellum America (Office xv). Americans sought a "native heroic age" in the time of New England Puritans, relying on the pilgrims' "sacred mission." Indeed, the "American way" was imagined by many to have originated in New England (33). Thus, negotiations of national identity were given a Puritan "language of prophecy" which imagined a peaceful, organic development of the nation towards liberty (37). In this context, the Puritan myth describes a civic mythology: It is the story of a new settlement (and later, of a new nation) "dedicated to the 'principle of liberty'" (53). Its mythemes included notions of religious piety, sin, justice and forgiveness, voyages to gain freedom, and a community that is chosen, destined, and united. Here, the basic myth is the story of a Christian group of radical dissenters who flee religious decadence, oppression, and set out to establish a true Christian kingdom on Earth.

This myth offers a number of core meanings. One of them is based on its inherent theology and highly consequential for societal belonging in the covenant. This mytheme is worked on in the *The Scarlet Letter*, a mytheme best described as *Sin-as-Sign*. According to Calvinist doctrine, sins are *signs*, visible manifestations of the depraved status of a human being. Ignoble acts, therefore, were not seen as instances of transgression and much less as "sequential parts in the building of a mor-

---

8   For an authoritative text and select criticism, see Wall: *The Pilgrim's Progress* (2009); Dunan-Page: *The Cambridge Companion to Bunyan* (2010); Sharrock (ed.): *The Pilgrim's Progress: A Casebook* (1976); Furlong: *Puritan's Progress* (1975).

al life." Colacurcio reminds us that in Puritan thought, sins presented clues towards a fundamental depravity: They become evidence of the *inner* self and a person's status regarding salvation (327f). In the context of predestination and the idea of visible sainthood, sin presents a revelation through action. Sinners are sinners by *nature* and must be shunned.

Indeed, the letter on Hester's gown offers the metaphorical and indexical realization of this mytheme: Here is a sinful woman. However, Hester's actions throughout the novel refute the tenets of Sin-as-Sign. She will change the letter's meaning and disprove the idea that sin must be indexical to a person's character. The text's mythological resignification works on this specific signification of the Puritan myth. It elaborates on legal and theological discourses of sin, guilt, and atonement, and thereby reworks the Sin-as-Sign mytheme. The basic Puritan myth will thus experience a variation that renders it compatible with Antebellum America.

The Puritan myth is imagined as *the* founding mythology of Antebellum America. In the world of New England Puritanism, Hawthorne and his contemporaries perceived a "native heroic age" which embodied the "origins of the American way" (Office 33). As such, the Puritan age produced a "cultural meta-identity" describing and cementing Antebellum notions about the genesis of the American polity, its political culture, rules for citizenship, and belonging (ibid.). Inherent to this myth is a sanctification of the founders, a filiopietistic perspective that renders Puritans as morally steadfast, unblemished culture heroes.

Here, Puritans become prophets of the American idea; they are protagonists of a myth that told of a group of dissenters who fled tyranny and sought freedom on new shores. Importantly, there was a tendency to read the Puritan story in a teleological manner. This interpretation not only depicted the pilgrims as founders of the nation but also as carriers of democratic citizenship. According to the basic myth, it was "freedom-loving Pilgrims, who on the ground of their new colonies found a more fertile soil for civic participation" (Thomas 182).

This teleological reading has its pitfalls. How can democracy evolve from a theocratic state? Or, to turn the question around, how can American democracy rely on principles forged by pious radicals who equated law and religion? There are inherent paradoxes in the development of America national identity, and the fact that it was based on Puritanism accounts for many of these discrepancies. These paradoxes were intolerable for Hawthorne for two reasons. First, he held that Antebellum America required a compelling civic myth in order to overcome the struggles that threatened to tear the nation apart. Second, a romantic *Weltbild* informed his musings on the development of American democracy: the organic perspective.[9] In this context, America grows out of its past, is the result of gradual development in the ongoing succession of life-cycles. But how could a liberal democracy grow from theocratic roots? Where was the seed in the Puritan past that allowed for the development of Hawthorne's America?

I believe that the answers to these questions lie in the mythological treatment of the Puritan myth in *The Scarlet Letter*. In producing a variant myth, Hawthorne effects two things. First, he denaturalizes the basic Puritan myth, thereby complicating the perspective on Puritans and writing, to say it with Blumenberg, Achillean heels on the image of the founding fathers. Second, he naturalizes an alternative to the founders: He focuses on dissenters, creating an alternative set of ancestors. It is the variant myth – the mythological naturalization of an alternative set of founders – that allows for the recuperation of the Puritan narrative as a civic myth for the 19th century. This variant, however, entails very different consequences for American national identity.

Certainly, the early settlers are not entirely discredited in Hawthorne's novel. But Boudreau is correct in noting that Hawthorne had a very ambivalent opinion regarding Puritanism. He was torn between patriotic filiopiety and ethical condemnation of his ancestors' deeds, a position shared by most of his contemporaries (365). But it may have been this ambivalence that motivated him to ultimately salvage the founding fathers' relevance for a democratic America. At first, however, *The Scarlet Letter* presents the forefathers in a rather unflattering light, which reflects the novel's ethical judgment of the perpetrators of witch-trials and intolerance – sins which the author, as their "representative," wished to amend and remove (SL 11).

The Planters of the Black Flower

Hawthorne's writing is deeply informed by organicism. The vegetative metaphoric used in *The Scarlet Letter* is directly associated with the Puritan Fathers, and their description attests to the novel's ambivalence towards the settlers. It is in the first chapter and with a vegetative metaphoric that Hawthorne begins his mythological resignification; here, he offers the preparation (Ia & IIa) of the basic myth and its

---

9   Male notes that in organicism, we find a vegetative view of history that holds the entirety of reality as connected on a fundamental level. Everything in this system occurs gradually and grows naturally. The universe is seen as a coherent and living unity, and the laws that govern the universe are bound by the recurring cycles of birth, life, and death (218). For a detailed elaboration on organicism in Hawthorne see Male: *From the Innermost Germ* in ELH Vol. 20.3 (1953).

variant. In this novel, the first three stages of mythological resignification (I) are intertwined and occur almost simultaneously. While the preparation of basic and variant myth is given in vegetative metaphors which will accompany the entire text, the denaturalization (Ic) of the basic myth begins on the very first page.

Here, the reader is presented with the supposed harbingers of American democracy. It is also here that we are offered an alternative, a second principle that will guide us through the story. The emerging tension between the basic Puritan myth and the alternative set of founders creates the very space in which ambiguity can effect a reevaluation of Puritan and, by extension, American identity. The preparation and simultaneous denaturalization of Boston Puritans sets the stage for the gradual emergence and final assertion of pluralism and legitimate dissent in a formerly coercive society.

But the initial preparation (Ia) presents the Puritan founders in a more than ambivalent light:

A throng of bearded men, in sad-colored garments, and gray, steeple-crowned hats, intermixed with women, some wearing hoods, and others bareheaded, was assembled in front of a wooden edifice, the door of which was heavily timbered with oak, and studded with iron spikes. The founders of a new colony, whatever Utopia of human virtue and happiness they might originally project, have invariably recognized it among their early practical necessities to allot a portion of the virgin soil as a cemetery, and another portion as the site of a prison. (SL 36)

The *Et in arcadia ego* motif used in this passage illuminates how the utopian Puritan project clashes with the realities of crime and death. The dream of a colony "of human virtue and happiness" finds immediate restriction by reality's absolutism: not just by death but by the fact that man is fallible. The garments worn are of central importance here, especially their color; the grayness and sadness of Puritan life is reflected in their attire. Further, their legal system is "studded with iron spikes" (ibid.). Indeed, these denaturalizing descriptions recur throughout the novel: The "general tint" of Puritan life "was the sad gray, brown, or black of the English emigrants" (148); the period is imagined as an "iron age" (165), its belief systems as "an iron framework" (83). The narrator may at times exaggerate "the gray or sable tinge," but he nevertheless uses said tinge to characterize "the mood and manners of the age" and presents us with a coding of the Puritan character: hard, cold, gray, and sad (146).

The aforementioned iron framework is of special significance. If the Puritan legacy is portrayed as one of gray radicalism, its harshness in fact counter-acts something darker and stronger: human depravity. Indeed, Puritanism is imagined as a nominal space in Schmitt's sense: A space fenced against the onslaught of human nature, which – from the nominal point of view – is tainted by depravity and sin.

Faced with the facts of life, the settlers erect two new sites, both reactions to realities outside their control: death and crime. The latter receives particular attention here, as it is with the transgression of law that the novel begins.

[T]he wooden jail was already marked with weather-stains and other indications of age, which gave a yet darker aspect to its beetle-browed and gloomy front. The rust on the ponderous iron-work of its oaken door looked more antique than anything else in the New World. Like all that pertains to crime, it seemed never to have known a youthful era. (SL 36)

The prison seeks to control what must be seen as threat to the covenant: sin and transgression. In Puritan Boston, crime is not just a legal concern. Crime shakes the very foundation of the community of saints. If the Puritans sought to find fertile soil for a sinless life, the world did not hesitate to prove their utopia nothing but a dream, for crime and death never knew a "youthful era" (ibid.). They are an unconquerable part of reality's absolutism.

The institution to control crime, however, is not presented as a holy (or wholesome) answer. The text is rather pragmatic about the prison, which is, after all, one of life's "practical necessities." But it imagines it as one of the darker outcomes of social order: the "black flower" of civilized society. Puritan treatment of the feared aspects of human nature is clearly given a sad-colored tinge. What is more, the supposedly dark and uncivilized realm of nature reacts toward the planting of such a flower. As if resonating its purport, "unsightly vegetation" grows around the prison (SL 36). Nature echoes the institution and renders its own verdict on the matter.

The black flower of civilized society is the Puritan flower, an image that prepares (Ia) and accompanies the ongoing denaturalization (Ic) of the basic myth. That is not to say that the settlers are condemned completely. But it is decisively the way they view (and react) to human imperfection that is depicted in negative terms. The founding fathers are associated with the black flower and its signification: judgment.

Simultaneously, the reader is given an alternative. Here, the variant myth finds its preparation (IIa). It is important to note that this alternative does not deny the human ability for crime – but it answers it differently. A second flower is offered, one that will also color the entire narrative:

But, on one side of the portal, and rooted almost at the threshold, was a wild rose-bush, covered, in this month of June, with its delicate gems, which might be imagined to offer their fragrance and fragile beauty to the prisoner as he went in, and to the condemned criminal as he came forth to his doom, in token that the deep heart of Nature could pity and be kind to him. (SL 36)

The text's focus switches from the prison to the roses. Here, the reader is prepared for the conflict that is to be resolved in the novel: the tension between justice and mercy. The black flower and the red roses become emblems for Puritans and dissenters respectively.

This vegetative and preparatory imagery takes us back to Hawthorne's organic perspective. The question that arises is this: Which of these flowers sired the American generations to come? Two points may be given to illuminate the issue. First, the "rose-bush," we are informed, "has been kept alive in history." In this case, the roses are associated with Ann Hutchinson, a reference which will receive my attention at a later point. What is crucial here is that the rose-bush has survived, has come down, almost as if by evolution, to the present. It may have done so as an heirloom of the "sainted Ann Hutchinson" or by the efforts of "the stern old wilderness." Second, at the close of the first chapter, the reader himself is addressed and offered one of the roses. "It may serve to symbolize some sweet moral blossom" which may be of use to "relieve the darkening close of a tale of human frailty and sorrow" (SL 37). Nature's mercy cannot deny the frailty of the human condition. But instead of punishment, it offers relief.

The basic Puritan myth experiences a denaturalization from the very beginning. Instead of sanctified heroes we are presented with a "throng of bearded men, in sad-colored garments" (SL 36). The forefathers are depicted in organic terms and assigned the black flower of civilization. At the same time, the text offers alternatives: the instance of mercy and the rose-bush. It is the roses and the idea of mercy that prepare for the introduction of the novel's main transgressor.

Primacy of Justice and Popular Judgment

The scene in which Hester faces her fellow Puritans for the first time tentatively begins the usage of witchcraft imagery. Here, the tension between justice and mercy is elaborated. Further, the reader is reminded of the black flower vs. rose-bush dialectic and given analogous notions (town vs. forest and orthodoxy vs. heterodoxy). Importantly, the Puritan's negative depiction and their association with the realm of law and justice continue in a proper exposition of the basic myth (Ib). The manner of representation further entails a continued denaturalization process (Ic).

The inhabitants of Boston assemble on Prison-lane in front of the jail. Their gaze is "fastened on the iron-clamped oaken door," their appearance one of "grim-rigidity" and in tune with the "severity of the Puritan character." The settler's overall aspect prefigures the sentence that the tribunal shall pass on the woman about to emerge. Indeed, there is little distinction between the punishment of petty and serious crimes for the onlookers; the "mildest and the severest acts of public discipline were alike made venerable and awful." Very early, we are made to understand that there exists but little discretion in the Puritan mind regarding acts of transgression. Here is "a people amongst whom law and religion were almost identical," a statement which the politically minded reader immediately understands as the identification of Puritan Boston as a theocracy. In Boston, religion and law conflate (SL 37).

The exposition is contrasted and thereby given a sharper edge by representatives of other spheres. The narrator guesses at the cause for the settlers convention and imagines "an Antinomian, a Quaker," "other heterodox religionists," and a "vagrant Indian" being prepared for permanent exile. "It might be, too," he continues, "that a witch, like old Mistress Hibbins, [...] was to die upon the gallows." We are presented with contrastive sets of individuals, a variety of dissenters and undesirables, which share one final destination: exile. Whatever their offense, their punishment hurries them back "into the dark forest" (SL 37). The forest, in fact, marks them for what they are perceived to *be*, revealing their innermost nature as other.[10] Antinomians, Quakers, Indians, and witches are not merely imagined as persons who sin; their sins reveal themselves as *essentially* sinful and therefore unfit to remain in society.

As mentioned, sins were imagined as *signs*, visible manifestations of the depraved status of a human being; they were seen as evidences of the *inner* self (Colacurcio 327f). However, we should not suppose that every transgression immediately marked a person as saint or sinner. Especially for the latter, a return to the fold was possible, as long as punishment, public confession, and repentance were observed. Puritan doctrine taught that the personal and societal covenant remains unbroken even if the saint possesses "infirmities." Still, there were transgressions that were unforgivable, sins which, in John Preston's words, "untye the marriage knot" (in Colacurcio 328). The marriage knot in this context means the covenant, but one does not need to think far to apply this to other relationships. The crux lies in the idea that sinners who enact an unforgivable sin are not only unable to return to the covenant; this kind of transgression reveals these individuals as radical *others* who never partook of the covenant in the first place (329).

The exile of Antinomians, Quakers, Indians, and witches referred to in the passage enforces the perception of Puritan Boston as a closed community. These individuals were not only exiled for their deeds but for the fact that their deeds ousted them as *non-covenanted*. Their sphere lies outside Puritan religion and law: in the dark forest. They are sent to the place that seems to be their natural habitat. Further, the practices of public punishment, confession, and banishment attest to two notions. First, there exists a conflation of performance and identity, outer action and

---

10 Person notes that Ann Hutchinson, for instance, was not only expelled for preaching a covenant of grace; it was the very action of dissentious preaching which revealed her to be a sinner, a person, in John Winthrop's words, "not fit for [Puritan] society" (in SL 37).

inner nature. Second, Puritan Boston suffers from an inability to integrate heterodox elements due to a deep-seated anxiety regarding the covenant's survival. Both these notions are rooted in Puritan theology, which formed the basis for legal and political practice.

The Scarlet Letter denaturalizes the Puritan myth aesthetically as well as politically. Indeed, the novel is a testing of Puritan ideology, a "literary exercise in moral theology." And Puritanism ultimately fails this "pragmatic test." In fact, the novel becomes an argument against the utopia of Calvinism: In its political dimensions, it reveals the inadequacy of theocratic governance (Warren in Colacurcio 319). Puritanism's inability to integrate dissent is rooted in its theological foundations; as such, it becomes impractical as a civic myth for the Antebellum. Ethically, the novel discards Calvinism, but it also tests Puritanism as a civic myth for a free polity. In the end, it fails to pass the democratic test: the successful systemic accommodation of dissent and pluralism (Cohen and Arato 568).

I hold that the novel imagines the reason for this failure to be a radical *primacy of justice*. The negative imagery attached to Puritanism is the result of an imbalanced theology turned law. Thus, the basic Puritan myth is denaturalized because Puritan strategies to cope with dissent are held inadequate for Antebellum democracy. However, Hawthorne is able to produce a variant myth which promises to alleviate the tensions between justice and mercy. In recommending a balanced approach in the novel, he salvages Puritanism as a civic myth.

When it comes to the enactment of mercy that can balance justice, the novel differentiates between popular and magisterial judgment. Central to the balancing is the character of Hester and her association with the imagery of witchcraft. The conflation of crime and heresy in witchcraft is analogous to the Calvinist conflation of outward act and inner nature: Sinners sin because they are by nature sinful; a person betrays their heretical nature by acts of witchcraft. As seen above, the text gives a number of possible points of association to produce the image of a radical other. But the novel does not use Indian or Quaker imagery to describe the protagonists. Hawthorne invests in witchcraft to focus on a historical notion that is able to represent a demonized form of dissent. The novel will transform the transgressor and mold the attached witchcraft image. In the end, the dissent that would have earned Hester a demonized status will be able to legitimize the heterodox subject.

First, however, the transgressor feels the full force of the Puritan either/or mindset in the exposition of the basic myth (Ib). The exposition reveals Puritanism's primacy of justice, and Hester is subjected to two forms: popular and magisterial judgment. In 'The Market-Place,' the first stands in the foreground, while magisterial judgment – like Hester's transgression itself – remains in the background. At this point, the novel exposes the basic myth while simultaneously denaturalizing it (Ib & Ic). Passages like the following also prepare for the gradual introduction of the elements that will help to constitute the variant (IIb). As Hester faces her fellow

Puritans, she is subjected to what her punishment was designed to achieve: shame through popular judgment. This is formulated by a group of gossips:

'Goodwives,' said a hard-featured dame of fifty, 'I'll tell ye a piece of my mind. It would be greatly for the public behoof, if we women, being of mature age and church-members in good repute, should have the handling of such malefactresses as this Hester Prynne. What think ye, gossips? If the hussy stood up for judgment before us five would she get off with such a sentence as the worshipful magistrates have awarded?' (SL 38f)

Indeed, Hester's trespass is of public concern. Its publicity is mirrored in her public shaming and the judgment passed by the populace. To them, the magisterial sentence seems insufficient, and another "autumnal matron" calls for a more suitable punishment: "At the very least they should have put the brand of a hot iron on Hester Prynne's forehead. Madame Hester would have winced at that, I warrant me. But she—the naughty baggage—little will she care what they put upon the bodice of her gown!" (39).[11]

The brutality of such punishment may shock the reader; but the "ugliest as well as the most pitiless of these self-constituted judges" is yet to speak, and she calls for another penalty: "This woman has brought shame upon us all and ought to die. Is there no law for it? Truly there is, both in the Scripture and the statute-book. Then let the magistrates, who have made it to no effect, thank themselves if their own wives and daughters go astray!" (SL 39).

Hester's sin is not a private matter; it has societal implications. What this speaker suggests is that the continued life of a sinner would bring others (especially young women) to give in to temptation. Hester as the temptress is one of the first witch references in the novel.[12] What is important in this passage is the explicit fear

---

11 The practice of branding sinners with letters which indicate their crime was common at the time. Hawthorne himself reports on it in *Young Goodman Brown* (YGB 174). Again, we find the conflation of sin and personal nature at the core of this practice. The branding of a person with a marker of their sin illuminates how Puritans saw the nature of sin itself. Branding a sinner, just like one would brand cattle to assert ownership, testifies to the perception of sin as the sign of a person's inner nature. The sin and the subsequent branding reveal the status of the sinner. The sin, quite literally, *owns* the person.

12 Karlsen explains that the idea of witches as recruiters of young women was among the most pronounced fears of Puritan settlers (5, 10). Moreover, although not hereditary, witchcraft was thought to be contagious. In order to explain the existence of male and child witches, Puritan doctrine held that husbands, children, and especially daughters could receive their wife's or mother's magical powers. A witch's close family members were indeed likely suspects.

of contagion and the belief that only Hester's death could prevent the settlement from falling into moral darkness. To what extent witchcraft is conflated with societal categories becomes clearer if we ask why a private sin receives such a harsh and public judgment in the first place.

Elias' concept of the *We-Ideal* is helpful here. New England, like any other community, awarded membership in exchange for the paying of a prize. The consent to a group's fundamental beliefs (and subsequently adherence to its laws) is an indispensable requirement for membership. The prize to pay, therefore, is a *Lustopfer* [Lust-Sacrifice], a control of such affects which go against given norms; membership and the gains of belonging are the awarded *Lustprämie* [Lust-Gain] (18f).

Now, if religion and law are separate, the transgression of theological boundaries may affect one's belonging to a religious community. But in theocratic Boston, Wall notes, religion and law are one, and church membership is prerequisite for freemanship, a status carrying the ability to vote (6). Hester's adultery is a transgression of societal *and* religious law, and its punishment is set down in "the Scripture and the statute-book" (SL 39). By transgressing, Hester violated one of the basic values of the community. Her guilt and the consequences are therefore not only assessed by the magistrates but also by the public, whose anger is fueled by a subjective feeling of injustice. Why should someone be allowed to partake of the *Lustprämie* if they did not pay the *Lustopfer*? Why should the "church-members of good repute" suffer the presence of one who transgressed the rules that grant membership (38)? A logic of emotions is at work here which does not regard objective considerations. The gossips' judgment stems from a conviction of having been hurt *personally*. They respond to an attack on societal rules as if they had been attacked themselves. As carriers of the group's values and beliefs, they are the most outraged and the most injured by Hester's sin. In their either/or mindset, the transgressor has no place in a sainted community. Because of her sin, Hester becomes an outlaw, outside of both societal and divine grace. She should die because the consequences of her enemy-presence would prove disastrous to the settlement as a whole. Societal reentry, in fact, is possible and would depend on public confession and public exhibition of repentance. The popular judges, however, do not even consider these options.

Until now, the novel exposed the basic Puritan myth (Ib) by focusing on the darker aspects of Puritan society: the primacy of justice and judgment. The ongoing denaturalization (Ic) will continue to draw on these negative notions. Nevertheless, there are aspects of mercy interspersed in the narrative, and there are redeeming and merciful instances that inform this very scene. These instances are restricted to the female young, the male, and to the magistrates.

The Scarlet Sign

Voices of mercy are a rare occurrence, especially at the beginning of the text. A "young wife" is the first person to speak, if not favorably, at least pityingly on Hester. "[L]et her cover the mark as she will," she states, "the pang of it will be always in her heart." Her ability to show mercy is contrastive and almost alleviates the gossip's harshness. Their accusations are further countered by a male voice. "'Mercy on us, goodwife," exclaimed a man in the crowd, "is there no virtue in woman, save what springs from a wholesome fear of the gallows?" (SL 39). Beneath these merciful statements, we find one of the central questions of the novel: Is there a possibility for good in a person who has been found a sinner? Can a sinner's life culminate in something virtuous? Hester's return and her social work will answer both questions with a definite yes, disproving the Calvinist presumption of Sin-as-Sign.

As Hester is introduced, we are once again reminded of the color-coded images that inform the narrative. Before she emerges from prison, the town-beadle, a stern representative of Puritan Law, is described by the now familiar imagery:

The door of the jail being flung open from within there appeared, in the first place, like a black shadow emerging into sunshine, the grim and gristly presence of the town-beadle, with a sword by his side, and his staff of office in his hand. This personage prefigured and represented in his aspect the whole dismal severity of the Puritanic code of law. (SL 39f)

The description of Puritan justice clashes with the young woman emerging from prison. "[O]n the threshold of the prison-door" she "repelled" his touch and "by an action marked with natural dignity and force of character […] stepped into the open air, as if by her own free will." From the moment she is introduced, Hester Prynne is described in terms that defy, both literally and pictorially, everything the black flower of civilization stands for. Indeed, Hester *is* dissent. She faces her fellow settlers "with a burning blush, and yet a haughty smile, and a glance that would not be abashed" (40).

As mentioned, the letter itself presents the embodiment of the Sin-as-Sign mytheme. But instead of accepting its original purport, Hester appropriates it from the very beginning and infuses it with her own signification. Indeed, the phase of mythemic elaboration (IIb) begins as early as this. Contrasting the settlers' "sad-colored garments" (SL 36), Hester's attire does justice to the luxuriant beauty of her own symbol, the rose:

On the breast of her gown, in fine red cloth, surrounded with an elaborate embroidery and fantastic flourishes of gold thread, appeared the letter A. It was so artistically done, and with so much fertility and gorgeous luxuriance of fancy, that it had the effect of a last and fitting decoration to the apparel which she wore; and which was of a splendor in accordance with the taste of the age, but greatly beyond what was allowed by the sumptuary regulations of the colony. (40)

What follows is a description of Hester's beauty, which seems an odd point to dwell on given the circumstances. But her beauty and its effect constitute her separation from other Puritans. Those who had already been familiar with her had expected the culprit to hang her head in shame and were shocked "to perceive how her beauty shone out, and made a halo of misfortune and ignominy in which she was enveloped" (ibid.). Sainted Hester, although a saint of misfortune, does not abide in the sphere of mortals anymore. It is the letter that takes her out of society and ascribes her to another realm: "that SCARLET LETTER, so fantastically embroidered an illuminated upon her bosom [...] had the effect of a spell, taking her out of the ordinary relations with humanity and enclosing her in a sphere by herself" (41).

That sphere is neither town nor forest but a *liminal space*. If Hester were indeed a creature of the forest in the novel's imaginary, she would have become a full-blown witch like Hibbins. But she has not, for reasons I will discussed later. Hester is *associated* with witchcraft but never portrayed as a real witch. She is stuck in the middle, caught on neither side of the fence. One should not forget that Hester, too, is a Puritan. A "burning blush" betrays her feeling shame at her transgression. Her spaces are the "threshold" between prison and market place (SL 40), Boston's "outskirts" between civilization and wilderness (56), and the "margins of the water" between the old and the new world (109).

Coercion and Conditional Mercy

In the exposition (Ib), we are introduced to the basic Puritan myth. Simultaneously, its mythological opposition is elaborated in the novel's main dissenter. Indeed, the mythemic elaboration (IIb) begins as Hester is worked out of the throng of sad-colored individuals and as the scarlet letter becomes visible. The text exposes the basic Puritan myth by means of the contrastive introduction of the variant myths' protagonist. Moreover, the act of imposing the letter on Hester constitutes the first appearance of the Sin-as-Sign mytheme. At the same time, Hester's appropriation of the symbol presents the first instance of mythemic elaboration (IIb) preparing for the variant myth. Indeed, Hester and the variant evolve from and against – are both result and effect of –the basic Puritan myth.

The Hester we encounter has an attitude of "desperate recklessness," one that seems primarily designed to hide her shame (SL 40). But her dissent is the direct result of the Puritan practice of public shaming. Similarly, the letter itself is not, as others have suggested,[13] an object designed to eliminate conflict (Office 8) but the agent of a punishment designed to coerce the culprit into submission. Confession and repentance were the preconditions for a return to the community. In the novel, a magistrate states that Hester's confession and "repentance" may serve "to take the scarlet letter off [her] breast." All he needs is the name of her lover. That confession, however, had to be public; a bargain Hester refuses to take, thereby salvaging her integrity but barring her societal reentry (SL 49). Thus, the wearer of the letter is depersonalized; she becomes a "living sermon against sin" (46). It is difficult to see the elimination of conflict in a punishment where consent is based on coercion.

Coercion is further imminent in the instrument of the scaffold. As Hester and Pearl are directed towards it, the narrator expresses his disgust at the practice: "There can be no outrage, methinks, against our common nature, – whatever be the delinquencies of the individual, – no outrage more flagrant than to forbid the culprit to hide his face for shame." Such punishments and the mindset that originated them are repudiated, and the narrator continues: the Puritan "penal machine [...] was held, in the old times, to be as effectual an agent, in the promotion of good citizenship, as ever was the guillotine among the terrorists of France" (SL 42). Interestingly, the narrator speaks of citizens here; Puritan settlers, however, were royal subjects. Thomas has commented on the use of this anachronism and links it to Hawthorne's participation in viewing the Puritan narrative as a fundamental civic myth (181f). I agree with this perspective but would like to refine it. I hold that the use of the term citizenship actually wrests legitimacy from the basic Puritan myth; it propels the reader into an Antebellum perspective and makes them reflect on whether Puritan policies might be applicable to a democratic America. In short, the denaturalization (Ic) of the Puritan myth is continued with this question: Are the scaffold, the pillory, public shaming, and radical justice the answers to Antebellum issues?

While the novel condemns the use of Puritan practices and thus denaturalizes the basic myth, it does not completely repudiate the founders themselves. The concept of mercy is in fact held inherent to Puritanism; at least to the Puritanism preached by the most famous Puritan Father: John Winthrop. Boudreau is certainly wrong to see the rose-bush as Winthrop's symbol and to label him as "angelic." But the governor and his legacy are woven into the novel. The capacity of balancing justice and mercy are found in Winthrop's writing, and one may argue that, as a political agent, he strove to achieve this balance. Hawthorne's recognition of the similarity between Antebellum and Colonial issues prompted him to adopt Winthrop's

---

13 Among others, Bercovitch argues in this vein. See Bercovitch: *The Office of the Scarlet Letter* (1991). For further commentary on the letter see Pringle: *The Scarlet Lever* in ESQ Vol. 53.1 (2007).

strategies, culminating in the design of rituals of consensus: solutions based on experience outside the realm of moral considerations (Boudreau 351-356).

Winthrop's influence on the novel can be summarized as the conviction that an insistence on radical justice was not an adequate way to govern. "Winthrop believed that severity was not necessarily the best instrument of government. Through he had little patience for sin, his compassion toward sinners was genuine" (Boudreau 348). Indeed, mercy as a *sine qua non* of governance is prevalent in his writing. So are peace, stability, and the primacy of the Puritan errand; in fact, the successful achievement of the latter trumps a strict adherence to the letter of the law (349). There existed mechanisms to alleviate conflict in the Puritan regime, some of which may be linked to Winthrop. The forgiving of sins and the sinner's restoration were possible, as the following excerpt from the *Platform of Church Discipline* (1649) testifies:

If the Lord sanctify the censure to the offender, so as by the grace of Christ, he doth testify his repentance, with humble confession of his sin, and judging of himself, giving glory unto God; the Church is then to forgive him, and to comfort him, and to restore him to the wonted brotherly communion, which formerly he enjoyed with them. (in Boudreau 350)

Forgiveness and restoration were not only possible but desirable. It is instances like these that may motivate Bercovitch's reading of the scarlet letter as an instrument of resolving conflict by restoring the culprit back to the fold. But given its dehumanizing effect and the production of consent by means of coercion, I find it hard to ascribe to that perspective. At the same time, there are instances of mercy in Puritan policy which may have been overshadowed by the events of the late 17th century. The fact that Puritans *intended* mercy is a point Hawthorne's novel tries to make, and Bercovitch is correct in noting that Massachusetts leaders had chosen "not to apply the letter of the law" but define law "through the ambiguities of mercy and justice" (Office 47). The novel therefore revolves around the "question of how to treat a single sinner, whether to exile or rehabilitate her," which for Hawthorne had "particular relevance to the larger political issues confronting antebellum America" (Boudreau 350). Whether the perception of Puritan mercy is a product of Antebellum (and contemporary) filiopiety is at this point irrelevant. Acts of mercy inform the decisions made in the novel, and they are enacted by the magistrates especially: Magisterial mercy safes the Puritan myth from complete denaturalization.

Magisterial mercy stands in opposition to the gossip's popular judgment. Only the young wife pities Hester: "Oh peace, neighbors, peace!" whispered their youngest companion; "do not let her hear you. Not a stitch in that embroidered letter, but she has felt it in her heart" (SL 41). Likewise, the magistrates employ discretion and do not sentence Hester to death. They pass a merciful sentence and levy arguments that consider Hester's character and personal situation. The judges, therefore, decide not to "put in force the extremity" of the law, but "in their great mercy and tenderness of heart" sentence Hester to public shaming and the wearing of the letter. It is only Chillingworth, Hester's cuckolded but incognito husband, who knows that the letter will depersonalize her, making her "a living sermon against sin" (SL 46).

The text, however, denaturalizes the sacrosanctity of Puritan magistrates in Governor Bellingham[14] and contextualizes their position:

They were doubtless, good men, and sage. But, out of the whole human family, it would not have been easy to select the same number of wise and virtuous persons, who should be less capable of sitting in judgment on an erring woman's heart, and disentangling its mesh of good and evil, than the sages of rigid aspect towards whom Hester Prynne now turned her face. (SL 47)

Still, the text claims that "whatever sympathy [Hester] might expect lay in the larger and warmer heart of the multitude." Considering the settler's judgment, this does indeed sound hollow. It is only the Puritan leaders who at least try to "disentangle [the] mesh of good and evil" before passing judgment (ibid.). Their use of discretion, rigid as it may be, trumps the simplistic judgment of the goodwives.

The elder that addresses Hester on the scaffold is Reverend John Wilson. Although described as a man of "kind and genial spirit," he is also famous for his part in the trial of Ann Hutchinson. In his description, the denaturalization process finds another continuation: "He looked like the darkly engraved portraits which we see prefixed to old volumes" (SL 47). Wilson offers to remove the letter in hope to extract her lover's name; but the mercy offered here is of Puritan coloring: Punishment, shaming, and public confession remain the prerequisites for forgiveness. Wilson thus adheres to doctrine and offers a merciful alternative on Puritan terms. He cautions Hester not to transgress "beyond the limits of heaven's mercy." The letter may have been intended to enable the transgressor to return to the community (on communal terms), but in its failure, it causes her exclusion. The letter lies outside magisterial power now: "Never!" replied Hester Prynne [...]. "It is too deeply branded. Ye *cannot* take it off" (49).[15]

---

14 Person notes that Hawthorne was rather liberal in his use of dates. Historically, John Winthrop would have been governor in 1642 (SL 47). The most sensible reason for this liberality seems to be the author's wish to disassociate Winthrop from the "grayness" that informs the Puritan's description. Moreover, Bellingham was involved in a scandal in 1642. He married a woman who was promised to another (Newberry 337). The irony sits deep if one considers that a magistrate persecuted for improper behavior now sits in judgment over Hester.

15 Italics MRD.

I wish to clarify three points here. First, mercy is indeed evident in magisterial policy. Magisterial discretion in judgment and their efforts to return the culprit to the fold point towards that conclusion. Second, magisterial mercy is *conditional mercy*. It makes a return to society possible only by absolute submission. But the failure of conditional mercy is obvious: Such absolute consent can only exist in a system that is inhabited exclusively by people who believe exactly the same things. Such a community cannot not exist; it would require total obedience and crumble at any instance of heterodoxy. Third, it is specifically this notion of ideological cohesion (and coercion) that the process of mythological resignification reveals to the reader. The basic myth is prepared for and exposed; then, the image of the Puritan fathers is denaturalized by means of historical critique focusing on the errors in their treatment of dissenters. Puritans are imagined as stern and harsh; but most importantly, as *old* and *overcome*.

Nevertheless, Hawthorne turns to Winthrop's notions of mercy to construct a Puritan model for Antebellum America:

Writing as civil war loomed, but before it seemed inevitable, Hawthorne too was wary of deep political differences: an expanding market economy, violent labor and political disputes, and a culture whose emerging ethos was based on individualism. He turned to Winthrop as a model of peace-maker. (Boudreau 341)

In fact, the notion of conditional mercy is rooted in Winthrop's doctrine. He upheld a primacy of communal affectation, i.e. he believed that mercy arises from affective bonds in a community (345). But if mercy is a product of affection, it is rendered mute if there is no affection. Conditional mercy is a sentiment restricted to an in-group bound by sympathetic feeling. Any outsider (or insider) who lacks those precarious bonds cannot expect a merciful treatment. If mercy is to balance justice, which applies to all, it fails in the case of individuals who do not possess the qualities that, for whatever reason, produce affection.

Hester is an apt example. In having refused Wilson, she transgressed "the limits of heavens mercy" and the limits of Bostonian belonging (SL 49). It is in this very moment that she is cast out. Wilson retracts mercy and lounges into

a discourse on sin, in all its branches, but with continual reference to the ignominious letter. So forcibly did he dwell upon this symbol, for the hour or more during which its periods were rolling over the people's heads, that it assumed new terrors in their imagination, and seemed to derive its scarlet hue from the flames of the infernal pit. (50)

Hester becomes a mere reference in the rhetorical upholding of doctrine. One will be hard pressed to find mercy in this treatment of a human being. Hester did not ascribe to the conditions that would have granted her mercy, so she becomes the outcast, the ultimate transgressor.

True to their either/or mindset, her fellow Puritans now perceive her approaching the realm of witchcraft. Standing on the scaffold, her letter "derives its scarlet hue from the infernal pit." As she is escorted back to prison, those who look after her believe "that the scarlet letter threw a lurid gleam along the dark passage-way of the interior" (SL 50). The transformation of the outcast to the witch begins with Hester's rejection of conditional mercy. Simultaneously, this transformation continues the mythemic elaboration (IIb). It is here that the Sin-as-Sign mytheme begins to be molded.

Why did Hester refuse the merciful alternative, conditional as it may be? Winthrop's mercy is restricted by the primacy of the errand. Given the New World situation, Winthrop was anxious about cohesion.[16] Communal interest had to overrule individual interest if the errand was to be fulfilled. For Winthrop, a community in the face of danger requires obedience, a clear-cut feudal hierarchy, and the divine sanction of magisterial power. Individuality and "the low estate of democracy" had no place in Puritan Boston (in Wall 10). Hester Prynne could not consent to that. In Boston's theocratic world, she holds on to individuality. Yes, she may feel shame, but the ambiguous circumstances of her transgression make it hard for her to believe her action to be truly sinful. It is the reliance on her *self* rather than on Puritan authority that causes her defiance. She will foster that feeling and arrive at a point of radical individualism later in the novel. At the beginning, however, Puritan mercy failed her, just as she failed to be an obedient Puritan.[17] Conditional mercy, it appears, was unsuccessful. This notion, like many other Puritan concepts, seems impracticable for Antebellum democracy.

---

16 His anxiety is made manifest in a journal entry repudiating the plea of colonists to leave Boston and pursue their own opportunities: "Ask again, what liberty thou hast towards others, which thou likest not to allow others towards thyself; for if one may go, another may, and so the greater part, and so church and commonwealth may be left destitute in a wilderness, exposed to misery and reproach, and all for thy ease and pleasure" (in Boudreau 355).

17 The failure of conditional mercy in the novel reflects the historical failure of Winthrop's policy. Boudreau comments that upon Winthrop's death, the settlement turned to Endicott as governor, an election which hailed a decade of ruthless persecution of Quakers, witches, and other dissenters (356). After Endicott's rule, the situation did not improve; "for the next few decades at least, orthodoxy was to hold sway, and after Winthrop died in 1649, it was to be uncompromising and harsh" (Wall 233).

The Democratic Applicability of the Puritan Myth

At this point, Hawthorne's mythological resignification has accomplished a number of things. First, it has prepared (Ia), exposed (Ib), and begun to denaturalize (Ic) the basic Puritan myth. Second, it has prepared the protagonist for the production of a variant mythology (IIa). The text positions Hester in a liminal space between society and nature and begins to associate her with dissent, individuality, and the imagery of witchcraft. In Hester and her roses, the novel has prepared for the mythemic elaboration (IIb) in which the Sin-as-Sign mytheme will be continuously worked on. Third, the resignification process has refuted Puritan strategies of dealing with dissent as adequate policies for the Antebellum. This was achieved by derogating Puritan penal practices and focusing on their anxieties regarding justice and community. At the same time, the text has endeavored to present mercy as inherent to Puritan governance by elaborating on magisterial policy. Before I move on to the production of the variant myth, I wish to explain on what grounds the basic myth fails as a democratic civic myth.

In 1630, Bellingham and Wilson were present on the *Arabella* when Winthrop unfolded his ideas regarding the settlement in the New World. Boudreau notes that in his famous sermon *A Model of Christian Charity*, the reverend set up the blueprint for the covenant to be. Mercy is undoubtedly one of the pillars of this sermon (344). But one should not forget other, more immediate notions put forth concerning the ruling of Massachusetts. Winthrop was aware of the special circumstances the settlers would find themselves in. Consequently, he considered mercy of paramount importance: "[I]n the infancy of plantations, justice should be administered with more lenyte than in a settled state" (in Boudreau 345). Still, Winthrop and other Puritan magistrates had other, very particular ideas about the organization of the new commonwealth.

The *Arabella* sermon puts forth the basic idea of a covenant; *two* covenants to be precise, one between the settlers and God, the other between the settlers themselves. The settlers entered into a divine and a social covenant, the latter being

> a contract between the settlers under [Winthrop's] care and God—a bond which made them a people and commanded them to live by God's law. If obedient, the covenanted people would enjoy the fruits of God's creation in all their abundance. If stiff-necked, the results would be destruction. (Wall 2)

This covenant was destined to be ruled by a specific class of men. These were men of high birth and wealth – i.e. the magistrates – whose success was a *visible* blessing from God. The magisterial office, in sum, "was divine in origin—judges were gods" (ibid.). The covenanted, on the other hand, remained subjects. Their duty was to obey.[18]

The idea that Puritans brought the nucleus of democracy to the New World is problematic at best. Mythologically, however, America claimed New England founders as their ideological and political ancestors. Wall comments that the Antebellum's civic myth was grounded on a Puritan covenant which was "in many ways merely a New England deification of the political realities of old England" (4). Indeed, Puritans did not pretend towards democracy. The government set up in 1630 was clearly arbitrary, and it was due to the efforts of freemen that this arbitrary government was somewhat restricted.[19] The fact is that Puritan magistrates doubted that "God's law and the covenant" could "be upheld in a democracy," which was seen as a rather debased form of government (10).

Yet if democratic government arises from the people, and laws are derived from the democratic process, then New England governance presents an antithesis.[20] The novel's Puritan Boston was, historically speaking, a theocratic regime. Deriving a democratic civic myth from Puritan New England seems impossible if one regards

---

18 Wall notes that regarding social hierarchy, the covenanted ascribed to a divinely sanctioned feudalism. First, obedience was paramount for the success of the errand. That obedience was to be attained by coercion, if necessary. "Man," they argued, was irreparably "corrupted by original sin" and could therefore never "successfully abide by his promises to God without coercion" (10). Second, they held that human beings were not created equal but were born into a natural hierarchy. Winthrop was a devoted disciple of William Perkins, who established this mode of thought: "Persons are distinguished by order, whereby God hath appointed, that in every society one person should bee above or under another; not making all equall, as though the bodie bee all and nothing else; but even in degree and order, hee hath set a distinction, that one should bee above the other" (in Wall 2f).

19 For a detailed political and institutional history of the first decade in New England see Wall: *Massachusetts Bay: The Crucial Decade* (1972).

20 Here, it is important to differentiate between New England Puritans and their contemporaries in Europe. Wall notes that the "most pronounced differences between English and New England Puritanism lay in their attitude toward heresy." As English Puritanism was a fractured community, toleration became a necessity (121). But for New Englanders, the term 'tolerationist' held almost insulting connotations. The New World covenant had no patience for any kind of heterodoxy. Least of all welcome was any sort of heretical (read differing) religious enthusiasm (33). Puritan New England was not the best place for pluralism, let alone democratic culture.

its governance and political culture.[21] So how does Hawthorne produce a variant myth given the basic myth's inapplicability for the Antebellum? We have already seen that the instance of mercy in Winthrop's system was restricted to in-groups and designed to affirm the regime's stability. Conditional mercy failed even in Puritan times. It simply "dried up" after a while, replacing "mercy and charity […] with adamant justice" (Boudreau 344). However, there is a way to salvage Puritanism as the provider of a new civic myth. Instead of focusing on Puritanism, one may write the variant mythology around those who resisted it.

2.3 THE ORDER OF ROSES

The variant myth in *The Scarlet Letter* elaborates an alternative set of founders. By highlighting the shortcomings of the basic myth and confronting the founding fathers with a group of heterodox Puritans, the novel presents a variant myth that focuses not on the traditional founders but on those whom they persecuted. The imagery used to describe these dissenters is based on witchcraft. The use of witchcraft imagery and the organic metaphoric of civilization vs. nature allows the text to situate the dissenters outside the frame- and fencework of Puritanism and serves to mark their status of societal transgressors.

The alternative set of founders aids in the construction of an independent social space that gradually succeeds in transforming a coercive regime into a community able to tolerate a specific amount of pluralism. At the end of the novel, the protagonist lays the foundations for democratization and prepares for a pluralistic civil society by means of legitimizing her dissent, thereby disproving the anxiety about transgressing individuals. By means of a mythic elaboration (IIb), the novel works on the Sin-as-Sign mytheme and transforms it into the variant myth's *Sin-as-Possibility* mytheme. This mythic elaboration centers on Hester Prynne, her conduct and perception in society. Ultimately, the Sin-as-Possibility mytheme will include other dissenters and finally naturalize the variant (IIc), the *Order of Roses myth*. The final reincorporation of the demonized subject allows for the introduction of pluralism and paves the way for democratic change.

---

21 How closed this system was becomes clear if one considers the following excerpt from the Minister's convocation of 1648: "The doors of the Churches of Christ upon earth, doe not by Gods appointment stand so wide open, that all sorts of people good or bad, may freely enter therein at their pleasure; but such as are admitted thereto, as members ought to be examined and tryed first, whether they be fit and meet to be received into Church society, or not" (in Wall 226).

The alternative founders are with one exception Puritans. Besides Hester, it is also Pearl who is included in the production of the variant. Further, two other heterodox founders are presented: the Antinomian Ann Hutchinson and the Tolerationist William Blackstone. These characters, like Winthrop, remain in the background of the novel's action; but their legacy infuses its meaning. They provide the historical sources for the coloring of Hester's organic symbol, the rose. Hutchinson and Blackstone function as the forgotten founders: They present the historical possibilities refuted by the Sin-as-Sign mytheme and serve as forerunners for Hester's dissent. A third pair of dissenters completes the alternative set. Arthur Dimmesdale and Roger Chillingworth are dissenters in their own right, similarly marked by the imagery of witchcraft. But unlike Hester and Pearl, they ultimately fail.

The variant production is again prepared for (IIa). Every character in the set of alternative founders bears a vegetative emblem. Arthur and Roger approach the Puritans black flower, but they transform it into an "ugly weed" (SL 87). The other members (Hester, Pearl, Ann, and William) share the symbol of the rose. The variant myth contrasts the traditional Puritans (the black flower) with an *Order of Roses*. It is this order that effects the mythological pushing of horizons, thereby gaining spaces for the imagination of new realities and, as a civic myth, for the building of a more inclusive and civil American national identity.

The Pact and the Beginnings of Exclusion

After the scaffold scene, we encounter Hester and Pearl back in prison. Her association with witchcraft is continued here; yet instead of the devil, she faces her own husband. Chillingworth is immediately associated with witchcraft, the wilderness, and its Indian inhabitants. His liminality is further evident in his garment: "By the Indian's side, and evidently sustaining a companionship with him, stood a white man, clad in a strange disarray of civilized and savage costume." But it is not just his "heterogeneous garb" that associates Roger with witchcraft (SL 44). Although liminal in attire, he is not yet a transgressor. It is the recognition of his wife's crime that triggers his transformation. Here, like in *Young Goodman Brown*, the text employs the Edenic image of the snake to mark devilish influence: "A writhing horror twisted itself across his features, like a snake gliding swiftly over them." Roger has been a captive of the Indians, and he introduces himself as a "stranger" and a "wanderer" (45).[22]

---

22 Similarly, a character named Doctor Melmoth appears in Hawthorne's *Fanshawe*. This character is reminiscent of Maturin's *Melmoth the Wanderer*, a Faustian story of a young student who sells his soul to the devil.

On attending Hester in prison, his devilish depiction intensifies. He is described as an occult alchemist but also as a physician who has augmented his knowledge whilst living with the Indians (SL 51). He is the apocalyptical thief in the night (87),[23] a gatherer of herbs (80), and a "leech" (79). Most tellingly, however, is his relation to the scarlet letter itself. As mentioned, the devil touches his disciples and leaves a mark. Similarly, Roger touches the letter, which reacts to his touch as if branding itself onto Hester's skin: "As he spoke, he laid his long forefinger on the scarlet letter, which forthwith seemed to scorch into Hester's breast, as if it been red-hot" (52). This begins a series of images suggestive of the devil's pact. Not only has Roger marked Hester, he makes her swear to keep his identity secret. Further, she seems to be aware of the situation's import and shrinks from tying this "secret bond." She ultimately takes "the oath" (54) but fears its outcome: "Art thou like the Black Man that haunts the forest around us? Hast thou enticed me into a bond that will prove the ruin of my soul?" (55).

Hester's initiation to the realm between civilization and forest prepares the mythological pushing of horizons. It enables the work on the Sin-as-Sign mytheme and is telling of two aspects. First, Hester is outcast from society on the grounds of refusing to cooperate towards her social restoration on communal terms. Her relocation confirms the space allotted to those marked by sin. Second, she binds herself to Roger in a pact that will frustrate any future possibility to pursue her restoration by revealing her husband's identity. A return on communal term is made impossible. Hester is trapped; but she does not leave the fence behind to venture into the forest. Indeed, her liminality will be of importance for the renegotiation of her branded status.

Roger, too, transgresses received boundaries. But unlike Hester, he takes a malefic path:

In a word, old Roger Chillingworth was a striking evidence of man's faculty of transforming himself into a devil, if he will only [...] undertake a devil's office. This unhappy person had effected such a transformation, by devoting himself, for seven years, to the constant analysis of a heart full of torture. (SL 110f)

His transformation begins in the prison scene. Roger's zeal for justice and his inability to show mercy will prove his destruction. Indeed, Roger shares in the Puritan

---

23 cf. KJV 2 Peter 3:10: "But the day of the Lord will come as a thief in the night; in which the heavens shall pass away with a great noise, and the elements shall melt with fervent heat, the earth also and the works that are therein shall be burned up."

primacy of justice; but his is an egotistical justice.[24] He thus serves as antithesis to other transgressors and exemplifies the results of radicalism.

Hester and Roger become outcasts, the first on account of her societal condemnation, the second by his own choice. Roger transforms himself into a fiend, which results in his loss of humanity. He is indeed an "unhappy man" to have followed the road of radicalism and become a 'real' witch. Yet, as the narrator notes, "to all these shadowy beings, so long our near acquaintances [...] we would fain be merciful" (SL 164). Hester, too, will become one of these shadowy beings. She will live a marginalized life and come very close to the kind of radicalism that proved fatal to Roger.

Hester and Life on the Fence

The idea of Sin-as-Sign causes Hester's marginalization. But the space she now occupies will be paramount to her ability to transform the mytheme. To do so, she must retreat to a sphere outside of Boston: She must live at the fence. Indeed, Hester Prynne settles in a space that is telling of her liminal status:

On the outskirts of the town, within the verge of the peninsula, but not in close vicinity to any other habitation, there was a small thatched cottage. It had been built by an earlier settler, and abandoned, because the soil about it was too sterile for cultivation, while its comparative remoteness put it out of the sphere of that social activity which already marked the habits of the emigrants. (SL 56)

The conditions of her life in the cottage are reminiscent of another outcast. Like Hester, the Greek king Sisyphus was punished and exiled because he refused to adhere to the powers that be. Zeus sentenced him to roll a boulder up a hill, only to see it roll back as soon as he reached the top (Hamilton 423). Hester's situation is described by referring to this Greek myth:

Tomorrow would bring its own trial with it; so would the next day, and so would the next: each its own trial, and yet the very same that was now so unutterably grievous to be borne. The days of the far-off future would toil onward, still with the same burden for her to take up, and bear along with her, but never to fling down. (SL 55)

---

24 Thomas notes that Roger's vendetta harks back to earlier, individual forms of justice. He ignores Puritan law and perpetrates his own vindication, reclaiming the personal "responsibility of punishing wrongdoers" (190). At the same time, he refuses his "legal responsibilities as a father." From a legal perspective, Pearl was Roger's daughter (192). His vengeance serves none but himself and is ruthless in its execution.

This referential treatment of myth illuminates the effect the scarlet letter has on Hester's life. The exclusion and shaming inherent in the punishment are of a permanent nature; they divest her life of the possibility of change. A better life cannot be imagined, because she "could no longer borrow from the future to help her through the present grief" (ibid.). Agency is forestalled by the letter; so is individuality. The letter dehumanizes, and Hester becomes

> the general symbol at which the preacher and moralist might point, and in which they might vivify and embody their images of woman's frailty and sinful passion. Thus the young and pure would be taught to look at her, with the scarlet letter flaming on her breast—at her, the child of honorable parents—at her, the mother of a babe that would hereafter be a woman—at her, who had once been innocent—as the figure, the body, the reality of sin. (ibid.)

Hester becomes the *sign* of her sin. While the Sin-as-Sign mytheme has been implicit until now, it is fully exposed in this passage. Also, its consequences are made visible: The mytheme effects a dehumanization of the individual, who loses subjective and societal agency.

In order to regain agency, the easiest course would be exile. Hester is "free to return to her birthplace, or any other European land" (SL 55). She may also turn to the "passes of the dark, inscrutable forest." If she had, Hester would indeed walk in the footsteps of Hutchinson and Blackstone, both of which left Boston. But Hester does not flee. She is still a Puritan and partially adheres to Puritan values. She feels a "force of doom, which almost invariably compels human beings to linger around and haunt, ghost-like, the spot were some great and marked event has given color to their lifetime." The Puritan in her feels the "iron links" that "can never be broken" and bind her to Boston (56).

Her reasons to remain are "half a truth and half a delusion." Hester is bound, on the one hand, by her partial belief in the Sin-as-Sign doctrine. Indeed, part of her believes herself guilty. On the other hand, she was transformed by her trial, given a "new birth," which had converted the "forest-land, still so uncongenial to every other pilgrim and wanderer, into [her] wild and dreary but life-long home." A decision would be possible if Hester could ascribe to one or the other. But she cannot. She finds herself negotiating her belonging and settles for neither. She lives on the fence between civilization and nature, in a space between the realm marked by "the habits of the emigrants" and the "forest-covered hills" (SL 56). From the settlers' perspective, Hester's new abode looks out of place, and being of Puritan mind, they attach "a mystic shadow of suspicion" to the cottage. That feeling is motivated by a "strange, contagious fear" (57).[25]

Trapped in a space between nature and society, Hester moves in a sphere of her own. But why would the population, if fear of Hester is so pronounced, allow her to remain?

The Taming of Puritan Anxiety

A comparison of Hester and Ann Hutchinson is helpful here. Ann functions as alternative ancestor that transforms the Puritan myth. Hester following in Ann's footsteps without continuing her Antinomianism effects a legitimation of dissent and a refutation of its radicalized forms.

The similarities between Prynne and Hutchinson lie in their role as dissenter and in the nature of their dissent. The "Hester-Ann analogy" portrays Hester as walking

---

[25] I have already elaborated on the notion that witchcraft was held to be contagious and that it affected primarily the witch's next of kin. Hester's husband has already been associated with witchcraft. Her daughter Pearl and her lover Arthur will share that fate. Yet it is not witchcraft per se that is feared by the settlers. The Puritans, anxious about their theocracy's stability, fear dissent itself. They dread what Elias termed *anomic contagion*. Hester, Pearl, even the space they inhabit, are demonized by the in-group members. The dissenter appears as an infected individual, and society at large will shy away in fear of contagion. Public demonization allows for the dissenter's dehumanization, which in turn protects the in-group's values and norms (Elias 19). Fear of contagion further explains the recurring image of an empty space around Hester. We know that the scarlet letter has "the effect of a spell, taking [her] out of the ordinary relations with humanity and enclosing her in a sphere by herself" (SL 41). As witchcraft acts as the foil for dissent, that sphere is imagined as a magic circle: "As was usually the case wherever Hester stood, a small vacant area—a sort of magic circle—had formed itself about her, into which, though the people were elbowing one another at a little distance, none ventured" (149). A further instance is given when the people gather around Hester on Election Day. Even their curiousness "could not bring them nearer than a circuit of several yards. At that distance they accordingly stood, fixed there by the centrifugal force of the repugnance which the mystic symbol inspired" (SL 156). Thus, a witch/dissenter produces a contagious space around them. Consequently, the witch-lady Hibbins has her own sphere of contagion. In conjunction with Hester, that space (and the fear of it) expands: "[T]he crowd gave way before [Mistress Hibbins], and seemed to fear the touch of her garment, as if it carried the plague among its gorgeous folds. Seen in conjunction with Hester Prynne [...] the dread inspired by Mistress Hibbins had doubled, and caused a general movement from that part of the market-place" (153).

in Ann's footsteps but not hand in hand with the "famous lady heretic" (Colacurcio 305). I agree that their relationship is not one of identity, but I will suggest a typological relation. Ann presents a *type* upon which Hester is built.[26] Ann is a type of Hester in the sense that the latter will fulfill the promises the first was unable to enact. In the manner that Mary presents the fulfillment of Eve, Ann prefigures the coming of Hester. Both women are depicted as prophetesses, albeit only one will be able to prepare for a prophetic change.

The figuration commences at the novel's beginning in the preparation of the variant (IIa). The symbol for mercy, the rose-bush, is said to have "sprung under the footsteps of the sainted Ann Hutchinson" (SL 37). Moreover, both women had significant relationships to eminent pastors, Hester to Arthur and Ann to John Cotton (Colacurcio 306). Both elaborated individualistic ideas and disrupted the traditional perspective. Hutchinson preached a covenant of grace, the "belief that God's gift of grace relieved Christians of responsibility for obeying the moral law of the Old Testament" (Karlsen 15). Thus, her doctrines went against the covenant preached by Winthrop (and Dimmesdale). Hester, indeed, thinks along the same lines. The following is taken from the forest scene, where Hester consoles Arthur and shows him (Antinomian) alternatives for a happier life:

'You have deeply and sorely repented. Your sin is left behind you in the days long past. Your present life is not less holy, in very truth, than it seems in people's eyes. Is there no reality in the penitence thus sealed and witnessed by good works? And wherefore should it not bring you peace?' (SL 123)

Hawthorne's sketch *Mrs. Hutchinson* is helpful at this point. Here, Ann is presented as "a woman of extraordinary talent and strong imagination, whom the latter quality […] prompted to stand forth as a reformer in religion." As Ann emerges from prison, one is reminded of *The Scarlet Letter*: "A crowd of hooded women, and of men in steeple hats and close cropt hair, are assembled at the door and open windows of a house newly built. An earnest expression glows in every face" (MH 168). Similarly, the air with which Ann faces her tribunal is reminiscent of Hester: "[Ann] stands loftily before her judges, with a determined brow, and, unknown to herself, there is a flash of carnal pride half hidden in her eye, as she surveys the many learned and famous men whom her doctrines have put in fear" (171). In descriptive terms, Hutchinson is a clear prefiguration of Prynne.

---

26 For a detailed explication of typology see *Figura* in Auerbach: *Scenes from the Drama of European Literature* (1984); Miner: *Literary Uses of Typology from the Late Middle Ages to the Present* (1977).

Still, Hawthorne is all but enthusiastic about Hutchinson's "irregular and daring thought." Her dissent is portrayed as societal threat, and her doctrines as undermining the errand itself. Ann was too radical for Hawthorne's taste, because her dissent threatened disunion.[27] Torn between allegiance to the "blessed Fathers of the land" and simultaneous criticism of those who were "ready to propagate the religion of peace by violence," his perspective on Ann is ambivalent (MH 168). This is translated into an equally ambivalent judgment of Hester. Indeed, "Hawthorne will have nearly as many reservations about Hester's sainthood as John Winthrop had about Mrs. Hutchinson's" (Colacurcio 304).

Yet Hester is not Ann. The fact that her dissent is successful lies primarily in the way that Hester differs from her precursor. Had she indeed been a Hutchinson, Hester

might have come down to us in history [...] as the foundress of a religious sect. She might, in one of her phases, have been a prophetess. She might, and not improbably would, have suffered death from the stern tribunals of the period, for attempting to undermine the foundations of the Puritan establishment. (SL 108)

But she did not. There are fundamental differences in Hester's dissent when compared to Ann. These differences form part of the novel's mythemic elaboration (IIa). Ann is imagined as the dissenter who failed to appease Puritan anxiety and refute the Sin-as-Sign mytheme. Hester, in contrast, is able to do so because of her *legitimation* of dissent. First, Hester achieves a societal position by economic efforts. Second, she performs merciful deeds that benefit society. Third, she never antagonizes the populace or the elites. Fourth, instead of choosing exile, she returns and establishes her own sphere of influence. Finally, her dissent is of individualistic, not theological nature.

Bercovitch reminds us that visible sainthood included the belief that a blessed status is reflected in a person's economic welfare (Assent 33). Wealth and power were considered visible signs. But Hester is, for better or worse, branded: Her sinful nature is made visible by the scarlet letter. Yet the fact that she is allotted a place in society originates in her economic occupation. Hester's gift for needle-work situ-

---

27 To Hawthorne, Hutchinson's Antinomianism was "a most remarkable case, in which religious freedom was wholly inconsistent with public safety, and where the principles of an illiberal age indicated the very course which must have been pursued by worldly policy and enlightened wisdom. Unity of faith was the star that had guided these people over the deep, and a diversity of sects would either have scattered them from the land [...], or perhaps have excited a diminutive civil war among those who had come so far to worship together" (MH 170).

ates her in the realm of domesticity and femininity. It is an occupation seen as 'fit' for a woman, which conforms to Puritan (and to Hawthorne's) notions of gender. Twenty-five years before his famous rant against female writers, the author introduces the story about Ann Hutchinson with the following:

The hastiest glance may show, how much of the texture and body of cis-Atlantic literature is the work of those slender fingers, from which only a light and fanciful embroidery has heretofore been required, that might sparkle upon the garment without enfeebling the web. Woman's intellect should never give the tone to that of man, and even her morality is not exactly the material for masculine virtue. (MH 167)

Hawthorne clearly saw embroidery as a female employment.[28] Hester is assigned a gendered occupation; it is this occupation that allows her an amount of agency.

Indeed, her needle-work is advertised by her token of punishment. By means of the "curiously embroidered letter" she exhibits her "delicate and imaginative skill." She attains a broad customer-base, because there was a "demand for such labour as Hester Prynne could supply" (SL 57). Gradually, her work infuses society at large but for one exception: Not "in a single instance, her skill was called in to embroider the white veil which was to cover the pure blushes of a bride" (58). Still, embroidery serves as a marker of Hester's economic success. Additionally, this occupation carries a mythological import that foreshadows Hester's future as prophetess and councilor.

The text employs a referential treatment of myth in this instance. Spinning, embroidery, and needle-work are strongly related to the Germanic concept of *wyrd*, i.e. fate and the becoming of life. Here, human existence is seen as a process of spinning, usually governed by three maidens (*Norns*) who spin the threads of fate beneath the tree of life (*Yggdrasil*) (Guerber 87). The Norns are analogous to the fates (*Moirae*) in Greek mythology (Hamilton 48). The reason why I focus on Germanic myth is that Frigga (or Freya) – goddess of conjugal and motherly love – is also im-

---

28 Hawthorne's explicit sexism in this passage, later made famous by his "mob of scribbling women" remark (in Winship 418), gives evidence to a "significant woman-problem in Hawthorne's larger career" (Colacurcio 310). His discomfort regarding professional women is oftentimes related to women encroaching on a supposedly male domain. Female writers constituted a serious competition for Hawthorne in the 1830s; apparently, he saw women like Ann, and to some extent Hester, as forerunners to the public ladies that caused him so much trouble. At times, his sexism was motivated by something as "plebeian" as the dislike of competition, a reaction to the "triumph" of female authors in the Antebellum (Weinauer 383).

agined as a needle-worker (Guerber 26).²⁹ The fates and the needle-worker Frigga illustrate the ongoing process of becoming, and Hester's occupation illuminates her character as an evolving individual. Her status, her social influence, and her dissent are developmental, just as Massachusetts Bay is in a developmental state. The needle-worker Hester has pivotal influence on that development.

It is with embroidery and the benevolent Frigga that the imagery of witchcraft begins to change. It is also with Hester's economic occupation that the mythemic elaboration continues to transform the Sin-as-Sign mytheme. Hester's needle-work allots her a "part to perform" in the world (SL 58). Her embroidery accompanies the settlers' lives from birth to death, and embroidery's mythological significance foreshadows the social function that Hester will perform in the development of Puritan society: Hester, mythologically speaking, spins the fate of the Puritan project. Her influence will prepare the "brighter period" that is to come (166), and her embroidery serves as a marker for the continuous work that will be necessary for the attainment of that future. Simultaneously, her occupation and economic success disprove the Sin-as-Sign mytheme: Hester is *visibly* successful, *visibly* blessed by means of her work. Economic success in a sinner, however, disproves the Puritan mindset. Slowly but surely, Hester's actions begin to denaturalize the mytheme and pave the way for the variant.

Her economic success, however, do not effect societal reentry:

In all her intercourse with society, however, there was nothing that made her feel as if she belonged to it. Every gesture, every word, and even the silence of those with whom she came in contact, implied, and often expressed, that she was banished, and as much alone as if she inhabited another sphere. (SL 58)

Despite society's rejection, Hester does nothing to avenge herself. This, too, continues the mythemic elaboration (IIb). Instead of performing the *malefici* expected from a transgressor, Hester does the opposite and turns to charity. She bestows "all her superfluous means" on others and aides those "less miserable than herself" (ibid.). This charity effects a change in societal reception, yet none that would

---

29 In some stories, Frigga resides in a mountain instead of her palace in Asgard. This tradition has produced various names for the same concept of the female spinner; in Germany, for instance, she is called Frau Holle (Guerber 31). There are various legends informing on her capabilities: She will provide flax for peasants or help overworked servants. As a mother goddess, she takes a particular interest in children, especially those who are in need, like orphans and *Heimchen*, infants who have no guiding spirit (30, 32). Further, she was "very fond of dress" (26) and preferred an extravagant attire, very much like Hester, who shared Frigga's "taste for the gorgeously beautiful" (SL 58).

achieve complete communal acceptance. Still, she does not fulfill Puritan expectations. Her deeds oppose the traditional beliefs regarding a dissenter's nature. If sin is a sign, so is charity. A benevolent sinner, however, challenges either/or notions. Her charity is highly significant in the mythemic elaboration. There was

> [n]one so ready as she to give of her little substance to every demand of poverty, even though the bitter-hearted pauper threw back a gibe in requital of the food brought regularly to his door, or the garments wrought for him by the fingers that could have embroidered a monarch's robe. (105)

Hester's charity presents the first of various steps in the taming of Puritan anxiety. Gradually, she achieves a partial reentry to societal life, and her actions complicate the beliefs regarding dissenters. As dissent and witchcraft are conflated, Bostonians expected Hester to behave like a witch, i.e. to antagonize, harm, and corrupt the community. But her ongoing defiance of communal law (she is still silent regarding her lover) and her marginality do *not* result in malefic actions. The sinner transforms herself into a charitable person, who lives not in but *for* the community:

> She was self-ordained a Sister of Mercy, or, we may rather say, the world's heavy hand had so ordained her, when neither the world nor she looked forward to this result. The letter was the symbol of her calling. Such helpfulness was found in her,—so much power to do, and power to sympathise,—that many people refused to interpret the scarlet A by its original signification. They said that it meant Able, so strong was Hester Prynne, with a woman's strength. (SL 106f)

Hester's charity is one step in a didactic process to reeducate Boston: Her actions serve as general model. Instead of presenting a sermon on sin, she becomes an example of mercy. Yet it is not only her charity that effects that change. This process, which will result in the elaboration of a new mytheme, has several steps and offers practical polices that inform the civic myth under construction. Indeed, it presents a manual for the Antebellum situation: The first step to incorporate dissent and appease a community threatened to dissolve is adopting a primacy of mercy and the enactment of charity.

A second step is assuming a policy of non-irritation. Hester "never battled with the public." It is due to her charity *and* her non-interference that she was able to remain in Boston. Dissent functions best and influences most if it is present and visible in the system. In contrast, outer or aggressive dissent is easily derogated. The fact that the dissenter was both visible *and* defied common assumptions about her nature caused a change in reception. After seven years, Hester becomes a "familiar object," as "is apt to be the case when a person stands out in any prominence before the community and, at the same time, interferes neither with public nor individual interests and convenience." Therefore, "a species of general regard had ultimately grown up in reference to Hester Prynne" (SL 151). Familiarization, the visibility and presence of dissent, and non-interference have gradually changed the Puritan perspective.

Those instances, however, remain insufficient. A third step in the education of Boston taps directly into the town's belief in visible sainthood. Indeed, it is "the blameless purity of [Hester's] life during all these years in which she had been set apart to infamy [which is] reckoned largely in her favour." Hester lives according to standards the town itself embraces. Yet a blameless life contradicts the Sin-as-Sign perspective and complicates the perception of dissenters as heretics and traitors. The case of Hester, her charity, humility, and purity of life challenge basic Puritan beliefs: not by means of agitation but *in themselves*. The dissenter/witch concept is transformed, and the dissenter perceived as sister of mercy. One should not, however, mistake that change as a possibility for Hester's reentry. The "gloomy twilight" remained the only "medium in which she was entitled to hold intercourse with her fellow-creatures" (SL 105). She remains an outcast and will occupy that position all her life. But she has not become a witch, and her conduct has challenged Boston's either/or notions and prepared for the possibilities of both/and.

In terms of mythological resignification, the basic myth's core meaning has been transformed by Hester's actions. As the Sin-as-Sign mytheme is refuted, a new mytheme is installed. Sin cannot be a sign anymore: Hester's person, conduct, and mercy have refuted that perspective. The model of sin has become a model of charity, and a new mytheme is produced: *Sin-as-Possibility*. While Hester can never legalize her original transgression, she is able to reestablish her individuality in the face of an ideology which had her branded as inherently depraved. Her sin has pained her, but it has also opened up positive possibilities and developments. The Sin-as-Possibility mytheme will continue to inform the text, especially in Pearl and in the forest meeting.

Hester's success marks the main difference to Ann Hutchinson. Ann's dissent could not be abided by Puritan Boston and resulted in her banishment. But Ann, I suggested, acts as a type whose shortcomings will be overcome and whose mission is to be fulfilled by Hester. Ann exemplifies the manner of dissenting that in the novel's perspective cannot effect societal change. In order to comprehend how Hawthorne understood ineffective dissent, we may once again turn to *Mrs. Hutchinson*.

The mission that Ann and Hester share is the introduction of mercy to an unbalanced, judgement-focused society. But Ann failed to establish a space in which mercy could balance justice. Hester, on the other hand, was successful in establishing such a space, a fact that will occupy the analysis at a later point. It is the *manner* in which their dissent was enacted that resulted in different outcomes. Hester follows a policy of non-interference; Ann, however, attacked society at large. While

Hester enacts charity, Ann's doctrines aggressively defied the established order. Ann becomes something Hester will not: the "foundress of a religious sect" (SL 108). The threat that Hawthorne perceives in this is one that Winthrop would have shared: Ann's sectarianism carried the danger of separatism and the collapse of the covenant. Colacurcio notes that by claiming a "totally self-sufficient private illumination," Ann's doctrines stood in radical opposition to Puritan thought (313). The result was Ann's demonization by Puritan elites.[30] The case of Ann Hutchinson is perhaps the best example of the heretic/witch and dissenter/traitor conflation.

Hester is spared that fate. Yes, she is associated with witchcraft; especially during her time of "moral wilderness," she entertains thoughts that come very close to Ann's Antinomianism (SL 118). But she overcomes these impulses, remains in and later returns to Boston, where she, "with important modifications of tone and in separation from all traces of antinomian self-justification," expresses are more seasoned dissent (Colacurcio 310f). Indeed, the reason for this difference in outcome lies in the existence of a child. I will devout a separate section to the analysis of Pearl.

A second difference between Ann and Hester is that the latter's dissent is private, while Ann's is of theological and political nature. Hester has political and theological thoughts, but they are neither public nor dogmatic. They apply to herself, her own situation, and later to the people she counsels. While Ann's dissent is political but inefficient, Hester's private dissent has fundamental political consequences.

A last difference lies in Hester's return. Ann could not rid herself from the Puritan either/or mindset. By establishing her dissent as dogma, she suffered the treat-

---

30 Colacurcio notes that Cotton Mather sexualized the Antinomian issue and presented Ann as the seductive female (316). It is but a small step from the issue's sexualization to its conflation with witchcraft. This theological antifeminism peaked in the description of Ann's heresies as "monstrous births" (317). Hutchinson's doctrines were imagined as the result of a witch's sexual intercourse with the devil. The fact that Ann's last pregnancy ended in spontaneous abortion cemented the notion of Antinomian heresy as witchcraft. Ann's misfortunes were interpreted as visible signs of her sinful nature. Thomas Weld elaborated on the image: "Mistris Hutchinson...brought forth not one... but... 30. monstrous births or thereabouts, at once; some of them bigger, some lesser, some of one shape, some of another; few of any perfect shape, none at all of them (as farre as I could ever learne) of human shape" (in Karlsen 17f). This minister went as far as to recognize divine intervention in Hutchinson's misfortunes: "God himself was pleased to step in with his casting voice... in causing the two fomenting women in the time of their height of the[ir] Opinions to produce out of their wombs, as before they had out of their braines, such monstrous births as no Chronicle (I thinke) hardly ever recorded the like" (in Karlsen 18).

ment reserved for radical opposition. Exiled, she has no choice but to live outside of Massachusetts. Hester, on the other hand, has the opportunity to leave but remains. And when she leaves, she returns. Ann's failures are indeed amended by Hester's creating the possibilities for systemic change. The latter manages to enact her dissent by pushing the boundaries of society. The Puritan treatment that conflated Ann's heresy with witchcraft cannot apply to Hester, as she disproves the theological grounds of that conflation by acts of mercy.

Floods of Sunshine and the Nature of Hester's Dissent

Some scholars doubt the sincerity of Hester's merciful deeds. Yet if one reads Hester's behavior in terms of her of own dissent, one arrives at a satisfactory explanation. Hester's character complicates the question of whether noble deeds must be motivated (or necessitated) by a noble nature. While the settlers receive her actions as motivated by mercy and penitence, the narrator has his doubts. One must fear, he states, that there was "no genuine and steadfast penitence but something doubtful, something that might be deeply wrong, beneath" (SL 58). Colacurcio argues that Hester merely plays at sanctification because she is aware of the Puritan belief that "the true Self is the sum of all its outward works" (322). I agree that Hester's mercy is sometimes motivated by something other than genuine repentance. Aware of the Sin-as-Sign rules, she indeed plays the game, yet only as a survival strategy. One may condemn her behavior, but it is important to remember that her inability to be true to her feelings stems from systemic circumstances, not from a desire to deceive.

Her true feelings are revealed in the forest meeting with Arthur. This meeting cannot occur on the market place; what will pass here stands in contrast, even opposition to Boston's received ideas. For this, the lovers require a primeval space outside city limits. The forest is the only place where Hester is free to speak as she thinks fit; it is also a place representative of her struggling inner self:

[The path] straggled onward into the mystery of the primeval forest. This hemmed it in so narrowly, and stood so black and dense on either side, and disclosed such imperfect glimpses of the sky above, that, to Hester's mind, it imaged not amiss the moral wilderness in which she had so long been wandering. (SL 118)

However, that Hester is not at home in the forest becomes clear as nature itself retreats from the scarlet letter: "'It runs away and hides itself, because it is afraid of something on [her] bosom'" (119). Still, this space frames Hester's climax of dissent. Here, witchcraft associations are particularly strong.

While Hester and Pearl wait for Arthur to pass by, the child describes "the Black Man" who

haunts this forest, and carries a book with him,— a big, heavy book, with iron clasps; and how this ugly Black Man offers his book and an iron pen to everybody that meets him here among the trees; and they are to write their names with their own blood; and then he sets his mark on their bosoms. (119f)

Pearl continues, relating how "a thousand and a thousand people" had already put their names down, and that Mistress Hibbins was one of them. Finally, she inquires as to the mark on her mother's breast, and Hester, in responding, continues the witchcraft associations: "'Once in my life I met the Black Man! [...] This scarlet letter is his mark!'" (120). This self-identification serves to prepare for her upcoming, radically dissenting speech on freedom. Also, it designates a second character as witch. When Hester affirms the meeting and the mark, she is referring to her adultery. In doing so, the witchcraft concept involves Arthur in the representation. He soon appears on the forest path, and we may rely on Pearl's keen observation again: "'[H]e has his hand over his heart! Is it because, when the minister wrote his name in the book, the Black Man set his mark in that place?'" (121).

The discussion of Hester and Arthur's signs of sin continues the mythemic elaboration (IIb). Yet Pearl's words question rather than affirm the signification of her mother's letter and the reverend's mark. This critical treatment will result in the transformation of the mytheme: The focus on visible sin will be shifted towards a celebration of possibility.

Hester and Arthur's meeting is the meeting of two ghosts. Their burden has exhausted them, and Hester's appearance has conformed to the "gray" and "sad-colored garments" typical of Puritanism (SL 36). Arthur discerns a form, not a person, "clad in garments so sombre, and so little relieved from the gray twilight" that he believes her to be a specter. The fact, however, that society was only superficially successful in coercing Hester into submission is about to become very clear.

It is here, "in the world beyond the grave," that Hester voices her most radical dissent (SL 122). The reader has been prepared for this climactic transgression by the strong witchcraft imagery used in the last paragraphs as well as by the forest setting. But they were prepared to *sympathize* with Hester's dissent, not condemn her. The description of what Puritanism has done to these individuals does not offer legalization but certainly legitimizes their transgression. We are made to understand the reasons for dissent, reasons which are largely systemic and societal, not solely personal. What follows is a speech infused with a powerful and radical individualism. Despite claims to the contrary,[31] this radical dissent, tamed and seasoned as it will be later, is not mourned but *celebrated*.

Hester's dissent unfolds on the grounds of Arthur's weakness. His cowardice has made him "most miserable," and his Puritan mind regards his "soul" as "ruined." The contrast between what he seems and what he supposedly is have driven the minister to desperation (SL 123). Hester disagrees and – reminiscent of Hutchinson – focuses on forgiveness through grace:

'You wrong yourself in this,' said Hester gently. 'You have deeply and sorely repented. Your sin is left behind you in the days long past. Your present life is not less holy, in very truth, than it seems in people's eyes. Is there no reality in the penitence thus sealed and witnessed by good works? And wherefore should it not bring you peace?' (ibid.)

Hester insists on intra-personal forgiveness: "Let God punish! Thou shalt forgive!" (125). This push of (and retreat into) individuality is motivated by her societal condition. Unable to live an actual social life in Boston, she had to retreat into herself. Arthur, the other, albeit secret outcast, remains her last connection; one she desperately holds onto:

All the world had frowned on her,—for seven long years had it frowned upon this lonely woman,—and still she bore it all, nor ever once turned away her firm, sad eyes. Heaven, likewise, had frowned upon her, and she had not died. But the frown of this pale, weak, sinful, and sorrow-stricken man was what Hester could not bear, and live! (ibid.)

A *primacy of individuality* is established by Hester's legitimation of their adultery. At this point, Hester's innermost convictions are revealed. It is also here that Hutchinson's doctrines and Hester's beliefs most strongly concur: "'What we did had a consecration of its own. We felt it so! We said so to each other'" (126). This is not an attempt to legalize their crime; but it is the establishment of a parallel truth, a *private* truth at odds with the legal framework. Private truths, however, cannot exist in Boston; they have to be voiced in the forest. But in the forest, the outcasts are free:

No golden light had ever been so precious as the gloom of this dark forest. Here seen only by his eyes, the scarlet letter need not burn into the bosom of the fallen woman! Here seen only

---

31 In this instance, I argue against Bercovitch, who insists on an ironic reading of these passages. He claims this scene to portray Hester's dissent as misguided (Office 9, 118f). Nevertheless, Bercovitch also acknowledges the "enormous hope invested in [Hester's] dissent, a hope that remains compelling" (117).

by her eyes, Arthur Dimmesdale, false to God and man, might be, for one moment true! (ibid.)

Arthur, however, cannot free himself from the "iron framework of his order" and dreads the "judgment of God" (ibid.). But Hester insists on grace, trying to convince the minster: "'Heaven would show mercy [...] hadst thou but the strength to take advantage of it'" (127).

Hester's *Begin-All-Anew* speech is the central dialogue of the novel and the epitome of the Sin-as-Possibility mytheme. For the construction of the variant myth it is the expression of an American idea that is based not on the darker sides of Puritanism but on the dissent towards it. It is worth considering in some detail. The Sin-as-Possibility mytheme is best described in Hester's own words:

'Is the world, then, so narrow?' exclaimed Hester Prynne [...] 'Doth the universe lie within the compass of yonder town, which only a little time ago was but a leaf-strewn desert, as lonely as this around us? Whither leads yonder forest-track? Backward to the settlement, thou sayest! Yes; but, onward, too! Deeper it goes, and deeper into the wilderness, less plainly to be seen at every step; until some few miles hence the yellow leaves will show no vestige of the white man's tread. There thou art free! So brief a journey would bring thee from a world where thou hast been most wretched, to one where thou mayest still be happy!' (SL 127)

In contrast, Arthur's responding voice is the voice of the basic myth, informed by predestination, judgment, and the Sin-as-Sign mytheme:

'It cannot be!' answered the minister, listening as if he were called upon to realise a dream. 'I am powerless to go. Wretched and sinful as I am, I have had no other thought than to drag on my earthly existence in the sphere where Providence hath placed me.' (ibid.)

Hester counters his desperation by refuting the idea of a sealed destiny. Her reliance is rooted in the individual capacity for new beginnings and the ability to leave sin behind. Again, a belief in possibility and individual agency is paramount here.

'Leave this wreck and ruin here where it hath happened. Meddle no more with it! Begin all anew! Hast thou exhausted possibility in the failure of this one trial? Not so! The future is yet full of trial and success. There is happiness to be enjoyed! There is good to be done! Exchange this false life of thine for a true one. Be, if thy spirit summon thee to such a mission, the teacher and apostle of the red men. Or, as is more thy nature, be a scholar and a sage among the wisest and the most renowned of the cultivated world. Preach! Write! Act! Do anything, save to lie down and die! Give up this name of Arthur Dimmesdale, and make thyself another, and a high one, such as thou canst wear without fear or shame.' (127f)

It is the radicalism of Hester's speech and her reliance on the individual that is "too partial a truth" for Hawthorne (Colacurcio 322). Her ideas stem from a "latitude of speculation" born of the powerful mind of a woman who has been an outcast for too long. Hester's dissent is "untamed," the result of the fact that she "had wandered, without rule or guidance, in a moral wilderness, as vast, as intricate, and shadowy as the untamed forest" and like a "wild Indian" had achieved an outsider's perspective (SL 128). In the narrator's view, this perspective is fallible:

For years past she had looked from this estranged point of view at human institutions, and whatever priests or legislators had established; criticising all with hardly more reverence than the Indian would feel for the clerical band, the judicial robe, the pillory, the gallows, the fireside, or the church. The tendency of her fate and fortunes had been to set her free. The scarlet letter was her passport into regions where other women dared not tread. Shame, Despair, Solitude! These had been her teachers,—stern and wild ones,—and they had made her strong, but taught her much amiss. (ibid.)

Hester's dissent will be more seasoned by the end of the novel. But at its peak, it is powerful enough to convince Arthur to begin a new life. The decision made, it is not only Arthur who feels "joy again." He finally breathes freely, even if it is "the wild, free atmosphere of an unredeemed, unchristianised, lawless region" (SL 129). Their joy is indeed only temporary. Yet in the forest, they receive a consecration of their own, even if that consecration is inapplicable to Boston standards. For now, and only for now, Hester flings away the scarlet letter and an immediate transformation takes place:

O exquisite relief! She had not known the weight until she felt the freedom! By another impulse, she took off the formal cap that confined her hair, and down it fell upon her shoulders, dark and rich, with at once a shadow and a light in its abundance, and imparting the charm of softness to her features. […] A crimson flush was glowing on her cheek, that had been long so pale. (130)

Here, freedom and self-affirmation, even if they are restricted to the forest, receive a consecration. I hold that the 'flood of sunshine' was not intended as irony or as a trap for romantic readers. It is a celebration of individualism in its most radical form; a form it can only take on in the forest. But here, it may receive a sympathetic, albeit spacially restricted sanctification:

All at once, as with a sudden smile of heaven, forth burst the sunshine, pouring a very flood into the obscure forest, gladdening each green leaf, transmuting the yellow fallen ones to gold, and gleaming adown the gray trunks of the solemn trees. The objects that had made a shadow hitherto, embodied the brightness now. […]. Such was the sympathy of Nature,—that wild, heathen Nature of the forest, never subjugated by human law, nor illumined by higher truth,—with the bliss of these two spirits! (ibid.)

The consecration of their plans will not survive their return to the city. But the flood of sunshine was not in vain: Hester's moment of radicalism was indispensable, a "stepping stone" on her way to a more effectual and pragmatic dissent. It was "necessary for Hester to reach this stage of self-affirmation and release from shame before she can settle into anything approaching final peace" (Colacurcio 322).

Now that the nature of Hester's dissent has become clear, and the Sin-as-Possibility mytheme has been established, one may answer the doubts regarding the nature of her charity. Hester never fully accepts the norms that effected her punishment. Colacurcio is correct as he notes that Hester feels shame, but believing in the subjective legitimacy of her actions, she does not feel *guilt* (320). Therefore, indeed, her penitence has "something doubtful" (SL 58). The motivation for her charity may lie in both, the wish to survive in a hostile environment *and* the enactment of a different form of penitence. Hester holds that there is "good to be done" (127) and claims a "reality in the penitence thus sealed and witnessed by good works" (123). She assents to societal value *and* insists on individual dissent. She focuses on benevolent works as the expression of penitence, while at the same time trying to remain true to her conviction that her transgression was legitimate.

Thus, it is the motivation of her charity that justifiably arouses suspicion. Her deeds are not solely grounded on the moral demand for penitence and the possibility of social reentry. She is charitable because she believes in her ability to effect good despite her fallen state. Mercy for Hester is not Winthrop's conditional mercy. It is a subjective stance. The individual chooses to be merciful regardless of circumstance. Hester's mercy is unconditional, safe for the positive affirmation of her own self. Indeed, one may discuss the ethical dimensions of both perspectives, but the fact remains that she *is* charitable. Winthrop's conditional mercy has done little to stabilize the colony. But unconditional mercy will bring democratic change.

The forest scene is a crucial step in Hester's individuation. It may be a radical move, but it helps this character to affirm her own right to happiness and to later reflect on the balance between subject and society. The consecration between Hester and Arthur presents a bond that cannot hold in a theocratic society. A democracy, however, must allow for these inter-subjective bonds and the spaces that make them possible. The balancing of private and public interest can only succeed if spaces exist that allow for both their subsistence. Hester's experience of the flood of sunshine and her dissent will create such a space and lay the foundations of forest-freedom in a theocratic town.

2.4 The Recuperation of Mercy and the Foundations of Civil Society

The Scarlet Letter as civic myth is not a narrative about an American family. It does not provide a happy ending for Hester, Pearl, and Arthur, because its significance is primarily political, not private. Still, the forest meeting imagined a possible reunion of a family torn apart by society: The characters could have fled Boston and started a new life, but that development would have had consequences for Boston. Dissent as the motor of democratization would have been removed, Boston would have returned to the *status quo*, and the basic myth could not have been resignified. So, Hester's plan for happiness is frustrated by her own lover. Colacurcio reads Arthur Dimmesdale's betrayal and his subsequent death as the confirmation of theological steadfastness in the face of worldly temptation (330). In contrast, I hold that his death is a necessity for the development of civil structures. Dimmesdale forms part of the alternative set of ancestors; like Roger, he presents a failed dissenter who cannot serve for the embodiment of a new civic myth. This variant finds its source in more humane and hopeful characters.

Dimmesdale and the Delusions of Religious Fanaticism

Roger Chillingworth, as mentioned, does not partake of the roses' symbolism; in fact, he surpasses the harshness of the Puritan black flower. Arthur Dimmesdale holds a similar position in the mythological resignification: Both represent the *Flower from the Grave*, an organic image describing their characters and futures. These men are motivated (and tormented) by an exaggerated pursuit of justice. I have used the term radicalism for Roger; Arthur, on the other hand, is religiously radical, for which I will use the term fanaticism. Legal radicalism and religious fanaticism are similarly rooted in Puritanism; yet these men's fervor surpasses the Puritan mindset. Therefore, the text assigns them their own vegetative emblem. As representatives of an exaggerated Puritanism, their emblem offers another representation of the Sin-as-Sign mytheme.

After Roger returns from herb gathering, he produces a peculiar weed. Curious, Arthur inquires as to its nature and the physician explains:

'I found them growing on a grave, which bore no tombstone, no other memorial of the dead man, save these ugly weeds, that have taken upon themselves to keep him in remembrance. They grew out of his heart, and typify, it may be, some hideous secret that was buried with him, and which he had done better to confess during his lifetime.' (SL 87)

This weed reveals inner depravity and is once again a product of nature. Indeed, nature offers revelations throughout the novel. Earlier, it reacted to the prison with "unsightly vegetation" (36) and to Hutchinson's footsteps with the "rose-bush" (37). As nature sympathizes with the prisoner, it now sympathizes with the man in the tomb. But given his "hideous secret" it produces "ugly weeds" (87) Nature, too, judges. But in contrast to society, which left no visible sign of the man's life, it shows mercy by remembering him. Indeed, nature reveals sin and gives it a sign; but it is merciful while doing so and does not suggest general condemnation of the sinner's character. It is rather instrumental in extracting what should have been cast off long ago. Nature typifies sin, not the sinner.

This particular weed serves three functions. First, it marks Arthur and Roger as different from both, Hester's roses and the Puritans' black flower. In contrast to the rose's mercy and the black flower's judgment, this weed signifies death and unresolved guilt. Second, its ugliness is telling of the men's actions. Third, the weed foreshadows their demise and passing into anonymity. Roger "almost vanished from mortal sight" at the end of the novel (SL 164), and Arthur will likewise rest in an "old and sunken grave" (166).[32]

Arthur, like the unknown man in the grave, suffers from an unrevealed sin. In addition, the minister's societal position heightens his predicament. Dimmesdale is part of Boston's religious elite. He is the representative of Puritan civilization *par excellence*, "a young clergyman, who had come from one of the great English universities" (SL 48). The cleric is trapped in his world view, even thrives on it: "[I]t would always be essential to his peace to feel the pressure of a faith about him, supporting, while it confined him within its iron framework" (82f). Further, there is a "vast power of restraint" in the clergyman (48), a "hot passion" that is continuously checked by his religious beliefs (90). He is "a true priest, a true religionist" (82), whose character complicates his dissent.

---

32 Although both men are bigots, they express their bigotry in opposite directions. Roger's radicalism is outward; he devotes his energy to the torture of another. Arthur, on the other hand, works inwardly. He seeks justice but tortures himself. He lives in constant "anguish" and weakens himself through "fast and vigil" (SL 97, 142). Further, his fanaticism is rooted in inner weakness. He is "tremulous" and suffers from a "nervous sensibility" (48). He cannot confess his adultery because he "lacked the strength," being the "most sensitive of all beings" (111, 112). Arthur is a "pale, weak, sinful, and sorrow-stricken man" (126). His predicament is simple: He is too weak to bear his own dissent. "Crime," the narrator notes, "is for the iron-nerved, who have their choice either to endure it, or, if it press too hard, to exert their fierce and savage strength for a good purpose, and fling it off at once!" (98). Arthur was unsuccessful to endure his crime and proved too weak to confess it.

That he is a dissenter is not just evident in his "sin of passion" but in his decision to escape with Hester (SL 128). There is, indeed, a streak of Antinomianism in Arthur, and his "decision to 'seize the day'" presents "the crassest sort of antinomian response possible for a Calvinist to make" (Colacurcio 327). While Hester's new beginning is a decision made for the sake of freedom, Arthur's decision is a "pitiful retreat" (328). Both are trapped; but he is too weak to be either Nomian or Antinomian. Indeed, his final betrayal of Hester is not, like Colacurcio would have it, "moral honesty" but a turncoat move based on a convenient moral economy in his last moments of life. The forest did *not* free him from his "Calvinist entrapment" but rather cemented his religious fanaticism (330). Too weak to bear the burden of crime, he retreats into the Puritan mindset and exaggerates it.

What divests the hypocrite Arthur from any moral authority is that he ultimately sacrifices his family for the sake of what he calls higher truths. On Election Day, Hester relives her punishment at the scaffold (SL 156). While her suffering continues, Arthur finds himself

on the very proudest eminence of superiority, to which the gifts or intellect, rich lore, prevailing eloquence, and a reputation of whitest sanctity, could exalt a clergyman in New England's earliest days, when the professional character was of itself a lofty pedestal. (158)

Here, the bigot is celebrated as divine medium. It seems curious that Hawthorne's use of irony is often said to apply to Hester but rarely to Arthur. Nevertheless, I shall take the following as it stands:

[N]ever had man spoken in so wise, so high, and so holy a spirit, as he that spake this day; [...]. Its influence could be seen, as it were, descending upon him, and possessing him, and continually lifting him out of the written discourse that lay before him, and filling him with ideas that must have been [...] marvelous to himself. (157)

Why refrain from reading these lines as ironic? Because they do not pertain to Arthur's moral character but to his role as prophet: It is his *function* "to foretell a high and glorious destiny for the newly gathered people of the Lord" (ibid.). Dimmesdale becomes the overcome prophet of the basic myth. The minister repeats the credo of a divine errand and then dies. It is important to remember the context here: We are faced with a man who is the epitome of hypocrisy. With this in mind, it seems remarkable that, to my knowledge, no one has ever claimed the above lines to be ironic. Simultaneously, I hold that they are not, because Arthur stands for everything Hawthorne wished to see in the Puritan fathers: Inspired settlers who came to build a New Jerusalem. Indeed, Thomas reminds us that Arthur repeats the belief in the errand, and in doing so, perpetuates a theocratic society. He "teleologically projects a utopian vision of a cohesive—and, it is important to emphasize, closed—Puritan community into the future" (197).[33]

What follows is Arthur's death and the revelation of the letter on his breast. The minister enacts what will emerge as one of the morals of the story: "'Be true! Be true! Be true! Show freely to the world, if not your worst, yet some trait whereby the worst may be inferred!'" (SL 163). That perspective is one that Hawthorne shares with the Puritan magistrates. Boudreau notes that narrator and Puritan ideology are one for this moment (341).

Once again, the clergyman requires Hester's support and ascends the scaffold. He is a "dying man," who decides to confess now that societal punishment is muted (SL 160). He asks Hester if this is not better "than what [they] dreamed of in the forest" (the question remains: For whom is this better?). Then, Arthur reveals his own scarlet letter. What society had done to Hester, he now does to himself: He generalizes his individuality. But he does so not to acquit Hester, nor to ensure a future for Pearl, but to preach a sermon against those who "question God's judgment on a sinner" (161). He thereby breaks the inter-subjective bonds between himself and his family and goes back on his promise. Here, the minister sacrifices his family in order to serve judgment. Whatever was individualistic in Arthur is lost; he opts for the town's norms and betrays his duties towards his lover and daughter. There is no mercy in his treatment of his own family, and I find it hard to elevate such a person to represent moral standards. His fanaticism is most evident in his final words. When Hester asks him if they will meet in the afterlife, he denies her that consolation. Instead, all he has left for her is yet another sermon:

'Hush, Hester--hush!' said he, with tremulous solemnity. 'The law we broke—the sin here awfully revealed!—let these alone be in thy thoughts! I fear! I fear! It may be, that, when we forgot our God—when we violated our reverence each for the other's soul—it was thenceforth vain to hope that we could meet hereafter, in an everlasting and pure reunion.' (162)

In his last moments, the only things Dimmesdale knows are torture and castigation. He imagines divine mercy as an instrument of pain and punishment. The fact that

---

33 One should remember that is was the forest meeting that caused Arthur's "revolution in the sphere of thought and feeling" (SL 138). That meeting inspired "knowledge of hidden mysteries" (142). It is then that he writes his celebrated sermon, all the time wondering why "Heaven should see fit to transmit the grand and solemn music of its oracles through so foul an organ pipe as he" (143). Hawthorne believed in the destiny the Puritans preached; at the same time, the reader understands that the man who preached them was a fraud. Once again, filiopiety and criticism produce an ambiguous text that can only be appeased by a both/and perspective.

he perceives his death not as the result of life-long hypocrisy but as a triumph attests to his delusion:

'God knows; and He is merciful! He hath proved his mercy, most of all, in my afflictions. By giving me this burning torture to bear upon my breast! By sending yonder dark and terrible old man, to keep the torture always at red-heat! By bringing me hither, to die this death of triumphant ignominy before the people!' (ibid.)

The Puritan prophet is a deeply troubled and disturbed character. Here, indeed, one finds the ugly weeds of a "sad man," whose dissent failed utterly and whose failures effect a retreat into a fanatical exaggeration of Calvinist doctrine (146). Arthur preached New England's theocratic destiny, a future that would never be. Boston's transformation into a more civil polity is prepared by the woman he betrayed.

Hester's Return and the Establishment of Free Spheres

Hester Prynne's trial began at the scaffold, the Puritan instrument for the "promotion of good citizenship" (SL 42). But coercive strategies fail to return Hester to a complete acceptance of the law. The letter's "office" was fulfilled on her return to Boston, albeit with a radically changed import (109). Not only had the meaning of the letter changed from adulteress to angel and able; the wearer returns to establish a sphere that counteracts the polity's shortcomings. Thomas is correct when he states that the dissenter now supersedes the scaffold in promoting good citizenship and thereby changes the parameters of what citizenship entails (197).

While Arthur opts for total submission, Hester decides to search elsewhere for happiness. However, her eventual return to Boston must not be read as an act of compliance, although in returning she "acknowledges the civil law in a way she did not in her rebellious earlier days" (Thomas 197). She comes back to put in effect a seasoned dissent and does so with popular admiration as well as magisterial tolerance. Remembering Elias' elaborations on the fact that in-group members adhere to the We-Ideal to define communal values, the following illuminates to which degree Hester has become accepted by Boston's populace:

Individuals in private life, meanwhile, had quite forgiven Hester Prynne for her frailty; nay, more, they had begun to look upon the scarlet letter as the token, not of that one sin for which she had borne so long and dreary a penance, but of her many good deeds since. 'Do you see that woman with the embroidered badge?' they would say to strangers. 'It is our Hester,—the town's own Hester,—who is so kind to the poor, so helpful to the sick, so comfortable to the afflicted!' (SL 106)34

Hester has become *representative* of the community. Popular forgiveness has been effected by her merciful deeds to such a degree that she serves as civic figurehead: The branded becomes the town's own brand.

Elitist acceptance is more guarded than the popular. Yet remembering the "inquisitorial watch" Hester was subjected to, even magisterial perception underwent a change (SL 57). The magistrates had doubts, which

> were fortified in themselves by an iron frame-work of reasoning, that made it a far tougher labour to expel them. Day by day, nevertheless, their sour and rigid wrinkles were relaxing into something which, in the due course of years, might grow to be an expression of almost benevolence. (106)

The change in Hester's position enables her to return without having to completely submit to the Puritan *status quo*. The story "of the scarlet letter had grown into a legend" (164); but its protagonist resumes the letter "of her own free will, for not the sternest magistrate of that iron period would have imposed it" (165). The process of mythemic elaboration (IIb) is most evident in the letter itself: The token was designed as stigma but becomes a "badge," a symbol to be cast off, resumed, and changed in signification (105, 106, 110, 133, 156). This transformation is the result not only of Hester's dissent; it is the result of her interaction with her fellow Puritans. The transformation of meaning is based on her dealings with others, whose minds are changed by the wearer's conduct. Of course, Hester's individuality plays into that process by keeping the letter as a sign of her constant defiance. Thus, she elevates it to a position where it "ceased to be a stigma" and becomes "a type of something to be sorrowed over, and looked upon with awe, yet with reverence too" (165).

The change in the letter is representative of the mythemic transformation effected by the mythological resignification. An instrument of the basic myth's Sin-as-Sign mytheme, the letter was designed to brand and reveal the dissenter's essential depravity. Hester transforms the sign by means of her actions, a transformation which occurs in concert with society. So, the letter's changed significance disproves the Sin-as-Sign idea and molds it into something new: the Sin-as-Possibility mytheme. The subsequent social acceptance of Hester will have paramount consequences for Boston as a polity.

---

34 Italics MRD.

Hester has made the letter her own, thereby taming Puritan anxiety regarding dissent. She is far from legalizing free spaces in Boston, but she is able to establish a tolerated space of council and interpersonal relations at its margins. Her cottage becomes a *free sphere*, where those at odds with the town's regulations may seek her guidance. Her fellow settlers "brought all their sorrows and perplexities, and besought her counsel, as one who had herself gone through a mighty trouble" (SL 164). It is with this establishment of the first free space in Boston that Hester's dissent triumphs. In contrast to Arthur, who falls back to celebrating a closed society, Hester breaks open the community's fences. Instead of submitting with "childlike loyalty," she erects a new space between town and forest to alleviate the tensions between public and private (158). Her "counseling and comforting" in the cottage "extend the parameters of good citizenship to an interpersonal realm concerned with affairs of the heart that no affairs of state seem capable of remedying." Thus, Hester "dramatizes how important it is for the state to promote spaces in which the capacity for sympathy can be cultivated while simultaneously guarding against the dangers" of an egotistical approach towards liberty (Thomas 197).

This sphere is of crucial importance for the development of Boston. Hester's success in creating the possibility of mercy "helps to bring about a possible structural realignment of Puritan society by having it include what we can call the nascent formation of an independent civil society" (Thomas 197). Here we find the first instance of openness in a closed system, one of the central "non-political transformations that for Hawthorne were necessary for democratic rule to emerge from the Puritan's authoritative rule" (198). Thus, the novel credits not the Puritan fathers but a dissenter with the act of laying the foundations for the development of American democracy.

It is in the final chapters that the variant supersedes the basic myth and experiences its naturalization (IIc). In Dimmesdale we are presented with an orthodox Puritan vision, a vision that is nothing more than a projection of the theocratic polity into the future. Arthur does not change anything; he celebrates the *status quo* and repeats existing convictions. Hester, on the other hand, returns as reformer. She provides a space of freedom, one that is at least partially free of systemic loyalties, nurses individual hurt, and furthers the development of *civil* ties. This turn from systemic obedience towards civil concerns constitutes a first step in the process of democratization (Thomas 197).

Hester's prophecy is different from Arthur's. She becomes the prophetess of the variant myth. Her prophecy is one of gradual development towards equality, a "brighter period, when the world should have grown ripe for it, in Heaven's own time." Indeed, Hester is not the ultimate prophetess. Yet the "angel and apostle of the coming revelation must be a woman, indeed, but lofty, pure, and beautiful, and wise" (SL 166). Hester, like Ann, becomes a *type*. Ann Hutchinson served as type for Hester, who by her return succeeds where Ann failed. In turn, Hester herself is but figurative of the freedom that is to be fulfilled in the future. Whether Hawthorne had a specific person in mind, or if the coming angel is to be understood metaphorically, is a question that cannot be answered coherently.[35]

Nevertheless, the novel credits Hester with the foundations of a free American polity. Her liminal sphere of life – the space between town and nature – is given an institution, ending its association with witchcraft. Spatially, the realm between civilization and nature, public and private, now becomes accessible territory for Bostonians. The transgressor was able to push a theocracy's horizon, tamed its fear of what lies beyond the fence, and now offers a space where public and private can coexist. It is a small change, but it is the beginning of civil society, which can now evolve until the complex sphere of social interactions is strong enough to support a democratic system. This is the core meaning of the variant myth: The foundations of American democracy are indeed Puritan, but it is to the credit of those who resisted Puritanism that democratization was possible.

This democratization process entails the reinterpretation of dissent and its previous association with witchcraft. Witchcraft has served to mark dissenters of any kind, generalizing their individual transgressions in the image of the ultimate religious and political opponent. As heretics and traitors, the witch/dissenter needed to be removed from civilized territory and was assigned the realm beyond the fence. Hester's cottage changes this either/or geography. By establishing the cottage as a social space, the opposition between statist loyalty and private self-interest is ended. Individual content is made possible in the realm of the *social*, in interpersonal communications which may exist in the civil sphere between town and forest. Hereby, the conflation of dissenters and witches is terminated. Neither Hester nor the people she councils are associated with it; the cottage is presented as a legitimate sphere. We may remember the narrator's presentation of Hester in the novel's preface. It indicates that Boston would remember Hester Prynne as angel, nurse, and councilor:

It had been her habit, from an almost immemorial date, to go about the country as a kind of voluntary nurse, and doing whatever miscellaneous good she might; taking upon herself, likewise, to give advice in all matters, especially those of the heart. By which means, as a person of such propensities inevitably must, she gained from many people the reverence due to an angel. (SL 27)

---

35 I will, however, dare to propose the goddess Liberty as the "lofty," "beautiful," and "wise" woman who is to fulfill Hester's prophecy (SL 166). Thus, the American attainment of liberty may be read as a process of ongoing dissent: From Ann Hutchinson's radical Antinomianism, through Hester's sympathetic and civil dissent in the cottage, to the final establishment of dissent as basis of a polity devoted to freedom itself.

Hester's description as a "very old, but not decrepit woman, of a stately and solemn aspect" is once again reminiscent of Frigga (ibid.). This deity was known as a wandering councilor, aiding especially young women and couples (Guerber 31). Hawthorne's novel, intentionally or unintentionally, recaptures a pre-Christian meaning of the witch, just as it recaptures the forest as a space of freedom.[36]

Hester Prynne's story naturalizes a new civic myth. This variant, the *Order of Roses* myth, is based on mercy, individuality, and the celebration of dissent. It further allows for democratic policies regarding the treatment of heterodoxy. This myth calls for a balance of private and public by relying on the individual's capacity to both adhere to societal values and restrict their dissent to civil spaces. In a democracy, values are defined by the people, not by their government. But even if the democratic process is able to produce general laws, there must be spaces where dissent is possible and able to articulate itself. Democracy is, after all, not just a political system but a way of life. The ability to deal with dissent in a way that upholds the polity, while at the same time incorporating private concerns, is crucial to any form of democratic culture. The tension between private and public can be resolved in civil society, which not only allows for pluralistic opinions but channels them to influence decision making. Puritan Boston simply did not allow for such a sphere, because pluralism of opinion is impossible in a theocratic regime. It is the civic myth in Hester and the Puritan dissenters that allows for the imagination of civil spheres in an otherwise closed community.

Hawthorne rewrote the Puritan past so as to produce an adequate civic myth for Antebellum America. Beside Hester, a second character is successful in her dissent. She, however, never returns to Boston. The construction of an American national identity based on the variant myth is not complete without Pearl. She is the only American character in a novel populated by Englishmen. While other characters are imagined as the nation's past, it is in Pearl that the novel offers an American future.

Pearl and the Aesthetics of Catholicism

Pearl presents migration in an essential, transatlantic way, unbound by either politics or geography. In Blumenberg's sense, she illustrates the pushing of horizons: She is pure and individualistic dissent in a world that seeks to fence her in. She

---

36 The wandering councilor Hester leaves behind the darker associations of witchcraft and finds a place in the tradition of lay healers, the "leading therapeutic operatives of pre-Reformation rural Europe" (Klaits 64). Her character may be loosely attributed to the *benandanti* (the good wanderers), i.e. witches who serve their community (63). She remains a creature of the liminal but is able to transform that liminality by institutionalizing social and sympathetic interactions.

pushes fences so far that she returns to where the story began. Although dislocated, Pearl is nothing less than the first American, a true American Eve and crucial to the variant myth's construction of national identity. She is also the Sin-as-Possibility mytheme made flesh.

The fact that Pearl is representative of Hester's sin is first expressed in the mother's impulse to cover the letter with the infant as she stands at the prison door, but she realizes that "one token of her shame would poorly serve to hide another" (SL 40). Throughout the novel, Pearl is presented as another form of the scarlet A: In prison, the child will not stop screaming; she "writhed in convulsions of pain, and was a forcible type [...] of the moral agony which Hester Prynne had borne." Her existence is the visible sign of sin, and her very body seems to be infused with that heritage, as if she had drunk "all the turmoil, the anguish, the despair, which pervaded the mother's system" (51). As an infant, Pearl is also representative of her mother's punishment. Like the letter, she is of "fantastic ingenuity" (58). Pearl, "the scarlet letter endowed with life" will share the fate of her textile counterpart: Her signification will change (69).

Very early, the girl is associated with the novel's symbol for mercy (the rose) and thus attributed to the alternative founders. She describes herself as "plucked by her mother off the bush of wild roses" (SL 76). While visiting Governor Bellingham, she is named "Ruby", "Red Rose", and "little bird of scarlet plumage" (74). These associations with dissent immediately link her to witchcraft.

The strongest witchcraft image in Pearl is the *demon-child*. I have already elaborated on the notion that witches were thought to produce demonic progeny, and I agree with Colacurcio that Pearl, a child born out of wedlock, presents a child born from a witch/dissenter (317). The townspeople see her as "demon offspring," and the narrator links her origin to that of Martin Luther: "Luther, according to the scandal of his monkish enemies, was a brat of that hellish breed; nor was Pearl the only child to whom this inauspicious origin was assigned" (SL 67). Even the magistrates entertain the notion that she may be of infernal origin (68). Yet there is something about Pearl that undermines these accusations. The child possesses an endearing charm. Therefore, she is linked to a more sympathetic imagery: fairies. Bellingham recognizes elfish influences in Pearl, and her supposedly demonic nature becomes playful wickedness:

'What have we here?' said Governor Bellingham, looking with surprise at the scarlet little figure before him. 'I profess, I have never seen the like since my days of vanity, in old King James's time, when I was wont to esteem it a high favour to be admitted to a court mask! There used to be a swarm of these small apparitions in holiday time, and we called them children of the Lord of Misrule. But how gat such a guest into my hall?' (74)

John Wilson echoes this sentiment, linking Pearl to the realm of fairies, the old world, and, significantly, to Catholicism: "Art thou a Christian child,—ha? Dost know thy catechism? Or art thou one of those naughty elfs or fairies whom we thought to have left behind us, with other relics of Papistry, in merry old England?" Both men, however, are yet unaware of Pearl's parentage; as they learn that this is Hester's daughter, Wilson immediately recurs to Puritanism's go-to response for transgressors: "Nay, we might have judged that such a child's mother must needs be a scarlet woman, and a worthy type of her of Babylon!" (ibid.).[37]

The association with mythological material – witchcraft, elves, and fairies – is again used to mark dissent. For Pearl, however, there are instances in which she is linked to a real oppositional force: Catholicism. Catholic imagery serves to contrast the dreariness of Puritanism, and Pearl plays a significant part in this strategy. The world of superstitions was supposed to have been left behind; yet it was left behind in *merry* old England. Bellingham, for instance, was invited to a masquerade by the Catholic king James I in his days of (overcome) revelry. Moreover, the Catholic possibilities of forgiveness may also play into the use of Catholic imagery to oppose Puritanism, both aesthetically and ideologically. Indeed, the use of a central Catholic image foreshadows Pearl's messianic destiny.

The novel presents Pearl as a quintessentially unruly child:

'There is no law, nor reverence for authority, no regard for human ordinances or opinions, right or wrong, mixed up with that child's composition,' remarked [Roger], as much to himself as to [Arthur]. 'I saw her, the other day, bespatter the Governor himself with water at the cattle-trough in Spring Lane. What, in heaven's name, is she?' (SL 89)

We may answer Roger's question: Pearl is the embodiment of a dissent that will be imagined as constitutive to American national identity. The "chaos of Pearl's character" is at constant odds with the regulations of Boston (116). Her very nature is dissent: "The child could not be made amenable to rules. In giving her existence, a great law had been broken; and the result was a being whose elements were perhaps beautiful and brilliant, but all in disorder" (62).

That chaos, however, is not always disruptive. On Election Day, Pearl's positive influences are evident. The holiday's attendants "had not been born to an inher-

---

37 cf. KJV Revelations 17:3f: "I saw a woman sit upon a scarlet coloured beast, full of names of blasphemy, having seven heads and ten horns. And the woman was arrayed in purple and scarlet colour, and decked with gold and precious stones and pearls, having a golden cup in her hand full of abominations and filthiness of her fornication: And upon her forehead was a name written, Mystery, Babylon The Great, The Mother Of Harlots And Abominations Of The Earth."

itance of Puritanic gloom" but were in fact "native Englishmen," accustomed to a more "stately, magnificent, and joyous" lifestyle (SL 146). Yet unwilling to follow their "hereditary taste," all "branches of jocularity" are repressed." The narrator laments this loss of merriment: The "generation next to the early emigrants [...] wore the blackest shade of Puritanism, and so darkened the national visage with it, that all the subsequent years have not sufficed to clear it up. We have yet to learn again the forgotten art of gaiety." Indeed, this passage attests to the Puritan element in American identity; but that heritage is not solely grim. The "great, honest face of the people smiled—grimly, perhaps, but widely too," and one has to ask what they are smiling at (147).

Color, gaiety, and the *liveliness* of the Election Day celebration are once again provided by outsiders. It is the Indian spectators and "their savage finery of curiously embroidered deerskin robes" that enlivens the "the sad gray, brown, or black of the English emigrants." The *forest*-men are joined by *sea*-men, the sea being another unregulated space which "swelled, and foamed very much at its own will" (SL 148). Attire marks outsiders in the novel, and the sailor's appearance stands out:

They were rough-looking desperadoes, with sun-blackened faces, and an immensity of beard; their wide short trousers were confined about the waist by belts, often clasped with a rough plate of gold, and sustaining always a long knife, and in some instances, a sword. From beneath their broad-brimmed hats of palm-leaf, gleamed eyes which, even in good-nature and merriment, had a kind of animal ferocity. (ibid.)

Their otherness is not confined to apparel but includes conduct: The sailors "transgressed without fear or scruple." But even the magistrates "smiled not unbenignantly," because the sailor was believed to be able to "relinquish his calling, and become at once, if he chose, a man of probity and piety on land" (ibid.).

Flanked by sailors and natives, Pearl flutters through the scene and makes "the somber crowd cheerful by her erratic and glistening ray" (SL 153). Her connection to outside realms is made clearly visible, and the settler's recognize something essentially alien in the girl but are nevertheless amused by her otherness:

The Puritans looked on, and, if they smiled, were none the less inclined to pronounce the child a demon offspring, from the indescribable charm of beauty and eccentricity that shone through her little figure, and sparkled with its activity. She ran and looked the wild Indian in the face, and he grew conscious of a nature wilder than his own. Thence, with native audacity, but still with a reserve as characteristic, she flew into the midst of a group of mariners, the swarthy-cheeked wild men of the ocean, as the Indians were of the land; and they gazed wonderingly and admiringly at Pearl. (155)

Witchcraft imagery remains prevalent in this scene. Hibbins situates Pearl in "the lineage of the Prince of Air" and the sailor's captain calls her a "witch-baby," at which Pearl, invoking a traditional witch-power, answers: "If thou callest me that ill-name, I shall tell [the devil] of thee, and he will chase thy ship with a tempest!" (154, 156).

Pearl's association with otherness illuminates a crucial point. While still linked to witchcraft, Pearl attains a positive imagery. Her elves and fairies point to merry old England, and the narrator's mourning of the loss of gaiety is answered by the girl's merriment. She represents the cheerfulness of the unregulated, lawless spheres of life. That cheerfulness, however, is linked to Catholicism. There is, indeed, no promotion of Catholic theology; but the novel's warmer, happier, more merciful imagery is linked to the Roman faith. The sailors are Spanish (read Catholic), and especially the captain's attire and conduct, him being the "most showy and gallant figure" of the scene, is reminiscent of Catholic smells and bells. The strongest association, however, is found earlier in the novel and serves to foreshadow Pearl's destiny.

As Hester stands on the scaffold, the narrator assumes a Catholic perspective:

Had there been a Papist among the crowd of Puritans, he might have seen in this beautiful woman, so picturesque in her attire and mien, and with the infant at her bossom, an object to remind him of the image of Divine Maternity, which so many illustrious painters have vied with one another to represent; something which should remind him, indeed, but only by contrast, of that sacred image of sinless motherhood, whose infant was to redeem the world. (SL 42)

A Catholic perspective in theocratic Boston can only be imagined; there were no Catholics. But the fact that a Catholic perspective is given at all illuminates the function this image serves. Although the world is "darker" and "more lost" for it, and "Divine Maternity" can only be deduced by contrast, the image nevertheless draws upon the original's signification (ibid.). If we see Hester as a darker because tainted version of Mary, we must read Pearl as a version of Jesus. The image reverses the original signification and casts mother and child as impure. But Pearl as a demon-child is disproven in the course of the novel. Pearl, indeed, becomes a savior figure and elaborates on the good that can result from sin: Pearl embodies the Sin-as-Possibility mytheme. Moreover, she dramatizes a new American beginning.

In opposition to the Sin-as-Sign mytheme, the visible, physical sign of Hester's adultery defies its categorization as sinful. Pearl is "a lovely and immortal flower, out of the rank luxuriance of a guilty passion" – she is the good that may come out of sin – and as such continues the symbolism of the rose. Her name indicates a treasure bought with great pain, and her character is penance as well as salvation for Hester.[38] The demon-child is designed to answer Ann Hutchinson's miscarriage, a tragedy that was interpreted as God's punishment.[39] In Hester's case, the divine intervenes as well, only differently: God "had given her a lovely child, whose place was on the same dishonored bosom, to connect her parent forever with the race and descent of mortals, and to be finally a blessed soul in heaven" (SL 61). Pearl's existence is divine counteraction. She becomes a child of *possibility*, of "outward mutability," "depth" and "infinite variety." It is this both/and perspective, the possibility to unite the diverse, that the variant civic myth seeks to establish for the Antebellum: "In this one child were many children" (62). Such a perspective may overcome the forces that threaten to tear the nation apart, and Pearl embodies this new national identity. Indeed, her very function is salvation.

Pearl saves Hester in that she balances and restricts her dissent. It is for her daughter that Hester resists Hibbins' invitation to the forest. The mother had just successfully fought for the child's custody and remarks on the consequences of Pearl's removal: "Had they taken her from me, I would willingly have gone with thee into the forest, and signed my name in the Black Man's book too, and that with mine own blood!" (SL 79). Pearl saves her mother from open rebellion; she grounds Hester and hinders her adoption of Antinomianism:

Yet, had little Pearl never come to her from the spiritual world [...] [Hester] might have come down to us in history, hand in hand with Ann Hutchinson, as the foundress of a religious sect. [...] But, in the education of her child, the mother's enthusiasm of thought had something to wreak itself upon. Providence, in the person of this little girl, had assigned to Hester's charge, the germ and blossom of womanhood, to be cherished and developed amid a host of difficulties. (108)

The Catholic image of Divine Maternity foreshadows Pearl's role as savior.[40] Simultaneously, she presents the fulfillment of a Puritan prophecy. She is the promised

---

38 cf. KJV Matthew 13:45f: "Again, the kingdom of heaven is like unto a merchant man, seeking goodly pearls: who, when he had found one pearl of great price, went and sold all that he had, and bought it."

39 cf. footnote 27.

40 Hester is aware of her daughter's role. In Bellingham's mansion, she fights for the right to keep her and explains: "'God gave me the child!' cried she. 'He gave her in requital of all things else which ye had taken from me. She is my happiness,—she is my torture, none the less! Pearl keeps me here in life! [...] See ye not, she is the scarlet letter, only capable of being loved, and so endowed with a millionfold the power of retribution for my sin?'" (SL 76).

new beginning, a Utopian character able to leave the past behind. Yet in contrast to Puritan expectations, this new being, the *American*, is not born in the confines of Puritanism but is a child of nature and passion. Pearl's character is of paramount importance for the variant myth, because she offers the tenets of American national identity. Hawthorne has the first American emerge from the lawless forest and links her being to a Puritan settler whose arrival predates the Mayflower.

A New Eden and the Terms of National Identity

Foundational myths do not begin in the streets of a city. Beginning belongs to the forest, to the earth, to the darkness of chaos, or the bottom of the sea. Human civilization may try to overcome nature, but it is always imagined as deriving from organic beginnings. Pearl presents such a beginning and is accordingly depicted as a child of the primeval.

Like her namesake, Pearl is a product of nature, an "immortal flower" of "native grace" and "faultless beauty." She is "worthy to have been brought forth in Eden; worthy to have been left there, to be the plaything of angels" (SL 61). As an Edenic being, she is full of possibilities, "a creature that had nothing in common with a bygone and buried generation, nor owned herself akin to it. It was as if she had been made afresh out of new elements, and must perforce be permitted to live her own life, and be a law unto herself" (90). Pearl is the emissary of the American, the beginning of something new. Unlike all other characters, she is born outside of English Puritan politics and geographies. She originated in the New World and outside Puritan law. That she is not even connected to Puritan children ("sombre little urchins") is evident in their recurrent confrontations (64, 69). Pearl is never characterized as Puritan. She is, indeed, a break in the hereditary line. In a community that had to bury its Utopian expectations, Pearl is born a child of Eden.

This does not mean that she was born without sin. Hawthorne certainly could not go as far as to deny human depravity, and to think of Pearl in terms of an immaculate being is contradicted by the darkened image of Divine Maternity. She is a savior, even a founder, but certainly post-lapsarian. But her relation to nature and reality's absolutism is of Adamic innocence: Pearl is not afraid of death. The Puritans built a cemetery to accommodate death in their New World paradise; Pearl, on the other hand, skips "irreverently from one grave to another" (SL 89). Her interaction with the world is experimental: As Hester speaks with Roger by the seaside, Pearl flirts "fancifully with her own image in a pool of water, beckoning the phantom forth" (115).[41] Later, she will start throwing pebbles at nearby seabirds, injur-

---

41 Pearl is reminiscent of Eve in Milton's *Paradise Lost* (1667), who also flirts with her reflection. Compare Eve's report on the experience of looking into a pool of water for the

ing one severely. There is no moral discretion in the child yet, save the ability of identification and therefore sympathy: At realizing that she had hurt the bird "the elf-child sighed, and gave up her sport, because it grieved her to have done harm to a little being that was as wild as the sea-breeze, or as wild as [...] herself" (ibid.). Pearl is the mythological primordial human, representing the beginnings of a new civilization. Her character contains elements which will allow for her development, but for the moment, all we are given is the experience of an infant state:

In the little chaos of Pearl's character there might be seen emerging and could have been from the very first,—the steadfast principles of an unflinching courage,—an uncontrollable will—sturdy pride, which might be disciplined into self-respect—and a bitter scorn of many things which, when examined, might be found to have the taint of falsehood in them. She possessed affections, too, though hitherto acrid and disagreeable, as are the richest flavours of unripe fruit. With all these sterling attributes, thought Hester, the evil which she inherited from her mother must be great indeed, if a noble woman do not grow out of this elfish child. (116)

This last description of Pearl may be taken as a description of a nascent American identity. It includes dissent, self-reliance, courage, and, importantly, the young nation's infant and rougher qualities which are yet to ripen and result in greatness. From a romantic perspective, nature and authenticity are of importance for American identity negotiations. Pearl serves that purpose.

Pearl is a child perfectly attuned to nature. While she exhibits her wild, destructive self at the seaside, she reveals her communion with nature in the forest. Sunlight in the woods "lingered about the lonely child, as if glad of such a playmate." Pearl "had not the disease of sadness, which almost all children, in these latter days, inherit, with the scrofula, from the troubles of their ancestors" (SL 119). Nature embraces Pearl's presence because she is untouched by the darker aspects of civilization. So, while her parents discuss their sadness, the forest becomes "the playmate of the lonely infant," and she amuses herself by playing with wild animals (131). Her mythological depiction is fortified by the following imagery. She makes a wreath of flowers and crowns herself, becoming a nymph at play. Simultaneously – and here we find another instance of *myth-then-ratio* – her play is reminiscent of a

---

very first time: "As I bent down to look, just opposite, a shape within the watry gleam appeard, bending to look on me, I started back, it started back, but pleas'd I soon returnd, pleas'd it returnd as soon with answering looks of sympathie and love; there I had fixt mine eyes till now, and pin'd with vain desire, had not a voice thus warnd me, what there thou seest fair Creature is thyself" (Milton IV 460-468).

messianic prophecy, the coming of the savior from the roots of Jesse.[42] Here, a child restores the peace of Eden, and man is returned to a state of natural innocence:

A wolf, it is said,—but here the tale has surely lapsed into the improbable,—came up and smelt of Pearl's robe, and offered his savage head to be patted by her hand. The truth seems to be, however, that the mother-forest, and these wild things which it nourished, all recognized a kindred wilderness in the human child. (ibid.)

Hester attributes the girl's flowery attire to "one of the fairies, whom they left in dear old England," and again, Pearl serves as savior as she insists on Hester's resuming the cast-off letter (132). Here, the child is transfigured to assume the stance of guardian. Standing by the brook, the water creates a second image of the child and reflects her "little figure, with all the brilliant picturesqueness of her beauty, in its adornment of flowers and wreathed foliage, but more refined and spiritualized than the reality" (133). Pearl's description is one of transfiguration:

It was strange, the way in which Pearl stood, looking so steadfastly at them through the dim medium of the forest gloom, herself, meanwhile, all glorified with a ray of sunshine, that was attracted thitherward as by a certain sympathy. In the brook beneath stood another child – another and the same – with likewise its ray of golden light. (ibid.)

Arthur is correct in recognizing "that this brook is the boundary between two worlds," but he errs when he sees Pearl as "an elfish spirit, who [...] is forbidden to cross a running stream" (ibid.). Pearl is not arrested by a boarder but rather hinders her mother from trespassing. We are given another fence, one that must not be crossed if Hester wishes to return to town. The flood of sunshine is over and not resuming the letter would only cement Hester's radical dissent. Pearl, once again, bars Hester's way towards radicalism. Her insistence on resuming the letter is neither societal nor primeval. It is both:

At length, assuming a singular air of authority, Pearl stretched out her hand, with the small forefinger extended, and pointing evidently towards her mother's breast. And beneath, in the mirror of the brook, there was the flower-girdled and sunny image of little Pearl, pointing her small forefinger too. (134)

---

42 cf. KJV Isaiah 11:6: "The wolf also shall dwell with the lamb, and the leopard shall lie down with the kid; and the calf and the young lion and the fatling together; and a little child shall lead them."

Town and forest demand the resumption of the letter. In her accusation, Pearl foreshadows the necessary balance between societal duty and individual integrity which will be attained by Hester upon her return. Nature, too, "does not love" the bearer of the letter, even if it is sympathetic towards her (SL 119). Pearl, however, seems aware of the importance of the badge, especially as it has changed its meaning. The letter, just as the rose, is her symbol as well. The letter connects her to Hester. Yet as the first American rose, she is connected to another alternative ancestor.

New England's First Gardener

Ryskamp notes that Pearl's character becomes more substantial when read against William Blackstone (298). Blackstone, a scholar and clergyman, arrived in what is now Boston three years before Winthrop landed at Plymouth Rock (Lind vi). He first aided the settlers in establishing themselves near his own land (today Boston Commons), but it became clear that William could not accept the rising theocracy. The fusion of public and religious law infuriated the reverend (10, 20). In 1634, he sold most of his land, moved to Rhode Island, and later described his predicament with Winthrop's theocracy: "I left England to get from under the power of the lord bishops, but in America I am fallen under the lord brethren." Further, Rhode Island records summarize William's time in Boston: "At a point upon Shwamut, or Trimontaine, since Boston, lived Mr Blaxton, who had left England, being dissatisfied there and not a thorough conformist; but he was more dissatisfied with the non-conformity of the new comers" (in Lind 21).

Lind notes that William Blackstone grew famous throughout New England for reasons which enabled his legendarization.[43] He was received as a Tolerationist and non-conformist who liked living off the beaten tracks (31, 36). Among his eccentricities, his habit of riding a white bull stands out (21). With Hutchinson, this character informs the background of the novel. Blackstone is mentioned in Bellingham's mansion while discussing the governor's failed attempts to cultivate English garden ornaments. The soil itself seems to resist the imposition of English seeds. Instead, the earth produces its own vegetation:

[The governor] appeared already to have relinquished as hopeless, the effort to perpetuate on this side of the Atlantic [...] the native English taste for ornamental gardening. Cabbages grew in plain sight; and a pumpkin-vine, rooted at some distance, had run across the interven-

---

43 Blackstone was the very first settler in the Massachusetts Bay area and a known scholar and hermit. He was celebrated for his orchards and gardens, both in Massachusetts and Rhode Island, and developed the first American apple variety, the Yellow Sweetling (Lind 1, 13, 27).

ing space, and deposited one of its gigantic products directly beneath the hall window, as if to warn the Governor that this great lump of vegetable gold was as rich an ornament as New England earth would offer him. (SL 72)

What follows is the reference to William, who is presented as a mythological personage that informs New England's history. He is linked not only to apples but, significantly, to roses; indeed, Blackstone was famous for his apples, but he was celebrated for his rose-gardens (Lind 1, 13).

There were a few rose-bushes, however, and a number of apple-trees, probably the descendants of those planted by the Reverend Mr. Blackstone, the first settler of the peninsula; that half mythological personage who rides through our early annals, seated on the back of a bull. (SL 72)

If we inquire about the signification of the rose as a symbol of dissent, we may of course include Ann, Hester, and Pearl. But the symbol originates with William Blackstone, the planter not just of the rose but of the dissent which the emblem will represent. As an alternative ancestor, he serves the naturalization of the variant myth (IIc) by offering a historical founder of Boston who preceded Winthrop's company and dissented from their form of Puritanism. The variant myth traces Puritan dissent from Hester and Pearl, through Ann, to originate in William Blackstone. If Winthrop planted the black flower, Blackstone was the rose-gardener.

Pearl thus stands at the end of an organic development that was initiated by Blackstone. She is the rose of dissent, the first that has sprung from American soil. Just as William cultivated a first all-American apple variety, Pearl is imagined as the first all-American dissenter. Yet if Pearl is indeed the American Eve, than the development of the nation is to be traced back to both, Winthrop's black flower and Blackstone's roses. With Blackstone, Hawthorne enthrones a Puritan dissenter as a founding father who predates the Mayflower Puritans and whose organic influences have been "kept alive in history" (SL 37). In Pearl and Blackstone's genealogy of dissent, the variant myth is ultimately naturalized (IIc). The variant thereby balances the heritage of Puritanism by the inauguration of a heritage of tolerance, mercy, and dissent: Antebellum America receives a second set of forbearers, which finds its genesis in William Blackstone and its revelation in Pearl Prynne.

There is an extra-textual connection between William and Pearl worth mentioning. This connection refers to Pearl's description as a child of nature and a legend that has formed around William's daughter Sarah.⁴⁴ Regarding the legend, Lind quotes:

> It was long believed that Blackstone had an only daughter who was borne away from the abodes of society, – educated by her father alone, – who had grown up in communion with nature and was graced with the simplicity of nature's charms, a child of the forest and the field, a flower of the wilderness. (Dagget in Lind 50)

Sarah was in fact the name of Blackstone's stepson's sister and had no direct relation with him whatsoever (Lind 50). The legend nevertheless strengthens the depiction of William as a man attuned to nature, who raised a daughter whose description is highly reminiscent of Pearl.

The legend proved a ready literary subject. *The Humours of Eutopia* (1828), a romance in two volumes, illustrates that the Blackstonian legend was alive during Hawthorne's time. The author Ezekiel Sanford wrote his own tale "of Colonial Times" (i) and offers another, albeit more humorous account of the Puritan settlements.⁴⁵

I am not claiming that Hawthorne was aware of Sanford's romance. What I am saying is that the legend of William Blackstone presents material that was used to rework the Puritan past by focusing on the era's rebels. In 1947, Conrad Aiken comments on Blackstone in his foreword to *The Kid*, a poem dedicated to the set-

---

44 It is important to note that this legend is fictional, and that I am not claiming that Hawthorne based Pearl on Sarah. Still, there are similarities that illustrate Pearl's importance for the construction of American identity.

45 The narrative revolves around settlers who establish their own settlement called Eutopia. Central to the plot are the descendants from "one William Blaxton, a dissenting clergyman of the church of England, who came to America prior to the arrival of Winthrop's company" (Sanford 43). The imagery of William as dissenter is prevalent: "But the Rev. William Blaxton was something of an Ishmaelite in religion. To use the cant of the day, he symbolized with no denomination of Christians. Much pains were taken to puritanize him, but as he was a non-non-conformist to the church of England, so he was a non-conformist to all other non-conformists. He quitted England, he said, 'because he did not like to lord bishops;' and avowing that he equally 'disliked the lord brethren,' he departed from Boston" (44). William's prodigy seems to have inherited his dissent. Abijah Blaxton, for instance, "did not belie his origin by the slightest manifestation of conformity" and his daughter Mary was named to defy the Puritan expectations of his wife (46). Mary, like William, is an ardent reader, and most importantly, a "great rambler" (47f). She would spend her time in "the field and woods." The girl's reading and rambling produce queer ideas, thoughts which repeatedly shock her mother (71).

tler, who is still held to have influenced the construction of American national identity:

He is a tantalizing figure, in many respects the true prototypical American; ancestor alike of those pioneers who sought freedom and privacy in the 'wide open spaces,' or the physical conquest of an untamed continent; and those others, early and late, who struggle for it in the darker kingdom of the soul. Daniel Boone and Johnny Appleseed were his grandchildren. But so, too, were Thoreau, Melville and Henry Adams. And the outlaws, the lone wolves, the lost souls – yes, these as well. (in Lind 94)

Blackstone's influence, however, was marginal. By removing himself from Boston, the Tolerationist had no further political influence on Massachusetts Bay. Yet Pearl does not have to be read as William's legendary daughter to see the ancestral line that is drawn from the first Bostonian dissenter to the elf-child. Pearl dramatizes the Puritan errand but strips away its theology, replacing divinely ordained obedience with individuality. The new being in Pearl is not Puritan anymore. She is, like Blackstone, free to follow her own discretion. It is that idea which will constitute the identity of the 'proto-typical' American.

A primacy of individuality causes the first American to leave America. Chillingworth bequeathed all his wealth on Pearl, making her "the richest heiress of her day in the New World," a fact that would have facilitated Pearl's marriage to a Puritan (SL 164). Apparently, that fate seemed undesirable to the young woman. Hester returns to Boston alone, and any information regarding Pearl's destiny is based on hearsay. The novel indicates that she chose a life far from her native home. She became an "inhabitant of another land" who communicates with her mother through letters "with armorial seals upon them, though of bearings unknown to English heraldry." Thus, the novel is explicit in stating that Pearl returned to Europe but not to England. She may have settled on the continent, in France, Germany, or Spain. Regardless, she is the only character who finds true happiness: "In fine, the gossips of that day believed […] that Pearl was not only alive, but married, and happy" (165).

If we consider the members of the Order of Roses, it becomes clear that, except for Hester and Pearl, their dissent ultimately fails. The predecessors, Ann and William, are removed; Arthur and Roger cement or exceed the Puritan primacy of justice; only Hester is able to effect real change in Boston. But there is no true *private* happiness for her. These characters remain fenced by the Puritan world; they are all part of it and all trapped by it. It is exclusively Pear who succeeds in living a happy and fulfilled life, albeit on the old continent. Here lies the core of the paradox inherent in Pearl: She embodies the American pursuit of individual happiness at a time when America itself was not ready for it.

Thus, Pearl combines the Puritan errand with the American idea. She is a new being that tips the scales of duty. Instead of being trapped in a theocracy that demands submission to a communal errand, Pearl dramatizes the same errand on an individual level by leaving. She enacts the errand: She leaves a coercive realm and crosses the Atlantic in search for freedom. Yet she does it for *herself*, not for the sake of a divine covenant. Pearl's migration presents a redefinition of the Puritan migration and reverses its direction. Her leaving mirrors the voting with one's feet performed by the Puritan's themselves, only now it is Puritan Boston that has to be fled, and her quest for free shores constitutes the American primacy of individuality. The search for freedom is not restricted to specific (American) geographies; it is an individual idea that motivates and legitimizes the establishment of a happy life, regardless of spaciality. Thus, Pearl *globalizes* the errand. The Promised Land is where the person is able to pursue happiness, not where a community dictates its terms. In turning her back on Boston, Pearl is a descendant of William Blackstone indeed.

Pearl and Hester serve two functions for the naturalization of the variant myth (IIc) and its inherent national identity. Hester illuminates the importance of a pragmatic dissent for the construction of a democratic society. Her role is communal by creating spaces for individuality in society. But Pearl dramatizes the transformation of a communal errand into a subjective pursuit of happiness. She thereby divorces the quest for freedom from both theology and geography, opening the possibility of religiously and ethnically generalizing national identity. The American becomes a rebellious human being in search for freedom and happiness, free of any specific religion, ethnicity, and geography.[46]

The latter is not without its problems. The terms of identity set in the novel are able to incorporate pluralism in society and diversity in terms of belonging in theory. But the displacement of the first American is telling of the fact that the process of opening these categories is slow. Boston is not ready for Pearl and her individualism. Likewise, Antebellum America struggles with the incorporation of new identities, may these be immigrants or ex-slaves. Bercovitch notes that the incorporation of ever new identities to the American is an ever-ongoing process; revolution becomes a "controlling metaphor" enabling every new generation to continue the Puritan errand (Assent 38). I agree that dissent towards that goal cannot be radical, as radicalism would forestall its effectiveness. But it needs to be *active*. By removing Pearl, her influence is nullified. Hester, on the other hand, the character who works

---

46 The personalization and globalization of the Puritan errand will be of importance when discussing Abolitionist literature. Very much like Pearl, Brown's characters in Clotel will enact a reversed Puritan voyage and strip the errand of spaciality by pursuing happiness in Europe.

towards change, must forgo a happy life. While the novel is successful in balancing (because restricting) public and private demands, it fails at providing a third way of effectively marrying political dissent and personal happiness.

The Apotheosis of Hope and a New Coat of Arms

Hawthorne not only constructs an alternative set of forefathers, he also designs an escutcheon to represent the variant myth. When Hester is laid to rest next to Arthur, they are not allowed to share a grave but are given the same tombstone. Their stone is unmarked but bears a heraldic emblem telling of their role as New World nobility. On the stone

> appeared the semblance of an engraved escutcheon. It bore a device, a herald's wording of which may serve for a motto and brief description of our now concluded legend; so sombre is it, and relieved only by one ever-glowing point of light gloomier than the shadow: — 'ON A FIELD, SABLE, THE LETTER A, GULES' (SL 166)

Here we find the final balancing and ordering of the forces that contested throughout the novel. The Puritan black (the sable field) is and remains the background of American development. Yet the red A (the gules letter) contrasts the Puritan heritage and conceptualizes the novel's import. While the Puritan past forms the nation's background, this coat of arms honors dissenters with the concretization of what developed from a theocratic past: *A*merica. The binaries that compete throughout the novel – justice/mercy, society/individual, orthodoxy/heterodoxy – are brought together to symbolize a nation whose identity is, in Bercovitch's words, one of "fragmentation and dissent" (Assent 29). This escutcheon elevates dissent to the fundamental notion in American ideology – as long as it centers on the individual, seeks independence, group pluralism, and progress (Office 30). It highlights the possibility of uniting a fragmented and diverse society by celebrating differences and the merciful treatment of ambiguity (25). Finally, it credits those who dissented with the illumination of a dark past, now relieved by their "ever-glowing point of light gloomier than the shadow" (SL 166).

The scarlet dissenters framed by the black of Puritanism are, however, not the last word. In a novel that insists on color symbolism, one has to consider an A of a different hue. Again, Pearl serves to describe a brighter American future. She is the scarlet letter in another form; yet at the end of the novel, that burden is lifted from her: A "spell was broken" as she kissed her father, an act of sympathy which will lead her to "grow up amid human joy and sorrow" (SL 162). It is here that the bounds of her past are severed; she will have to rely upon herself in the future and "must gather [her] own sunshine" (70). By now, the reader knows that she will, albeit not in Boston. But Pearl will give the letter a final and significant turn. She transforms its color: "Pearl took some eel-grass and imitated, as best she could, on her own bosom the decoration with which she was so familiar on her mother's. A letter—the letter A—but freshly green instead of scarlet" (115). Pearl transforms the letter and thereby reorients the new nation towards hope. Thus, the survivor of the story may indeed provide a brighter moral blossom to be plucked and offered to the reader.

3. Karl Gutzkow's *Wally, die Zweiflerin* and the Despair of Artificiality

> Der germanische Geist ist der Geist der neuen Welt.
> HEGEL/VORLESUNGEN ÜBER DIE PHILOSOPHIE DER
> GESCHICHTE

In 1835, Zacharias Löwenthal planned to establish a new press devoted to liberal literature in Mannheim. He turned to his friend Karl Gutzkow, asking him to provide a novel that may launch his enterprise. Three weeks later, Wally, die Zweiflerin [Wally the Skeptic] was published (Kaiser 186).

Gutzkow's novel was notorious. The scandal that followed its publication not only led to the Young Germans' prohibition but also to Gutzkow's incarceration. Eke notes that *Wally* wrought a deep change in Young German policy after 1835 (52). But while Gutzkow's debut novel remains his most famous work, little attention has been paid to the narrative itself. The text has remained in the shadow of its societal impact, and the following chapter endeavors to alleviate that critical deficit. I would like to ask *how* the text effects its singular force, for the critical focus on its reception may have clouded the perspective on the mythological elements in *Wally* (63). Indeed, the novel's critique is reinforced by Germanic myths, which are appropriated, denaturalized, and transformed. A novel concerned with the present, *Wally* looks to narratives of the past to comment on Germany's disempowered citizens.

The mythological resignification in this text foregrounds a female dissenter who shares certain characteristics with Hawthorne's Hester Prynne. Wally and Hester are both rebels. They insist on "freedom of speculation," and their dissent is of a personal *and* political nature (SL 107). It is the way in which they cope with their dissent that differentiates these women. Yet their position and conceptualization is almost identical: Wally is another hedgerider. She also pushes horizons in Blumenberg's sense and lives on the borders between conformity and individuality.

Gutzkow's novel is representative of a Young German author's endeavor to merge literature and politics; it offers a complex, at times confusing narrative which critiques German social reality. Importantly, its variant myth gives an alternative to Wally's ultimate despair and advocates the transition from disempowered subject to empowered citizen. However, before turning to *Wally*, I need to explicate the material through which it employs its mythological resignification. As *The Scarlet Letter* worked on the Puritan myth, *Wally* recurs to material that informs Vormärz Germany's most fundamental civic narratives: Germanic mythologies.

3.1 GERMANIC MYTHS AND THE AESTHETICS OF *DAS JUNGE DEUTSCHLAND*

Germany's national identity was informed by narratives best described as *Germanic myths*.[1] The Vormärz was an age of political uncertainty, and the negotiators of national unity inquired about the historical foundations of the future nation state. For answers regarding origin, character, and history of the German people, cultural elites turned to myth. Wiwjorra explains that this "archaic strategy" served to legitimize unification and to negotiate lifestyle, political culture, territorial borders, and social cohesion. Indeed, this mechanism was not restricted to Germany. It has pervaded European history for the last 200 years (8).

German identity began to take a national shape in the Vormärz, and Wiwjorra describes the Germanic myth as a system of ideas which serves political orientation (9). This orientation was desperately needed at the end of the 18th century, as originally elitist myths began to spread among the public. With the rise of the bourgeoisie and an increasing demand for political participation, these myths produced a nationalism based on the imagination of an ancient Germanic culture; but German nationalism in this early stage was different from its later forms. Wehler points out that in the Vormärz, nationalism was "a liberal-oppositional and emancipatory ideology, which sought to overcome feudal inequality, the supremacy of the nobility, German absolutism, and member-state egotism" (in Eke 26).[2] Indeed, the recur-

---

1 Germanic myth entails a vast number of stories, legends, and fairytales, all of which revolve around the imagined forbearers of modern Germany, the Germanic people. Wiwjorra notes that the trajectory of the Germanic myth is almost infinite. While some narratives are situated in primeval ages, myths of civic momentum usually recur to the Middle Ages and the era of the Holy Roman Empire (36).

2 [eine liberale Oppositions- und Emanzipationsideologie, welche die ständische Ungleichheit, die Vormacht des Adels, den deutschen Spätabsolutismus, den partikularstaatlichen Egoismus überwinden wollte].

rence to myth for the construction of a national identity was a rational approach: myth's emancipatory fight against reality's absolutism enters politics as it strives to fight statist absolutism.

The Germanic myth evolved from a patriotic-national to an ethnic (and racist) concept at the end of the 19th century. This turn was informed by imagining the superiority of the forefathers, who were now constructed in terms of race (Wiwjorra 15)[3]. In the Vormärz, however, liberal authors recurred to the Germanic myth in a different manner. They worked with cultural and historical continuities regarding the forefathers, not with questions of race. Indeed, the myth itself made instrumentalization likely: Freedom was imagined as an intricate element of the Germanic myth.

The Germanic Forefathers

The idea of the Germanic people as freedom-loving individuals is one the most prevalent motifs of Germanic myths (the *Inherent-Freedom* mytheme).[4] This idea revived at the beginning of the 19th century, as German territory was invaded and occupied by French forces. During the Napoleonic Wars, the recurrence to a German *Urfreiheit* [Original Freedom] carried the imagination of an authentic, free, and united nation. Thus, contemporaries sought a "recuperation" of freedom motivated by a romantic idealization of the Germanic past (33). In 1806, during the French occupation, Schlegel wrote: "For now, I as a writer know but one goal: To show Germans the image of their old glory, their old dignity and liberty in the mirror of antiquity, and fan every spark of national feeling, wherever it may rest" (in Wiwjorra 33).[5]

The Germanic myth imagines a set of natural characteristics which inform the image Schlegel's contemporaries had of their forefathers. Based on these character-

---

3   The development of the concept of race is, of course, not restricted to Germany but must be regarded as a transnational process. Taine, for instance, regards race as a prerequisite of cultural identity. For more see White: *Taine on Race and Genius* in *Social Research*, Vol. 10.1 (1943); Weschenbach: *Philosophie des Hippolyte Taine* (1992); Atkin: *The Philosophy of Race* (2003).

4   Wiwjorra notes that this motif was nurtured by the history of the Roman-Germanic wars. Germanic resistance to Roman colonization and the subsequent establishment of Germania Magna present the earliest historical sources for the idea of *Deutsche Freiheit* [German liberty] (33).

5   [Für jetzt kenne ich als Schriftsteller nur ein einziges Ziel: den Deutschen das Bild ihres alten Ruhmes, ihrer alten Würde und Freyheit im Spiegel der Vorzeit vorzuhalten und jeden Funken von Nationalgefühl, der irgendwo schlummern mag, anzufachen].

istics, a specific national identity is elaborated: First, the typical German excels in simplicity, virtue, loyalty, and bravery and is endowed with a natural will to freedom, the most essential quality of the Germanic tribes (Wiwjorra 109f). Indeed, the idea of free tribes consisting of free individuals would have consequences for the imagination of the modern German polity.[6] Vormärz Germans would imagine a socio-political continuity between ancient Germanic tribes, the Holy Roman Empire, and modern Germany.

There is a vast literature on the Holy Roman Empire.[7] For my purposes, I will focus on the mythological aspects that informed one of Europe's oldest polities. In this context, Wilson explains that the concept of German freedom shaped the empire's political organization; its system recurred to ancient and medieval narratives. The idea of German liberty was so ingrained in the Reich's political structure, that it was imagined as a divinely sanctioned political order (1). While the Kaiser held the highest position, territorial sovereignty presented the supreme principle, so that electors, princes, landgraves, and margraves shared power with the emperor (6). Moreover, the elective standards of the Germanic past were maintained in the imperial context: The Kaiser was a non-sovereign ruler chosen by the College of Electors. Here, the elective character of the *Thing* found a mytho-political continuation

---

6   Krüger notes that the tribe constituted the central political category in this context and was defined regionally as well as by ancestry. The tribes were cultural communities with distinct traditions. Differences in dialect, clothing, and armament served to distinguish one tribe from another (29f). The tribes' political organization advocated a political process based on equality and collective decision making. But Germanic freedom also entailed the will towards tribal independence. The historical organization of the Germanic tribes offered material for liberal writers bend on the construction of a democratic polity. The Germanic tribe was based upon two institutions. The *Thing* [People's Convention] comprised all men able to bear arms as well as their elected leaders. It was the most important political body. It was complemented by the *Stammesrat* [Tribe's Council], a body constituted of the *principes*, leaders elected in the convention (30f). Tribes rarely formed alliances but remained autonomous. It was only later that a cohesive tribal organization emerged on German-speaking soil. In fact, Roman invasions presented a driving force towards unification. Thus, history not only enabled the imagination of a territorial and linguistic continuity between the forefathers and modern Germans; it paralleled Germany's situation during the Napoleonic Wars and furthered cohesion. It also imagined a 'natural' because 'original' egalitarianism of Germans (32).

7   For an introduction see Ewans: *The Holy Roman Empire* (2012); Whaley: *Germany and the Holy Roman Empire* (2012); Schneidmüller and Weinfurter (eds): *Heilig – Römisch – Deutsch* (2006).

in modern structures. The territorial equality of regions, likewise, harks back to Germanic standards (8).

The concept of Germanic liberty had consequences for the development of a modern German identity. In the 18th century, elites based an early form of *Reichspatriotismus* [Imperial Patriotism] on this concept, which imagined the imperial system as a cohesive state (Whaley 438). Indeed, its obvious diversity was not received as hindering to the development of a unified national identity. The Holy Roman Empire was perceived as a German nation, both during its existence and after its collapse in 1806 (443). The early 19th century would therefore mourn the *loss* of a nation in the dissolution of the Reich, and democratic writers would call for a *re*unification of Germany, albeit on democratic terms.

But why would a literary group such as the Young Germans employ Germanic myths if their aesthetic and political values were so radically rooted in the present? Gutzkow, like most Young German writers, opposed a recurrence to romantic content. So how can the use of mythological resignification be reconciled with the Young German *Poesie des Lebens*?

The Poetics of Life

The recurrence to mythology in Young German literature may appear paradoxical. Young German authors – however loosely bound in their aesthetics and politics – were united by one significant factor: the rejection of romanticism. Indeed, the romantic idealization of the past constituted an idea against which Young Germany was originally formed. So how can mythology play a role in their literary endeavors? Before turning to *Wally*, we need to clarify how mythological resignification is possible, even commendable, for the Young German's central aesthetic and political stance: *Poesie des Lebens* [*Poetics of Life*].

The Vormärz was a period of transformation. Aesthetically, it presents a time between romanticism and the era of realism. Politically, it stands at the beginning of the national development that will end in German unity in 1871. As such, the Vormärz is riddled with conflict and contradiction.

Goethe described the emergence of a new time as an *ex negativo* process: A new age is born out of the friction with the preceding age. In this spirit, and not to the amusement of the old master, Heine proclaimed the Vormärz to be an "insurrection against Goethe" (in Eke 8).[8] Heine and his Young German colleagues perceived the classic and romantic period as backward. First, both were epochs of the past that had no connection to the needs of the present. Second, they held that romanticism entailed a backward glance: It was a world of idealized illusion resulting

---

8   [Insurrekzion gegen Goethe].

in an unworldly aesthetics. In this context, Heine sought to end art's romantic perspective on reality. He wished to do away with a conceptualization of art that insisted on the separation from worldly concerns. His idea of the "end of the art period"[9] became constitutive to the Young Germans and the Vormärz as a whole:

> It was no coincidence that Heine's notion of the 'end of the art period,' written in 1831 and enclosing both classicism and romanticism, would become the guiding spirit of the time, which sought its identity in the renunciation of an art-autonomous poetic and found it in the affirmation of a 'Poetics of Life' […] i.e. a political and life-centered art which nevertheless harbored ongoing literary tendencies and aesthetic processes beneath its surface. (Eke 12f)[10]

The literary Vormärz found its identity in the renunciation of a romanticized aesthetics. Wabnegger notes that the construction of romanticism as the historical Other[11] culminated in the development of Young Germany's central tenet: the *Poesie des Lebens* and its postulation of a conscious merging of art and life. It complicated conceptions of artistic autonomy and sought to marry idea and reality (106f).

Thus, the Young Germans changed the rules of the literary game. The Poetics of Life influenced content, style, and genre standards. New ways of writing evolved: Journalism and creative writing came closer; notes, letters, and tracts found their way into the literary narrative (Eke 49). Literature aspired to be "the present rendered text,"[12] espoused an accessible style, and tried to build bridges between art, politics, and science (Brendel-Perpina in Eke 49). New forms of writing refuted the primacy of beauty and aristocratic prerogatives; poetry and prose were now regarded equals (Eke 49). Moreover, the novel became the dominant genre in the 1830s (Wabnegger 43).

Prose was received as the perfect vehicle for a literature that sought to merge art and life. It sought to mirror reality and society, while simultaneously influencing society by disseminating ideas. The novel became the genre of influence, exemplifying the functional character that literature acquired in the Vormärz (Steinecke

---

9 [Ende der Kunstperiode].
10 [Nicht zufällig wurde Heines Wort vom ‚Ende der Kunstperiode,' geschrieben 1831 und dabei Klassik und Romantik umfassend, zum Leitgedanken einer Epoche, die ihre Identität in der Abkehr von einer kunst-autonomen Dichtung und der Hinwendung zu einer „Poesie des Lebens" […], d.h. einer politisch und eben lebensbezogenen Kunst finden sollte, auch wenn unter der Oberfläche literarische Tendenzen und ästhetische Prozesse weiterliefen].
11 A notion perfected in Heine's *Die romantische Schule* [The School of Romanticism] (1836).
12 [verschriftlichte Gegenwart].

18f). The romantic chasm between literature and politics was leveled, and literature became a force in the political negotiations pertaining to Germany's national future.

The Poetics of Life opposed art for art's sake: It wanted, needed to be political. This development was connected to the emergence of a new socio-literary situation in the German states. Eke notes that, accompanied by the progress in printing, public communication grew denser in the early 19th century. Reading habits changed from the intensive study of select classics to a broader, more extensive reading culture. Thus, literature's societal function shifted: once a culture-stabilizing factor, it now furthered dissent and became a vehicle for the destabilization of the *status quo*. As values were destabilized in a growing public consciousness, they were re-evaluated in journals, novels, and poetry. New genres emerged, such as the essay, the journal, the serial novel. And while statist powers perceived readers (and authors) as potential threats, liberal writers found ready instruments in the realm of literature (44). A "war of ideas"[13] was under way, and Heine elevated literature, especially its journalistic forms, to the "strongholds"[14] of the liberal opposition (in Eke 47).

In this oppositional spirit, Karl Gutzkow sought to wrest art from its pedestal and situate it in the world. Accordingly, his rejection of romanticism was absolute. He criticized its tendency to reject reality and find solace in what he saw as aesthetic escapism. For Gutzkow, a 'pure' aesthetics was a denial of reality (Eke 10f). He also opposed apolitical literature and claims towards artistic autonomy (12). Art, in his view, was *part* of reality; any separation was, in Gutzkow's words, "artistic masturbation" (in Eke 59).[15]

This position is grounded in the perception that the Vormärz – politically and aesthetically – suffered from *Zeitferne* [backwardness]. Gutzkow and his colleagues blamed this on the romantic mindset: Romanticism's idealization of the past posed an obstacle to societal development (Wabnegger 39). Instead of living in the now, the romantics preferred to live in the then. The Young Germans held that living in the past restricts the subject's agency; it creates an "elegiac indifference"[16] to present concerns. At the same time, a fixation on the future has similar effects: It neglects the needs of the present (Eke 62). For the Young Germans, art constituted the spirit of the time. The poet becomes a servant of the present, and the aesthetic revolution prepares and accompanies the political (63). These writers saw themselves as *Zeitschreiber* [time-writers], both in a historiographic (Wabnegger 43) and in a reality-creating sense (Lauster 66). For them, the present enjoyed absolute primacy.

---

13 [Ideenkampf].
14 [Festungen].
15 [Kunstonanie].
16 [elegische Indifferenz].

In order to develop such a nostalgic society, the Young Germans resorted to critique. In 1833, Laube writes: "Here revolves a world in its becoming; her flag is assessment, her scepter is verdict. The warming sun rarely shines in such times of development; all is seeking the guiding moon – critique" (in Eke 50).[17] This critique was meant to be devastating; it sought to shatter all that hindered Germany's catching up with the *Zeitgeist*. The Young Germans pushed for the unforgiving destruction of the old, a policy that in turn was criticized by contemporaries of all political colors (Eke 50).

But the "Young German ire"[18] was not solely destructive (in Eke 51). They held that all decayed elements had to make way for new ideas, but they imagined this critique to be a literary and political *interregnum* which would usher in the new age. The Young Germans saw their endeavor as destructive to the old and constructive to the new (Eke 51). Gutzkow and his colleagues did not only employ art to further political ideas and improve their turbulent age; they made use of the age to further the development and societal significance of art itself.

Young Germany's Use of Myth

In order to understand Gutzkow and Heine's mythological resignification, their recurrence to myth needs to be seen in their conception of critique. Indeed, critique is an inherent part of mythological resignification. A critical treatment of myth it is employed especially in the exposition (Ib) and denaturalization (Ic) of basic civic myths.

Gutzkow and Heine's tapping into myths serves their denaturalization and the refutation of overcome values and norms. By denaturalizing myths, *Wally* and *Wintermärchen* seek to illuminate their incompatibility with Vormärz Germany. The recurrence to myth does not constitute a romantic idealization of Germanic forefathers but criticizes their usage for the Vormärz situation. As such, mythological resignification in Young German texts presents a critical treatment of myth in the context of national values, origins, and identity. The accusation of *Zeitferne* finds its literary elaboration in the usage *and* criticism of dominant civic myths. Indeed, refuting the Germanic myth by *using* the Germanic myth presents an attack on social, cultural, and political norms. Thus, the resignification of Germanic myths is rooted in the Young German principle of critique through literature. Gutzkow and his colleagues did not employ a romantic strategy when using myths; their main ob-

---

17 [Es rollt jetzt eine werdende Welt, ihre Fahne ist die Prüfung, ihr Scepter das Urtheil. In solcher Periode der Entwicklung scheint selten die wärmende Sonne; alles sucht nach dem leitenden Monde – Kritik].

18 [jungdeutscher Zornmuth].

jective in recurring to such narratives is to be found in their exposition and denaturalization.

Simultaneously, the Germanic myth is not completely refuted by the texts. Very similar to Hawthorne's approach in *The Scarlet Letter*, the basic myth is never completely denaturalized. Hawthorne used aspects of the Puritan myth for the writing of a new civic myth; Gutzkow does the same. In using a Germanic myth, he not only denaturalizes it but uses its imagery and plot structure to construct a new civic myth for Vormärz Germany. Indeed, the denaturalization (Ic) in *Wally* exceeds Hawthorne's criticism of the Puritan myth. Yet one has to bear in mind that the author of *The Scarlet Letter* espoused an organic perspective regarding history and human progress. The Young Germans, on the other hand, largely rejected the organic principle.

Young German literature partook in a larger cultural debate that pitted organic determinism against the potential of human agency in the course of historical development. Here, the possibility of dissent depends on whether one sees history as an organic-deterministic process, or if one believes that humans can intervene in history. If we remember Wienbarg's elaborations of what it meant to write for a young Germany, it becomes clear that some Young German authors adopted organicism but with a twist to its deterministic elements. Eke notes that Germany was imagined to *unnaturally* resist historical development. Intervention and revolution could therefore mean putting Germany back on the organic track. Revolution in this context is seen a principle of nature. Those who support it become "agents of a historical process identified with the *Weltgeist*" (22).[19] Thus, the organic perspective could indeed be used to legitimize intervention.

Gutzkow supported interventionism: He held that literature needs to be revolutionary in order to establish an improved present and future (Kaiser 197). This last point may illuminate how mythological resignification is fundamental to Gutzkow's aesthetic tenets: Denaturalization of the old and naturalization of the new are essential to his interventionist approach. This elucidates a fundamental difference between Hawthorne and the Young German writers. As an organicist, Hawthorne refuted drastic dissent and revolutionary intervention; Hester's radicalism is seasoned by the end of *The Scarlet Letter*. But in her time of radical dissent, she is linked to those who believe in revolution. Hawthorne allocates her ideological contemporaries in Europe and would certainly have included authors like Gutzkow in the ranks of the "terrorists of France" (SL 42).

Wally, die Zweiflerin and *The Scarlet Letter* are stories of women at odds with society. Both novels tell of personal development and growth, yet instead of consenting to societal norms, both women remain dissenters. In the following, I will

---

19 [Agenten eines mit dem Weltgeist identifizierten Geschichtsprozesses].

analyze Wally's dissent and the mythological resignification in Gutzkow's text. *Wally* presents dissent in a modern German context, and its analysis will reveal the denaturalization of civic myths of love, marriage, and courtship, and the construction of a variant.

The mythological resignification in *Wally* can be divided into three parts. The first is the preparatory use of interspersed narratives (Ia). These stories tap into the *Falcon myth*, a myth that serves as background to the love plots and foreshadow Wally's trajectory; they are *Schauergeschichten*, gothic tales which are informed by the romantic imagery of the genre. In recurring to the Falcon myth, they present a topos popular in medieval German poetry. *Wally*, especially at the beginning, is a love story that discusses social norms of courtship, love, and marriage. The Falcon myth pervades the preparation of the basic myth (Ia) and represents the mythological foundations of 19th century norms of romance.

Second, Wally's and Cäsar's characters are informed by a basic Germanic myth, the *Sigune myth*. Here, elements of Wolfram's *Parzival* and *Titurel* are used to guide the novel's plot. Parzival, Sigune, and Tschionatulander play a crucial part in the lover's development and expose the basic myth (Ib). At this point, the civic myths of marriage, love, and courtship are denaturalized (Ic).

The third and last component constitutes the naturalization (IIc) of a variant myth in Cäsar. This character serves the construction of an individualistic German national identity. While Wally is unable to develop an independent identity, Cäsar is successful in offering a modern tale of individual freedom. Here, the novel transforms the basic *Love-is-Consolation* mytheme and molds it into the variant's *Love-is-Choice* mytheme. This mythemic elaboration (IIb) results in the naturalization (IIc) of a variant: the *Inner Poems myth*.

3.2 THE ABANDONED LOVERS AND THE WAILS OF *WELTSCHMERZ*

A fact that is often overlooked when discussing Gutzkow's debut novel is that *Wally, die Zweiflerin* is a love story. The romance between Wally and Cäsar dominates the plot. But as their relationship fails, Cäsar finds a more suitable partner in Delphine. Wally, on the other hand, is left alone to face her loss. Their romance is accompanied by a number of smaller narratives, all of which offer stories of unsuccessful, insane love. These stories serve as an elaborate preparation (Ia) of the basic myth. They contain a mythological element that refers the reader to an image that merges the romantic and political dimensions of the text, thus refining the perspective on Wally's situation. The image in question is the *abandoned maiden*.

The Interspersed Narratives

Eke notes that the Vormärz was an age of *Weltschmerz* (15). Contemporaries mourned the loss of ideals, a loss that produced pain and despair. Usually, this emotion can be overcome by accepting the world's limitations or replacing old ideals with new ones. Sometimes, however, we are unable to face the incongruence between idea and reality. Then, *Weltschmerz* can have disastrous effects. In that context, *Wally* offers a number of *Weltschmerz* tales that accompany the main plot. Here are stories of shattered dreams, romantic betrayal, and a love that results in insanity. In *Wally*, love stories are used as a foil upon which larger societal issues can be discussed. At a fundamental level, they speak of the clash between reality and its idealized versions; and of individuals who cannot bear said collision.

There are five of these interspersed narratives. All of these stories are informed by gothic-romantic imagery, and Kaiser notes that their function is twofold. On an intra-textual level, these "gothic-romantic intermezzi"[20] are meant to entertain Wally. On an extra-textual level, they seek to entertain the reader (190). There are, however, additional approaches to their interpretation. For Kruse, these stories are "secondary tales," narratives of "destroyed and 'insane' love"[21] which end in death and prepare for Wally's despair (Kolloquium 47). Further, Horrocks summarizes his take on the narratives as follows: "The stories present women who – because of a romantic relationship – are driven to madness and subsequent suicide, both of which are infused with a generous helping of gothic-romantic creepiness" (157).[22]

While this is true, the stories' function transcends entertainment. Indeed, Kaiser describes them as "catalysts" that further the novel's meaning (190), and Kruse reads them as stories foreshadowing Wally's death (47). In addition, I read the interspersed narratives as a group of stories that, by elaborating a Germanic myth, prepare for the novel's basic mythological narrative. Indeed, the mythological re-signification in *Wally* entails an extended preparation (Ia) which includes the elaboration of the Falcon myth. It is therefore worthwhile to consider these narratives in some detail.

The *Bärbel narrative* is set in Schwalbach, the resort to which Wally and Cäsar repair in the summer. Cäsar relates how Bärbel, a young girl of low social status, falls in love with a nobleman. The nobleman wins her by promising marriage upon

---

20 [schauerromantische Intermezzi].
21 [zerstörter oder ‚verrückter' Liebe].
22 [Die Geschichten handeln von Frauen, die infolge einer Liebesbeziehung in den Wahnsinn und schließlich in den Selbstmord getrieben werden, und beide sind mit einem reichlichen Maß an schauerromantischer Gruseligkeit versehen].

his return (WDZ 25).[23] However, he returns a married man and refuses to acknowledge any previous relation to the young woman. Heartbroken and unable to deal with her loss, Bärbel goes mad (26). Later in the novel, the fictional account is revealed to be factual: Bärbel commits suicide while Wally and Cäsar are in Schwalbach. What was told as a gothic story gains further factuality in the circumstance that Cäsar's friend Waldemar is revealed as Bärbel's inconstant lover (38).

Despite the tragic nature of the story, the incident is received as entertaining by the aristocrats. Cäsar comments that the story pains him, but only because of what it signifies in a historical context (WDZ 39). He interprets the incident as a commentary on human nature, compares other famous suicides to Bärbel, and draws rather abstract conclusions. Bärbel's suicide, he holds, attests to the fact that the present is an age without values. Indeed, Bärbel's death is met with a scholarly treatise on history:

'Die Unzulänglichkeiten der Erhabenheit,' sagte er, 'die Furcht vor dem Tode, der Schmerz, nicht wie Brutus, der alte und der junge, töten, nicht wie Cato sterben zu können, die Bitte des Prinzen von Homburg, ihn leben zu lassen: das ist das Tragische unsrer Zeit und ein Gefühl, welches die Anschauungen unsrer Welt von dem Zeitalter der Schicksalsidee so schmerzlich verschieden macht.' (39f)

'The inadequacies of noble feelings,' he thought, 'the fear of death, the agony of not being able to kill like Brutus, both the older and the younger, not being able to die like Cato, the plea of the Prince of Homburg to be allowed to live: all this is the tragedy of our times, a feeling which makes the views of our world so painfully different from the age dominated by the idea of fate.' (WTS 57)

Here, Cato and Brutus' heroic behavior is contrasted with the Prince of Homburg, a 17th century figure who first pleaded for his life, then accepted his death sentence, only to be spared in the end. A similar conflict between death-fear and death-longing seems to have infused Bärbel. Cäsar, always the cynic, decries the to-and-fro of his own age. He parallels the Vormärz's fractured *Zeitgeist* with the girl's inability to die like the old ones: devoted to the "idea of fate" (ibid.). Interestingly, Wally will ultimately share Bärbel's destiny.

The second story is the *Drummer narrative*. Again, Cäsar tells the story of a love gone awry, yet this time, it is the man who is left heartbroken. The story is set

---

23 For quotation purposes in German (marked WDZ), I use an annotated reprint of Gutzkow's original 1835 edition edited by Heintz: *Karl Gutzkow. Wally, die Zweiflerin* (1979). For the English translation (WTS), I rely on Joeres: *Wally the Skeptic* (1974). All unmarked translations are my own.

in Wiesbaden and tells of a soldier and his love for a bourgeois girl. He serves in the infantry and is the regiment's best drummer. Yet the object of his devotion ultimately prefers a higher ranking soldier, a trumpeter serving in the artillery. Unable to cope with his loss, the drummer slowly deteriorates. On the night before her wedding, he serenades her one last time, and then throws himself into the Rhine (WDZ 27f). Later, the married couple moves from Wiesbaden to Schwalbach. Cäsar comments that even in Schwalbach, the drummer's ghost still follows his unfaithful lover and torments her with the constant playing of his drums (29f).

The Bärbel narrative's plot is reversed in the Drummer narrative. The male suffers the loss, goes mad, and commits suicide. Again, the story is connected to Schwalbach, and it is Cäsar who tells it in order to alleviate Wally's boredom. These two stories offer the material from which the other three narratives will derive their content. The Bärbel narrative presents the female, the Drummer narrative the male perspective on romantic loss. Both characters love above their social station, and while the recipients first indulge in the connection, they finally opt for a more suitable match. The tragic result is the destruction of the other's existence. Indeed, the lovers become victims of societal love constructions. But Kaiser is correct in stating that they are also victims of their own passions. Incapable of controlling their affections or reflect constructively upon the situation, they lose themselves in "radical subjectivity."[24] They feel *too much* and thereby serve as a contrastive foil for Wally and Cäsar's incapacity to feel anything (191). Indeed, Bärbel and the drummer offer the opposite of that inability: They ground their selves *exclusively* on the romantic Other. The Bärbel and Drummer narrative thus prepare for a crucial point: the utter artificiality of Vormärz love rites. This notion will later serve to expose (Ib) and denaturalize (Ic) the basic Sigune myth.

Wally displays an emotional coldness in responding to the narratives.[25] This depiction is continued in her reaction to the third story. Cäsar once more functions as narrator; he is, however, unaware that Wally had witnessed the events firsthand (WDZ 47). The *Trumpeter's wife narrative* picks up where the drummer's story ends: with the trumpeter's wife's torment. At this point, Wally already suffers from sinking spirits, a depression that will only increase in the course of the novel. Her boredom in Schwalbach is added to by an inability to regain her usual happiness

---

24 [absolute Ich-haftigkeit].

25 That Wally is not able to grasp romantic love is evident in her lack of sympathy for Bärbel. On being told her story, Cäsar is shocked at Wally's lack of compassion; she simply complains that the story has no real ending (WDZ 26). When the ending finally manifests itself in Bärbel's suicide, and Waldemar is revealed as the inconstant nobleman, Wally – instead of showing sympathy – aids Waldemar in procuring an acceptable explanation why the girl was wearing his ring (38).

(44). I have described the narratives as gothic tales, and this scene may give representative evidence to that claim. Kruse notes that the tone and imagery of the following contrasts with the otherwise dry and austere style of the novel (Kolloquium 44). Unable to write a letter to her friend, Wally looks out the window, where a romantic landscape unfolds before her eyes:

Der Mond beleuchtete hier und dort einen Teil des engen Tales und seiner Umgebungen. Er war mit Wolken bedeckt, die aber nicht eilten, sondern schwer auf ihm hafteten. Es wehte kein Wind. In sanfter, nächtlicher Stille ruhte die malerische Natur. Ein tannenschwarzer Bergrücken begrenzte auf der einen Seite die ovale Rundung des schlummernden Tales. Nirgends die Ahnung eines menschlichen Wesens. (WDZ 44)

Here and there the moon illuminated a section of the narrow valley and its surroundings. It was covered with clouds which did not scurry by but rather clung heavily to it. No wind was blowing. Picturesque nature lay in a gentle evening stillness. A mountain ridge black with pine trees circumscribed the oval curve of the sleeping valley on one side. Nowhere was there any sign of human life. (WTS 55)

Restless, she decides to go for a walk. After a few steps, however, the silence is interrupted by a "strange noise." Hiding behind a tree, Wally sees a woman walking up the alley, screaming and pressing her hands against her ears so as to "ward off something invisible." Finally, the woman falls to her knees and tries to burrow "her head in the loose sand," while Wally runs back to her quarters. The next morning, Cäsar completes the tale by relating the trumpeter's wife's death. She has been reported to have run through the streets – trying to escape the drumming in her head – and was found dead with her head buried in the ground. Hearing this, Wally decides to leave town at once; as her aunt inquires as to the reason for their hasty departure, she gives a telling answer: "I am weary of a place that will be the death of me (56).

The Trumpeter's wife narrative, more strongly than the previous stories, emphasizes death through madness. Also, the description grows more gruesome. There is an *increase of intensity* which will continue in the subsequent narratives. Bärbel and the drummer go mad before they die, but the trumpeter's wife is an extreme elaboration on the image. The next story will further increase the narrative tension.

The *Jeronimo narrative* is part if the novel's main plot. It mirrors the trumpeter's wife's death as well as the narrative of Alfred the sleep-walker. The trumpeter's wife and Jeronimo share fundamental elements: First, both are driven insane by a former lover. Second, their deaths are connected with Wally's window and the alley in front of her quarters. Third, they continue the representation of lack of affective control. Lastly, Wally's reaction is once more of an unfeeling and, importantly, escapist nature.

Jeronimo is introduced after Wally married the diplomat Luigi in Paris. He is described as an eccentric sentimentalist whose speech relies on hyperbole and dead metaphors (WDZ 72). In fact, the young Italian is a "master" of these "delightful exaggerations" and does not hold back in showering Wally with flowery compliments (WTS 66). With time, he falls deeply in love with her, despite the fact that he is her husband's brother. There is little motivation offered that might explain the young man's infatuation, and the text portrays Jeronimo's advances as highly artificial. It is not until Cäsar uncovers Luigi's plot to disinherit his brother that we are given any sort of explanation for Jeronimo's infatuation. But even the fact that Luigi causes his brother's romantic delusion does not explain the supposed depth of his feelings (WDZ 72). Jeronimo's declarations remain most tacky and attest to a desperate wish for romantic immediacy. Indeed, Jeronimo claims an unmediated intimacy with Wally:

'Ich kannte Sie schon, als Sie nur noch ein Gedanke waren, der im Schoße Gottes schlummerte. Meine Liebe zu Ihnen ist nur die Erinnerung eines alten Glückes. Diese schwellenden Lippen, diese jetzt so spröde Brust: ich weiß es, ich habe sie schon einmal geküßt, ich habe sie schon einmal umarmt.' (66)

'I already knew you when you were still just a thought slumbering in the bosom of God. My love for you is only the memory of a past happiness. Those swelling lips, that breast now so prim – I know that I kissed them once, I once embraced them.' (WTS 69)

Jeronimo's artificial sentiments are rooted in Luigi's manipulations. Yet for Jeronimo – just as for Bärbel and the drummer –imagined love quickly becomes his only *raison d'être*. So, rejected and unable to see Wally for months, the Italian nobleman goes insane. Like the other abandoned lovers, he deteriorates physically, becomes "pale and gaunt," while his eyes emanate a "strange fire" (72). Finally, driven to complete madness, Jeronimo ends his life.

Reminiscent of the trumpeter's wife narrative, this death scene is set at night and in front of Wally's apartment (WDZ 84). Yet while the scene in Schwalbach was suffused with the imagery of "[p]icturesque nature," the Parisian alley is moonless and plagued by "frost" and "snow" (WTS 55, 81). Again, the description effects an increase of intensity. It is not only the deaths' violence that increases with the plot's procession; the stories' romantic imagery also darkens, paralleling Wally's situation. In Schwalbach, she encounters death by coincidence. In Paris, however, she is the cause of Jeronimo's insanity. In terms of proximity, this narrative allocates the suicide significantly closer to Wally. Death does not simply occur in the alley; it comes to seek her out. Jeronimo climbs the walls as the young woman is – like in Schwalbach – drawn to the window (81). But instead of witnessing the night's moonlit calm, she literally finds death at her windowsill:

Da störte sie ein Geräusch am Fenster. Sie sieht auf und erblickte durch die angelaufenen Scheiben die ganz undeutlichen Umrisse einer menschlichen Gestalt. Sie eilt hinzu, wischt so viel von dem Tau des Fensters ab, um ein gräßlich verzerrtes Antlitz wahrzunehmen, das im Nu beim Knall eines Pistols zerschmettert ist. (WDZ 85)

Suddenly a noise at the window disturbed her. She looked up and saw the very blurred outlines of a human form through the misty windowpanes. She ran over, rubbed off enough of the frost from the window to perceive a terribly distorted face which was in the next instant shattered by the burst of a pistol shot. (WTS 81)

Death increasingly closes in on Wally. The Jeronimo narrative describes the young lover's demise not just in terms that involve her personally but locates the event much closer to the protagonist.[26]

The last of the interspersed stories, the *Alfred narrative*, is once again a tale related by Cäsar, and it continues the approximation of death. With this last narrative, madness and suicide do not simply approach Wally physically. Here, death becomes psychological. The Alfred narrative is without a doubt the odd bird in this set of stories. But it entails the same gothic-romantic imagery and mirrors the preceding tales. We are once more presented with the death of a lover; death again occurs in an alley and features the climbing of walls and an encounter at windows. Also, Wally reacts with escapism, but this time, and in keeping with the increase of intensity, her trying to flee reality catapults her to the realm of dreams.[27]

Horrocks notes that the Alfred narrative offers a direct elaboration of the Jeronimo story (157). These two stories, together with the Drummer narrative, present the male perspective on lost love, complementing the female perspective in Bärbel and the trumpeter's wife. At the same time, the Alfred story is different from the other narratives, given its position in the main plot and its content. The sleepwalker Alfred appears in the section devoted to Wally's journal. Here, the novel abandons the third-person authorial perspective of Book I and II and offers journal entries in

---

26 Wally's reaction to this incident mirrors her reaction to the trumpeter's wife's suicide in Schwalbach, where she arranges for her departure the next day (WDZ 46). In Paris, we find a similar situation, yet with an emotionally heightened import. Wally faints but recovers quickly; she orders the servants to prepare for her immediate departure and packs her bags in a room where "bloody pieces of a skull" lie scattered on the floor; she even forbids the servants to collect the body that lies in the alley. The narrator comments on Wally's coldness: She acts "as if bewitched," she commands "majestically, coldly, in a northern fashion, like an absolute Moscovite monarch" (WTS 82). Wally, it seems, grows colder the more she is faced with death.

27 cf. Heine's elaboration on dreams as the realm of German escapism in chapter 5.2.

the protagonist's own hand. It resorts to a first-person narration, which naturally offers a more personal, albeit less reliable insight.

At this point, Wally is already in a state of intense reflection. She has become a recluse, bent on thought and inwardness (Horrocks 156). Meditating on the distinction between rationality and madness, she remembers a story once told by Cäsar (WDZ 102). That the Alfred narrative is given at this specific point is significant with regard to the preceding narratives. It is also telling that the last story is a perfect *Schauergeschichte*. It belongs completely to the realm of the sublime, is informed by the irrational, and soaked in gothic imagery.

The story begins at midnight. Alfred woke and observed "cloudy circles" painted on the wall by the night lamp. For some time, he just watched the ghostly play, trying to grasp the images and give them materiality. It made him think of the world outside, his first thought being that of his lover Julie. He rose and saw himself in the mirror, a "pale" and "ghostly" figure. Suddenly and against his will, he was dressed and resolved to go to Julie's window and "draw back" the "curtain." He walked down the alley, but the "moon was concealed" and the street "deserted." Not even Alfred "could be seen." Still, he was sure to be standing in front of Julie's "window" (WTS 94) He tried to open it, but it would not yield. Laughing at his own "vivid imagination," he decided to ascend the stairs and knock at her door. All of a sudden, he stood higher than Julie's quarters; a "beam of light" blinded him, and he saw his beloved open the window. The girl "became frightened," she shuddered and screamed his name. Alfred, however, lay dead on the pavement beneath her window, his "body shattered" (95).

This story is important because it contains some of the main issues of the novel. Alfred is a "sleep-walker," and his endeavor to seek his lover occurs in the psychological realm of dreams but has real life consequences. Similarly, Wally will engage in pursuing the explication of the world through constructed terms. Indeed, Alfred's initial but unsuccessful wish to give materiality to the "cloudy circles" on the wall is not just reminiscent of Plato's cave allegory (WTS 95). It offers an image that describes Wally's wish to understand (and thereby master) her own existence. Earlier in the text, she complains at the "elastic" nature of the "ideas" that govern her life. Her complaints tell of an inability to successfully grasp reality, just as Alfred cannot grasp the shadows on the wall. Both are confronted with the "tyranny of withered concepts" and the despair in seeking but not finding answers (54).

This inability prompts Alfred to focus on his beloved, seeking her instead of dwelling on the shadows. The moment he thinks of the outside world, he thinks of her: The significant other becomes a substitute for reality. He seeks her out blindly, seemingly overcoming the laws of physics in the meantime. He, like Wally, approaches the question of finding a lover "mechanically" and still "ceremoniously" (WTS 94). Regarding love, Wally constantly follows the social protocol of romance without either understanding or actually caring about its meaning. What better image for her behavior than the somnambulist. Her quest, like Alfred's, is impossible because artificial, a dream-substitute that can only end in death.

The approach of death is paralleled by the increase of intensity in the narratives, and the Alfred narrative fortifies the expectancy of death in Wally. The fact that Alfred's story affects Wally psychologically is evident in her reaction. We are, as mentioned, in the journal section of the novel. This is already the closest the reader can get to Wally's inner world, and she reports a noteworthy response to the Alfred story: the emergence of nightmares (WDZ 105). She writes that the world seizes her like a "whirlpool" and "drags her down into a bottomless abyss" where "[d]espair" and "horror" gnaw at her soul. The approximation of death and the increase of horror in the narratives have arrived in Wally's mind: Her nightmares drain her of all hope, until she perceives reality as a mocking place full of "horrible, unspeakable things" (WTS 96).

Here, Wally returns to the "tyranny of withered concepts" mentioned before, a sensation that has found its image in Alfred's inability to grasp the shadows on the wall (WTS 54). Her despair is caused by an incapacity to grasp reality; in other words, she despairs of the human condition itself. How this despair is transmitted in religious terms will occupy the analysis in the next subchapter. For now, let it suffice to say that with the Alfred story, Wally has reached the point of complete disorientation. Her inability to cope with reality's (and society's) absolutism in a constructive or creative way has resulted in hatred of reality. Unable to understand the given terms of existence and incapable of creating her own, she is plagued by visions of "torsos" and "black hall[s]," "coffins" and "scaffold[s]," and lastly, is haunted by the walking dead (96). She will become a living corpse herself, a person who has but death-in-life and sees no path but self-destruction. Indeed, in the dreams inspired by the Alfred narrative she foresees the loss of Cäsar:

Er dreht sich um, und Leben, galvanisches Leben regt sich in dem Körper und der Leichnam erhebt sich, ein blasser, schöner Jüngling und schleicht zur Pforte hinaus. Dort, dort — eine grüne Flur — ein Mädchen, das Rosen bricht und im Schatten der Allee ausruht. Ein bleiches, gespenstisches Bild schleicht zu ihr heran, spricht nicht, sondern lächelt. Sie umarmt ihn, sie scherzt, sie lacht; er hat auf sich warten lassen, er sei untreu, er gehe zu Doris, er gehe zu Galathee, du Lieber! (WDZ 106)

He turns around, and life, galvanic life surges into the body, and the corpse arises, a pale, lovely young boy, and slips out of the gate. There, there a green meadow, a girl who gathers roses and rests in the shadow of the garden path. A pale, ghostly image creeps up to her, not speaking but smiling. She embraces him, she teases him, she laughs: he has certainly been a long time in coming, he is unfaithful, he has gone to Doris, to Galatea, my goodness! (WTS 96f)

This dream concludes her journal entries, and she ends them on a prayer: "Jesus, what is happening to me?" (97).

The five interspersed narratives accompany and foreshadow Wally's suicide, yet they also trace the advent of death and madness and depict Wally's tendency to rather escape than face existential questions. The stories offer differentiated narratives of unhappy love, despair, and death, thereby enriching and accompanying the main plot. Importantly, they introduce and develop the image of the abandoned and despairing lover, thus preparing for the Sigune myth (Ia).

These stories also define and critique courtship rites. The characters' comport is strictly gendered and adherent to traditional stereotypes. The male characters are active, men of the public realm, while female lovers are restricted to passivity.[28] The social dialectic of male activity/female passivity infuses these narratives. Indeed, it is the gendered structure that *effects* the stories' outcomes. Gutzkow thereby not only elucidates on traditional norms of romantic love, courtship, and marriage but depicts these standards as *inadequate* bases for the development of loving relationships. As such, these preparatory narratives also partake in the process of denaturalization (Ic). There is criticism of individual behavior in each story; but that criticism is paired with the revelation of a structural violence that guides the characters' decisions.

Especially the female characters are presented as both perpetrators of their own misery *and* victims of societal circumstances. In fact, Gutzkow's usage of these narratives transcends the issue of gender. It rather highlights subjective agency, a universal (and political) *equality* in the matters of love and marriage. The image of the powerless and abandoned female becomes the image of the powerless and abandoned *human*. It is used so as to present the material upon which the author can heave his Young German instrument of change: societal critique. That material, however, points to a medieval myth which informs the gender politics and courtship rites of Vormärz Germany. This myth, the Falcon myth, prepares (Ia) and simultaneously aides in denaturalizing (Ic) the basic Sigune myth.

---

28 Bärbel's lover, for instance, is a nobleman who casts her aside to fulfill social expectations while she is restricted to perpetual waiting. Alfred seeks Julie, who is confined to her bedroom and then left to be consumed by her sorrows. Jeronimo takes matters into his own hands and seeks Wally out to end his life in her presence. Similarly, the drummer reaches out to his lover before ending his life. The girl becomes the passive victim of a gruesome memory; even her final suicide is not portrayed as active but as a reaction to her constant torment.

The Falcon Myth and Mental Dominion

In German medieval poetry, the motif of an abandoned and mourning woman is intimately connected with the image of the falcon. The abandoned maiden and the falcon are part of the socio-poetical discourse of the Middle Ages, concepts that prepare and inform the emergence of *Minne*, a form of secular love poetry, practiced in and for aristocratic circles.[29]

Wapnewski notes that Minne became constitutive to medieval social reality and set the rules regarding love and romance. The idea of Minne is one of *submission*, the loyal service of the male towards the idealized female. It becomes clear that Minne and *eros* are two very different things. Love as an erotic-physical relationship contrasts the artful system of rites of submission, chastity, and service. The latter is highly abstract, a world of the imagination. Further, there usually is no physical gratification in Minne. Rituals enjoy primacy and reflect the medieval hierarchies of feudalism. In short, Minne is an artistically organized *game* (Minnesänger 15ff).

This poetry sought to describe and legitimize courtly society. It was short, lyrical love poetry which – in contrast the theological concept of love (*caritas*) – established a secular love conception. The genre reached its peak with poets such as Wolfram von Eschenbach, Hartmann von Aue, and Walter von der Vogelweide; their writings already recur to the abandoned maiden image. But in order to get to the beginnings of the image and thus contextualize the Minne representations in *Wally*, we need to go back to the poetry of a German nobleman called Der von Kürenberg[30](Wehrli 326f).

Weil notes that Kürenberg is the oldest German poet known by name (9). He is the author of one of the earliest poems that uses the abandoned maiden image. A short analysis of this poem will clarify the nature of the image and serve to illustrate its socio-political dimensions; it will illuminate the connection between what Wapnewski describes as the medieval institution of falcon-taming and the democratic politics of Vormärz author Karl Gutzkow (Minne 7). The poem in question is Kürenberg's *Falkenlied* [Song of the Falcon]:

---

29 Minne is an erotic form of "sublimation" which enacts itself in stylistic rites of adoration. Adoration flows from the male towards the female in a one-sided idealization of the latter. Central to the concept is the *Minnedienst*, the love-service of the male, which constitutes a spiritual exercise (Minnesänger 18f). Minne is poetically systematized love and central to the building of medieval societal structures in Western Europe.

30 For the sake of clarity I will refer to this poet as Kürenberg.

Ich zoch mir eine valken mere danne ein iar.
Do ich in gezamete als ich in wolte han
Un ich im sin gevideremit golde wol bewant
Er huob sich uf vil hohe un fluog in anderiu lant.

Sit sach ich den valken schone fliege.
Er fuorte an sine fuosse sidine rieme.
Un was im sin gevidere alrot guldin
Got sende si zesamene die gelieb welle gerne. (Codex Manesse 63r)

Ich zähmte einen Falken länger als ein Jahr.
Als ich ihn gezähmt hatte, so wie ich ihn haben wollte,
und als ich ihm sein Gefieder mit Gold geschmückt hatte,
erhob er sich sehr hoch und flog in andere Länder.

Seitdem sah ich den Falken schön fliegen:
Er trug an seinem Fuß seidene Bänder,
und sein Gefieder war rotgolden.
Gott führe zusammen, die sich herzlich lieben wollen! (in Weil 12)

I tamed a falcon, for more than a year.
The moment I had tamed him, the way I wanted him to be,
as I adorned his coat with gold,
he soared very high and flew away to other lands.

Since then, I saw him fly in beauty:
On his foot, he wore silken ribbons
and his coat was red and gold.
May god unite those, who want to love from the heart!

I will follow Wapnewski's interpretation of a text that proves as elusive to academic investigation as the falcon itself. The predatory bird occupies the central position, and the motif is evident not just in Germany but throughout Europe (Minne 23f).[31]

---

[31] Wapnewski notes that the falcon motif is also found in the Italian sonnet of the 13th century and the French chanson of the 15th. It presents an "international wander motif" that equates the male lover with the falcon and falconry with the *ars amandi*, the art of love (Minne 24).

The Falcon myth includes the abandoned maiden image, which points to its inherent mytheme: *Love-is-Possession*.[32]

The *Falkenlied* tells of a situation of loss, and it is the poem's idea of a mourning lover that informs the interspersed narratives in *Wally*. In Minne (and in the *Wally* narratives) the man does the courting, he is the tamer; but in the poem, he is also the falcon that leaves the lover behind. The woman, on the other hand, is the one who waits, loses, and mourns. This has a very specific reason which carries socio-political consequences with regard to Vormärz norms of love and possession.[33]

The falcon image was prevalent in medieval politics, for falconry was more than a diversion for aristocrats. The *Falkenlied* entails the Love-is-Possession mytheme, a notion which unfolds in Minne, in the unadulterated love between a knight and a maiden, a love that knows neither the desire of the flesh nor its fulfillment. This idea will have consequences for the politics of love in the Vormärz. Courtly love not only genders Wally and Cäsar's positions; it also transforms an emotional and physical relationship into an abstract affair of the mind. The rituals of love become spiritualized, its rules defined by courtly standards.

Wapnewski notes that falconry was a cultural institution in the Middle Ages (Minne 7). Karl der Große, Heinrich I, II, and III, as well as Friedrich II were enthusiasts, and the animal imagery as well as the sport's technical terms influenced poetical production (27). The poem's expression "to other lands," for instance, is such a technical term.[34] Another instance is the idea of possession. Wapnewski ex-

---

32 Weil notes that the poem has a female perspective. The *Falkenlied* is proto-Minne, a prelude to the later, idealized Minne style. In Kürenberg's poetry, the female traditionally plays an active role; it is the maiden who tames the falcon (10). This narrator is far removed from later maidens shyly awaiting their princes. Love is nevertheless thought of as possession.

33 The abandoned lover and the falcon were very much alive in the cultural consciousness of the Vormärz. Wilhelm Müller, for instance, wrote tragic-romantic epic poems which employed the imagery. In *Die schöne Müllerin* (1821), the protagonist gains a maiden's love only to be replaced by another man; a plot reminiscent of the Drummer narrative. Love will indeed prove the wanderer's destruction. But in his days of bliss, he finds a "young starling" that he wants to "tame" so as to act as envoy to his beloved. The bird is to learn to speak, so as to profess his love "in his own voice" at the maiden's window (Müller 55). Such a bird may also act as a companion, faithfully sharing the road with the wanderer until the journey's inevitable end (22).

34 This term describes the situation in which a tamed falcon loses his way. First, it will remain in its accustomed hunting grounds but after a while abandons that space (and thereby its owner). In the song, this term allows for a definition of the falcon's flight as an event happening against the speaker's will, rendering the flight as a voyage towards free-

plains that the bird's garment (the gold and the ribbons) are not symbolic of a new falconer (read new lover). A falcon was never without these insignia, which constituted legal signs that enabled recognition of the animal's owner (Minne 35). It does not take much to imagine other sparkling objects with which people adorn themselves (and their significant other) to express romantic possession. In Kürenberg's poem, it is the woman who adorns the bird. Wally, for instance, reverses the practice and signals her romantic possession by collecting her suitor's rings. The question of who adorns (and who is adorned) carries gender-political consequences, and the first instance of such gender-coding through falconry occurred in the reign of Kaiser Friedrich II.

In 1248, the German-held city of Parma was sacked by Italian forces while Friedrich II was out flying falcons (Minne 39). During the sack, his two volume treatise entitled *De arte venandi cum avibus* [*On the Art of Hunting with Birds*] was stolen. The book, first published in print in Augsburg in 1596, not only proved the Kaiser to be one of the most eminent natural scientist of the Middle Ages (Weil 17). It also gave evidence to the moral significance of falconry at the time (Minne 39f). Falconry, Friedrich writes, has a profound moral function. It is an art restricted to the nobility that elevates the human being to moral perfection. "The chapter concerning the ideal falconer is essentially one concerning the ideal human; it is a teaching of virtue and a catalog of perfections."[35] Indeed, Cäsar will also unite the courting/taming of Wally with the attempt of educating her. The degree to which Friedrich equated falconry and education is evident in the treatise's dedication: He dedicated the book to his favorite son Manfred, future King of Sicily and a boy of sixteen at the time (41).

Wapnewski notes that the moral theology connected to falconry lies in the "adoration of the power of the human mind."[36] In this perspective, the ingenuity of the mind lies in the capability of an earthbound creature (a human) to tame and subjugate the freest living thing of all (a falcon). According to Friedrich, man does homage to himself in dominating such a creature by means of his *ingenium* (Minne 44). Here, the Kaiser develops a theory of *Geistesherrschaft* [mental dominion]. While men and women were involved in falconry, this new politicized perspective restricts the power of mental domination to the male. In *Wally*, the narrator attests to the prevalence of male mental dominion in commenting on the novel's most imperial character: "It wasn't love that drove [Caesar], it was the task imposed by his vanity,

---

dom (Wapnewski 29, 36). The bird seeks liberty from being possessed. In *Wally*, it is the abandoned lovers who see their falcons fly to other lands.

35 [Das Kapitel über den idealen Falkner ist im Grunde eines über den idealen Menschen, ist eine Tugendlehre und ein Katalog der Vollkommenheiten].

36 [Verehrung der Kraft des menschlichen Geistes].

that of conquering Wally, this untamed and ebullient creature! Ladies, beware! For most men, love is no more than the homage they pay themselves" (WTS 48).

Weil notes that Friedrich's moral elaborations spilled over into the realm of Minne (17). It is a telling fact that a poem by Heinrich VI opens the famous *Codex Manesse*. The following lines ring even more significant considering the position of the Holy Roman Emperor:

Höher noch den mächtig fühl ich mich all die Zeit,
wenn so liebevoll die Liebe bei mir liegt.
Sie hat mich mit ihren edlen Eigenschaften,
befreit vom Leide. (in Minnesänger 46)

Higher than just powerful I feel all the time
when love so lovingly lies by my side.
By her noble attributes
she has freed me from all suffering.

Here, the highest form of power is the power of the mind, and love, similarly, is pushed into the mental realm. Love becomes the abstinent love of Minne: an aristocratic, honor-centered, chaste endeavor. Medieval politics attached the imagery of an avian sport onto the spiritual-romantic game of courtly love. Friedrich's mental approach to power finds its application in gender relations.

Wapnewski notes that the last line of the *Falkenlied* is a prayer. Indeed, the maiden's sorrow over the falcon is palpable throughout the poem, but in the last line, her subjective situation is transformed into an objective one. As she sees the falcon fly, she *abstains* from claims of possession. What we witness here is a deliberate "objectification"[37] of sorrow and a subsequent "overcoming of the subjective self" (*Selbstüberwindung*). The maiden, unlike so many of the characters in *Wally*, is able to control her affect. She prays for *all* lovers: God may unite those who *want* to love – if they both want it (Minne 45). Here, Kürenberg celebrates the ability of the lover to perceive a higher because unselfish love. But unlike Friedrich II, the poet celebrates the *maiden's ingenium*, the sovereignty of a woman who makes the bitter realization that a "human heart can fail to become the life-element of another."[38] Her inner genius is evident in the fact that she "understands in a state of abstinence and then abstains in understanding."[39] Thus, she recuperates dominion – not

---

37 [Objektivierung].
38 [das schmerzvolle Bewußtsein, daß ein Herz zuweilen nicht stark genug ist, sich zum Lebenselement eines anderen zu machen].
39 [die in Entsagung erkennt, und in der Erkenntnis entsagt].

over the falcon – but over herself (46). In this manner, the *Falkenlied* and the abandoned maiden inform the *Wally* narratives. But the falcon maiden achieves what the *Wally* characters fail to do: She regains individual sovereignty.

The Regaining of Sovereignty

I have shown how the interspersed narratives accompany, foreshadow, and comment on Wally's development. Subsequently, I have traced the narratives' topos to its medieval origin, the Falcon myth (Ia). It includes the imagery of the *Falkenlied*, the development from gender-equal romantic agency to gender-specific Minne, as well as the idea of *Geistesherrschaft*. Before moving on, I need to elaborate on the connection between mental dominion and the text's portrayal of insanity and suicide.

It is noteworthy that none of the abandoned characters in *Wally* are able to achieve what the falcon maiden achieved. Instead of overcoming loss, the narratives' protagonists remain in states of desperation. The reason for this is threefold. First, none of the lovers succeed in objectifying their situation and thus transcend their subjective feelings. They fall into "absolute subjectivity"[40] without being able to establish an individual feeling of self-worth (Kaiser 191). Their selves dissolve in the social identity of 'lover,' and their only reason to exist is found in the romantic relationship. Second, the characters are unable to transcend their grief because they confuse *eros* with Minne. They cannot perceive the difference between the socially constructed game of courtship and an emotional (and sexual) connection between two people. The lovers loose themselves in the rules of the game, refuse to see social reality as it is, and mistake their relationships for real love. Third, they exaggerate the consequences of loss.

Bärbel's relationship to Waldemar is socially unacceptable from the start. The latter is a nobleman, and Bärbel misinterprets his artificial advances. Waldemar adheres to the rules of Minne: He courts her, 'tames' her, and 'adorns' her by giving her a ring, signaling his romantic possession. But his courtship is *unreal*: a summer game played by an aristocrat to amuse himself and fortify his mental dominion. The nobleman, of course, does not return to marry Bärbel but finds a suitable wife instead. Bärbel, on the other hand, mistakes courtly love for love.[41]

---

40 [absolute Ich-haftigkeit].

41 The drummer suffers a similar fate. He courts his maiden only to be replaced by a more talented musician. We approximate a *Sängerkrieg* [minstrel contest] here, a competition between Minne artists. The trumpeter – who knows more songs and performs them better – wins (WDZ 28). The drummer, on the other hand, mistakes real affection with the theatrics of a socially constructed courtship game. His last serenade is not just his curse on

This confusion is also found in Jeronimo. In fact, Jeronimo is an aristocrat fully aware of the rites of courtly love. Yet being prone to hyperbole, he hypercorrects: He inflates the game and also mistakes artifice for reality. His love for Wally is, once again, socially unacceptable: Wally is married, to his brother none the less. But Wally *plays* along and encourages his courting (WDZ 61). For her, his courting is a game; to him, it becomes the foundation of his existence. As she retracts her affection, he loses his will to live. Unable to 'let the falcon go,' yet also incapable of claiming her, he takes his life at her window.

Here, the novel's dissent is expressed in a fundamental social critique. Certainly, all these characters may be held accountable for their suicides due to their inability to control their affects. At the same time, their actions are informed, if not controlled, by a social protocol they do not understand but nevertheless follow. Indeed, it is (also) the rites of courtship that push the socially inferior and mentally unstable to desperation.

But how can one overcome existential loss? In fact, the *Falkenlied* answers its own predicament: The maiden first accepts the fact that she will be unable to hold on to the falcon. Yes, the bird was tamed by her, but it escapes nevertheless. The taming, the possessive symbols, they are all part of the game of Minne. But the game does not guarantee, it does not even aim at actual love. Understanding that, she abstains from any claim in the falcon. Moreover, she achieves a new perspective on love, ultimately defining real love in the last line. This love is divorced from social taming and imagined as something individual, a voluntary and relational emotion. The falcon maiden is able to let go, able to heal because she now occupies a transcendental position. Indeed, Kürenberg foreshadows the idea of love's higher, consolatory power evident in Heinrich's poem. This power is therapeutic: "By her noble attributes / she has freed me of all suffering." By adopting this position, the falcon maiden regains self-possession. Her last line, however, is represented as a prayer and hints at the therapeutic function of religion; religion will be crucial for the connection between Wally and the Sigune myth.

The Falcon myth presents the preparation phase (Ia) in the ongoing mythological resignification. This myth offers the background to another, a myth that brings a more distinct narrative to the novel which will inform the relationship between Wally and Cäsar directly.

---

the unfaithful lover; it is the desperate attempt to recapture the falcon. Unable to do so and unable to transcend his subjective situation – or accept the girl's decision – he commits suicide.

3.3 THE SKEPTICAL MAIDEN AND THE RULES OF THE GAME

Gutzkow's novel begins with an image that immediately recurs to myth so as to describe the female protagonist. We are presented with a sovereign, confident young woman. Timeless beauty and modern artificiality come together in the depiction of Wally:

Auf weißem Zelter sprengte im sonnengolddurchwirkten Walde Wally, ein Bild, das die Schönheit Aphroditens übertraf, da sich bei ihm zu jedem klassischen Reize [...] noch alle romantischen Zauber gesellten: ja selbst die Draperie der modernsten Zeit fehlte nicht, ein Vorzug, der sich weniger in der Schönheit selbst als in ihrer Atmosphäre kundzugeben pflegt. (WDZ 5)

A white saddle horse being ridden at full gallop, a forest pierced by sunlight, Wally, more beautiful than Aphrodite, imbued not only with every classical charm [...] but with all the magic of a romantic age and even the trappings of her own time, this last a virtue seen less in her beauty itself than in the atmosphere enveloping it. (WTS 30)

The forest scenery, the Aphrodite reference, the romantic imagery that surrounds Wally are added to by the "trappings of her own time," odd drapery changing the scenic "atmosphere." From the first page, Gutzkow differentiates between true, natural beauty and its modern, artificial copy. That Wally is a true representative of modern artificiality is made clear very quickly. Her "coquetry" is an act, "appropriate" only in terms of social standards; her effect is calculated and constructed. Wally is not intent on beauty but on its "atmosphere." This endeavor is successful: Dashing through the forest, she is surrounded by "numerous cavaliers." Yet none of these suitors see past her artifice; none is able to see the "flashes of fear" that riddle her self-presentation (WTS 30).[42]

Wally, in fact, is not in control of her self-representation. Despite her intention to seem beautiful (and be powerful in beauty), she is unaware of riding a blind horse. She gives "an impression of confidence" but misses this vital element. While her performance is "convincing enough," she is still a "being whose acts are more studied than inborn." Wally believes to be in control but ultimately trusts a blind

---

42 Butler has defined gender as performance, and Wally's enactment of expected gender norms plays in the same vein. Gutzkow seems to highlight the performativity of gender, while at the same time insisting on a natural, authentic inner nature which is the true source of beauty. His contrastive descriptions evoke Hegelian notions of *Sein* [being] and *Schein* [appearance]. For more see Butler: *Gender Trouble* (1990); Theunissen: *Schein und Sein* (1978).

animal. The notion of acting mechanically – of going through the motions – will resurface in the text. Indeed, the revelation of individual control as socially determined behavior is part of the novel's dissent. Wally is ignorant of that fact: She does not realize that her performance of beauty – however natural she may think it to be – is but beautiful fake complying with social standards. The same holds for her suitors, who cling to her like "imitation to creativity" (WTS 30). Wally and the cavaliers confound true beauty with its socially mediated depiction. Of course, all conception of beauty is, to a certain extent, socially constructed. The point is that Wally and her suitors have not come to that realization. They perform without being aware of performativity.

Only the male protagonist, Cäsar, sees through her veil. He is a true individualist, a skeptic who is able "to grind" others "against the millstone of his own personality." He is a man of the mind but jaded and bored; an aristocrat able to assess society with a quick "triumphant look." Indeed, Cäsar is the epitome of *Geistesherrschaft*. Also, he is a static character, a man whose education and personal development are "complete" and who carries with him an "entire cemetery of dead thought, glorious ideas in which he had once believed." His perspective on the world is absolute; whatever he sees only serves to "strengthen but not to change" his preconceived notions (WTS 30f).

Cäsar is certainly an emperor, even a seducer, but most importantly a critical *seer*.[43] His skeptical perspective does much to uncover the social trappings of Vormärz Germany. In Cäsar, one may very well recognize the Young German movement itself. Horrocks notes that he is a tragic character and representative of his age in his aggressive masculinity (156). At the same time, he is a man stripped of individual power and forced to resort to irony, skepticism, and critique (Kaiser 188). Here is the epitome of Germany's young male generation, which was "cut off from the field of activity" and can do no more than "smile, sigh, ridicule, and if [they] love, make the ladies unhappy." Critique and skepticism, the cores of the Young German aesthetic, are presented as the consequence of social-systemic op-

---

43 Indeed, Gutzkow's Cäsar is an Emersonian character. His radical insistence on individuality and primacy of inner truth evoke the imperial individual Emerson describes in *Self-Reliance*: Cäsar is indeed the "center of all things" and "measures you, and all things, and all events" (Emerson 126). His conduct is one that absolves himself; this nonconformist believes in his "own thought" (121), and his arguments, cynical as they may be, have the "edge" which for Emerson defines a subjective and true relation to society (123). Even in his inconsistency of opinion, Cäsar evokes Emerson's "great soul" which has "simply nothing to do" with consistency (125). Cäsar prefigures Gutzkow's metaphysical elaborations in *Wahrheit und Wirklichkeit* at the end of the novel, where the Young German, like Emerson, champions the adherence to the inner, subjective self.

pression. They become apotropaic acts: "As he wandered alone, Caesar felt that he should cry, and laughed instead to drive away the tears" (WTS 30f).

As he encounters Wally, Cäsar also constructs an artificial atmosphere.[44] He recurs to an old legend, the "princess in the forest," and takes "pleasure in believing" that their encounter was infused by ancient magic: A "strange glitter ran through the air and five costly rings" suddenly rest at his feet. These rings hung on Wally's "riding whip," another image reinforcing the young woman's (artificial) power position (WTS 31). Now, with the reference to *The Sleeping Princess in the Forest*,[45] the novel begins its recurrence to tales of courtly love. Importantly, Wally's rings and the events which develop from their loss present a second instance of preparation (Ia). The ideas which will be resignified in the Sigune myth find another preparation in the whip and the rings; the latter invoke the process of taming as well as the possessive adornments in the *Falkenlied*. The manner in which they were procured and later dispensed of not only informs on Wally's expertise in the *ars amandi*; they illuminate one of her basic characteristics regarding love: Wally is a player.

The rings, indeed, are reminiscent of the falcon's adornments in Kürenberg's poem. As such, they belong to the discourse of romantic conquest and control. The latter notion is reinforced by the original location of the rings: Wally does not wear them but uses them to adorn her riding whip. During her second encounter with Cäsar at a country ball, she explains how she procured the jewelry:

'Ich bin gewohnt,' sagte sie 'für jeden Monat im Jahre einen andern Anbeter zu haben, und ich nehme niemanden an, der sich nicht durch einen Ring in meine Gunst einkauft. An meinem Finger will ich die Ringe nicht: ich trage sie an meiner Reitgerte und mache mir ein Vergnügen daraus, wenn ich von Juli zu Juli ins Bad reise und armen preßhaften Leuten sie alle zwölf nacheinander in die heißen Sprudelbecher werfe.' (WDZ 8)

'I am accustomed,' she said, 'to having a different admirer for every month in the year, and I accept no one who does not give me a ring in payment for my favors. I have no desire to wear that rings; I carry them on my riding whip, and every July when I got to the spa I derive great

---

44 It is important to note that Wally and Cäsar are complementary characters. Both protagonists are used to describe social constraints on dissenting individuals. Wally offers gendered perspectives on a socially defined love and marriage culture that oppresses individuality (Kaiser 187). By treating the issue from a male and a female perspective, the novel's dissent furthers general emancipation. Wally becomes a skeptic that despairs at the reality surrounding her, and Cäsar's behavior, imperial as it seems, is but a consequence of the same oppression. Both offer a common social type, and their relationship gives insights into the gendered "wars of conquest" of the time (Horrocks 151f).
45 A French precursor to the Grimms' *Sleeping Beauty* that features the loss of a ring.

pleasure from throwing all twelve of them, one after the other, into the poor, oppressed people's cups of bubbling spring water.' (WTS 31)

Here, the rings' traditional signification is reversed. Instead of following courtship rituals, in which jewelry signals male possession of a female lover, the tokens embody the maiden's claim in Kürenberg's text. Wally becomes the tamer and possessor. What is more, she *collects* lovers, conquers them, and displays her ownership on a whip. The image is telling of the way she sees herself in the courtship process: Power, possession, and control are hers; the whip becomes the scepter of the female sovereign. Love becomes a status one can 'buy into' – a status, however, that Wally is not deeply invested in. For her, love and its rituals are a game she knows exactly how to play.[46]

Courtship Rituals and Emotional Power Strategies

The Cäsar-Wally relationship is an artificial romance. From its beginning, it is a connection defined by social protocol. The lovers go through the motions of what they think may be love, but their inability to form an intrapersonal relationship bars the possibility of *eros*. Their relationship is dominated by the rituals of societal mediation, and Wally and Cäsar make the same mistake as Bärbel, the drummer, and Jeronimo: They confuse the rites of courtship with love.

In this context, Cäsar comments on the calculated nature of human behavior: "Our actions are supposed to be calculated, but it is our feelings which really are" (WTS 34). Indeed, Cäsar himself is most calculating when it comes to his feelings for Wally. After having witnessed the "flashes of fear" in her self-performance, he approaches her for his own amusement (30). True, he finds her distracting, even fascinating, but it is not in Cäsar's nature to take a real interest in anything that does not serve his own pleasure: "He was interested in heaven, hell, earth, and what is inside, on top and down below only for the sake of [his entertainment] or to turn a fancy phrase" (36). All he sees in Wally is a "humorous cappricio of animal na-

---

46 Wally's play is not restricted to love. She is also an ardent gambler. She regularly tries "her luck at faro," a popular card game. The gambling table is "a place she loved most of all." The young woman is accustomed to winning and embodies that fact that "audacity is the only secret of the game" (WTS 41). Yet her playfulness will later spill over to more existential spheres. She will begin to follow Cäsar's example and regard other human beings as playthings, objects to be analyzed for the sake of diversion (WDZ 87). Her superficiality will find an apex as she revels in fashion and card games: "Who cares about religion? Or the creation of the world? Or immortality? To wear red or blue, that is the question!" (WTS 58).

ture;" he "bathe[s] in the shallow foam which was all that Wally allowed to exit of ideas" (38). Indeed, "Wally had enchanted him" but only to "the extent that people of his makeup can love" (40). Cäsar cannot love in the sense of *eros*. Very much like Hawthorne's Roger Chillingworth, he is an anatomist of the human soul. While the first uses his intellect to pursue vengeance, Gutzkow's male protagonist seeks diversion.

In fact, Cäsar is a telling name. With his dissecting intellect he conquers the world, including human beings. Horrocks describes both protagonists as complementary in their inauthenticity, and Cäsar leads an existence that reduces life to an "aesthetic phenomenon" (151).[47] Some critics go further and interpret his conquering as acts of mental terrorism. Because of his higher education, he is able to win Wally by following a terroristic strategy: He uses his talent as storyteller, enters the gaps in Wally's self-performance, and wounds the young woman by expressing dissentious theories, and, importantly, by telling the interspersed narratives. In this context, Moi describes his storytelling as "phallic probings of masculine thought" (in Horrocks 154).

I hold this view to be unbalanced, because it renders Wally the powerless victim of Cäsar's supposed probing. Cäsar's words, Horrocks notes, have a two-fold function: to emancipate and to shackle. There may be parallels to Goethe's *Faust*, but Wally is no Gretchen (155). She is a confident, educated noblewoman, who is familiar with philosophical and theological thought and a forward critic of the literary publications of the time (WDZ 9, 13). Horrocks is correct when he states that there is a gap between Wally and Cäsar, albeit of an intellectual, not social nature (154). Wally is incapable of "speculation;" her ideas are "momentary" and she refuses to "playing the intellectual because she knew she was pretty" (WTS 38). Yes, she is vulnerable to Cäsar's theories but not to the same degree as Gretchen was vulnerable to Faust. It is wrong to depict Wally as the unsuspecting victim.

In fact, Cäsar's stories – as well as his "boring theories" – put Wally on the path towards emancipation (WTS 36). Horrocks admits that Cäsar aids Wally in developing "the ability to combine logically,"[48] thereby enabling her subsequent pursuit of personal freedom. That Wally only partially succeeds in freeing her mind and only mimics Cäsar's "masculine" mode of thought can hardly be described as the result of a terroristic act (154). Moreover, Cäsar's relating of the interspersed narratives is certainly not a 'phallic probing' to conquer Wally. Horrocks defines them as instruments that "penetrate into those 'flashes of fear' which Cäsar discovered on

---

47 [ästhetisches Phänomen].
48 [Entwicklung logischer Kombinationsfähigkeit].

meeting Wally" (157).[49] I understand that it is rather tempting to recur to a Freudian reading and attest a "literary tyranny" on Cäsar's part (158). Yes, Cäsar is a conqueror and yes, he conquers Wally. Here, we may return to the Falcon myth: Courtship is the taming of the falcon, the exercise of man's mental dominion. And Cäsar is nothing if not an expert at *Geistesherrschaft*. But a Freudian reading blinds us to the societal sources informing this behavior and suggests a conscious motivation in the alleged perpetrator. Yet the novel explicitly states that Cäsar is unaware of the pain he is causing. He is completely ignorant to the fact that he is hurting his paramour (WDZ 14, 21). Similarly, the notorious content of his theological discussion with Waldemar was not meant for Wally's ears. Yet she overhears the men talk and almost faints (37). Most importantly, Cäsar's religious tract, the text that will give Wally the last push towards suicide, was written upon Wally's explicit request (100).

The point here is that a reading of Cäsar as an emotional terrorist blurs the perspective on the social-systemic situation. This perspective blames the male protagonist for Wally's death. But terroristic acts require purpose and intention, both of which Cäsar lacks. There is but one thing for which one could justifiably blame the skeptic: his inconstant because "lighthearted treatment of religion" and his incapacity to see how much his incoherent teachings confuse Wally (WTS 91).[50] By making religion an intellectual game, he causes Wally to despair, because she *did* take religion seriously. Indeed, there is a "massive masculine power strategy," as Horrocks notes. But it lies not with Cäsar as an individual. I will later show how Cäsar is the only character who is finally able to overcome systemic restrictions. But – and here I agree with Horrocks – the skeptic presents a gendered *type* of the Vormärz, the product of a culture informed by the gendered rituals of courtly love (159).

In fact, Cäsar's conduct is motivated by a wish for authenticity, a desire for "truth and immediacy"[51] (Kaiser 190). His taming is not just conquest; it is the endeavor to form an equal partner by means of education. He seeks to emancipate Wally from her constraints, especially from her religious and romantic preconceptions. Thus, he assumes the role of teacher-lover. Here is a selfish, subjective endeavor to educate another person so as to achieve romantic immediacy. This endeavor fails, because Cäsar's egotism finally harms Wally (WDZ 11f). His attempt at educating climaxes in the tract *Confessions Concerning Religion and Christiani-*

---

49 Indeed, the penetration metaphor is not without substance. While discussing philosophy, Cäsar will tell Wally: "If I bury myself in the innermost furrows of your soul [...], when I imagine myself to be in your soul, I am certain that I shall bring about the effects that I was already able to predict a minute ago"(WTS 35f).

50 cf. my comments on Cäsar as an Emersonian character in footnote 39.

51 [Wahrheit und Unmittelbarkeit].

ty, which will prove disastrous. But Cäsar's failure in attempting to free Wally does not change the fact that his endeavor was benevolent. It was based on the assumption that a new, free identity can be built on criticism. The fact that criticism cannot be the foundation of a person's identity did not occur to the skeptic. He ultimately masters his life by settling in a dissentious but stable relationship. Cäsar transcends skepticism; Wally cannot do this. She is trapped in the world of critique.

Wally shares Cäsar's wish for truth and immediacy. But Kaiser is correct in noting that truth and immediacy are rather unspecific terms (190). So, both characters remain guided and trapped by the myth of courtly love and its rites. Certainly, these "wars of conquest" were part of the German cultural system and their effects were catastrophic (Horrocks 160). As romance is thought of as mental dominion, any romantic advance must tend towards a taming and controlling of the lover. The wish for an equal, emotional partnership inevitably clashes with rituals of conquest and possession. At the same time, the subject's political powerlessness encourages the enactment of mental dominion in the private. Men, educated and raised for dominion, are politically impotent; dominion in the romantic realm can therefore serve as an *Ersatz* arena. Women, however, are doubly disempowered. Agency is denied in both public and private realms (Kaiser 192). Thus, their only societal *raison d'être* is being the courted, the conquered, and the possessed. They may, of course, choose a life of dissent. Indeed, at the end of the novel, Wally and Cäsar are both dissenters. Yet at the beginning, the protagonists escape into artifice. They follow the social protocol of courtly love without taking love seriously. Their end is the game itself and its distraction from reality.

The Escapism of Laughter

Wally and Cäsar are aristocrats and plagued by a common disease of their class: boredom. The novel presents boredom as the foundation of artifice. The escape to shallow occupations results from the perpetual monotony Wally and Cäsar face. Their lives not only lack identity, they lack purpose and meaning, and their search for truth and immediacy stems from the social position of having absolutely nothing else to do. They are not philosophers out of passion or curiosity; they dissect the world because they are idle.

Boredom is repeatedly paired with a counter-strategy to escape constant ennui: laughter. On being introduced to Cäsar, we are told that he would like to weep but escapes melancholy by laughing instead (WDZ 6). Similarly, Wally answers her pain with laughter (43). Even before her despair, she employs escapist laughter and exaggerates: "Wally was able to laugh and did so excessively" (WTS 11). In Schwalbach, Cäsar tells Wally the interspersed narratives to relieve her from ennui; creative imagination becomes an instrument in the fight against boredom (WDZ

24). Yet Cäsar does not only tell stories for Wally's sake. He has a tendency to fictionalize his life, thus giving his existence a romantic shine. As he meets Wally, he conjures fairytale images to enchant the scene (2). In Paris, Wally comments on a meeting that was "not so miraculous as Caesar will make it seem" but which will serve to quench his "everlasting ennui" (WTS 71). For Cäsar, only fictionalized life is worth considering, and his skepticism runs in the same vein. The dissection of the world ("one must dissect people in all aspects of their being") serves academic interest but also the alleviation of ennui (83). For both, love and love stories (like the interspersed narratives) serve diversion. Here, Gutzkow uses romanticism's literary enchantments to make a modern point. Kavanagh notes that Cäsar tells these gothic tales *because* they are romantic. His recurrence to these stories illuminates his own reality, a disenchanted, tedious world (165, 169).

Thus, reality becomes a diverting game. Wally plays with men, Cäsar plays with education. The reason for the characters' boredom is systemic: Kaiser notes that "the game"[52] becomes a way of life were responsibility is no longer possible. Responsibility presupposes personal agency, but these Vormärz characters are *subjects*. The strategy to deal with the world (and with one's self) in an *insincere* manner is a direct consequence of the person's disempowered status in the monarchic polity (192). The game, indeed, is the expression of the perfect subject: For a monarchic system, individual responsibility is undesired. The individual is only a category, a product of societal mediation. The real world is transformed into a playing field designed for self-exertion and self-affirmation (189).

Again, the Falcon myth becomes relevant and prepares for the denaturalization of the basic civic myth (Ic). Romance in *Wally* is the expression of the larger political issues of artifice. By relating the stories of couples that lose themselves in artificial love rituals, the novel imagines a more authentic love conception that lies outside the socially constructed. People play by the rules of Minne, but Minne is represented as a spiritualized theatrics that aims at transcendence, not at the attainment of *eros*. The characters mistake the game of love with love, just as they revel in shallow occupations which substitute reality. The consequence of the novel's dissent is evident: It is only a systemically unmediated, individual identity that can overcome the status of monarchic subject and constitute a real and free existence.

An example may be helpful to clarify this point, and the clearing scene will serve as such. The clearing scene presents an apex of romantic artifice in the novel. Indeed, it is geographically and structurally related to the forest meeting between Hester and Arthur in *The Scarlet Letter*. Both scenes are located in nature, feature the expression of love between the protagonists, and present a dissent aimed at the establishing of individual truths.

---

52 [das Spiel].

Wally and Cäsar take a carriage ride in the forest. Unable to "resist the temptation of a patch of grass in the midst of the woods," they decide to leave their fellow travelers and the road and head for the clearing. This clearing may be thought of as a *locus amoenus*, a natural and idealized space for the expression of love. But despite the fact that civilization (the road) and social expectation (the fellow travelers) are left behind, nature does not offer them a realm of love, immediacy, and truth. On the contrary, artifice dominates the description. Shortly preceding this scene, the narrator defines the upcoming enterprise as an endeavor to tame the falcon: "It wasn't love that drove [Cäsar], it was the task imposed by his vanity, that of conquering Wally, this untamed and ebullient creature!" So, the characters sit and face each other, but their behavior is "mechanical, as if a tryst had been arranged" (WTS 48).

It is Wally who begins to speak, and she does not speak of love but of gender categories. She denounces women as cruel and states that they "thrive only because of men;" a woman's nature is "animal fear" and contrastive to men's "reflections of a noble soul" (WTS 48f). Wally taps into stereotypes of female naturalness and male rationality and thus opens a romantic dialogue with a gendered self-positioning: The woman signals her will to be tamed. Cäsar is quick to follow protocol and inquires as to what feeling could possibly effect the "transformation of women." Here, Wally answers and Cäsar reacts; the exchange, however, is not the expression of subjectivity but a socially mediated communication: "She hesitated, then *looked* at him. He *guessed* the answer and sank at her feet" (49).[53] An actual exchange of words is not necessary here: Society is doing the talking.

As he kneels at Wally's feet, Cäsar enacts a Minne pose of adoration. What passed here is a contract, the willingness of one party to be tamed, i.e. transformed by the other party's agency. Whoever criticizes Cäsar's mental dominion and efforts to educate Wally should bear in mind that the latter explicitly asked to be educated. Love, however, is represented as the attempt to civilize the female, and the Falcon myth and its notion of male mental dominion over the natural woman informs this representation.

However, their "happy emotion" only lasts as long as they remain in this position of adoration. The "warm mood" dissipates the moment they begin to talk. Wally states that love is indeed the "magic wand which first awakens the feelings slumbering in a woman's heart."[54] Then, Cäsar takes her hand and proposes an arrangement that would be of mutual benefit. He throws himself at her feet, overcome by a "genuine feeling" (WTS 49). That feeling, however, is not love:

---

53 Italics MRD.

54 That this wand is an instrument of control and discipline is more evident in the German original "Zauberrute" [magic *rod*] (WDZ 33).

Aber was warf ihn nieder? Nicht die Liebe, sondern [...] der Gedanke an jene Augenblicke, wo wir, überdrüssig der konventionellen Formen des Lebens, zu aller Welt herantreten möchten und ihr zurufen: 'O warum dies Gehäuse von Manieren, in welches du Spröde dich zurückziehst? Warum diese Verhüllung des Menschen in und an dir? Warum Zurückhaltung, du, mein Bruder, du, meine Schwester, da du doch gleichen Wesens mit mir bist, eine Hand wie ich zum Drucke, einen Mund wie ich zum Kusse hast?' (WDZ 34)

But what had thrown him there? Not love, but [...] the question that comes in those moments when, sated with conventional formalities, we long to stand up to the whole world and cry out to it: 'Oh, why this shell of manners into which you prudishly retreat? Why mask that humanness which is at the core of your being? Why this reserve, my brother, my sister, who are after all of the same nature as I am, have a hand to be pressed as I do, a mouth like mine to be kissed?' (WTS 49)

These lines present some of the most direct social dissent to be found in the novel. They are a call for human immediacy, the transcendence of social restrictions, and the general equality of humanity. It is, indeed, a beautiful sentiment. But is has nothing to do with Wally. This is a manifest of human brotherhood, a philosophical, a political idea, but nothing related to *eros*. Cäsar is thrown to the ground by philosophy, not by love.

Wally also re*acts*. She "collapsed in tears" and felt the "ecstasy of being a human instead of a woman," trembling at this "genuinely philanthropic idea" (WTS 50). Once again, she revels in the beauty of an ideal, not in the ecstasy of love. As she allows Cäsar to embrace and kiss her, she does not embrace a lover but hopes to be included in the greater, universal scheme of things. Her lover's kiss is not personal. It is received like Schiller's famous kiss in *An die Freude* (1785), a kiss meant for the entire world:

Sie ließ die Umarmung Cäsars zu: nicht, weil sie ihn liebte, oder aus Egoismus, aus Stolz, einen Mann überwunden zu haben, sondern weil sie sich als das schwache Glied der großen Wesenkette fühlte, die Gott erschaffen hat, weil sie wußte, daß sie ja vor der Wahrheit und Natur ganz nackt und bloß und mitleidswürdig war, weil sie zuletzt glaubte, daß diese heißen Küsse, welche Cäsar auf ihre Lippen drückte, allen Millionen gälten unterm Sternenzelt. (WDZ 34f)

She allowed Caesar to embrace her, not because she loved him or out of egotism or of pride of having conquered a man, but because she felt herself the weak link in the great chain of being which God had created, because she knew that she was indeed quite naked and exposed and pitiable in the face of truth and nature, and finally because she believed that the burning kisses which Caesar was pressing on her lips were for all the millions beneath the firmament. (WTS 50)

This scene not only prepares (Ia) for the exposition of a basic myth which champions two Minne lovers, it also explicates its mytheme: *Love-is-Consolation*. In the Sigune myth, love is imagined as an emotion which consoles the fundamental pain of the human condition: loneliness, disorientation, doubt, and adversity. Further, by means of this consolation, the lover attains a place in the world and in society. In this context, Wally and Cäsar seek refuge in love so as to appease their skepticism. Unfortunately, they seek refuge in the *rituals* of love, not in love itself. The scene closes with a telling reader address. This form of love, the narrator comments, is "artful, contrived, born from the inner disharmony" of the age. The traditional conceptualizations of love fail to appease the emotional and societal turmoil of the Vormärz. But what, the narrator asks, "is the truth of Romeo and Juliet compared with this lie! What is selfish sexual love compared with the enthusiasm of ideas which can hurl two souls into the most wretched of confusions!" The narrator is both amazed and repulsed by the scene, and he trembles "before a century that is so tragic in its errors and yet worthy of adoration even in its accursedness" (WTS 50).

The Falcon myth in the interspersed narratives offered the preparation of the basic Sigune myth (Ia). Here, the rites of courtship that Wally and Cäsar employ in their relationship are explicated. But despite their search for truth and immediacy, the lovers fail in attaining *eros* as they confuse the games of Minne with love. Thus, the novel stresses a modern artifice born out of love rituals based on the Falcon myth. Simultaneously, it presents the incapability of the paramours to articulate their own individual love conceptions. Wally and Cäsar are stuck: They are tired of medieval rites and unable to produce contemporary ones. Their escape is a desperate celebration of the game and of artifice. The question is whether (and how) they may be able to break the despair of artificiality and attain a more genuine perspective on life. The novel will further elaborate on this question, but before it gives answers, it recurs to another myth. The Sigune myth presents the basic myth in the process of mythological resignification. It will not only be retold; it will be exposed, staged, and enacted so as to finally be refuted.

3.4 THE SIGUNE MYTH AND ALTERNATIVE PATHS TO SALVATION

Among the most controversial passages in *Wally*, the Sigune scene was denounced by critics as licentious (Flavell 550). But this crucial scene presents the text's climax of artificiality, an imaginative enactment rather than a pornographic performance. Further, it offers the exposition of the basic myth (Ib) and further works towards its denaturalization (Ic). Prepared by the interspersed narratives and the Falcon myth, the Sigune scene epitomizes the artificiality of the Wally-Cäsar relationship and has strong political undertones in its call for gender equality and artistic autonomy (Zeller 212).

The Veiling of Absence

A tête-à-tête between the lovers prefigures the exposition (Ib) of the Sigune myth. Wally had just informed Cäsar that she is to marry a Sardinian ambassador (WDZ 48). However, she promises that they will talk again soon, and Cäsar finds himself invited to an interview (49). On his way, he encounters friends and discusses marriage concepts. Their exchange is an apt precursor to a scene which oversteps social boundaries. The text prepares the interview with Wally by critiquing and ridiculing contemporary marriage norms.

Cäsar's elaborations on marriage range from criticism to ridicule.[55] By neglecting the romantic components of marriage and restricting the relationship to its material/societal aspects, Cäsar divorces romance and marriage. He refutes societal marriage norms and begins to hint towards a more individualistic approach to the issue. Granted, his elaborations border on the absurd; nevertheless, a shift from societal to individual marriage conceptions, and therefore a first instance of mythological elaboration (IIb), is evident in his arguments. Simultaneously, his friends' reactions suggest that they do not take Cäsar's elaborations seriously because Cäsar himself is not entirely serious. The reader just witnessed an intellectual game: critique *qua* diversion. Further, Cäsar's elaborations on marriage effect the denaturalization (Ic) of courtship rites and marriage norms. His critical treatment exaggerates the Love-is-Possession mytheme of the Falcon myth and complicates it. By separating romantic love from the notion of possession in the marital covenant, Cäsar dissents from traditional concepts and opens them up for further reflection. The skeptic will himself re-negotiate marriage relations later in the novel and thereby suggest an alternative to the tenets of the Falcon and Sigune myth. In the upcoming interview scene, however, he will partake in the exposition of the basic myth (Ib).

Zeller is correct in noting that the interview between Wally and Cäsar is suffused with theater metaphors (211). It presents a continuation of the clearing scene, where Wally and Cäsar began the dramatization of an artificial relationship. On entering the room, Wally is already in costume. She wears a "fanciful black dress,"

---

55 Marriage has become frivolous to the skeptic; he proposes to disallow marriages before a child enters the equation, making premarital sex a prerequisite. He further comments on the fact that women could more easily find men through newspaper announcements (WDZ 50). One of his friends just lamented that his fiancé is poor, so Cäsar prompts a solution that would aid the "revolutionizing" of society: "The girls should play themselves in a lottery" (WTS 60).

her eyes are filled with tears, which Cäsar interprets as a plea for "forgiveness, warmth," and "conquest" (WTS 60). It is again the atmosphere that moves him, not having expected such a tragic setting (WDZ 51). Their conversation, however, is painfully evasive: They talk about the "discovery of gunpowder" and the "law of gravity" (WTS 60). If there ever was phatic language, this is it. And the theatrics continue:

[Er nahm Wallys Hand] und legte sie sanft auf die Lehne des Sofas, um sie als Kopfkissen zu brauchen. Sie lächelte dazu und warf ihm das ganze Polster ihres elastischen Körpers, sich selbst in aller ihrer Anmut nach. Sie hielt ihn umschlungen, während sie unwillig glaubte, daß er es täte. (WDZ 51)

He took Wally's hand and laid it gently on the arm-rest of the sofa so that he might use it as a pillow for his head. At this she smiled, and offered him all of her supple body as a cushion, her entire self with all her charm and grace. She held him in a tight embrace, indignantly believing the while that it was he who was embracing her. (WTS 60)

On top of the shallow conversation, the scene depicts the failure of physical closeness. Who is embracing whom? Is there real sentiment in the gestures? Whatever may be behind it, the gross of the action is artifice, a conscious process of veiling: Wally closes her eyes, which is described as a "lowering of the curtain," a "closing of the shades of femininity," a "veiling [that] is the charming opposite of what it appears to be, since it is only the signal of gradual capitulation" (60f).

Zeller reads the veils in *Wally* as acts of "veiling to unveil" (211).[56] Indeed, these acts of veiling reveal something that lies underneath. However, I hold that the veil is *dominant*; not the *eros* at the core of the relationship, not the wish for truth behind the romantic shine in Cäsar's imagination, nor the wish for true poetry behind Wally's enactment. The veils, in fact, present the expert performance of courtship rites. The point of the Wally-Cäsar relationship is not the unveiling of love but the revelation of love's *absence* in rituals of courtship. Yes, Wally will come to truly love Cäsar (WDZ 66). But both remain unable to express genuine sentiment because they lack the adequate terms to express real love. They must make do with the palls of courtship rites.

During their embrace, Cäsar is again overwhelmed by the situation; but this time, he does not sink to his knees. Knowing that he can never *possess* Wally's "divine body," he asks for something else: for a look (WTS 61). Here, we are given an explicit refutation of *eros*: Cäsar does not wish to possess Wally physically, all he wants is the *Schein*, her body's visual revelation *qua* adoration. Indeed, we are very

---

56 [Verhüllung zur Enthüllung].

close to Minne's chaste love conceptualization here. Accordingly, he tells of a German medieval epic that introduces the Sigune myth. Here, the exposition (Ib) of the basic myth occurs:

'Da gibt es ein reizendes Gedicht des deutschen Mittelalters, der 'Titurel,' in welchem eine bezaubernde Sage erzählt wird. Tschionatulander und Sigune beten sich an. [...] Nur jener Zug ist so meisterhaft schön, wo Tschionatulander, als er in die Welt hinausmuß [...] Sigunen anfleht um eine Gunst–[...] daß Sigune – in vollkommener Nacktheit zum vielleicht – ewigen Abschiede sich ihm zeigen möge.' (WDZ 52f)

'There is a charming German medieval poem called Titurel which relates a bewitching legend. Schionatulander and Sigune worship one another. [...] Only that scene is so brilliantly beautiful, the one in which Schionatulander, when he must go out into the world, [...] implores Sigune for a favor... [...] that Sigune ....might reveal herself to him in complete nakedness in a – perhaps eternal – farewell.' (WTS 61)

Wally does not answer his request and leaves without a word. This passage further illuminates the absence of *eros* behind the rites of courtship, because it is only the *Schein* that Cäsar requests of Wally, not a truly romantic connection. Both lovers are playing a game but its end cannot be real love. Indeed, the Sigune story is a Minne story. By its means, their game attains the spiritual dimension of medieval courtly love. But Minne, too, is a game: Behind the lover's theatrics, there lurks little truth. This is most evident in the following denaturalization (Ic), in Wally's reenactment of Sigune's nakedness.

The Dramatization of Physical Immediacy

The Sigune scene offers the cornerstone of the mythological resignification employed in *Wally, die Zweiflerin*. Prepared by the Falcon myth's abandoned lover, Wally stages the romance between Sigune and Tschionatulander. The basic myth's denaturalization (Ic) focuses on two points. First, the basic myth connects Wally and Sigune's attempts to deal with despair and loss, offering a contrastive structure regarding the possibilities of female identity in their respective historical contexts (a referential treatment). Second, it highlights the incompatibility of mediaeval notions with the Vormärz (a critical treatment). The Sigune figure suggests a distinctly female-coded path to worldly fulfillment and spiritual salvation. While that path may have been applicable to a medieval context, it cannot fulfill its identity-stabilizing function in the 19th century. The Sigune scene allows the reader to connect Wally and Sigune's trajectories, working towards a rejection of gendered (female) identity and outdated love conceptualizations. Indeed, the idea that allowed Sigune to overcome her despair (Love-is-Consolation) will no longer be able to assist Wally. Thus, the value system inherent in the Sigune myth is presented as incompatible with the age: Wally's death is the result of trying to live a life based on the values of the past.

Wally's enactment of the Sigune scene illuminates her desire for immediacy. This desire is checked by a socially conditioned inability to genuinely express feelings. Cäsar and Wally are too invested in social standards to effectively free themselves from the same. The only way to express their wish for immediacy is to give it an artificial veil by recurring to the Sigune narrative. The reader is offered a complex merging of political and social critique, as well as an aesthetic call for a free and individual approach to life and art.

Indeed, Wally submitted to social expectations in originally refusing Cäsar's request. Then, she decides to recant her submission. She quickly realizes that her initial refusal is based in her consenting to social virtue and morality. Suddenly, this consent seems vulgar to her "Schon im nächsten Augenblicke, als sie gegangen war, war sie sich mit ihrer Tugend recht abgeschmackt vorgekommen" (WDZ 54). Thus, she decides to give way to a force that transcends societal law: poetry. It "tormented her, to be subordinate and basically less innocent than poetry" (WTS 62). Wally puts aside social concern and bows to what she feels to be the power of natural beauty. She gives herself to what makes nature graspable: art.

Wally beugte und wand sich mit all ihren schönen Grundsätzen und den Lehren, die sie ihrer Erziehung, ja selbst ihrer vernünftigen Überlegung verdankte, vor dem Ideale des Naturschönen. Sie ging noch weiter. Sie gab die Natur auf, sie hielt sich an die Kunst, an das Gebilde der Phantasie, das in sich abgerundet und hier so richtig gezeichnet war wie jeder logische Zirkel ihrer tugendhaften Entschlüsse. (WDZ 54)

With all her fine maxims and principles which she owed to her upbringing and to her own rational judgment Wally bowed down before the ideal of natural beauty. She went still further. She abandoned nature and clung to art, to this creation of imagination that was as perfectly rounded as the logical circle of her own virtuous decisions. (WTS 62)

Wally makes a choice between social constructions and the constructions of art. Art, too, is a way of understanding and shaping reality. But Wally does not stop here. She turns from art's "divine power," goes farther than the "beauty of nature," and focuses on its *mediation* (ibid.). Again, Wally is fixated only on the veil itself.

It is not a poetic desire that motivates the young woman; it is that she cannot bear the thought of not being an *object* for poetry. Thus, by re-enacting the Sigune scene, she makes "herself such an object" and counteracts Cäsar's disgust at her virtue (WTS 62): "Sie ist ohne Poesie [...] Sie hat nicht mich, sie hat die Poesie beleidigt!" (WDZ 53). Wally and Cäsar recur to art as an apotropaic act: Instead of facing their personal deficits, they escape into artistic rituals to alleviate their inadequacy. Unfortunately, instead of being truly artistic they become artificial. Both desire the *Schein*: He recurs to the myth to produce a tragic love scene; she will ultimately enact it. But this, too, is nothing more than quotation. Still, Cäsar finds a self-affirming stability in his idealist position towards beauty. Wally, on the other hand, loses the first barricade against the assault of reality's absolutism: her belief in social standards.[57]

Thus, she gives in to Cäsar's request; but she does so on her very own terms. It would be naïve to disregard Cäsar's influence over Wally, but it is important to remember that it is exclusively Wally who produces, stages, directs, and enacts the Sigune scene. Her gesture is superficial, her motivation selfish, but the fact that she feels the need to *do* something betrays her inner processes. Wally yearns for something *real*. Her artifice is conditioned by an inability to create but motivated by a desire for immediacy. The enactment of the love between Sigune and Tschionatulander is, in short, the best she can do.

Wally not only stages the Sigune scene, she has specific instructions for the audience. Cäsar receives a note detailing time and place of the enactment. He is to present himself to her fiancé's hotel at 10 pm sharp; then, he will be ushered to a place he is not to leave under any circumstances; at exactly 10:10 pm, he is to draw back the curtain but not step out of his designated viewing area. Spatially, Wally designs a theater – a stage and a patron's box – in order to best enact the *Schein* that is to follow (WDZ 56). Again, no physical intimacy can take place in this setting. Wally remains on stage, Cäsar in the stalls. This is performance *qua* performance, not an erotic display aimed at a physical connection (or action).

In her rejection of social convention and the enactment of the Sigune scene, Wally makes clear that she has replaced societal values with the ideals of art. Her earlier shame at Cäsar's request is replaced by a shame of feeling poetically inadequate: "Ich schäme mich vor Ihnen, daß ich Scham hatte" (WDZ 56). Now, she hopes that this enactment will express a truly poetic feeling. Her earlier coldness is to be replaced with a poetic idea: that she might be able to love "ardently, eternally, unspeakably." The fact that unspeakable love resists an expression does not occur to her. So, the lovers engage in an artistic endeavor: the painting of a medieval sce-

---

[57] That the poetic perspective is not without its own power politics is illuminated by the character's behavior after the original request. Cäsar's espousing of art gives him superiority: "Er konnte das Auge erheben, das Ideale hub es in ihm!" But Wally cannot help feeling ashamed. "Ihre ganze Tugend war armselig, seitdem sie ihm gleichsam gesagt hatte, die Tugend könne nur in Verhüllungen bestehen, die Tugend könne nicht nackt sein" (WDZ 55). Shaming, an instrument of socio-political control, also works in artistic constructions of reality.

ne. "And on Wally's wedding day the unseen artists sketched a charming picture, a painting in the old style, tender, loving, like the pure groups of colors which are found on the satin-soft parchments of golden medieval prayerbooks" (WTS 63).

Wally and Cäsar, whose names are not mentioned during the scene, become the "unseen." This is not the convention of two individuals; they lose their identities in the act of quoting and produce an image "in the old style" (WTS 63). Zeller notes that their artistic efforts reproduce the idealized clichés of how Vormärz Germany imagined the Middle Ages (213). The artists wish to quote the style of bygone ages but naively use contemporary colors to do so. Further, Eke comments that the contemporaries' scandalized reaction to the description of female physicality tells us much about the Puritanism of Germany's guardians of public morals (78). But the scene is not *erotic*. It is fundamentally un-erotic, in fact. The following is a *failed* attempt at expressing romantic physicality due to the use of an outdated aesthetics:

Rings, wie Rahmen und noch hineinrankend in die Szene, Epheu und Weinlaub. Auf den Ästen sitzen Paradiesvögel in wunderbarem Farbenspiel, auf den breiten Blättern der Arabesken schlummern Schmetterlinge, in den Kelchen der Blumen saugen Bienen. Oben schwebt der Vogel Phönix, der fußlose Erzeuger seiner selbst; unten blicken die spitzschnäbligen Greifen und hüten das Gold der Fabel. Bezaubernd und märchenhaft ist die Verschlingung aller dieser Figuren. (WDZ 56)

Framing the scene, yet extending into it, are ivy and grape leaves. On the branches Birds of Paradise are perched in a wonderful array of color. On the broad leaves of the arabesques butterflies slumber, in the calyxes of the flowers bees are sucking. Above hovers the bird Phoenix, the footless begetter of itself; below, the sharp-beaked griffins glare and guard the gold of the fable. The intermingling of all these figures is mythical and fantastic. (WTS 63)

The failure of the attempt again furthers the denaturalization (Ic) of the myth that is portrayed here. The scene is inauthentic, just as the lovers (and the Vormärz) are imagined as inauthentic. Medieval material cannot do justice to modern love, just as modern depictions cannot approach medieval love. Such an attempt is doomed to become artificial. The artificiality of the whole is emphasized by the perspective. There is a real-life spectator, and if this were aimed at building a connection to Cäsar, Wally would offer her bodily beauty to him. But she does not. There is a *painted* Tschionatulander gazing at Wally: "Zur Rechten des Bilds aber im Schatten steht Tschionatulander im goldenen, an der Sonne funkelnden Harnisch, Helm, Schild und Bogen ruhen auf der Erde" (WDZ 56). Cäsar is excluded from the scene's universe. The direction of Wally's display is intratextual, aimed at the *representation* of the knightly lover. Wally unveils herself to the *idea* of Tschionatulander, not to her flesh-and-blood paramour.

Her unveiling, however, is a romantic (albeit failed) depiction of the medieval myth:

Zur Linken aber schwillt aus den Sonnennebeln heraus ein Bild von bezaubernder Schönheit: Sigune, die schamhafter ihren nackten Leib enthüllt, als ihn die Venus der Medicis zu bedecken sucht. [...] Sie steht ganz nackt, die hehre Gestalt mit jungfräulich schwellenden Hüften, mit allen zarten Beugungen und Linien, welche von der Brust bis zur Zehe hinuntergleiten. Und zum Zeichen, daß eine fromme Weihe die ganze Üppigkeit dieser Situation heilige, blühen nirgends Rosen, sondern eine hohe Lilie sproßt dicht an dem Leibe Sigunens hervor und deckt symbolisch, als Blume der Keuschheit, an ihr die noch verschlossene Knospe ihrer Weiblichkeit. (WDZ 56f)

To the left a picture of magical beauty arises from the misty sunlight: Sigune, who reveals her naked body with more modesty than the Medici Venus in her attempt to conceal hers. [...] She stands quite naked, the noble form with swelling hips, with all the gentle curves and lines which glide down from her breasts to her toes. And as a sign that a pious consecration sanctifies the immense voluptuousness of this situation, roses bloom nowhere, but a tall lily shoots up close to Sigune's body and as the flower of chastity conceals symbolically the still closed bud of her femininity. (WTS 63f)

The scene lasts only a moment. Then, the ambassador enters, causing the curtain to fall and leaving Cäsar to make his way home. The fiancé Luigi suspects nothing of the "[d]eep secret" between Wally and Cäsar (64).[58]

The Sigune scene presents a radical and conscious dissent. It may be artificial, it may be a failed attempt at *eros*, but it celebrates a (misunderstood) allegiance to "irresistible" poetry, which "stands above all laws of morality and breeding" (WTS 62). Wally has denounced societal restrictions including the institution of marriage. Indeed, she was never really serious about it. Her upcoming nuptials with Luigi, we will learn later, were based on a frivolous contract that excluded a sexual relationship (63). Cäsar's critique of the frivolity of modern marriage has come true in

---

58 Zeller notes that later, under the pressure of Restoration authorities, Gutzkow will claim that the Sigune scene hints at a secret marriage between Wally and Cäsar (214). There is, however, nothing that would suggest a marriage at this point. Only later will the narrator inform us of Wally's genuine love for Cäsar (WDZ 66). Moreover, the scene is not a marriage scene in the original myth, so that an inter-textual argument falls flat as well. On the contrary: The context of Wally's situation point towards a crass dissent from marriage conventions. Wally is not only engaged at the moment of the Sigune scene, it is her wedding day. Zeller is correct in noting that Gutzkow's attempt to soften the scene's dissent is to be seen in the context of his prosecution (214).

Wally. But Wally's enactment of the Sigune scene represents the desperate attempt to give shape to a romantic feeling which has no other way of expressing itself. On trying to express her love for Cäsar, she can only recur to cliché. But there *is* something she wishes to express: her wish for an intimate, immediate connection. The fact that she could not help but focus on artifice does not mean that there was nothing behind the veil. It means that she had no way of expressing truth except through hyperbolic artifice.

It is this fundamental difficulty of expressing individuality which will finally drive Wally insane. That problem, however, is a systemic one. Wally does not possess the ability for creative self-expression because she lacks the tools of self-expression. The novel is very clear in this regard: This lack is the consequence of a gender-structure and a love-culture that divests women from the power to self-articulate. Wally aspires to education, agency, and individuality, but is unable to attain them in Vormärz Germany.

Instead, Wally recurs to myth. Sigune, too, is a woman who has to redefine her position in society. She also confuses social protocol with love and ultimately suffers because of her fixation on the game of Minne. But Sigune is able to make sense of the world and of her fate by relying on love and religion. Wally will try the same; but love and religion as the female domain for consolation fail to provide for Gutzkow's 19th century skeptic. The artificiality of Wally's enactment continues the denaturalization (Ic) of the basic myth. Wally, a woman of the 19th century, cannot follow Sigune's path to peace and salvation.

The Grail Maiden and the Path to Salvation

The Sigune scene in *Wally* harks back to a 13th century poem entitled *Der Jüngere Titurel* by Albrecht von Scharfenberg. This poem is based on two epic poems by Wolfram von Eschenbach: *Parzival* and *Titurel*. While the *Parzival* manuscript survived in its entirety, all that is left of *Titurel* are fragments. Considering sources, the story of Sigune thus draws on three texts: Her youth and the early romance between her and Tschionatulander are found in *Titurel*; her loss, suffering, and death are described in *Parzival*; the nude scene is found in *Der Jüngere Titurel*. Gutzkow and his contemporaries, unaware of Albrecht's authorship, attributed all three texts to Wolfram.[59] Thus, Gutzkow regarded *Der Jüngere Titurel* and its nude scene as part

---

59 For the original Middle High German texts and German and English translations see: Bumke und Heinzle (eds): *Titurel* (2006). Martin (ed.): *Parzival und Titurel* (1976). Edwards (ed.): *Parzival* (2004). Nyholm (ed.): *Albrechts Jüngerer Titurel* (1995). Hahn (ed.): *Der jüngere Titurel* (1842). Simrock (ed.): *Parzival und Titurel: Rittergedichte von Wolfram von Eschenbach* (1883).

of a unified narrative complex by the same author. I will also treat the Sigune myth as one narrative that draws on three highly interconnected texts.[60]

Wally's trajectory parallels the life of Sigune. Similarly, the characters in the interspersed narratives draw on the life of the medieval grail maiden. Sigune is a noblewoman and member of the Grail family. As a young girl, she falls in love with Tschionatulander, son of a lesser knight. Their relationship is seen as socially unacceptable; nevertheless, Sigune becomes a sovereign *Minnedame* [Minne lady] and Tschionatulander her devoted lover. Tschionatulander eventually becomes a knight and starts questing. On one of these occasions, he asks Sigune to reveal her breasts to him, so that he may gain strength and courage for the journey. On another occasion, a hound falls into their hands, upon whose embroidered leash they begin to read two love stories. But the animal escapes before Sigune can finish reading, and she demands the hound's return. As Wally promises love to the one who returns her stolen rings (WDZ 7), Sigune promises Tschionatulander her everlasting love if he returns the hound. But the quest fails and Tschionatulander is slain. Heartbroken, Sigune despairs; her exemplary love turns into exemplary mourning. With time, however, she is able to alleviate her grief. She leaves court, becomes a recluse in the woods, and lives in a cottage. Blaming herself for Tschionatulander's fate, she decides to make up for the love she denied him in life by loving him in death. Thus, Sigune opts for a religious life and finds consolation in her ongoing love for the fallen knight. She dies and is buried with her lover, thus ending a romance that would become the epitome of ideal love in the Middle Ages (Braunagel 6ff, 29ff; Kragl 139ff).

Indeed, Sigune's despair is the most obvious parallel to Wally's story. But if we follow the maiden's trajectory, it will become clear how intimately connected Wally and Sigune's fates really are. The Sigune scene in the novel enables and demands

---

60 One may regard Wolfram's *Titurel* as a prelude and addendum to *Parzival*. This prelude tells the story of two young lovers, Sigune and Tschionatulander. Their love's tragic end is then related in *Parzival*. *Parzival* contains four Sigune scenes ([1] 138-142, [2] 249-255, [3] 435-442, [4] 804-805). Here, the despairing maiden plays the central guiding instance for the hero's attainment of *saelde* [bliss] (Braunagel 5, 34). So, while *Titurel* relates a young, socially sovereign Sigune (54), *Parzival* tells the story of Sigune the prophet and recluse (55). Further, Albrecht's draws on Wolfram and embellishes the Titurel poem to over 5000 stanzas (Baisch 7). The nude scene alluded to in *Wally* is found only in Albrecht's poem ([1] 1247 and further referenced in [2] 2502 and [3] 4104). This fact prompted scholars to disassociate it from Wolfram's oeuvre, as the depiction did not seem courtly enough (Leitzmann 121f). The overall narrative, however, is largely identical. For the sake of clarity, I will refer to the *Titurel-Parzival-Jüngerer Titurel* complex as *Sigune myth* and treat is as a unified mythological narrative.

further reflection on the grail maiden. Sigune illuminates how *Wally* denaturalizes (Ic) this basic myth by working on traditional female gender positions, the artificiality of courtly love rituals, and the therapeutic function of religion to appease despair.

We may first regard Wally and Sigune's shared talent for love rites. Wally is an expert in the games of courtship. She dances though the night (WDZ 9), rides through the forest encircled by suitors (5), and like everyone else in her social circle seeks excitement (23). In Paris, a married woman now, she receives the attentions of numerous suitors, and triumphs with her expert "coquetry" (WTS 60, 64). A collector of hearts, she accumulates her suitors' rings and insists on their service to regain them (WDZ 7). Like Sigune, she is rather careless when it comes to the consequences of her romantic demands.[61] Wally is not just a flirt; she is a skilled *Minnedame*.

Like Wally, Sigune is an expert in the *ars amandi*. Braunagel notes that the *Titurel* fragments tell the story of the innocent love between the children Sigune and Tschionatulander (36). This love will evolve and render the young girl a sovereign Minne lady (54). But her education in the art of love and its inherent rituals – especially the *Minnedienst* [Minne service] – fails. Like Wally, she confuses Minne with *eros*. She misinterprets the rules of courtly love and hypercorrects their import; instead of focusing on the relationship, she fixates on the rituals. That misinterpretation will result in Tschionatulander's death (58). Braunagel further comments that the concept of courtly love is critically reflected in the fate of this female heroine (60f). *Wally* presents a similar critique of marriage and courtship norms. The Sigune myth, like *Wally*, works by means of a specific dialectic: real vs. societal love (42). Is there real love between Sigune and her knight, or are the immature lovers simply following social protocol? Is love naught but a social requisite? Five hundred years later, Gutzkow's *Wally* asks the very same questions.

As they fail to attain *eros*, Wally and Sigune turn to religion. We need to remember that Minne is a spiritual process meant to attain mental dominion and self-transcendence. Additionally, Kragl explains that Minne is the soul's *love of god* which paves the way to paradise. In contrast, *eros* is received as *Unminne* [Anti-Minne] (163). Unfortunately, this binary is not as clear-cut as it seems. Minne may

---

61 After Wally fails to extract the rings from Cäsar, she will turn to her suitors to restore her honor. The men oblige and challenge Cäsar to a duel (WDZ 8). But while these gentlemen risk their life for her, Wally chooses to "whirl around with the dull and mediocre" on the dance floor (WTS 32). That we are indeed presented with rites of courtly love is made clear by the text. The duel for the rings is suffused with Minne imagery: The five suitors are knights, "die Ritter von den fünf Ringen" (WDZ 11), and as Cäsar is challenged, he comments that he, "the dragon," is happy to face "St George" (WTS 31f).

pave the way to god, but *eros* grants strength and courage. This is exemplified by Sigune's nudity: to *behold* the beloved's naked body grants power (165). The medieval interplay between Minne and Unminne is complex and paradoxical, indeed. However, the dialectic between real and social love is of importance for the novel. Sigune and Wally both misinterpret courtly love, mistaking the rituals for the genuine article (164).

If we remember the confusion of love rites with real love in the Falcon myth, we see that this notion is continued in Sigune. All the characters in *Wally* fixate on the game, on the artifice. But as societal love cannot produce *eros*, all of them, including Wally, are abandoned and forced to face their loss. None of them, however, is able to cope, an inability that leads to their suicides. The medieval women, in contrast, are successful in overcoming their grief: The falcon maiden lets her lover go, and Sigune will find consolation in an ongoing religious love. The medieval maiden possess something the Vormärz lovers lack: religious faith.

Kragl explains that the love between Sigune and Tschionatulander is imagined as ideal love, a love that can shape the world and pave the way to paradise. Yet it can only do so if it remains free of *zwivel* [doubt] (154). Doubt shakes the foundations of the medieval value system, just as it rattles Wally's life. Indeed, the lovers in Gutzkow's novel are excessive characters. There is too much artifice, too much boredom, and, lastly, too much skepticism. Their endeavors are characterized by overcompensation, hypercorrection, and exaggeration. Sigune, however, does not fall short in comparison. She fixates on the service aspects of courtly love; she irrationally focuses on the hound; after her lover's death, she exaggerates her grief (155). Doubt, loss, and grief accompany these characters, and they all – Wally, Cäsar, Tschionatulander, Sigune – exaggerate. But while doubt and grief are transient for the medieval characters, Wally and Cäsar will insist on it. They finally elevate doubt and skepticism to their lives' maxim.

But how does Sigune transcend her grief? Indeed, the grail maiden is a perfect Bärbel at first; she is unable to control her affect. As Parzival meets his cousin for the first time, he is confronted with a woman approaching insanity: She sits on the ground embracing Tschionatulander's corpse; she wails bitterly and tears out her hair (Braunagel 7, 26). Sigune blames herself for her lover's death; at the same time, she understands that is has been her education in (and misinterpretation of) the *ars amandi* that caused her to send the knight on the fatal mission. Thus, she does not seek to return to court but opts for the life of an *inclusa* (58, 60). A retreat from society and a turn to religion aid her to conquer her grief. She ceases her crying and wears a penitent's garment; she buries her lover and prays incessantly at his tomb; she dies and is reunited with her knight in the grave. Her constant retreat from the world effects an ongoing decrease in misery. Sigune, like the falcon maiden, *tames* her grief (26). And like the falcon maiden, she turns to religion to transcend personal pain.

The turn towards religion and spiritual love as therapy goes hand in hand with Sigune's retreat from worldly spheres. It is further accompanied by a loss of the superficial markers of femininity.[62] Her retreat is gradual, parallels her taming of grief and eases her misery. This espousing of spiritual love is motivated by a central virtue of medieval Germany: *triuwe* [loyalty]. According to Braunagel, Sigune transcends societal norms by expanding her loyalty to Tschionatulander beyond the grave (27). She chooses love over social expectations and thereby achieves salvation by following the path of spiritualized love (*Gottesminne*) (55). That path ends in the grave; but it ends not through suicide but by means of a continuous retreat from a painful existence.

Braunagel notes that in the medieval mindset, Sigune offered a female way of overcoming skepticism and pain. This myth, indeed, offers the nucleus of Vormärz gender relations: The male's sphere is the world; his quest is taming and conquest. The female's sphere is love; and if love fails, a life of religion. In its medieval context, Sigune offers a gendered path towards salvation (60, 25). How to achieve earthly and heavenly bliss lies at the core of the Sigune myth: the Love-is-Consolation mytheme. Sigune adheres to this mytheme in overcoming loss and pain by means of a spiritualized love for Tschionatulander and a turn towards religion. Her ongoing loyalty to her lover and the adoption of a religious life console the grail maiden's grief and aid her in attaining perpetual peace.

Wally is the literary exemplification that the Love-is-Consolation mytheme is incompatible with the Vormärz. Sigune's reliance on love and religion presupposes an unwavering commitment to Christianity. While this might have been practical in the 13th century, the theologian Gutzkow leaves little doubt that this strategy must fail in the 19th. Wally's suicide is exemplary of what happens to an intelligent woman if she tries to ground her happiness exclusively on love and religion. The Vormärz was riddled with theological controversy, a fact that Gutzkow was very aware of. The ongoing denaturalization (Ic) focuses such issues, especially on the question of whether it is still possible to build a gender identity, and an *individual* identity, on religious notions. The Sigune myth's love conceptions, courtship rites, and gender roles do not aid Wally or Cäsar. Wally certainly walks Sigune's path, but her death is ugly, brutal, and certainly not spiritual. Indeed, it is her fixation on religion that will ultimately cause her suicide.

---

62 Note that likewise, Hester loses feminine attributes as she repairs to her cottage. The Puritan recluse had been "once a woman" and "ceased to be so" as she is forced to retreat from Boston (SL 107). Similarly, Sigune's lips lose color, her hair is cut, and her dress is replaced by coarse garments (Braunagel 28).

Wally's Path to Desperation

Whereas Sigune is able to find peace by turning to religion, Wally fails to come to terms with the world. In this context, Kaiser is correct in noting that Wally never possessed what could be called faith (195). Her despair is symptomatic of a general disorientation, an inability to resists what Blumenberg calls reality's absolutism: Wally, indeed, fails at *Lebenskunst*. On encountering Cäsar, her artificial world is shattered by his skepticism, and she is unable to reconstruct a stabilizing perspective on reality.

That Wally lacks faith is evident early in the novel. At home, she browses through a pile of books, happens on an illustrated bible, and marvels at the colorful prints. Again, her focus is on the *Schein*, although she seems aware that the prints only serve to distract from the book's contents (WDZ 10). Her relation to the bible is playful; she does not take religion seriously but peruses the bible for amusement: "It is nice to discover mistakes in the Bible" (WTS 33). Her religious engagement is insincere because she suspects that a deeper preoccupation with the topic may be dangerous. Later, Cäsar will inquire whether she believes in Christ's resurrection. Stomped, Wally expresses "great agony" and immediately changes the topic (40). Religion, clearly, is a sensitive spot.

Wally's period of skepticism begins in Schwalbach. Here, she overhears a discussion between Cäsar and Waldemar. This exchange continues the denaturalization (Ib) of the Sigune myth by refuting the idea that love and religion can offer consolation to a Vormärz subject. As Cäsar expresses his belief that religion is born of the human endeavor to make sense of a senseless world, Waldemar admits that he has lost his faith in politics and religion alike. His subsequent self-description foreshadows Wally's future situation:

'Ich bin ein kahler Hügel, jedem Windzuge offen und von jeder Wolke gleich bis tief unter die Augen bedeckt. Nach ideellen Schutzwehren such' ich ebenso vergebens. Die Politik ist nur imstande, meine Schwermut zu vermehren, und die Religion hat man mir durch meine Erziehung verleidet.' (WDZ 37)

'I am a bare hilltop, exposed to every breeze, quickly covered by every cloud, well below eye level. In vain I search for ideal bulkwards. Politics only increases my melancholy, and thanks to my upbringing I've taken a dislike to religion.' (WTS 51)

Here lies the crux of Wally's upcoming predicament. Cäsar and his skeptical lifestyle have torn her out of a shallow existence, but she had no other protection against reality's "cloud[s]" and "breeze[s]" than artifice. Religion and love were Sigune's "bulkwards," but Wally does not have that fighting advantage (ibid.). Indeed, Cäsar holds that religion cannot help in times of desperation, because it is a product of desperation (WDZ 37). However, the novel will differentiate here: The passage distinguishes between real religion, which is a "positive healing force," and institutionalized religion, an "elixir made up of hundred ingredients" overburdened by its own dogmas. In the Vormärz situation, religion has "no effect for the agonies of the soul" (WTS 51). The novel attacks the contemporary institution, and it is in Wally that it exemplifies that modern religion cannot offer solace to the degree that Sigune's medieval religiosity once did.

From this point on, Wally's doubts will intensify. She will begin to speculate, to philosophize. The Waldemar conversation touched a weak point in her, for in all other things, Wally was insincere: She never sought for a "center of gravity in her life," her being "was of the moment and capricious." Yet "only in religious matters did she often pause, like a wanderer on the road who thinks he has lost his way." The Waldemar conversation produced a "religious tic" in Wally, and her doubts begin to turn inward (WTS 53). She realizes that her life has been lived to no avail, that she has never been truly happy, and that her intellect is restricted by gender structures. She suffers from a "spiraling disquiet," which will become a downward "whirlpool" as the plot proceeds (54, 96). Additionally, she begins to understand that her predicament is a socio-mythological one: She is unable to make sense of the world, because no one has ever taught her to give shape to her doubts and anxieties. Indeed, she refers to Ulysses to express her own struggle with the gods:

Die Schilderung jener Zweifel, die eines Menschen Brust durchwühlen können, macht uns vertraut mit ihnen und die Wirkung derselben für uns weniger gefährlich. Aber ich fühl' es, daß sich in jedes Menschen Herzen innere Gedichte entwickeln, eine ganze Historie von Wundern, die wir zu erklären verzweifeln, Gedichte, in denen wir selbst der von den Göttern verfolgte, geneckte, scheiternde, irrende Ulysses sind. (WDZ 42)

The portrayal of the doubts that gnaw at a person's heart helps us understand him more and makes us understand [them] more and makes [their] effects less dangerous to us. But I feel that poems develop in every human soul, an entire chronicle of miracles which we despair of explaining, poems in which we ourselves are Ulysses, hunted by the gods, tormented, failing, erring. (WTS 54)

Wally cannot 'portray' and thereby control her doubts; an inability at mythology *par excellence*. This predicament is negotiated in the realm of religion but constitutes a socio-mythological problem: Mythological, because she lacks the tools to make sense of reality in an aetiological manner; social, because that lack is rooted in her gender position. Interestingly, Cäsar is able to control his skepticism. And he does so mythologically in Blumenberg's sense of *Lebenskunst*: He appropriates the world by means of fictionalization.

Religious skepticism worsens Wally's situation. She suffers from disorientation, then from inner doubt which results in outright desperation. Religious consolation is made impossible by the refutation of institutionalized Christianity. Further, a settling for a more positive and individual spirituality is also impossible because Wally was denied the tools to form existential tenets of her own. Even the recurrence to artificiality is muted as soon as she begins her period of reflection. A return to naivety is not an option anymore; so, she turns to diversion again. In a last escapist act she invests her whole being in her love for Cäsar. "A male heart that loves us is the guardian of all our thoughts" (WTS 86). This, of course, is the opposite of Cäsar's intention in emancipating Wally. Instead of living for and by herself, Wally now "live[s] and die[s] with Caesar." But she knows that this love is merely another way to keep her from reflecting: "Gott, ich glaube, fast brauch' ich Cäsar nur, um mich zu beschäftigen und meinen Gedanken eine unschädliche Richtung zu geben" (WDZ 93).

Indeed, Wally's development runs regressively to Sigune's. Sigune is first overwhelmed by despair and then calms herself by espousing religion. Wally, on the other hand, gradually refutes religion and thereby increases her despair. While Sigune's path to 'victorious death' begins with the loss of her lover, Wally's path to suicide ends with this loss. Wally's skepticism increases over the course of the novel. In the end, she will become a recluse just like Sigune, a reflective writer of diaries. But for Sigune, the retreat from the world meant peace; for Wally, it will mean despair. In the diary section of the book, Wally describes herself as completely lost. She will perceive the world as an arbitrary place, finds joy in ironies, and begins a fruitless search for meaning (WDZ 93ff). At the same time, she mourns the loss of the "childlike legendary saga" called faith (WTS 89). Bereft of religion (and of Cäsar) she has nowhere to turn to for solace: "Ich suche Trost. Wo? Wo?" (WDZ 96). Whereas Sigune could turn to religion, Wally has nothing left. Her last support (Cäsar's love) is gone, and she gives in to absolute despair: "Aber es erquickt mich nichts mehr. Cäsars Liebe war die schönste Zerstreuung meiner unglücklichen Seelenstimmung. Ich sinke immer tiefer in Nacht und Verzweiflung" (100). Finally, Cäsar's *Confessions Concerning Religion and Christianity* pushes her to the extreme.

I cannot go into detail regarding Cäsar's tract.[63] Let is suffice to say that after his critique of German religions institutions, Cäsar becomes political. It is instances

---

63 Cäsar's *Confessions* are informed by the reformist theology of Herman Samuel Reimarus. Reimarus called for a rational approach towards faith, demanded an exegetic treatment of the bible, and refuted pietistic notions. Cäsar adopts some of Reimarus' tenets but mostly critiques the politicization of belief and the inherent feudalism in institutionalized religion. His tract especially opposes religious dogmatism and recurs to pantheistic world

like these that further the denaturalization (Ic) of the Sigune myth: "Our age is political, but not godless," he writes. This age would gladly "couple the freedom of nations with belief in eternity." But Christianity, he continues, "get[s] in the way of political emancipation everywhere." So, Cäsar ends his tract with a call for a new religion based on the *Zeitgeist*: "We live in the time of the Holy Ghost, of whom Christ himself says that he would lead us to all truth and make us free" (WTS 106f).[64] But this freedom can only blossom if it is built on the realities of the now, on the necessities of an age in which one needs to understand that

der Weltgeist rastlos wirkt und in uns schafft und die Wahrheit zuletzt nur der Gottesdienst im Tempel der Freiheit ist. Wir werden keinen neuen Himmel und keine neue Erde haben; aber die Brücke zwischen beiden, scheint es, muß von neuem gebaut werden. (WDZ 124)

the world spirit works without pause and creates within us, and that truth is in the end only the religious service in the temple of freedom. We shall have no new heaven and no new earth – but the bridge between the two, it seems, must be built anew. (WTS 107)

This is not just a call for a new understanding of freedom and religion. It is also an appeal towards re-building the connections between the spiritual and the worldly. Cäsar in no way refutes religion *per se*; but he calls for the establishment of a contemporary religiosity. After Cäsar's separation of romance and marriage earlier in the novel, this passage presents another instance of mythemic elaboration (IIb). Cäsar suggest individual agency to be a sort of subjective "religious service," a true and authentic exercise in the "temple of freedom." There is a shift from dogma to individual liberty here, a turn to a new kind of subjective religiosity hinting towards

---

views to suggest a tolerant and individualistic approach. In his turn to the individual as source of spirituality, Gutzkow's critique is reminiscent of Emersonian tenets. At the same time, *Confessions* leans towards a developing Marxist atheism in its depiction of religion as therapy. However, Cäsar works for a shift from institutionalized religion to a subjective revelation of divine truth. He claims to be living in the "time of the Holy Ghost" and suggest a primacy of subjective inspiration in matters of religion (WTS 107). For more see Groetsch: *Hermann Samuel Reimarus* (2015); Graf: *Profile des neuzeitlichen Protestantismus* (1990), especially Vol. 1 *Aufklärung, Idealismus, Vormärz*.

64 The influence of Hegelian notions regarding the teleology of history is evident in Gutzkow's Wally. The ongoing process of history itself opposes the adoption of medieval realities but demands a focus on the present. Here, Cäsar adopts a Hegelian perspective and calls for the conscious edification of adequate realties for the Vormärz. For a detailed discussion of Hegel see chapter 1.

a new mytheme (*Love-is-Choice*). This mytheme will later establish the variant in Cäsar.

However, Wally misunderstands Cäsar's argument. Instead of realizing the potential for a new beginning in the tract's closing paragraph, she receives the pamphlet like a deathblow. Desperate, she resolves to die (WDZ 124). Her suicide will take another six months, but in that time, Wally achieves complete exclusion from the world. Sigune, too, retreats from the world but dies a natural death. Wally, however, dies based on a purely societal assumption: "Within herself she had a deep conviction that without religion the life of a human being is desolate" (WTS 108).

Does Wally end her life because she felt that a life without faith was not worth living? No: She thinks that life without faith is worthless because society preaches that idea. Despite all her reflections, Wally is still bound by her upbringing. In the end, the skeptic turns to prayer, a last confession that reveals the true reason for her suicide. It is not so much her skepticism that kills her; it is a desperate feeling of loneliness. Comparing her own situation with Jesus in the Garden of Gethsemane, she weeps at the fact that she, too, is utterly abandoned. "Ach, um mich schlafen sie alle, und niemand kennt den Schmerz, der mich verzehrt, niemand wacht mit mir, niemand betet für mich!" (WDZ 125). Later, she will wish the world would "set itself on fire" and thus mock the "hatred of heaven." Wally's hate is again focused on one notion: the human condition. Unable to peak behind the veils and behold truth, she discards the whole human project. Even if humans were able to behold the deity, Wally imagines that deity as someone who "sits behind a curtain and now as before hides his obstinate face and hesitates to come an reveal himself" (WTS 108f).

Wally's trajectory ends in death. She is unable to tame her grief or transcend her despair. On the contrary, her grief increases, and she will ultimately call for the death of all humankind. But while the Wally-Sigune connection clearly foreshadows her death, her suicide is different from Sigune's peaceful passing. Further, their connection reveals the *societal* function of Wally's suicide. Sigune is not only a grail maiden but the medieval formulation of an ancient mythological figure, a half-goddess that brings both death and consolation. In Sigune, Wally the skeptic becomes Wally the Valkyrie.

Wally the Valkyrie and the Guides of the Heroes

One of the central questions of Gutzkow's novel is whether meaning can be assigned to Wally's suicide. Is there a message in her despair? Or is Wally no more than the literary exemplification of a noblewoman incapable of coming to terms with the world? Some contemporary commentators thought so. An English review reads Wally as a representation of German skepticism, a representative citizen of a nation plagued by religious indifference and speculative error. Germany, so the reviewer, is a "whole nation of Wallys" (in Flavell 565). Indeed, even this pessimistic view hints at Wally's dissent and function. Yes, the novel is more critique of the old than a definition of a new social order. But Wally as a social type offers the elaboration of a *status quo* to be overcome (Flavell 565). By describing the consequences of a life lived according to the backward definitions of Vormärz womanhood, the novel calls for a new understanding of love, marriage, and gender relations. The same holds for the male protagonist. Both gender representatives struggle because the traditional, i.e. Germanic terms of identity are incompatible with modernity. If they are taken seriously, they amount to an artificiality that drives anyone, male or female, to desperation.

Wally becomes a living jeremiad. Her despair and suicide are a literary wake-up call aiming at guiding the reader to the realization that a new social order is necessary. Thus, Wally becomes a prophetess. Signne, as mentioned, offers the medieval answers to the overcoming of loss and grief. But Signne's character has both individual and societal functions. While her self-transcendence offers personal identity terms, she also suggests political ones. If we understand Signne as prophetess, we understand Wally's prophecy. And in Wally's prophecy, we are offered the final denaturalization (Ic) of the Signne myth.

Braunagel notes that Signne's function as prophetic guide is evident in her meetings with Parzival. She gives him an identity by telling him his name and informing him of his royal heritage (7); later, as the knight renounces god, the grail maiden acts as teacher and restores his faith (10f). Indeed, Parzival is not just a cousin. In the grail knight, Wolfram constructs the standards of medieval society (3). Parzival embodies the ideal of knighthood, and on his rather unsteady path to salvation, Signne acts as his guide (47). Her overcoming of loss has rendered the grail maiden a wise woman, and she will finally follow the maxim that was embodied by the hound: *Hüete der Verte* [Beware the paths] (37). She disregarded that advice when she sent Tschionatulander on the fatal mission; later, she guides her royal cousin to the fulfillment of his destiny.

I have already introduced the Germanic idea of the wise woman while discussing Hawthorne's Hester Prynne.[65] Grimm notes that the function of these demigoddesses was to guide humanity and prophesize the future, for the ancients held that destiny is always foretold in a female voice. The basic idea is that while men earn their immortality by the sword, women attain immortality in moral and spiritual matters. So, the role of prophet and guide falls to Signne, and she is adored accordingly. Indeed, the nude scene in *Der Jüngere Titurel* and *Wally* is not meant for the male's sexual satisfaction: It is a rite of *adoration*. Grimm explains: The hero receives divine blessing on beholding his naked lover, on thinking of her, and on call-

---

65 cf. chapter 2.3 and 2.4.

ing her name in battle (369f). Tschionatulander asks Sigune to reveal herself in this context; even Cäsar bases his request on the fact that he will travel and may never see her again (WDZ 52). The demigoddesses are the male's guides; they control the hero's fate. Sigune is certainly one of these goddesses: In *Titurel*, she aids in the attainment of victory; in *Der Jüngere Titurel*, she grants power through her nudity; in *Parzival*, she holds and consoles the dying knight in her arms. Thus, Meyer notes that Sigune reveals herself to be one of the war maiden who descend on storm clouds, the envoys of Odin, and the angels of death. In short, Sigune is a valkyrie (176).

Grimm describes a valkyrie as a militant demigoddess, a *Schlachtmädchen*. Her main function is reflected in her name: In Old High German, *wal* means 'the slain' and *kiosa* 'fetch'. The 'Chooser of the Slain' would fly over battlefields, grant victory and strength, but also carry the victorious dead to Asgard, were the heroes would feast with Odin in the Hall of the Slain (Val*halla*) (389). As the warrior dies, he would see

Maidens excellent in beauty
Riding their steeds in shining armor
Solemn and deep in thought
With their white hands beckoning. (Hamilton 439)

But unlike the wise woman Hester, who will hail a new age for Puritan Boston, Sigune tells of endings. Grimm explains that valkyries are not just battle spirits but prophetesses; as spirits of destiny they predict the future (396).

Gutzkow taps into the significance of Sigune-as-Valkyrie and produces a modern variant of the ancient figure. Wally does not overcome her grief, and her religious desperation does not grant the hope for happy endings. Instead, Wally represents a valkyrie gone mad in a time that is not made for valkyries, an age that is not "dominated by the idea of fate" (WTS 53). Gutzkow makes it very clear that he does not believe in the Vormärz as a time of heroes, for the concept of the victorious dead is lost: "das ist das Tragische unsrer Zeit und ein Gefühl, welches die Anschauungen unsrer Welt von dem Zeitalter der Schicksalsidee so schmerzlich verschieden macht" (WDZ 40). Wally's despair cannot be overcome because she is everything *but* a medieval grail maiden; she cannot be a Sigune because Sigune is confined to another epoch. Wally, a creature of the Vormärz, lacks the ability of making sense of the world through faith. She is a skeptic who cannot overcome her skepticism, a true representative of the age. Interestingly, *doubt* becomes the new religion. The divine is imagined to reside in skepticism:

Die Glocken läuteten, aus der nahen Kirche brausten die Töne der Orgel herüber. Wally war in Tränen aufgelöst. Kann man dem Himmel ein schöneres Opfer bringen? Diese Tränen flossen aus dem Weihebecken einer unsichtbaren Kirche. Die Gottheit ist nirgends näher, als wo ein Herz an ihr verzweifelt. (WDZ 10f)

The bells rang, and the tones of the organ thundered from the nearby church. Wally was reduced to tears. Can one offer a more pleasing sacrifice to heaven? These tears flowed from the baptismal font of an invisible church. God is never nearer than when a human heart despairs of his existence. (WTS 33)

The valkyrie in Wally is a prophetic swan maiden whose death in despair contains the call for a new order built on the tenets of the inner "invisible church" (ibid.). Her quest is for individuality, the ability to make sense of the world on her *own* terms. This endeavor is reflected in her wish for romantic immediacy, in her attempts to conquer the "tyranny of withered concepts," and in her effort to overcome the passivity of her gender role. Indeed, she seeks to combat the "plant-like unconsciousness" and the "fortuitousness" of ideas which are inherent to Vormärz femininity (54):

[M]an verlangt nichts von uns, man will gar nichts, es kömmt gar nichts drauf an. Auch dies noch: wir haben einen Ideenkreis, in welchen uns die Erziehung hineinschleuderte. Daraus dürfen wir nun nicht heraus und sollen uns nur mit Grazie wie ein gefangenes Tier an dem Eisengitter dieses Rondells herumwinden. Diese Gefangenschaft unserer Meinungen – ach, war Spreu für den Wind! Rechte will ich in Anspruch nehmen, für wen? für was? (WDZ 42)

[N]obody demands anything of us, nobody wants anything, it's not important at all. And also this: we have a cage of ideas into which our upbringing has tossed us. We are not allowed to leave it and are supposed to move inside the iron bars of this rondel with graceful charm, like a captive animal. This prison of our opinions – oh, we are like chaff before the wind! I want to claim certain rights – for whom? for what? (WTS 54)

In her jeremiad of desperation, Wally becomes the prophetic valkyrie. The novel criticizes the lack of education in German women and holds society responsible for their degeneration to objects of diversion and physical pleasure. Women's intellect is systemically restricted, and Gutzkow laments that his female contemporaries "ceased to comprehend" (in Heintz 197).[66] Thus, Wally is further conceptualized as an ideological dissenter, as a *witch*. In 1852, Gutzkow writes that he designed Wally, or "Walpurgis," as a "little witch" that was to wreak societal havoc (Beigaben

---

66 [sie verstehen uns ja gar nicht mehr].

144).[67] But *Wa*lly the *va*lkyrie is the 'slain' from the start. Further, Walpurgis is the name of an herb that has a very Wally-esque effect: It causes disorientation and insanity (Grimm 1161). But in this disorientation, Wally embodies the call for individuality. Her life exemplifies the fate of the Vormärz female; her suicide is the result of societal oppression. She clashes with statist absolutism and its policies, and her prophecy is a prophecy *ex negtivo*: A jeremiad exemplifying how society should *not* be.

But the question remains whether *Wally, die Zweiflerin* goes beyond criticism. Does it offer alternatives or does it climax in representing the consequences of living according to overcome civic myths? Indeed, there is a variant myth in the novel. That variant is built on the espousing of individuality as a *sine qua non* for an authentic modern existence. In Wally-Sigune, we have been offered the unacceptability of the *status quo*. In Cäsar, however, we will find a variant that resists traditional love conventions and pushes the idea of skepticism as a prerequisite for the enactment of individual agency.

3.5 CÄSAR AND THE CONQUEST OF INDIVIDUALITY

The variant myth in *Wally* is found in the marriage between Cäsar and Delphine. In Delphine, the novel imagines an individual free of societal imprint, an authentic and natural human being. Thus, Cäsar is successful in his search for authenticity and romantic immediacy. Importantly, Cäsar's skepticism finds a tangible expression in his love for Delphine. While the Wally-Cäsar relationship fails because of its artificiality, the Delphine-Cäsar romance succeeds to overcome the civic myth of courtly love and exemplifies a more equal coming together of individuals. In the following, I will present the variant myth and conclude the textual analysis with a discussion of Gutzkow's tract *Wahrheit und Wirklichkeit*.

The Undefined Glimmer of Feeling

Wally introduces Delphine in the diary section of the novel and describes her friend as an oppositional character. Again, Wally starts with the superficial: Delphine is not beautiful, but she "pleases people" by means of "her bearing." It is her "gliding walk" that makes men notice her, and her dress is of such "amazing simplicity" that is contrasts the fashion choices of the protagonist (WTS 83). Delphine is, indeed, a simple woman and differs from Wally not only in beauty but in character. What

---

67 [unsere kleine Hexe Walpurgis].

makes her different is her "peculiar turn of mind:" She is a sentimental, rather naïve young woman, who would fall in love with whoever loves her (84).

Her friend loves for the sake of love, and Wally attempts to critique her naivety in intellectual terms: Delphine is able to "sustain the dialectics of a barely understood logical discussion for a few minutes" but cannot continue unless the discussion is given materiality by practical examples. Also, she cannot judge people abstractly, as she "considers all people good and judges everyone according to herself." It seems interesting that Wally, herself unable of abstraction, should find fault with her friend for the same deficit. At the same time, Delphine is more practical and less abstract in her confrontation with reality than Wally. In order to amend that deficit, Wally recommends that her friend read more: "[She] should try and mold herself by readings on various subjects that lie beyond music and that appeal to more than simple feeling." Is Wally talking about Delphine or about herself? Indeed, Wally will start to read on various subjects, but her studies will leave her disoriented and miserable. Her friend, in contrast, reads extensively but only in a "haphazard way" (WTS 84). Her studies seem to be guided by personal interest rather than external demand, and Wally consents that Delphine is still learning and evolving. However, Wally finds weakness in her friend, a characteristic which renders her "diametrically opposed" to Cäsar. At the same time, Cäsar once told her that he, too, would love any woman who loved him. Wally, however, does not fear an encounter because society would not condone the relationship: "Delphine is Jewish" (85).

There is another, fundamental difference between Wally and her friend: Delphine is not a religious person. She was never educated so as to heed sacred commandments; she has skipped social conditioning – including that of her Jewish heritage – and Wally marvels at the result: "How unique a girl is who never went through the whole process of education in Christian ideas" (WTS 85) In Wally's book, that makes Delphine not only a happy person but offers her friend a direct, immediate connection to the deity:[68]

Glücklich ist Delphine zu nennen, denn niemals wird ihr die Religion irgendeine Ängstlichkeit verursachen. Ein gewisses unbestimmtes Dämmern des Gefühls muß für sie schon hinreichend sein, die Nähe des Himmels zu spüren. Sie braucht jene Stufenleiter von posi-

---

68 Indeed, Wally's predicament can be subsumed by turning to Schleiermacher's subject/object division in the perception of reality. While Wally is unable to negotiate a subjective self in relation to reality, Delphine is imagined as transcending this division, thereby attaining true religiosity. Delphine represents an untainted "Sinn und Geschmack fürs Unendliche" (in Spalding 297). Again, Emersonian notions of transcendence and connectivity to an Oversoul find a parallel here.

tiven Lehren und historischen Tatsachen nicht, die die Christin erst erklimmen muß, um Einsicht in das Wesen der Religion zu bekommen. (WDZ 90)

Delphine can be called happy because religion will never arouse any feelings of anxiety in her. A certain undefined glimmer of feeling must be quite sufficient for her to sense the nearness of heaven. She does not need that latter of positive dogmas and historical facts that the Christian woman must first climb in order to gain insight into the essence of religion. (WTS 85)

Delphine's approach to reality is based on her personal, inner self; the text imagines her free of social mediations. Thus, Wally presents the reader with a person that is not artificial but immediate. Indeed, that immediacy remains ungraspable – it is but a "glimmer" – yet it becomes the foundation of Delphine's happiness (ibid.).

This is why Wally considers her friend's love, the "love of a Jewess," especially interesting for dissenting Christian men. These men will not need to make "allowance for bigotry" but can "delight in [a] pure, unsullied natural femininity." The young Jewess is "swollen with love." Not a socially negotiated love but real love; and Wally knows that Cäsar will find this agreeable (WTS 85). For Cäsar, of course, refuses to see love and marriage as religious institutions. Love, he holds, does not require a priest's mediation but is the "sacrament of marriage" *per se*. This stands in direct opposition to prevailing Vormärz norms, and in loving Delphine, Cäsar would be able to cut the societal middlemen: Courtship rites, gender positions, even church rituals would be nullified. Theirs would be a *civic* marriage, an "act of social agreement." Wally is aware of how much this would appeal to Cäsar. In time, she realizes that Cäsar and Delphine get closer and dreads the effect of their relationship on her own sanity. Yet she would not mourn the loss of love; she would mourn the fact that "everything will then collapse," as it is only Cäsar who can give her thoughts a "harmless bend" (86). Indeed, her lover's therapeutic effect will cease as he announces his engagement to Delphine. His marriage is possible because Delphine's parents are "not prejudiced," and he will move to German territories under French law (89). There will be no church service but a simple civil ceremony (91). Thus, Cäsar will realize his dream of romantic immediacy.

The Inner Poems Myth

Cäsar's development runs parallel to Wally's. Yet while the latter drowns in doubts, Cäsar's trajectory ends in the realization of his wish for immediacy. Both protagonists work through the conditions of the basic myth, only to realize the inapplicability of its standards. Sigune's spiritual stance (Love-is-Consolation) cannot apply to the two Vormärz skeptics. Wally consequently rejects the world, but Cäsar negotiates his own terms of existence in the relationship with Delphine. He refutes medieval norms and shapes a world of his own, outside social expectations and marriage conventions. The Delphine-Cäsar romance presents the novel's attempt to elaborate a new civic myth: The coming together of two individuals regardless of social protocol. Indeed, the naïve Delphine and the jaded Cäsar do not represent the ideal figures of Minne, but it is their imperfection that makes them human, that makes them citizens of the Vormärz. In Delphine, we are given individual potential rather than perfection worthy of adoration. In Cäsar, we encounter a desperate figure searching for truth who finally comes to terms with reality by designing his own truth. These lovers offer the naturalization (IIc) of the variant: the *Inner Poems myth*. It tells of individual beings able to go beyond societal convention and base their romantic relationship not on artifice but on subjective, inner compatibility. Cäsar and Delphine follow personal motivations and subjective emotions; they attempt to realize the "poems" which "develop in every human soul" and which consist of "motifs that the outside world would never recognize" (WTS 54, 111). Instead of adhering to social expectations, Cäsar and Delphine decide to follow their own hearts. Importantly, Cäsar's path towards romantic immediacy is accompanied by a rejection of skepticism *qua* skepticism.

Wally is driven to suicide by her constant reflection on the social construction that is reality. Cäsar, on the other hand, is able to settle for a love construct outside social standards. Thus, he gives shape to a reality that remains ungraspable but that nevertheless requires articulation in order to be lived. Skepticism for Cäsar evolves from an escapist activity that ensured his survival to the foundation of a stable relationship; his marriage is based on dissent. Wally, on the other hand, espouses skepticism for its own sake and fails to generate meaning. Gutzkow's characters thereby offer a literary commentary on the function of Young German criticism. Doubt, critique, and skepticism can be but means to the edification of a new and improved social reality. If employed solely for their own sake, these instruments have disastrous effects, Wally being the tragic exemplification. The fight for the primacy of individuality, the material "emancipation of the flesh," and the rejection of overcome social standards requires critique, but critique is not an end in itself (Jones and Lauster 14). The same goes for the idea of freedom. Freedom is nothing more than the ability to make choices. But decision making requires skepticism in order to make the individually appropriate choice, and Cäsar's radical skepticism finds an end in his choice to marry Delphine. It is important to note that this is still a marriage: He does not refute the concept itself but re-imagines marriage norms to fit his own personal convictions.

One may, of course, argue that the Delphine-Cäsar romance is just as artificial as the Wally-Cäsar relationship; that Cäsar opts for Delphine only because he finds her social position refreshing and a marriage outside societal norms desirable. It may be that this new relationship is also built on a game rather than on *eros*. Unfortunately, the novel offers very little information on Cäsar's last conquest. We know nothing of the manner of his courting. In fact, Gutzkow keeps this new relationship veiled. Had the author given details, he would have been forced to determine exact courtship rites; yet it seems that he would rather see these rites developed individually. The Cäsar-Delphine romance is not meant to be a blueprint for love and happiness, another social codex by which to live. Just as Wally's death, it is a socio-poetic prophecy, a fictionalization of possibility.

The Inner Poems myth revolves around the confirmation of individuality, not its transcendence. This dissents from the traditional myths that informed the novel. The falcon maiden transcends her loss by objectifying herself, and Signe recurs to religion in order to find peace. Both mythological characters abjure their individuality in order to serve. Wally, unable to find anything she could base her identity on, commits suicide. But Cäsar and Delphine do not transcend their individuality in order to comply with societal norms: They celebrate it. In this relationship, the new civic myth advocates modern individuality in the face of a medieval understanding of subjectivity. Here, being your own person is not a "Luciferian act"[69] anymore, and bliss is not found in the conforming to social categories. In the Falcon and the Signe myth, the medieval "individual erases itself and finds happiness in the consciousness of heteronomy." But by refuting the objectification of individuality, Cäsar and Delphine follow an individual path. They become *modern* human beings, citizens of an age "where the individual discovers itself and pursues its bliss by insisting on autonomy" (Minnesänger 17).[70]

Courtship, love, and marriage thus attain a new center. While the Signe myth produces a protocol focused on societal value, the variant centers on the individual as its normative source. Courtship rites, gender positions, and notions of possession are thus no longer a social *a priori* but conditioned and designed by the individuals themselves. Indeed, this does not mean that social rites are overcome; it only means that they become subjectively negotiated and legitimized. Cäsar's marriage is still a marriage, albeit one of his own design. The novel presents a variant myth that offers a new civic tenet: the *Love-is-Choice* mytheme. In contrast to the Love-is-Consolation mytheme in the Signe myth, this new mytheme constitutes the primacy of individual choice in matters of love. Wabnegger notes that *Wally* discusses the shift from a classical-idealist conception of reality to something more pragmatic and worldly. It searches for meaning not in eternity but in the moment itself (45). In

---

69 [luziferischer Akt].
70 [Neuzeit ist da, wo das Individuum sich selbst entdeckt, und sein Glück im Pochen auf seine Autonomie sucht. Mittelalter ist da, wo das Individuum sich selbst auslöscht und sein Glück im Bewusstsein der Heteronomie empfindet].

its final bend, it allocates the legislative power regarding laws of love in the individual rather than in society.

This shift from societal cohesion (Love-is-Consolation) to individual sovereignty (Love-is-Choice) is of course deeply connected to the novel's political message. The basic Sigune myth (and its preparatory Falcon myth) can no longer sustain courtship rites and marriage norms. A new myth is necessary to adequately negotiate such values. At the same time, these negotiations are not restricted to the realm of love. In Wally and Cäsar, we find characters that desperately yearn for individuality, freedom, and human immediacy. Gutzkow's call for equal gender relations and female emancipation is also a call for general freedom and citizen emancipation. The oppressed female stands in for the oppressed human, the conquering male for the revolutionary citizen. Wally embodies a socio-prophetic warning and Cäsar recommends the establishment of individual sovereignty.

But what does individual sovereignty mean? What does the text envision for the future of a democratic Germany? What are the tenets of a democratic national identity? It is in Gutzkow's closing definition of truth, reality, and art that we find how inseparable art and life were thought of in the Young German mindset.

The Aesthetics of Truth

Throughout the analysis, we have discussed real love, true immediacy, and genuine feelings. Following the text, I have implied the existence of a reality and truth which contrast artificial and socially determined realities. It is time to discuss these notions, for as soon as we understand Gutzkow's conception of truth, we understand what it was the characters in *Wally* yearned for. The relation between truth and reality is discussed in the last pages of the novel in form of a tract entitled *Wahrheit und Wirklichkeit*. Eke notes that these pages were added in order to reach a page count that would free the novel of preliminary censorship (78). But *Wahrheit und Wirklichkeit* is more than that: It is a political-aesthetic manifest that allows us to better understand the novel itself. Here, Gutzkow offers a conceptualization of truth, a genuine truth that is internal and veiled. He does not deny a physical reality but postulates a realm which lies beyond the objective and socially constructed:

Unendlich ist das Reich der Möglichkeit, jenes Schattenreich, das hinter den am Lichte der Begebenheiten sichtbaren Erscheinungen liegt. Es gibt eine Welt, die, wenn sie auch nur in unsern Träumen lebte, sich ebenso zusammensetzen könnte zur Wirklichkeit wie die Wirklichkeit selbst, eine Welt, die wir durch Phantasie und Vertrauen zu combinieren vermögen. (WDZ 128)

Possibility, the realm of shadows that lies behind the visible manifestations in the lights of events, is an endless realm. There is a world which, even if it only exists in our dreams, could just as easily be pieced together to form reality, like reality itself, a world which we are capable of deducing through imagination and trust. (WTS 110)

Gutzkow postulates a "realm of shadows" that lies behind and is before the world's visible manifestations. However, the visible world is imagined as constructed, pieced together by "imagination and trust." The world of possibility, decidedly a first-order realm, offers the building blocks of reality. Gutzkow holds that if one had access to the realm of possibility, one could build one's own world. This is where the freethinking individual comes in: The "shallow" minds are aware and content with the given; the "gifted minds" sense what could be; but the "free minds" become creators of their own realities (ibid.): "Freie bauen sich ihre eigne Welt" (WDZ 128).

Gutzkow continues by discussing the "guarantees" of this realm of shadows. One is religion, which hopes to offer comfort against reality; the other is poetry, which seeks to explain reality. Both, he notes, are based on illusions, only that poetry has plausibility on its side: "It is easier to believe in a poem than in heaven." When he talks about poetry, he does not simply mean the art and craft of writing. Poetry is conceptualized as *Lebenskunst* in Blumenberg's sense, an empowering outlook on reality which elevates the human being to creator.[71] So while poetry deals with "motifs explaining reality" and uses analogy to make the shadow world graspable, religion remains abstract and confusing. "[H]eaven floats in the air and, despite all its philosophy, is measureless, like God himself" (WTS 110). At this point, we may remember Wally comparing herself to Ulysses: "But I feel that poems develop in every human soul, an entire chronicle of miracles which we despair of explaining, poems in which we ourselves are Ulysses, hunted by the gods" (54). For Gutzkow, these inner poems are individual truths, manifestations of the realm of possibility. There are millions of motifs in the inner world of the individual, and piecing them together is the poetic work on reality: "Whoever is attentive to his development must often confess to himself that whole poems are put together within him, consisting of motifs that the outside world would never recognize" (111). These poems are unreal but for Gutzkow nevertheless true: "Dies sollte nicht auch Wahrheit sein?" (WDZ 130). Indeed, Cäsar and Delphine succeed in creating a graspable reality by following their inner poems; Wally, on the other hand, fails in articulating them.

For the comprehension of such truth, Gutzkow differentiates between three types of individuals and elaborates this differentiation in three types of artists. First,

---

71 cf. chapter 5.1 for Heine's elaborations on the poet as *alter deus*.

there are the "shallow" minds who only see and seek what they call reality. Second, there are the "free minds" who opt for the invisible truth. Third, the "gifted minds," people of taste and education, opt for a middle ground, for probability. Of course, Gutzkow champions the free: "[O]nly the free minds decide without asking, because they feel that what does not happen is still truth, even if it cannot happen." In contrast, Gutzkow claims that the shallow and the gifted cannot deal in the poetics of truth, and artists of their brand, from "Walter Scott" to "Kotzebue," are as artificial as Wally's attempts towards the poetic. Their aesthetics is "bright, glossy and polished, because it is a mirror of reality that reproduces it faithfully." This literature, Gutzkow holds, is only for "the masses," nothing more than an attempt at "copying reality" (WTS 110). It is tame, dull, and autogamous: "Die Poesie ist jetzt Selbstbefruchtung" (WDZ 129). Naturally, the Young German calls for a different kind of poetics, one that will follow truth, not reality.

True literature, Gutzkow claims, has little to do with reality. It is creative, disruptive, and, most importantly, revolutionary:

Die Wahrheit selbst ist unsichtbar und liegt niemals in dem, was wirklich ist. Die poetische Wahrheit ist schöpferisch. Sie baut mit den geheimsten Fäden der menschlichen Seele, sie combiniert [...] revolutionär. Die poetische Wahrheit offenbart sich nur dem Genius. Dieser lauscht niedergestreckt auf den Boden der Wirklichkeit und hört, wie in den innersten Getrieben der Gemüter eine embryonische Welt mit keimendem Bewußtsein wächst. (WDZ 130)

Truth itself is invisible and never lies in what is real. Poetic truth is creative. It builds with the most secret threads of the human soul [...] in a revolutionary way. Poetic truth reveals itself only to the genius. Streched out on the ground of reality, the genius listens and hears how an embryonic world with an emerging awareness grows in the innermost workings of the mind. (WTS 111)

Yet this, Gutzkow holds, was not the way the German forefathers created; their literature "stands petrified in temples and Valhallas." A modern Germany needs to adopt a creative truth. The world as it is will have no place in literary creations, but authors will follow the "ideas that slumber in the bosom of the deity that silently effects and creates." Of course, they will be reproached, but Gutzkow notes that a true genius "has always been ahead of his century" (ibid.).

This aesthetic stance, he believes, will have political consequences. Literature devoted to truth is an "ideal opposition" which will have two very distinct enemies: first, reality itself in the form of authority (the state); second, the poetry of reality (other poets). While this seems a rather literary and therefore extra-societal issue, Gutzkow makes clear that this is not just an aesthetic problem. It is a "symptom" of the time, and the Young German ventures to advise a general notion to alleviate the chasm between truth and artifice: experimentation (WTS 112).

Experimentation is Gutzkow's policy for the development of a democratic national identity. Gutzkow fears that mankind is afraid of experimentation to a harmful degree. There are institutions, like "custom, opinion and political arrangement," that are deemed indispensable to an extent that approaches irrationality. As "if mankind had no inner resources;" as "if mankind will not always be the first to help itself, and the one that knows the best course to take" (WTS 112). He therefore advises courage to experiment in all areas of human existence, even if the results cannot be predicted. The age, so much is clear, needs something new, something contemporary, something *true*. And that truth can only be attained by re-evaluation, reform, and, if necessary, revolution:

Sie zucken die Achseln wie unvorsichtige Ärzte, sie fürchten für das Leben der Patienten und quacksalbern an den alten Schädeln herum; aber nehmt der Menschheit ein Bein ab: sie wird sich ein neues machen; nehmt ihr, um nur eines, was unmöglich scheint, zu nennen, z.B. das Christentum: glaubt ihr, daß sie untergehen wird? Nehmt ihr eure Gesetzbücher, eure Verfassungen – nehmt ihr zuletzt das, worauf gleichsam alles ankommen soll, nehmt ihr euch selbst! – und die Menschheit wird fortbestehen. (WDZ 131)

They shrug their shoulders like careless doctors, they fear for the life of the patient and doctor up the old wounds; but take a leg off of mankind, and it will grow itself a new one; take away, for example, Christianity, only to name something that seems impossible – do you think that it would come to an end? Take away your lawbooks, your constitutions, and finally take away what should really matter, take away yourself! – and mankind will persist. (WTS 112)

Gutzkow bases his call for change on his faith in humanity's ability to cope with loss. Simultaneously, he presents a novel whose protagonist is unable to do so. Wally's inability to make sense of her inner poems is rooted in a notion which Gutzkow refutes in his closing tract: the elevation of reality over truth. Wally's attempts fail because she relies on dogmatic vocabulary. Cäsar, on the other hand, chooses a poetic, i.e. creative strategy of dealing with an adverse reality: He designs his own world. This is the suggested path for Germany's national future: A radical redefinition of national identity based on cultural and political experimentation.

I have already mentioned that the mythological resignification in *Wally* focuses on the denaturalization of the basic myth (Ic) more than on the naturalization of a variant (IIc). The last paragraph of *Wahrheit und Wirklichkeit* explains this. Gutzkow does not offer a detailed variant that would render a distinct national identity; he rather postulates individual and societal experimentation so as to *create* such an identity. Gutzkow fears that a society stuck in overcome rituals, a culture that will not move with the *Zeitgeist*, cannot achieve truth. It simply starts to replicate itself and gradually elevates the situational to the universal. Wally failed for the same reason: She was a reader unable to write. Likewise, Germany seems to be stuck in trying to read a Germanic past instead of writing the German present. But Cäsar conquered because he opted for a creative approach; he wrote his own story. For Gutzkow, only the creative strategy is successful in producing the foundations of a free existence. His call for experimentation is the attempt to free his contemporaries from the structures of ages gone by. Indeed, the whole novel tries to argue that refusing the now and copying the past must lead to a life of artificiality and despair. But while Wally fails, Gutzkow has hope for humanity based on his belief that humankind, no matter the circumstances, will be able to draw on inner poems to make its way: "Sie wird alles ertragen und durch Felsen von stärkstem Granit noch immer einen Weg finden, der sie zu ihrem Ziele führt" (WDZ 132).

4. William Wells Brown's *Clotel* and the Puritan Voyage Reversed

> Until he write, where all eyes rest
> Slave of master on his chest
> EMERSON/ASTRAEA

In *The Scarlet Letter* and *Wally, die Zweiflerin*, we encountered dissenting individuals who by developing their own subjective freedom expanded their polity's horizon. While Hester opens the Puritan regime to the possibilities of mercy and dissent, Cäsar designs his life and marriage on the basis of a radical individuality meant to inform society as a whole. The following analyses will continue the focus on dissenters. I will examine characters that set out to find and fight for personal liberty. Their journeys once again resignify civic myths in a way that allows for the imagination of more inclusive and democratic realities.

Part II, *The Treading of Pathways*, will continue to ask how myth was used to sever the ties with the past while at the same time construct a future on given mythological foundations. The American and German texts in question focus on *personal* journeys; they offer variant myths that present new possibilities and the means for the construction of a more democratic national identity for the U.S. and Germany. These are stories of *Wanderschaft*, fictional as well as factual accounts of roads taken in the hope of finding freedom, liberty, and the possibility of individuality.

4.1 Establishing Individuality and the Roads towards Freedom

In 1847, Brown published his autobiographical account *Narrative of William W. Brown* in Boston. He thus contributed to the upcoming genre of fugitive slave narratives, tales made popular by Frederick Douglass' *Narrative* (1845) and later boosted by the popularity of Harriet Beecher Stowe's *Uncle Tom's Cabin* (1852). Andrews notes that slave narratives became epic in nature and played on the American imagination in a way that rendered them "modern odysseys," journeys that "gave expression to a romantic concept of the human spirit." Fugitives like Brown became American "culture-hero[es]" whose journey "exemplified the American romance" and directly touched upon "America's raison d'être" (98).

In contrast to his autobiography, *Clotel* was Brown's first attempt to write about and against slavery in the form of fiction. But the fact that he prefaced his novel with a version of his autobiography shows how entangled fact and fiction present themselves when discussing American slavery. The novel, indeed, is fictional, but it rests on historical facts which are related in a manner that goes beyond the strictness of objective historiography. *Clotel* is a novel that wishes to inform; in order to do so, it taps into myth yet not in the romantic manner which Hawthorne and Gutzkow adopted. It concerns itself with cultural scripts that define the nature, character, and norms of America as a polity and as a people. Brown works on myth in a *personalized* manner and his mythological resignification not only rewrites civic narratives but elevates the heroic life stories of enslaved individuals to the realm of myth. These individuals become American heroes, a transformation that aims at their incorporation into the myths of the nation. As Fabi notes, *Clotel* is a collection of lessons in interpretation. The novel critiques racist presuppositions and offers the "adequate tools to interpret" the nation's civic narratives (xv). Its characters move from one place to another and embark on journeys in the hope for freedom. Their stories are prefaced by Brown's own personal narrative, a narrative that prepares (Ia) for the novel's mythological resignification.

Hunting for a Name

Brown is often referred to as the author of the first novel by an African-American, a designation that pertains to literary history but also to literary African-American identity politics (Levine 3).[1] While it makes sense to define this author as founda-

---

[1] For a recent discussion regarding the genesis and nature of African-American literature, see Warren: *What was African American Literature* (2012). Regarding Brown's Pan-

tional to a genre, it is helpful to recognize a broader perspective in his work: Brown writes from, of, and for a national viewpoint. Modern and historical criticism has recognized the fact that he "labored for the good not only of Negroes but of all his fellow Americans" (Farrison xi). Like Hawthorne and Gutzkow, he does not focus on partisan politics but succeeds in taking a more generalized position. That does not mean that his writings are disinterested. Indeed, slavery and the ongoing suffering of the black population force the author to push for a more enlightened state of affairs in the American polity. But Brown's mythological resignification (just as his Abolitionist work) celebrates Enlightenment values.[2] Following Gould, I understand Antebellum literature such as *Clotel* as "part of an Enlightenment historical legacy constituting not only a seamless tradition but a period [...] characterized by points of continuity and transformative change" (119). In this tradition, Brown focuses on the life of individuals so as to critique the *status quo* and offer solutions for democratic improvement by recurring to myth. In addition, his stories carry an aesthetic of the personal.[3]

Africanism and African Nationalism, see especially chapters 2 and 5 in Archer: *Antebellum Slave Narratives* (2009).

[2] There has been much criticism regarding the Enlightenment in recent scholarship. Gates' *Figures in Black* (1989), for instance, highlights the Enlightenment's primacy of literacy and the necessity of authentification of black writers. Further, in *The Black Atlantic* (1995), Gilroy critiques the separation of modernity's positive development from the histories of slavery and race. Indeed, criticism regarding an (Eurocentric) Enlightenment is certainly justified. The brute facts of modernity, i.e. race discourses, colonialism, and slavery, must be part of any comprehensive analysis of Enlightenment ideas. Still, a general rejection is equally fallible. It is especially in the emancipatory notions of the Enlightenment, e.g. individuals rights, benevolent humanism, belief in progressive history etc., that Antebellum writers found a philosophical phalanx against the horrors of slavery. Contemporary judgment of such ideas, and the fact that Western rationalism is/was both compatible with and complicit in racism, does not obliterate the fact that it was Enlightenment values that were relied upon when furthering abolition. For more see Drexler and White (eds): *Beyond Douglass* (2011), herein especially Richards: *Anglo-American Continuities of Civic and Religious Thought in the Institutional World of Black Writing*; Gould: *Early Black Atlantic Writing and the Cultures of Enlightenment*; Saillant: *Aspirant Citizenship*.

[3] The aesthetic of the personal is based on Brown's notion of discourse history. Andrews notes that the autobiographical element in slave narratives highlights two particular notions. First, the fugitive's person and their personal experience are highlighted by the genre. Second, this kind of centrality is justified by the fugitives' specific personal experience which offers the opportunity of building a connection to readers. Indeed, the recon-

Brown's autobiography was a successful slave narrative. In the first six months alone, the book sold approximately 3.000 copies and fueled the demand for a second edition. All in all, four editions were published, selling approximately 10.000 copies in two years (Farrison 114). The fact that Brown prefaced *Clotel* with his autobiography is significant. First, the reprinting of *Narrative* elevated the author's subsequent (and fictional) elaborations by proving his real-life expertise. By revealing the effects of the South's "real chivalry" in his own life, he contextualized slavery in his own personal history (CL 6).[4] Prefacing *Clotel* with this account is an attempt at heightening the legitimation and truth-value of the novel; it grounds denunciations of slavery in biography and explains the author's comprehensive knowledge of slavery and the slave trade.[5] Importantly, the account includes reviews from several papers discussing Brown's literary endeavors (36-38). *Narrative* evidences his expertise in matters of slavery but also presents the once-fugitive as a man of letters. His status as ex-slave and his intellectual position thus legitimize and support the subsequent novel.

If fugitive slaves become epic travelers in the American imagination, then their establishing of personal identities carries an Adamic import. The mythological act to name reality and thereby assume control over it also applies to the act of self-

---

struction of a fugitive's life can only occur successfully if their life is taken seriously (by reader as well as authors). Consequently, said life story must construct and contain value for others. Thus, slave narratives are always subject to the poetic process, blurring the lines between fact and fiction (16). Also, the inclusion of the reader and their world into this poetic process adds to the narrative impetus. A slave narrative is also an attempt to open the channels of communication with the Antebellum world of whites. It is oratorical in character, persuasive in style, didactical in intent, and representative or allegorical in the description of a life (17). The importance of the implied reader in the process of writing proves advantageous to the modern researcher: Because black autobiography embodies the consciousness of its author and the (received) consciousness of the audience, it "offers special access to the myths, norms, ideals, and self-perception" of Antebellum culture (30). The personal aesthetics employed in Brown's texts includes a perspective on the foundational mythologies of the Antebellum.

4   For quotation purposes I use the annotated Penguin Edition edited by Fabi: *William Wells Brown. Clotel or, The President's Daughter* (2004). Quotations will be given as (CL) throughout. Other primary sources will be abbreviated in the same manner.

5   In Narrative, the reader learns that Brown witnessed violence against his mother and sister (CL 6), sought to escape with his mother and failed (13), and was then forced to work for a slave trader (7f). The account goes on to tell of his ardent "love of freedom" that inspired his successful escape (19), and later gives proof (in form of letters and recommendations) as to Brown's occupation as Abolitionist lecturer and orator.

naming and name-claiming. Of his first days of freedom, Brown wrote: "I was not only hunting for my liberty, but also hunting for a name" (in Andrews 105). Brown, who experienced slavery firsthand, knew how it felt to be without a true name; Farrison notes that his family constellation (and his light skin complexion) complicated the racist slave-freeman dialectic from the beginning. This early confusion regarding matters of color triggered critical reflection and a feeling of arbitrary discrimination in the young man. Growing up, Brown was ever more aware of slavery's blatant injustice; especially as the denominating factor – color – revealed itself as arbitrary when he considered his own person (5, 12). This sense of being wronged climaxed in a family episode described in *Narrative*. As a white boy named William joined his household, Brown was renamed Sanford. The young slave interpreted this as nominal theft, an act that no "logic of slavery" could possibly justify (14).

In this context, *Narrative* served, quite literally, to give Brown a cultural position and a *name*. When it first appeared in 1847, he employed a first-person narration throughout. The revised version which was used to preface *Clotel*, however, employs a third-person narration. This switch of narrative register served to preempt charges of unreliability and stressed objectivity, thereby making the story of an individual representative for the entire slave population. Simultaneously, the third-person narrator highlights the protagonist's identity and repeatedly refers to him by his full name. In a societal context, Brown' personal voyage was given as "living proof, against the claims of proslavery and racist ideology, of an African American's ability to become a learned man of letters" (Levine 5). Yet *Narrative* also stresses Brown's personal individuality, his name, and intellectual position. The fact that a former slave claims such a position and insists on his own name must be seen as a conscious statement of identity.

The fact that slave narratives aim to assert individuality and identity is important for the mythological resignification in *Clotel*. Indeed, the preface offers the preparation of the basic myths (Ia). It presents the preparatory story of a person seeking freedom through voyage and resistance. Also, the preparation illuminates another crucial point. The mythological resignification in *Clotel* differs from Hawthorne and Gutzkow's. In imagining fugitive slaves (and himself) as American culture-heroes and describing their modern odysseys, Brown employs an *affirmative treatment* of myth. The novel confirms civic myths and assents to rather than dissents from their mythemes of voyage and resistance. Brown makes use of this strategy in order to incorporate black subjects into the hero-categories of the basic myths: Fugitive and insurgent slaves are imagined as homologous to the Puritan and Revolutionary fathers. Brown's variant myths naturalize the black subject as American hero and heir to the founders of the nation. In fact, his treatment of the Puritan and Revolution myth denaturalizes Antebellum *interpretations* of these narratives but not the myths *per se*. His variants call for a *return* to the foundational values of the American geneses, because he imagines the despotic development of the U.S. to be rooted in a misinterpretation of its own civic myths. *Clotel* seeks to correct this by offering the interpretative tools for the return to a democratic and humanist mythological reading. Consequently, the resignification in this novel lacks a mythemic elaboration (IIb). The text stays true to traditional mythemes throughout.

Gutzkow and Hawthorne resignified myths to adapt them to a modern situation. Brown's novel, in contrast, aims at the *incorporation* of slave identities into American civic myths so as to *readapt* the modern situation to traditional myths.[6] While the novels discussed in Part I reject basic myths because of their incompatibility with modernity, Brown seeks to readapt the modern situation to once again adhere to traditional myths. Therefore, *Narrative* foreshadows the emergence of modern culture-heroes who re-enact given mythological narratives. These characters are elaborated by focusing on their voyages, instances of migration which develop and produce their freedom and identity.

In *Narrative*, Brown comments on identity and freedom when he describes his stay with Mr Wells Brown, a Quaker who aided his escape. For the first time, the fugitive feels that he is "no more chattel, but a MAN." This change is received as so radical that it produces an identity crisis: "The fact that I was a freeman—could walk, talk, eat, and sleep as a man, and no one to stand over me with the blood-clotted cow-hide—all this made me feel that *I* was not *myself*"(CL 20).[7] The Quaker explains that Brown has "become a man," and that "men always have two names." Brown wishes to express his gratitude by granting his benefactor the right to name him, with one reservation: "I am not willing to lose my name of William. It was taken from me once against my will, and I am not willing to part from it on any terms" (21). Thus, Brown both claims ('William') and receives ('Wells Brown') his name.[8]

---

6   The construction of a black Puritan and a black Revolutionary is not restricted to U.S. American literature. In the context of the Haitian Revolution (1791-1804), C.L.R. James' novel *The Black Jacobins* (1938) elaborates on Toussaint L'Ouverture, a Haitian revolutionary born into slavery and later adopting the ideals of the French Revolution in his fight against Colonial powers.

7   Italics MRD.

8   Pennington also comments on the nature of slave-names in *The Fugitive Blacksmith*. He elaborates on the fact that slavery "robbed him" of an early education, which had consequences for his personal and societal identity (TFB 56). Due to this theft, his name is nothing more than an item on a list of property: "When I was laid in my cradle, he came and looked on my face, and wrote down my name upon his barbarous list of chattels personal, on the same list where he registered his horses, hogs, sheep, and even his *dogs*!" (57). The "chattel relation" robbed him "of his manhood," and "no where" could he find "any record of himself as a man" (xii).

The significance of names is further revealed in an episode where Brown learns to write. He meets a boy who informs him that he had been writing his name incorrectly. The boy then writes the correct version on a fence with a piece of chalk. Brown proceeds to cover that fence "for nearly a quarter of a mile" with his name, until he succeeds in writing it correctly (CL 24). I read this as a repetitive nominal performance, an Adamic act of self-naming and self-assertion. Importantly, it entails the *publication* of a private identity. It is helpful to regard the repetitive writing of Brown's name and the prefacing of *Clotel* with *Narrative* as two expressions of the same desire: to articulate and create an emancipated *self*.[9]

In spelling out his name (and life) to the reader, Brown personalizes the novel's narrative mode and foreshadows the focus on personal life stories constitutive to *Clotel*. Throughout, we are faced with accounts of slavery that – because of the preface – are rendered in a personalized voice. Hawthorne, for instance, employed a similar strategy by prefacing *The Scarlet Letter* with *The Custom House*. But while Hawthorne offers a metonymic account of the state of the nation (exemplified by his hometown Salem), Brown invites us to share his own life voyage. This voyage foreshadows other voyages in the novel, and its account serves as both: a critique of slavery and an exemplification of the emancipated slave's potential. This has consequences in the context of mythological resignification. A personal history is generalized, and the fugitive's voyage thus enabled to touch upon the *Freedom-through-Voyage* mytheme of the Puritan myth and on the *Freedom-through-Resistance* mytheme of the Revolution myth.

Hawthorne focused on societal and national horizons; his goal was the improvement of society in which the subject may be free. Brown and Gutzkow, on the other hand, sought the liberation of the subject, which would free the nation. They invite us to share the road and recognize the larger design in the individual life. This is, without question, problematic. The objectification of a fugitive's biography may present yet another form of oppression.[10] Nevertheless, Brown employed this strategy in his multiple editions of *Narrative* and *Clotel*.

---

9   One may safely join Andrews in describing slave narratives as Emersonian. As writing that makes the self, these narratives uphold the living discourse celebrated by the Transcendentalists. In sum, they are stories that claim independence, insist on self-allegiance, and postulate a truth that is consistent with subjective intuition rather than objective facts (102f). Again, we are reminded of Gutzkow's elaborations in *Wahrheit und Wirklichkeit*, cf. Chapter 2.4.

10 cf. Andrews' elaborations on the narrator's objectification in chapter 3 of *To Tell a Free Story* (1986).

Clotel was first published in England in 1853. Like *Narrative*, it was revised multiple times throughout Brown's lifetime.[11] Indeed, Brown acts as author, collector, and editor of cultural material (Farrison 354). Levine comments that Brown's constant editing and rewriting bear witness to his understanding of what it means to write: "Appropriation and revision are part of an author's ongoing dialogue with the present and the past; arguably, these practices are central aspects of what could be termed authorial power" (292). This approach, however, employs mythologies, and Levine notes that it is useful to think of Brown as a plagiarist in this context, an author who regards plagiarism as a form of trickery. The author becomes a thief, a person who "abducts" meaning. Importantly, Brown's "taking of texts" can also be seen in terms of a literary *emancipation* of what was taken. Indeed, this strategy creates a nexus with slavery: Brown "steals the texts of a culture that steals black bodies" and "attempts to liberate a variety of texts by placing them in an 'improper' relation within his revisionary narrative" (6). Here, Levine describes the very core of mythological resignification. Myth, following Barthes, is "speech stolen and restored" (125). Similarly, Brown "subvert[s] and transform[s] the very discourses that he imports into his novel" (Levine 7). Like Gutzkow, the author of *Clotel* constructs his resignification as a revelation of inadequacy, with the significant difference that Brown sees the polity as lacking, not the myth. He attempts to reveal a "national disunity – not the meaninglessness of the national text but its meaningful incoherence" (Ernest in Levine 7). Thus, the reader is forced to reflect upon prevailing civic myths and "rethink the politics and deeds of the nation's Founding Fathers" (Levine 7).

Historical as well as literary material is appropriated, transformed, and reinstalled in order to educate the reader on slavery.[12] These acts of revising given material will be of importance when discussing the writing of variant myths in *Clotel*. Brown – the author-editor – "talks back" to U.S. culture by stealing its myths and thus challenges and rewrites the "nation's patriotic narratives" (Levine 3). Indeed, Brown is not alone in his authorial self-image as editor of history. He finds a fellow thief in Hawthorne, who also prefaced his novel with a detailed and personalized

---

11 For a detailed account of the revision process of Clotel and Narrative, see Levine: *Clotel* (2011), especially Chapters 3 and 4.

12 Georgina's liberation speech, for instance, is reminiscent of Jackson's well documented proclamation to black troops in New Orleans in 1814. Much of what we are told of the slave-rebel Picquilo is based on Turner's *Confessions* (1831). Weld's *American Slavery as it is* (1831) delivers the material for Peck's discussion of plantation slavery. On the literary side, Child's short-story *The Quadroon*, Greenwood's poem *The Leap from the Long Bridge*, and, lastly, Stowe's *Uncle Tom's Cabin* offered further material for Brown's work (Levine 295).

autobiographical account.[13] But once the individuality of the author-editor is established, they continue to revise, rewrite, and reinterpret history and myth in their novels. And just like Hawthorne, Brown looks to the Puritan fathers.

4.2 THE PURITAN VOYAGE REVERSED

Loggins notes that Brown's book offers material for a dozen novels (in Farrison 230). Indeed, *Clotel* is a text of multiple and interwoven plotlines, entailing a number of separate stories which may all stand by themselves. Consequently, the mythological resignification at work here is concentrated not on the over-all plot but on select instances. Further, Brown uses the Puritan as well as the Revolution myth as basic myths. The myth of the Puritan fathers offers the basic material for the first instance of mythological resignification in *Clotel*.[14]

Brown makes use of Puritan ship imagery throughout the text and unfolds it gradually so as to lead the reader to an ever increasing understanding of its meaning.[15] Thus, the text continues to prepare (Ia) for the subsequent exposition of the basic myth. The imagery in question is maritime and elaborates the *Freedom-through-Voyage* mytheme. It entails the idea of an emancipatory voyage, a journey of dissenters who flee oppression, embark on a quest, and seek freedom in a different geographical space. This voyage is transformative; it is the very act of journeying that transports the subject to a status of liberty, both spatially and subjectively:

---

13 In *The Custom House*, Hawthorne states that his "true position" is one of "editor." To a specific degree, he shares in Brown's aesthetics of the personal. Hawthorne allows any author wishing to tell the truth to be "autobiographical" yet only "without violating either the reader's rights or his own." At the same time, an author is well advised to safeguard "the inmost Me behind its veil" (SL 7f). He goes on to claim the sources of *The Scarlet Letter* to be the writings of Jonathan Pue, a local Salem antiquarian, like him a collector of stories. Pue's writings, however, were "not official, but of a private nature, or, at least, written in his private capacity" (26). Again, private and public interact in the writing of history. While Hawthorne's preface is easily situated in genre conventions, explaining how "a large portion of the following pages" came into his possession, it also means to give "proof of the authenticity therein contained" (SL 7ff). Brown and Hawthorne personalize the narrative mode so as to give evidence to the truth-value of their stories.

14 For a detailed description of the basic Puritan myth see Chapter 2.2.

15 It may be noted that one may read the appropriation of (positive) ship imagery in a Diaspora context and as an attempt to reinterpret the middle passage. Voyage, both as bondage and migration, is of crucial importance to diasporic and postcolonial perspectives. For more see Gilroy: *The Black Atlantic* (1993).

The voyage *makes* the freeman. In the Puritan context, such voyages are maritime. The crossing of water presents the act of gaining freedom, and the ship, of course, offers the vehicle with which to effect the transformation.[16]

The ship as a symbol for freedom carried cultural weight long before the Pilgrim's voyage.[17] In the Puritan myth, it is the *Mayflower* that bore the first settlers to the shores of New England. Further, it was on board of a ship that the foundations of the future colony were first articulated. The *Arabella* witnessed Winthrop's sermon *A Model of Christian Charity*, which would lay the groundwork for the American City upon a Hill.

In this context, the ship offers an image that embodies the human capacity to conquer nature. It allows for the discovery of the unknown and furthers the ability to progress in a geographical and civilizatory sense. It is a mythological, cultural, and technological locus were humans stand against (and journey with) space and time; it thus intensifies and reflects the human experience itself. A ship on its journey conquers, overcomes Blumenberg's fear-inspiring horizon (*hic sunt draconis!*), and arrives at new shores of possibilities. Noah's ark, the ships of Odysseus, Columbus' *Santa Maria*, and finally the Puritan *Mayflower*: These ships inspire the

---

16 Andrews notes that these journeys carry connotations in the context of African-American autobiography. Here, quest motifs are spiritualized and symbolize multiple layers of spiritual evolution. In the black spiritual narrative, the journey begins with an escape from sin and leads to the achievement of righteousness. In the black secular slave narrative, which better applies to Narrative, one finds an escape from bondage and the achievement of freedom and literary enlightenment. Here, we are offered the awakening of a true identity by means of finally participating in the cultural logos. Both, the spiritual and the secular narratives present complementary gospels of freedom. The secular celebrates political freedom, the spiritual evidences the fact that blacks, too, are god's chosen. Finally, quests that focus on the need to declare one's self, like *Narrative*, serve to make the unreal or unknown Other a reality. Here, we find declarative acts that reconstruct the past, appropriate empowering myths, and (re)define a place in the societal system for the newly created (or newly defined) subject. These quests are psycho-literary in nature (7). I suggest that both *Narrative* and *Clotel* present secular and psycho-literary journeys. In contrast, Pennington's *Blacksmith* veers toward the spiritual quest, if one regards his famous "moral dilemma" (TFB 21) and his realization that, being a "slave to Satan," he must "must make another escape from a tyrant" (52).

17 For a general overview see Dear (ed.): *The Oxford Companion to Ships and the Sea* (2006). For further material see Agius: *Ships, Saints and Sealore* (2015), Witt: *Eroberer der Meere* (2014), Bacci (ed.): *The Holy Portulando* (2014), Adams: *A Martinime Archeology of Ships* (2013), Krauskopf: *Seefahrergeschichten* (2011) and Bockius: *Schifffahrt und Schiffbau in der Antike* (2007).

human imagination and carry with them stories of journeys, conquests, and the acquisition of freedom.

That they do so is grounded in the nature of the element they travel. In the context of the Puritan myth, ships crossing the ocean signify freedom.[18] Yet those who journey the seas are usually rebels, individuals who dare to defy the gods.[19] They enter a realm that needs to be discovered and conquered. Again, Blumenberg comes to mind: The ship *per se* exemplifies the attempt to stand against reality's absolute sway over human existence. Its image is mythological in that it represents human sovereignty against the powers of nature: Odysseus returns to Ithaca and thus spites Poseidon (Hamilton 282); Utanapishti in the Gilgamesh epic – and Noah in Genesis – weather the deluge on an ark and continue human life on earth (George 88, KJV Genesis 6-9); Moses leads his people through the red sea to the promised land (KJV Exodus 14:14).

Indeed, the ship is not always necessary for the voyage. Crossing oceans (or seas, rivers, or any other kind of water space) is an act that entails fundamental subjective and/or societal transformations. This ancient meaning is continued in New World associations with the ship and maritime voyages in general. Crossing water and setting sail remains significant in Colonial and Antebellum struggles for freedom. Winthrop will proclaim a New Canaan on the *Arabella*, and Brown will refer to the same imagery when promoting abolition. It is not surprising, then, that Abolitionists took up the imagery for the sake of emancipation. In *Clotel*, George and Mary will cross the ocean and find freedom in Europe, and Clotel will cross a number of streams on her voyage only to find death at the bottom of the Potomac River.

The novels discussed in Part I push horizons. Spatially and ideologically, they enlarge the borders of their respective polities. Hawthorne's witchcraft imagery opens Boston's fences to the forest; Gutzkow's mythological resignification transforms love rituals so as to enable individuality. In this, *Clotel* does not differ: This text crosses the waters (and lands) of Antebellum America to reach a *Newer* Canaan. Its characters embark on journeys to re-enact the Puritan Voyage and redefine an ongoing American Revolution. They do not flee British kings but escape

---

18 It is crucial to understand that this meaning is not universal. In the context of international slave trade and the middle passage, the ship, indeed, became a *locus terribilis*. This interpretation is evident in the Steamboat scene, but later laid aside by assigning the ship's negative meanings to the South, thereby imagining a positive, Northern, and Puritan ship imagery. By a-historically separating Puritanism from slavery, Brown succeeds in constructing the Mayflower as a solely positive and truly mythological image.

19 We may remember the characterization of Spanish sailors in *The Scarlet Letter*, cf. Chapter 2.4.

Southern tyrants. Like the Mayflower Pilgrims, they follow the North Star and become pilgrims in their own right.

Brown taps into this mythological imagery to describe the fugitive's journey. He gradually introduces the ship imagery by means of several scenes, which prepare (Ia) for the exposition of the basic Puritan myth. He is able to write in the ship imagery tradition because the seas – and the ships that cross them – are constitutive of slavery itself. Thus, Brown begins his mythological resignification with stories pertaining to American slavery and the slave trade. Indeed, his critical treatment of slavery presents the first instances of denaturalization (Ic) in the novel.

Slavery and the Steamboats of Modernity

The U.S. abolished the importation of slaves to American soil in 1807. Trading slaves inside national borders, however, remained legal until the Civil War. In this context, *Clotel* opens with a chapter entitled 'The Negro Sale,' introducing the reader to a Southern slave auction. Before expanding on the auction itself, the narrator discusses the principle of chattel slavery, "where the slave is placed by law entirely under the control" of another. He then connects this principle with the "marriage relation." The latter – the "oldest and most sacred institution given to man" – is made legally impossible to the slave, thereby robbing them (and the slave state) of "the foundation of all civilization and culture" (CL 44f).[20] In pairing the slaves' subjective situation with the societal function of marriage, the chapter depicts the consequences of slavery for the individual and its moral repercussions for society at large. For Brown, the South's moral depravation is rooted in the very existence of slavery.

Moral deprivation is exemplified in the subsequent discussion of quadroons[21] and the sexual politics that arise from a situation where "no safeguard is thrown around virtue." At this point, we are introduced to some of the novel's main characters. The text thereby once again personalizes a societal issue. Immediately juxtaposed to the description of quadroons – mixed-race women "of fascinating beauty" – three women are introduced (CL 46). The first is Currer, "a bright mulatto," former slave and lover of no other than Thomas Jefferson.[22] Two daughters emerged

---

20 The centrality of the marriage discourse for early black writing is elaborated on in Chakkalakal: *Novel Bondage* (2011).

21 For a discussion of the mulatto woman see Mohammed: *But most of all mi love me browning* in *Feminist Review* Vol. 65 (2000).

22 Here, Brown comments on the Jefferson-Hemings case. The literary reworking of Jefferson's relationship with Hemings functions to question and re-evaluate the character of the founding fathers. Hemings, a young slave in the Jefferson household, was 14 when the re-

from this relationship: Clotel and Althesa (47). Their prominent paternity notwithstanding, they are separated and sold at the auction block. First, the narrator informs on the cruelty of such auctions, where families "were separated with a degree of indifference that is unknown to any other relation of life" (49). Then, he proceeds to highlight the illogic of slavery, a system of discrimination that Clotel's very appearance reveals as arbitrary:

The appearance of Clotel on the auction block created a deep sensation amongst the crowd. There she stood, with a complexion as white as most of those who were waiting with a wish to become her purchaser; her features as finely defined as any of her sex of pure Anglo-Saxon. (ibid.)

From the beginning, the text insists on a multilayered condemnation of slavery's racist logic. Clotel's parentage (and her skin complexion) complicates the question of race. Morally, the elaborations on marriage and the sundering of families speak against the institution. Finally, the narrator comments on two additional pillars of institutionalized racism. These are economic (read capitalist) motivations and religious (read Christian) hypocrisy:

This was a Southern auction, at which the bones, muscles, sinews, blood, and nerves of a young lady of sixteen were sold for five hundred dollars; her moral character for two hundred; her improved intellect for one hundred; and her chastity and virtue for four hundred dollars more. And this, too, in a city thronged with churches, [...] whose ministers preach that slavery is a God-ordained institution! (CL 50)

The narrator calls for outrage but not without providing detailed information on legal, moral, and cultural contexts. At the end of the chapter, the discussion is elevated to an international level: "What indignation is not due to the government and people who put forth all their strength and power to keep in existence such an institution?" (50f).

Why this turn to a global context? Indeed, Brown's call for abolition is not only an American's call. It offers a *universalized* call for freedom that defies national

---

lationship began. The couple had the first of probably seven children in 1790. The affair was discussed widely but largely dismissed until modern DNA analyses produced proof of Jefferson's parentage of at least one of Heming's children. See Foster: *Jefferson fathered slave's last child* in *Nature* Nov.5 (1998); Reed: *Thomas Jefferson and Sally Hemings: An American Controversy* (1997); Chase-Riboud: *Sally Hemings* (1979); Brodie: *Thomas Jefferson: An Intimate History* (1974); Farrison: *Clotel, Thomas Jefferson and Sally Hemings* in *CLA Journal* Vol.17 (1973).

boundaries and situates the slave's journey towards emancipation in an Atlantic age of revolutions informed by the *Zeitgeist*: The "age repels" it, Brown writes. Here, he echoes the Young Germans' perspective on modernity and their call for a new, historically adequate state of society (CL 51). The slave trade – and slavery in general – is depicted as a condemnable thing of the past.

Another scene – this time from the second chapter – introduces the ship imagery. In keeping with the text's aesthetics of the personal, this scene focuses on names and identity. Currer has been bought by a slave speculator named Dick Walker. The trader orders his servant Pompey to get "the Negroes ready for market" (CL 53). Brown draws on his own biography here: As related in *Narrative*, he was forced to work for a slave trader, and one of his duties was to "ready" slaves for re-selling (Fabi 257). This scene again highlights the chattel principle and with it the mercantile-capitalist aspects of slavery. The women, even Pompey himself, are imagined as a product, an "artekil," to use the servant's phrase. They are devoid of any claim towards individual identity. Any biographical history – name, birthdate, age – is cast aside to improve the sale. Thus, a slave's age is open for change; a forty-five year old individual turns thirty, for "dat is what marser says [he] is to be" (CL 53). Names, a paramount institution to Brown, are also permeable in the context of slavery. When asked, one slave gives his name as "Geemes," which Pompey molds to "Uncle Jim" (54).[23] Indeed, a true name would imply personal wholeness; it would constitute a *person* able to claim personal rights.[24] The fact that slaves do not hold such an identity is evident in the first scene on water.

Following the Pompey dialogue, the text relates a steamboat race on the Mississippi. Another boat nears the vessel that carries Currer and Althesa, and after a while, more and more material is given to the fire "for the purpose of raising the steam to the highest pitch" (CL 54). Finally, a boiler on Currer's ship, the *Patriot*, explodes, killing nineteen people. What happens next is meant to serve as proof of the South's moral degeneration and the consequences of chattel slavery. Instead of mourning the dead, the steamers are soon on their way, their passengers gambling in the saloons. "Thousands of dollars change hands during a passage from Louisville or St. Louis to New Orleans on a Mississippi steamer, and many men, even ladies, are completely ruined." But it is not only money that changes hands. During

---

23 The designation 'Uncle' was a generic term to designate and address older slaves (UTC 17).

24 Fabi notes that this real-life episode shows Brown's ability to fictionalize autobiographical material. She further holds that the slaves' ignorance regarding birthdates was a common strategy to "undermine the personal identity of slaves" (257). The act of keeping (Brown would have said 'stealing') this information from a person is symptomatic of the system's psychological oppression.

one of these transactions, a certain Mr Smith loses a game of cards to a fellow passenger, Mr Johnson. Smith, apparently short on cash, bets a young boy who "will bring a thousand dollars, any day, on the New Orleans market." So as to ascertain the exact sum of the bet, Johnson inquires: "Then you bet the whole of the boy, do you?" (55).

Indeed, the idea that Smith could bet only parts of the slave constitutes an actual possibility: A legal yet illogical consequence of chattel slavery. Fabi notes that the scene "implicitly contemplates the absurd possibility of betting only parts of the boy." And certainly, given the preceding Pompey dialogues, the reader is slowly being acquainted with the *explicit* and very *real* fact that parts of a slave – maybe not physiological but psychological parts – are at the disposition of the masters. The text gives evidence to the fact that this discussion pertains to more than "paradoxical consequences" (Fabi 258). When the boy is asked whom he belongs to the next morning, his answer gives proof of slavery's despotism: "When I went to sleep last night, I belonged to Governor Lucas; but I understand dat he is bin gambling all night, so I don't know who owns me dis morning" (CL 56).

The Mississippi steamboat scene offers a first step in the process of denaturalization (Ic). By highlighting the inherent despotism on board, slavery and the polity that supports it are criticized. Indeed, the steamboat scene introduces the aforementioned ship imagery *ex negativo*: The Southern vessels are soaked in aristocratic vices.[25] After all, this is a slave river: races, gambling, fraud and violence, excessive drinking, and chained slaves in the cabins are the norm. The boats on this river represent the South's aristocratic atmosphere and cultural degeneration. Simultaneously, the *steam*boat offers a telling image for an American modernity out of bounds. During the race, the narrator informs us: These boats are "burning more than wood." And in fact, the race will result in "killed and scalded" human beings (CL 54). The industrialized and boundlessly capitalist South (and the U.S. in general, for that matter) is imagined as sacrificing human lives to the races of modernity. The slave states burn through human beings in order to keep up with (Northern) competition. There is no other instance in *Clotel* that employs such powerful figurative language to criticize modern capitalism as one of the major forces behind slavery.

Of course, the steamboat image clashes violently with its romanticized counterpart, the basic myth's Puritan tall ships. But on the Mississippi, we are introduced to a geographical and ideological binary which will resurface in the mythological resignification: The aristocratic South as a place of tyranny *versus* the democratic North as a space of freedom. The latter is illustrated in form of the Puritan ship *par excellence*: the Mayflower.

---

25 cf. footnote 15.

Two Ships, Two Polities

The Mississippi steamboats offered a picture of the South's situation as Brown conceived it. America's South is depicted as suffering from aristocratic decadence, loose morals, and a boundless capitalism. The Mississippi runs through as space that is defined by tyranny and despotism. How can the nation as a whole then pride itself on its freedom? This is the question that Henry Morton, husband to Althesa and covert Abolitionist, poses in Chapter XX. This chapter, entitled 'The True Democrat,' presents a theoretical discussion of two opposing political systems: Morton weighs democracy against despotism.[26] This instance further denaturalizes the basic Puritan myth and critiques American exceptionalism. And it turns the tables on what Bercovitch termed "transatlantic contrast" (Office 35).

'The True Democrat' begins with a few lines by the Irish poet Thomas Moore. He criticizes America's "boast of perfect liberty," a claim belied by the fact that some Americans stand over others "with a tyrant's rod." Thoughts on oppression and tyranny introduce a chapter that will elaborate on what a democrat may say when faced with the peculiar institution, an issue that is once again discussed on a transnational (and transhistorical) level. Morton questions the nation's international prestige: "It is not our boasts of freedom," he argues, "that will cause us to be respected abroad." With this in mind, he turns to American conceptions of Europe: "We say much against European despotism; let us look to ourselves" (CL 151). But first, he gives a definition of despotism itself:

A government is despotic where the rulers govern subjects by their own mere will—by degrees and laws emanating from their uncontrolled will, in the enactment and execution of which the ruled have no voice, and under which they have no right except at the will of the rulers. Despotism does not depend upon the number of rulers, or the number of subjects. It may have one ruler or many. (151f)

He uses examples from Greek and Roman history to illustrate his claims and then allocates the U.S. in a genealogy of despotism.[27] Here, just as in ancient Rome and

---

26 For a detailed analysis of the novel's theorization of democracy, see Wilson: *Specters of Democracy* (2011).
27 Morton includes monarchies (one ruler) and aristocracies (a number of rulers) in his concept of despotic government. He further differentiates between the number of rulers and the oppression suffered by the subjects. The more despots, he claims, the more severe the oppression, as "responsibility is more divided." Also, the "smaller the number of subjects in proportion to the tyrants, the more cruel the oppression, because the less danger from rebellion" (CL 152).

Greece, slavery is defined as symptomatic of a "despotic citizenry" (Wilson 45). "In this government, the free white citizens are the rulers – the sovereigns, as we delight to be called. All others are subjects." Thus, slaves stand against the "seventeen millions of sovereigns" and hold "no rights, social, political, or personal." They are not simply serfs – a common status in despotic European countries like Russia – but "native slave[s]" stripped of every right. There is no assent to the laws of the nation for them; none of the rights of "God and nature" which "the high spirit of [the] revolution declared inalienable." "Is [the American slave] not then the subject of despotic sway?" Morton's answer is clear and, in keeping with the jeremiad tradition,[28] hyperbolic: "The slaves of America [...] lie under the most absolute and grinding despotism that the world ever saw" (CL 152).

What happened to the Land of the Free? Who is to blame for its despotic governance? According to Morton, one of the defining characteristics of despotic polities is the fact that (only) the rulers are free. Again, the argument turns to Europe: Nicholas of Russia, the Turkish sultan, the Austrian emperor; they are all free. But the American despots are neither princes nor emperors; they are the "rulers of the country—the sovereign people!" (CL 153). American despotism, Morton concludes, shall suffer the same fate as the despotic empires of old.[29] In a prophetic call reminiscent of Bercovitch's American Jeremiad, he foresees a national apocalypse:

Our nation is losing its character. The loss of a firm national character, or the degradation of a nation's honour, is the inevitable prelude to her destruction. Behold the once proud fabric of the Roman empire [...] The ramparts of her national pride were broken down, and Vandalism desolated her classic fields. Then let the people of our country take warning ere it is too late. (ibid.)

28　This is the first of numerous jeremiads in *Clotel*. Andrews notes that in prophesying the judgment of slaveholders and the slave nation, Morton speaks in the jeremiad tradition, which parallels social groups to the enslaved people of Israel during their captivity. Simultaneously, Morton's is a distinctly black jeremiad, focusing on the issue of slavery. Another topos of the (black) jeremiad is the idea of a "world upside down." Here, the civilizatory order is reversed, which results in chaos and apocalypse (14f).

29　Greece and Rome were thought to have fallen due to a growing cultural decadence. Here, slavery and racism are seen as signs for un-civilization (Gould 118). Morton calls for a return to progress and civilization. His jeremiad presents an attempt to re-civilize the once again uncivilized. In *The Fugitive Blacksmith*, Pennington argues similarly regarding Western progress: "In all the bright achievement we have obtained in the great work of emancipation, if we have not settled the fact that the chattel principle is wrong [...] then we have wrought and triumphed to little purpose, and we shall have to do our first work over again" (TFB xii).

This discussion of the U.S. as a despotic nation serves a number of purposes.[30] First, it is devoid of religious sentiment, presenting a purely secular and political argument against slavery. Second, it is didactical in providing a political education to the reader, studded with historical and contemporary examples. It thus aims at re-educating the reader on slavery and the mode of American governance, and it provides material for private and public debate. Morton gradually unfolds his claims and ends with a patriotic call for reform. The third significant aspect lies in this chapter's function as jeremiad. If the U.S. has become a despotic polity and lost its national identity, two questions arise. First, what is (or was) the national character? Second, what exactly caused the U.S. to become a despotic polity and how may one achieve (or return to) a democratic status? The novel answers these questions in the subsequent chapter by turning to (and affirming) the Puritan myth. Here, Brown transports the reader to the 17th century. He has them stand on the banks of the east coast, search the waters of the Atlantic, and behold the Mayflower. What follows constitutes the exposition of the basic Puritan myth (Ib).

Levine is correct in noting that in *Clotel*, America's national character is made manifest in the "mythic account" of the arrival of two ships (26). The first, landing on Northern shores, is the Mayflower.

On the last day of November, 1620, on the confines of the Grand Bank of Newfoundland, lo! we behold one little solitary tempest-tost and weather-beaten ship; it is all that can be seen on the length and breadth of the vast intervening solitudes, [...] one lonely ship greets the eye of angels or of men, on this great thoroughfare of nations in our age. Next in moral grandeur, was this ship, to the great discoverer's; Columbus found a continent; the May-flower brought the seed-wheat of states and empire. That is the May-flower, with its servants of the living God, their wives and little ones, hastening to lay the foundations of nations in the occidental lands of the setting sun. (CL 155)

The text situates the birth of the American nation in the arrival of the Puritan ship. This scene offers the material which will inform the reader on American identity. All the classical elements of the Puritan myth are found and affirmed: their maritime journey to the New World; the hardships endured; the singular ("one lonely ship") and prominent character of the journey ("eyes of angels or of men"); the voyage's exceptionalism when compared to the "thoroughfare of nations." Lastly,

---

30 Morton's elaborations are grounded in political philosophy. Throughout the chapter, he puts forth concepts that originate in classical texts such as Aristotle's *Politics* (forms of despotic government) and Locke's *Two Treatises on Government* (representative government). He also refers to the heavily Lockean Declaration of Independence when speaking of the natural and inalienable rights of man.

the text defines the future of a nation founded by the "servants of the living God" (CL 155). Here, the Puritans' spiritual and moral traits are focused on, elevating the founders (and the nation itself) to the sacred. Their spirituality, however, has political consequences for the state-to-be:

Here in this ship are great and good men. Justice, mercy, humanity, respect for the rights of all; each man honoured, as he was useful to himself and others; labour respected, law-abiding men, constitution-making and respecting men; men, whom no tyrant could conquer, or hardship overcome, with the high commission sealed by a Spirit divine, to establish religious and political liberty for all. This ship had the embryo elements of all that is useful, great, and grand in Northern institutions; it was the great type of goodness and wisdom, illustrated in two and a quarter centuries gone by; it was the good genius of America. (ibid.)

Brown imagines an American spirit which is concentrated in the Mayflower's passengers. These "great" men stand for values which America-the-slave-nation seems to have forgotten: justice and mercy, "respect for the rights of all," esteem for personal integrity, for labor, and law (CL 155). The Puritans become the source of a Christian humanism, a just work ethics, and the carriers of a strong commitment to *tyrannis*, the right and duty to stand against arbitrary government (Thiele 21).[31] Here are the original rebels whom "no tyrant could conquer" and who embody the divine American mission. Here, the establishment of "religious and political liberty for all" is a celestially sanctioned "commission:" the Puritan errand *par excellence*. The Puritans transplant the European spirit of freedom – which could not conquer Europe – to the New World; they bring the "seed-wheat" and all the "embryo elements" necessary to build the New Jerusalem (CL 155).

This New Jerusalem, however, is imagined as a *Northern* city. The Mayflower, the "great type of goodness and wisdom," founded a nation that was (and according

---

31 *Tyrannis* refers to the concentration of statist power in one person and is one of Aristotle's six forms of government. In the present context, however, *tyrannis* describes the fundamental right of a populace to rise against an unjust ruler. The differentiation between *tyrannis* and *regnum* – the unjust and the just rule respectively – emerged in the Middle Ages. For Locke, tyranny – the exercise of power beyond right – stood in crass opposition to the rule of law. Although the right to dispose of a tyrant has been contested (e.g. Hobbes equated tyranny with sovereignty), *tyrannis* as a basic right to resist [*Widerstandsrecht*] has been prevalent in Western culture. For a detailed account of the term's etymology and dynamic significations, see the entry in Ritter and Gründer (eds): *Historisches Wörterbuch der Philosophie* Vol. 10 (1998). For more see Libero: *Die archaische Tyrannis* (1996); Jordovic: *Anfänge der Jüngeren Tyrannis* (2005); Sreedhar: *Hobbes on Resistance* (2010); Manning: *Liberalism* (1976).

to Brown should be) infused with "all that is useful, great, and grand in Northern institutions." All that pertains to the "good genius of America" is said to pertain to the Puritan source (CL 155). If the nation would trace its heritage back to these Puritan beginnings (and live up to the tenets of its founders) it may truly claim a "firm national character" (153). According to Brown's exposition, the true America is the American North. But the Puritan genealogical line does not stand alone. Similar to Hawthorne, Brown imagines a second line of ancestry. However, this parallel genealogy results in the despotism of slavery. Again, the text turns to a ship.

The reader is removed from the Northern shores to the James River in the South. It is still 1620, and another ship is seen on the horizon. But it is the Mayflower's antithesis, transporting a very different cargo.

But look far in the South-east, and you behold the same day, in 1620, a low rakish ship hastening from the tropics, solitary and alone, to the New World. What is she? She is freighted with the elements of unmixed evil. Hark! Hear those rattling chains, hear that cry of despair and wail of anguish, as they die away in the unpitying distance. Listen to those shocking oaths, the crack of the flesh-cutting whip. Ah! it is the first cargo of slaves on their way to Jamestown, Virginia. (CL 155f)

The Southern slaver contrasts the Puritan tall ship: It is "low," "rakish," and hails American shores not from Europe but from "the tropics." Instead of carrying the good genius of the new nation, it is "freighted with the elements of unmixed evil" (ibid.). Whereas the Mayflower offers an image of freedom and justice, the slave ship represents the historic origins of the South's peculiar institution.

Clotel produces two ship images that summarize two competing civic myths. Here, "Brown presents a rather clear allegory (albeit an artful one, as the Puritans did have slaves) of the struggle between slavery and freedom in the nascent republic" (Levine 26). The Puritan myth (and liberal democracy) finds its embodiment in the Mayflower and its passengers, the harbingers of futurity, as Emerson called them (in Office 35). The slave ship, on the other hand, summarizes the despotic South. Bercovitch notes that Puritan freedom was traditionally imagined as opposing European despotism, and Hawthorne clearly thought and wrote in this dialectic. Brown, however, molds this "transatlantic contrast" and allocates the site of despotic tyranny in the American South (Office 35).

Morton's questions have thus been answered. First, America's national character is imagined to be based upon Northern values which hark back to Puritan beginnings. The cause for America's degeneration and despotic mode of governance is found in Southern slavery. Yet "a reformative social transformation can occur" in "the very spirit [...] that initially brought the nation into being" (Levine 27). The text claims that a *return* to Puritan values would set the American polity back on its original course. These ships stand as "representations of good and evil in the New World," constitutive to and interwoven in American history. Each of them is

a parent, one of the prosperous, labour-honouring, law-sustaining institutions of the North, the other the mother of slavery, idleness, lynch-law, ignorance, unpaid labour, poverty, and dueling, despotism, the ceaseless swinging of the whip, and the peculiar institutions of the South. (CL 156)

Yet even if freedom and slavery are part of the nation's founding, the novel compels the contemporary reader to make a choice. The U.S. cannot rely on both, one of these "parallel lines" needs to "come to an end" (ibid.).

The exposition of the basic myth (Ib) continues the mythological resignification in *Clotel*. It has been prepared (Ia) by the preface, the steamboat scene, and Morton's elaborations on slavery and the state of the nation. This preparation served to contextualize the concepts of freedom/democracy and slavery/despotism and further allocates them spatially. The realm of freedom is imagined as the North, whereas the South becomes the space of despotism. Two binary oppositions, an ideological and a geographical, are thus conflated: North/democracy vs. South/despotism. This geopolitical outlook is further infused mythologically. The Puritan myth is elevated to the true civic myth of America, whereas the South attains its own civic myth (one of slavery and despotism) which needs to be overcome in order to safeguard the nation.

Brown is not alone in employing such Puritan and maritime imagery. Likewise, James Pennington employs it in *The Fugitive Blacksmith* (1849). Once more, the narrator is forced to flee a space of oppression and opts for agency: "The bare possibility [of capture] was impressively solemn; but the hour was now come, and the man must act and be free, or remain a slave forever" (TFB 13). The consequences of failure, however, pale in contrast to the dread that the making of a new beginning entails. Indeed, the narrator's dissent is *active*, and the *becoming of a man* is contrasted to the passive and miserable life of a slave:

And then when I considered the difficulties of the way – the reward that would be offered – the human blood-hounds that would be set upon my track – the weariness – the hunger – the gloomy thought, of not just losing all one's friends in one day, but of having to seek and make new friends in a strange world. But, as I have said, the hour was come, and the man must act, or for ever be a slave. (TFB 14)

The narrator's transformative journey is guided by the North Star and saturated in maritime imagery. The following conflates the image of the fugitive and the image of a Puritan about to set sail:[32]

> I felt like a mariner who has gotten his ship outside the harbor and has spread his sails to the breeze: The cargo is on board – the ship is cleared – and the voyage I must make; besides, this being my first night, almost everything will depend upon my clearing the coast before the day dawns. I therefore set forth in sorrowful earnest, only now and then I was cheered by the wild hope, that I should somewhere and at sometime be free. (TFB 15)

Unlike Brown, Pennington does not repeat the Puritan ship imagery throughout his account. However, the imagery is used at the beginning of his journey north. Pennington's mythological image is indeed much more subtle than Brown's, but it nevertheless has a similar effect: The fugitive slave is depicted as homologous to the Puritan fathers. We find the basic Puritan myth *in nuce* in this significant passage.

In the case of *Clotel*, Chapter XXI presents the reader with the exposition of the basic Puritan myth (Ib). It elaborates on the myth, works on its ship imagery, and focuses on the Freedom-through-Voyage mytheme. Here, the genesis of American liberty is situated with the Puritan fathers. So as to contrast (and thereby highlight) the significance of the Puritan heritage, a Southern myth is offered. This myth focuses on the origins of slavery in a way that reduces Southern identity to this singular aspect, thereby rejecting all Southern influence in the construction of American national identity. Moreover, the slave ship's heritage and its inherent Southern-ness are given as undesirables to be overcome so as to prevent an American apocalypse. From Brown's Abolitionist perspective, the Northern narrative should be the sole victor in this battle of myths.[33]

---

32 In Brown's *The Anti-Slavery Harp* (1848), we find a similar depiction of the fugitive as a mariner. In 'The Flight of the Bondman,' written by Elias Smith and dedicated to Brown, the fugitive's escape is compared to a mariner's journey: "O, sweet to the storm-driven sailor the light / Streaming far o'er the dark swelling wave / but sweeter by far 'mong the lights of the night / is the star of the north to the slave" (14). Further, 'The Chase' invokes the Puritan Fathers directly, calling the pilgrims from their graves to aid the enslaved: "Will not your old sires start up from the ground / At the crack of the whip, and the bay of the hound / And shaking their skeleton hands in your face / Curse the germs that produced such a miscreant race?" (20f).

33 Bercovitch notes that Southern ideology was unable to produce a civic myth. It possessed a regional identity, which was indeed a peculiar one, given the constant tension between slavery and the notions of free enterprise (Assent 30). See also Woodward: *The Burden of Southern History* (1991), Fraser (ed.): *The Southern Enigma* (1981), Rubin: *The Ameri-*

Historically, however, the Southern line had all but ended. Slavery was an American reality, and its despotism generates a new generation of Puritans. The resignification of the basic myth occurs in the novel's slave characters, who (like the English Puritans), flee a despotic space, cross waters, and seek freedom in a new land. The Freedom-through-Voyage mytheme informs the Puritan fathers as well as the fugitive slaves.

The Puritan Voyage Reversed

The mythological resignification in *Clotel* renders the fugitive slave mythologically homologous to the Puritan fathers. The fugitives' journey North is cast as a reenactment of the Puritan voyage and thus steeped in maritime imagery. The resignification works on the basic myth, taps into the Freedom-through-Voyage mytheme, and constructs a new *black* hero-protagonist. The variant, the *Newer Shores myth*, champions a rebellious, freedom-loving individual who resists slavery's despotism, flees the South, and achieves freedom through voyage. This variant myth is expressed in Clotel and William's journeys.

Chapter XIX, 'The Escape of Clotel,' opens by fusing the categories of fugitive slave and American hero. "No country has produced so much heroism in so short a time, connected with escapes form peril and oppression, as has occurred in the Unites States among fugitive slaves." The fugitives' escape is portrayed as a geographical transition (South to North) that entails a personal transformation (chattel to freeman). Here, Brown relates an episode which refers to the aforementioned water imagery. On his journey, an anonymous fugitive needs to cross the "Ohio river" and employs "great shrewdness" to do so. He reaches the Northern border, crosses the "Niagara river, and for the first time in his life, breathe[s] the air of freedom" (CL 139). The crossing of water and the journey north not only signify a spatial relocation or the legal shedding of the slave status. This journey is presented as a conscious act of dissent, a rejection of "the tyrant's base control." This is *tyrannis par excellence*: It legitimizes the fugitive's escape and allocates them in a hero-category homologous to the Puritan dissenters. These fugitives, too, navigate waters "led by the North Star" (140). But unlike the English pilgrims, they are headed for "her Britannic Majesty's dominions" (141).

Brown parallels the motivations of Puritans and fugitives but *reverses* the geographical direction. While the English Pilgrims escaped British oppression and sought freedom on American soil, the American fugitives flee American slavery and seek sanctuary on British territory. The fugitive attains the same legitimation as

---

can *South* (1980), Taylor: *Cavalier and Yankee* (1979) and Cash: *The Minds of the South* (1941).

the Puritan; but history has changed directions. This reversal of free shores further denaturalizes the basic Puritan myth (Ic) while simultaneously adhering to its mytheme.

Clotel, in fact, first plans to escape to the United Kingdom. When her companion William offers her money, he tries to convince her to go to England, "where [she] will be free." Later, they decide to flee to Colonial Canada (CL 142). They use a steamboat for this purpose, cross-dress, and attempt their escape in broad daylight.[34] Again, the act of crossing a river accompanies their attainment of freedom: The "fugitives had now passed the Rubicon (CL 144);" a reference that, as Fabi notes, indicates their journey's point of no return (269). Clotel is a free woman for the first time in her life; yet compelled by the love for her still enslaved daughter, she decides to return South.

Again, an aesthetics of the personal informs the plot. Clotel's decision to return to the South is significant. Up until this point, she was denied to make decisions on her own; it was this status of oppression that prompted her and William to enact a journey homologous to the Puritan voyage. But the Puritan voyage is a civic myth, and Clotel embarks on a *personal* quest now. This turn from the universal (the escape of the oppressed) to the individual (the search for her daughter) connects two outlooks on freedom. The first imagines a universal human love of freedom; the second elaborates on freedom as a question of subjective decision making.

Once Clotel attains her freedom, she abandons the cultural script and voluntarily returns to the space of bondage. She does so motivated by a subjective category: family. Unlike Hester – who leaves her daughter in Europe – Clotel returns for the sake of her child.[35] Thus, she expands the Freedom-through-Voyage mytheme and freely decides to return. This act not only naturalizes (Ic) her into the pilgrim-hero category; it also affirms the basic tenets of the Puritan myth. Her return and death elucidate on the nature of freedom itself. Clotel's freedom is expressed in her decision to return to the South: She redefines freedom as a subjective quality which can

---

34 Levine notes that this episode is based on the escape of Ellen and William Craft, who fictionalized their journey in *Running a Thousand Miles for Freedom* (1860) (24). The Craft escape presents both race and gender as performance, while racial and gender 'passing' become active acts of dissent by assenting to traditional categories, thus revealing their constructed and perfomative nature. Here, Clotel and William re-enact Ellen and William's cross-dressing and Master-Slave performance. See also Chaney: *Fugitive Vision* (2008), Brusky: *The Travels of William and Ellen Craft* in *Prospects* Vol.25 (2000) and Blackett: *Beating Against the Barriers* (1986).

35 This comparison illuminates diverging approaches regarding female emancipation. While the white female's emancipative return necessitates her leaving her family behind, the black female freely opts for family as a category which was denied her as chattel.

exist *in* and *despite* oppression. In the basic Puritan myth, freedom is attained through migration, a conscious act of individual agency. It is imagined as a goal to be attained, something which is the *result* of voyages. But Clotel highlights the idea that it is the subject who brings freedom, not the soil which makes the subject free. Like Hawthorne's Pearl, Brown's Clotel *universalizes* the errand and divorces the Puritan voyage from geographical and national restrictions.

As mentioned, the mythological resignification in *Clotel* employs an *affirmative treatment* of the Puritan myth. The novel does not produce a new mytheme but stays true to the basic myth's fundamental tenet. Thus, *Clotel* does not offer a mythemic elaboration (IIb). But the heroine's journey raises the following question: If a nation restricts the subject's ability to realize freedom, is the nation free? Like Wally's, Clotel's suffering and suicide illuminate lager socio-political issues. Her voyage reveals that, in the Antebellum U.S., freedom for a black individual is impossible. This issue is further elaborated in William's ongoing voyage.

As Clotel returns to the South, William journeys north. His voyage is telling of a pan-American racism and continues to denaturalize the Puritan myth (Ib). His quest dampens the pathos expressed in the Mayflower episode and criticizes the racist structures of the free North. Yes, Northern racism may be caused by Southern slavery, but it does not cease to be "another form of slavery itself." Slavery and racism have a "withering influence" on the Free states, a fact that both William and Clotel experience during their journeys (CL 146). Here, the novel continues its earlier dismantling of the racist bias. The narrator gives a number of examples that reveal discrimination based on color as arbitrary.[36] Still, discriminatory practices follow "the colored man into every place he might enter." Even the Free States cannot claim true liberty; at least not for all their inhabitants. The text goes as far as denouncing Northern freedom as a "name" that does not approach "a reality" (150). Thus, Brown not only attempts to reveal Northern hypocrisy but again suggests a reinterpretation of freedom itself. While the North may legally offer a space of freedom, it cannot and does not guarantee actual freedom for persons of color. In the North, a form of cultural arbitrary governance is in effect.

Therefore, William leaves the U.S. altogether. He reverses the Puritan voyage and flees to British Canada. This reversal complements Clotel's return to the South. The denaturalization process (Ic) has revealed the U.S. as an inadequate space for the realization of black freedom. Consequently, William directs his voyage towards another space. Like Clotel, he returns; but the male black Puritan returns to British

---

36 The novel reports on an episode involving a member of Congress, Thomas Corwin. This congressman is "one of the blackest white men in the United States," and suffers the consequences of his complexion. Further, Daniel Webster is denied a hotel room based on "the dark features of the traveler" (CL 150).

territory. The errand still guides his journey, but it has been universalized and no longer adheres to a westward migration. William is thereby naturalized (IIc) into the hero-categories of the basic myth. He is able to gain his freedom, albeit on British soil. His naturalization does not refute the basic Puritan myth nor does it transform the Freedom-through-Voyage mytheme. On the contrary, his voyage affirms them. But his incorporation into the structure of the basic myth effects an opening of categories. This black Puritan can now be incorporated into the civic myth: He produces a variant which affirms the basic myth but includes a new, black protagonist and a universalization of migration. This variant, the *Newer Shores myth*, retells the Puritan migration, adds a black protagonist, and reverses the voyage's direction. The reversal of direction, however, entails a fundamental critique of the American *status quo*. Similarly, Clotel's voyage ends in a devastating commentary on American liberty.

Chapter XXV, in which Brown situates Clotel's suicide, opens with poet William Snelling: "'I asked but freedom, and ye gave / Chains, and the freedom of the grave.'" Then, the reader is introduced to "slave prisons" in the nation's capital, so called "Negro pens," where both fugitives and free blacks are incarcerated. The capital is represented as a despotic space where "many persons born in the Free States have been consigned to a life of slavery." The reader finds Clotel in one of these prisons; she was captured in Richmond, where she failed to locate her daughter and now awaits the next ship to New Orleans. The fugitive is desperate, "all hope" of finding her family "had fled," and she could "expect no mercy from her master" in the South (CL 183). Indeed, Clotel's personal quest failed and her situation in the capital may be read as a representation of the universal fate of blacks in the U.S. While the English Puritan's journey ended with freedom in America, it is now America that condemns the black Puritan. Nevertheless, Clotel escapes once more.

The geography of Clotel's final bid for freedom is noteworthy and naturalizes (IIc) this character as representative of the variant myth. The scene is set in Washington D.C. Clotel's flight is removed from the North/South binary that informed the fugitives' voyage in the rest of the novel. Instead, her final escape is enacted on a national stage, and the text explicitly refers to the founding of the nation in her final attempt to realize freedom. Here, the Puritan myth's water imagery and the Revolution myth come together. In a nutshell we are presented with the Puritan Freedom-through-Voyage mytheme *and* the fulfillment of this voyage by the fathers of the American Revolution.

Clotel escapes from her "prison" and runs to the nearby "Long Bridge," which leads her "across the Potomac" to "Arlington Place." The latter, we are informed, is occupied by a "descendant of the immortal Washington." Clotel's last run incorporates the two civic moments of the American genesis. She runs through history, seeking to cross water (Puritan myth) in order to arrive at a place that would promise freedom and liberty for all (Revolution myth). It is towards the "immortal Washington" and the promises of the Declaration that the "poor fugitive directed her flight" (CL 184). The capital's reaction to this flight, however, betrays the divided and uncertain state of the nation.

While Clotel runs towards the Long Bridge, the citizens' behavior is telling. The wardens but also civilians comprehending the "nature of the chase" "fall in with the motley mass in pursuit." Others, however, "raise an anxious prayer to heaven," refuse to join the chase, and hope that "the panting fugitive might escape, and the merciless soul dealer for once be disappointed in his prey." As she draws closer to the bridge, she hopes for success until she beholds men on the Virginian side of the river. These men – following their "Virginia instincts" – form a "line across the narrow bridge" to intercept the runaway (CL 184). Her escape fails, and the narrator combines national and celestial causations. Like Wally, Clotel is to be a martyr. The fugitive becomes an example of the human love of freedom and the impossibility of liberty on American soil. It is not just the mob that effects the tragedy. It is divine intervention:

But God in his Providence had otherwise determined. He had determined that an appalling tragedy should be enacted that night, within plain sight of the President's house and the Capitol of the Union, which should be an evidence wherever it should be known, of the unconquerable love of liberty the heart may inherit; as well as a fresh admonition to the slave dealer, of the cruelty and enormity of his crimes. (184f)

In the following suicide scene, two points are elaborated. First, it is the inherent and subjective love of freedom that prompts Clotel to go to the utmost extremes. Second, it is Antebellum America itself which impedes any "further effort to freedom" (CL 185). A nation built on the Puritan voyage and the declaration of universal liberty now stands in the way of those who wish to realize their inherent liberty. It seems that the Puritan errand and the spirit of the Revolution die with Clotel: Her "Death is Freedom" (183). While her white counterparts were able to cross the seas, the now fully naturalized black Puritan suffers death by water:

She clasped her hands convulsively, and raised them, as she at the same time raised her hands towards heaven, and begged for mercy and compassion there, which had been denied to her on earth and then, with a single bound, she vaulted over the railings of the bridge, and sunk for ever beneath the waves of the river. (185)

Clotel is unable to re-enact the Puritan voyage in the United States. While William and other characters are successful, she is driven towards suicide. The reversal of the Puritan voyage is again apparent here. All those able to realize freedom did so *outside* American borders, mostly on British territory. America, however, has turned into a despotic polity, the very space the Puritans fled.

Indeed, Clotel's death projects into the realms of the universal and signifies the death of the nation itself. The variant, the Newer Shores myth, imagines that 'America the Free' dies with the descendant of a founding father: "Thus died Clotel, the daughter of Thomas Jefferson, a president of the United States." Through Clotel, Brown allocates the demise of "the land of the free and the home of the brave" in the institution of slavery and its national and individual consequences. A nation that has "tears to shed" for Greece, Poland, and Ireland is depicted as effecting the suicide of a Revolutionary father's heir. Had she not been a slave, she would have been celebrated as a "heroic woman." In breaking the line to the ancestors – so the chapter's conclusion – America, the "cradle of liberty," may have "rocked the child to death" (CL 185f).

The novel's suicide scene refers to both the Puritan and the Revolution myth. Clotel as the black Puritan, however, is unable to re-enact the original Puritan voyage in the Antebellum situation. The variant myth produced in this character attributes the basic Puritan myth to the fugitive, paralleling their love of freedom, their hatred of oppression, and their journey for the sake of liberty. But it reverses the voyage, rendering the U.S. (not just the South) as the despotic polity that needs to be fled. Indeed, Clotel is unable to realize her freedom *because* she stays in America.

The Newer Shores myth points towards the fact that the nation's Puritan foundations are crumbling. But other characters are able to attain liberty, and they do so by adopting the values of the American Revolution and by reversing the Puritan voyage. The variant myth in Clotel is certainly a pessimistic one, its consequences for American national identity devastating. The Newer Shores myth imagines a despotic America, a nation where the promises of freedom and democracy "ceased forever" in the death-cries of Clotel's "drowning voice" (CL 187). However, the mythological resignification was successful in incorporating black individuals into the structures of the Puritan myth. Despite her suicide, Clotel and William are both fully naturalized enactors of the Puritan voyage and errand. And Brown's novel has hope for other fugitives who finally cross the Atlantic.

4.3 THE REVOLUTIONARY EMIGRANT AND EUROPA THE FREE

Clotel resignifies two civic myths. Whereas the Puritan myth is resignified in Clotel and William, other characters tap into the Revolution myth. Regarding the resignification of the latter, Thomas Jefferson deserves attention as a figure who – like Winthrop in *The Scarlet Letter* – is physically absent and yet immanently present. It is interesting that Brown and Hawthorne decided to have the most prominent representatives of their respective mythologies in the background. Yet if we bear in mind that the novels' work on civic myths is largely one of denaturalizing and rewriting, it becomes clear that we cannot do without the presence of the fathers, however implicit it may be.[37]

Clotel does little to discuss Jefferson *per se*; it rather concerns itself with his legacy. The novel elaborates on his arguments against slavery only to situate them in the paradoxical fact that Jefferson was a slave-holder himself. We meet Jefferson as statesman and as a private person. The statesman resounds in our minds as we find the first sentence of the Declaration adoring the novel's title page. Yet most importantly, we are confronted with Jefferson's flesh and blood legacy: his family. The full title of Brown's novel is *Clotel, or The President's Daughter*. Indeed, the novel traces the journeys of the president's kin: Currer, Althesa, and Clotel.

Levine notes that the novel's focalization on Jefferson's slave children explores the Jefferson-Hemings case. But most importantly, Brown traces the children of the American Revolution. For Jefferson's offspring, the revolution was indeed a "failed" and "unfinished" affair (14). *Clotel* thus offers a "genealogical fiction"[38] based on the Jeffersonian bloodline and thereby effects a denaturalization (Ic) of the Revolution myth (Quinby in Levine 14). This genealogical fiction traces the journeys of Jeffersonian (read American) children for whom the promises of the revolution ring hollow. While Hawthorne's Puritan filiopiety caused him to be lenient with the Pilgrim fathers, Brown did not share in such sentimental concerns. His offstage treatment of Jefferson did not hinder him to denaturalize the fathers' sacrosanct image, thus pointing towards the fact that "heroes – and especially presidents – are not gods or saints, but flesh-and-blood humans, with all of the frailties and imperfections that this entails" (Ellis and Lander in Levine 17).

Yet while the novel uses the Declaration to make Abolitionist demands, it also effects a denaturalization of its author. The culture-hero Jefferson is presented as a paradoxical figure, a president who held slaves and left his children to their fates. Brown thus partakes of a nationwide debate regarding Jefferson's character. His critique is echoed by this *Liberator* reviewer in 1854:

But it will be to his eternal disgrace that [Jefferson] lived and died a slaveholder, emancipating none of his slaves at his death, and, it is well understood, leaving some of his own chil-

---

37 In her analysis of *Clotel*, Wilson refers to Jefferson as the present/absent "ghost of democracy" (40).

38 Levine notes that Hawthorne wrote his own genealogical fiction in *The House of the Seven Gables* (14).

dren to be sold to the slave speculators, and thus to drag out a miserable life of servitude. (in Levine 17)

At the same time, the novel highlights Jefferson's rejection of slavery. Chapter XVII refers to his *Notes on the State of Virginia* (1785) and *Observations* (June 22, 1786) to make an Abolitionist point. Here, slavery is condemned as a "despotism" that destroys morality and *amor patriae*. Jefferson held that slavery produces despots and opposes the foundations of a free nation. The ongoing disregard of "god-given liberties," he feared, would eventually result in a revolutionary apocalypse fueled by god's "wrath" (CL 130f)

The chapter concludes with Jefferson's very own jeremiad, a passage preparing for Morton's elaborations in Chapter XX. Here, the president warns that slavery offends god and the natural rights of men; but gradual change and patience may "prepare the deliverance" of the enslaved population, because "a God of justice will awaken to their distress." This deliverance will come to pass either by "diffusing light" or "exterminating thunder." However, the possibility that the slaves may "attempt to gain their liberties by a revolution" worries the statesman: "I tremble for my country, when I recollect that God is just, and that His justice cannot sleep forever" (CL 130f).

The narrator welcomes Jefferson's "high-sounding words in favour of freedom" and rests upon them to make his own argument. Yet he does not fail to point towards the fact that Jefferson "left his own children to die slaves" (CL 131). We are once again faced with an aesthetics of the personal: The statesman's elaborations are contrasted with Jefferson's personal deeds. The fates of Currer, Clotel, and Althesa, and of his granddaughters Mary, Jane, and Ellen, are never related without mentioning Jefferson himself.[39] All their deaths (with the exception of Althesa's) are directly caused by slavery, a practice that Jefferson, while rejecting it in theory, partook of personally. In highlighting his role in slavery and contrasting his words with his deeds, the novel denaturalizes (Ic) Jefferson's mythological image. It is useful to think in the novel's allegorical context here. Levine notes that if "all Americans are in some ways Jefferson's children," then one may contrast the citizen-branch of this family with another: the enslaved Americans (275). Slaves are, indeed, imagined as Americans. They have, however, been neglected by their fathers and "left to die slaves" (CL 131). Thus, *Clotel* draws on the fate of Jefferson's other family. While the black Puritans claim their mythological descent on the

---

39 The auction scene, where Currer, Clotel, and Althesa are sold (49f), the chapter describing Mary's enslavement and psychological torture (120f), the chapter relating Jane and Ellen's suicide to prevent their rape (174f), and the passage reporting Clotel's suicide in the Potomac river (183f) all explicitly refer to their family connection with Jefferson.

grounds of homology with the English pilgrims, the black Revolutionary is imagined as a generic American.

Brown allocates the fate of the American experiment in the question of whether or not the enslaved children of the revolution will be emancipated. Abolition is indeed thought of as the American Revolution continued, and *Clotel*, like *The Scarlet Letter*, offers an instance of alternative history (Levine 14). While Hester's story presents an alternative set of Puritan ancestors, *Clotel* concerns itself with the forgotten and oppressed branch of the American family. Moreover, it situates its mythological resignification not solely in the American genesis but makes the reader reflect upon contemporary bids for freedom. Archer notes that the black descendants of Puritan and Revolutionary fathers receive the torch of the American errand for the establishment of a free nation. Echoing Winthrop's *A Model of Christian Charity* and Jefferson's *Declaration*, it is the black and oppressed branch of the family that is destined to fulfill the unfulfilled American promise: "If America is to be mankind's last, best hope [for freedom], it will be because there will be found ways of releasing the creative and revolutionary force of the American people. The black community will be in the forefront of those changes if they occur" (Archer 75).

This image of the black Revolutionary, heir to the founding fathers, is epitomized in the character of George Green. It is in this young rebel that Brown unfolds his mythological resignification with regard to the Revolution myth.

Rebels and Patriots

The generation of revolutionary rebels became legend in the Antebellum. Indeed, the civic myth evolving from the American Revolution remains most influential to this day.[40] Schachner notes that the age of the revolutionary founders presents "the most crucial as well as the most exiting" period for the American national imagination. Very much like the Antebellum, this period had a generative and transitional character and offered a "world of predatory powers, locked in mortal combat, daily threatening" the existence of the young nation. Here, the founders are held as heroes of their time, "men of talent and genius" who shaped the foundations of the United States (vii). Washington and Jefferson are cast as negotiators of unity, statesmen who worked for the political cohesion of "disparate and quarrelsome sovereign states" (4). The founders, indeed, were already venerated during their lifetime. Washington, for example, was greeted with the following in Trenton on his way to his inauguration as first president of the union: "Virgins fair and matrons

---

40 For a detailed and recent analysis of the influence of the Revolution on contemporary U.S. politics, see Sehat: *The Jefferson Rule* (2015).

grave / Those thy conquering arm did save, / Build for thee triumphant bowers; / Strew, ye fair, his way with flowers! / Strew your hero's way with flowers!" (in Schachner 6).

The mythologization of the Revolutionary fathers forms part of what Bellah termed *civil religion* (in Schocket 6). The Revolution myth offers a moment of national and political genesis in the Antebellum imagination which is intimately connected to the revolution's protagonists. In contrast to the Germanic myth, the Revolution myth highlights contemporary and/or recent personages of historical importance. The U.S., being a young nation, looks to events of recent history to establish its own and exceptional moment of foundation.

[M]ost countries trace their origins to ethnicity and language, rather than to the establishment of a particular political structure. The Unites States retains its governmental form from the federal constitution that served as the Revolution's crowning achievement, and so its citizens look to the people who established that form. (Schocket 6)

Bercovitch, however, notes that the very concept of revolution was molded in the myth surrounding the events of 1776. He claims that revolution became an "indefinitely self-renewing rite of passage" in American ideology (Revolution 608). In this context, revolution is not contained in historical events but presents a principle of organic development in which America attains an exceptional role.[41] Here is a "people in transition, advancing generation by generation through severe trials of character towards a consummation that remains forever beyond his grasp." In contrast to European revolutionaries, who pursue revolution for a "Promethean self-assertion" against "paternal gods," Bercovitch imagines American revolutionaries as enacting their revolution for the sake of "affirming order." An ongoing, "continuing revolution" thus presents the "condition of progress" which in itself controls the "revolutionary impulse." Revolution becomes a "*controlling* metaphor for [American] national identity" (609). This revolutionary spirit is represented by the Revolutionary fathers but finds its origin in Puritanism.

Bercovitch credits American Puritans with the establishment of an American kind of revolution which is continued by Washington and Jefferson. Instead of giving in to partisan politics, the Puritan revolutionary spirit expresses "defiance" in "the form of exodus," channels its "energy into the creation of a prosperous state," and invokes order and obedience against forms of extremism. Revolution, in this interpretation, disciplines its violent tendencies so as to establish a "tribal order"

---

41 Indeed, Gutzkow's conceptualization of revolution and Heine's revolutionary philosophy are based on very similar standards. What Bercovitch reads as an American perspective is in fact not restricted to the United States. For more see Chapter 6.

(Revolution 613). Indeed, the legendarization of the Revolutionary fathers only functions if their efforts are read as a continuation of the dissentious Puritan spirit. They are thus imagined as perpetrators of an ongoing American revolution.

But the process of such legendarization entails acts of simplification, patriotic moldings that, to say it with Barthes, transform "history into nature" (129). For "myth hides nothing," and while its "function" is certainly not the production of falsehoods, it does, however, "distort" history (121). The Revolution myth consecrates the American Revolution *per se*, disregards any critical momentum, and does so with a strong focus on the leading personages. Their revolution is depicted as a legitimate departure from a despotic polity in the name of freedom, independence, and self-determination. These values are upheld on a national *and* subjective level, and the notion of *tryannis* is central to this narrative. It describes the basic right to rise against a despotic mode of government, overthrow its systemic structures, and construct (or return to) a free polity. In this myth, the American patriots, fueled by their love of freedom and abhorrence of despotism, stood against the tyrannical rule of Britain. The right (and duty) of the oppressed to rise against a sovereign was taken up by the American rebels. The system to be overcome in their case was monarchic; the desired polity one of democratic and liberal character. Thus, indeed, one may interpret the American Revolution as the organic consequence of a Puritan nation, which in the act of declaring independence takes the next step towards the realization of the errand and the edification of a democratic Jerusalem (Revolution 613).

Revolutionary heroes are of central importance in this context. The founding fathers, from Washington to Jefferson, are the protagonists in the writing and signing of the myth's central document, the Declaration. They are culture heroes, imagined as a patriotic and morally upright aristocracy of the American republic. Their image merges the martial war-hero and the philosophical prophet of new beginnings. As the wording suggest, these founding fathers are thought of as national *sires*. The modern American nation and its citizens, therefore, are cast as heirs to and descendants of these legendary personages.

But the fiction of the Revolution myth is myth and can be dissented from by means of historical critique. Brown does so in order to assent to it under improved conditions. In *Clotel*, these conditions are the recognition of the revolutionary effort of blacks in the War of Independence, the consequent earning of civil rights for those who fought for freedom, and the subsequent incorporation (Barthes would say naturalization) of the black Revolutionary in the structures of the civic myth. Besides the rewriting of revolutionary history, the mythological resignification here further endeavors to interpret the efforts of Abolitionist rebels as a modern incarnation of the spirit of the American Revolution. In keeping with the Revolution myth's *Freedom-through-Resistance* mytheme, the fight for abolition becomes the legitimized continuation of the original stand against British oppressive rule.

Indeed, the variant myth produced in George Green, the *Ongoing Revolution myth*, is a narrative that celebrates the same ideals as the basic myth but which incorporates the black Revolutionary into the narrative, thus producing a more open, more democratic mythology. In fact (and in contrast to the other texts in this study), *Clotel*'s resignification of the Revolution myth does not produce a new mytheme. It rather stays true to the Freedom-through-Resistance mytheme and adds to the myth's protagonists. Moreover, the variant myth entails a social critique similar to the notion of the Puritan Voyage Reversed discussed before. For ultimately, the black Revolutionary must flee the Antebellum polity. His freedom cannot be lived in America, and Jefferson's heirs – his granddaughter Mary and her lover George – have to (re)turn to Europe.

The reader is introduced to George Green immediately after Clotel's suicide in Chapter XXV. While Clotel's Puritan voyage ends in death, the George Green plot begins with an escape that shall end in liberty, albeit on British soil. The topic of expatriation is foreshadowed in the chapter's epigraph, summarizing Clotel and William's journeys: "No refuge is found on our unhallowed ground / For the wretched in Slavery's manacles bound" (CL 188).

George's journey is entangled with that of Mary Green, Clotel's daughter and grandchild to Jefferson. George, like Mary, is a servant in the Green household and looks "as white as most white persons" (CL 189). Again, a racist outlook is cofounded by the figure of the mulatto. But importantly, George serves to resignify the tenets of the Revolution myth, especially its Freedom-through-Resistance mytheme. In the context of American independence, the justification of the revolution by means of *tyrannis* is of paramount importance. The Revolutionary fathers became not only the defenders but the very embodiment of this concept of legitimized resistance. The Declaration, of course, is an Enlightenment document born from the essence of the right to revolt. George will base his argumentation on this very document.

It is tempting to read in George Green's first name a reference to yet another founding father. And indeed, this connection prepares for the work on the basic Revolution myth (Ia). George Washington, like Thomas Jefferson, remains in the background of the novel. Still, he is referred to at crucial moments of civic momentum, e.g. Clotel's suicide scene (CL 184). It would certainly go too far to claim Green to be a modern/black embodiment of Washington. But his personal background is explicitly traced to the political sphere: "[Green], too, could boast that his father was an American statesman. His name was George" (188). Further, Green's military and oratorical talent may be read as hinting towards the founder. Green will later address his white audience as descendants of this statesman and describe the U.S. as "land of Washington" (191). The Green-Washington connection is part of the novel's attempt to establish a black American genealogy in its fugitive characters, while it simultaneously traces the nation's genesis to the principles of the American Revolution, and thus prepares (Ia) for the exposition of the basic myth.

George Green is described so as to connect this character to the American Revolution, and the slave revolt he partook of is used to expose (Ib) the basic Revolution myth. Chapter XXVI 'The Escape' tells of a "revolt amongst the slaves" in Washington D.C.; indeed, this event is imaged as homologous to the rise of revolutionary forces. However, the slave's revolt fails to succeed. Most "insurgents" had been "put to death or sent out of state," except for Green, who still awaits his trial (CL 188). Green's heroic character is evident from the beginning. The fact that he joined the insurgents is legitimized by his "love of freedom" and "zeal for the cause of his enslaved countrymen." But this man – whose appearance was so white that no one guessed that "any African blood coursed through his veins" – had proven his patriotic heroism long before the slaves rose against their masters.[42] The "local courthouse" had "taken fire," endangering "a small box containing some valuable deeds belonging to the city." The fire advanced and no one dared to venture into the building. George, however, "hearing that much depended on the contents of the box" ran into the burning building and saved it from the flames (189).

Here we have an individual whose character and actions are depicted as homologous to the Revolutionary fathers. Green, too, is motivated by his love of freedom and his resistance to oppression; he is as patriotic as he is selfless, daring all for the community's benefit rather than following egocentric motives. Lastly, even his appearance is designed to evoke the founders' "natural aristocracy" (Taylor 23).[43] This slave was so white, "he was often taken for a free white person" because of his "straight," "light," and "fine" hair, his "blue" eyes and "well formed head," and his "high and prominent" forehead. He is described as an educated person, familiar with the English language, taking advantage of the debates in his master's house, and enjoying "opportunities" "far greater" than those of most slaves (CL 189). This noble, freedom loving, and patriotic individual, however, is finally convicted of

---

42 Fabi notes that in subsequent American editions of *Clotel*, Brown will describe George Green as dark-skinned (275f). This change evidences different strategies to re-interpret the black character, which adapted to the audience's national context. In the U.K. edition, Brown whitens Green in order to lessen racial prejudice and connect him more strongly to the American Revolutionary fathers. In American editions, Green's change in skin complexion serves to reject racial prejudice by proving moral integrity in blacks. I have argued similarly and in more detail in Drescher: *The Publishing of Protest* in Arapoglou et al. (eds): *Racial and Ethnic Identities in the Media* (2016), and *A Home in a Native Land* in Gabrowski and Toth (eds): *The United States as a Divided Nation* (2014).

43 Thomas Jefferson agreed with John Adams that "there is a natural aristocracy among men" (Taylor 23).

high treason. But his sentence does not pass without an oration reminiscent of George Washington. Green, indeed, stands on revolutionary principles to denounce slavery.

Asked to explain his insurgent actions, Green employs a revolutionary rhetoric based on the Freedom-through-Resistance mytheme. Again, it is despotism against which the patriot is forced to take up arms. His speech serves as both, a denaturalization (Ic) of the traditional version of the Revolution myth and a naturalization (IIc) of a variant which incorporates modern Abolitionists and insurgent slaves into revolutionary hero categories. British oppression is paralleled with slavery's oppression, and the text describes how the spirit of *tyrannis* awoke in Green as he heard the Declaration discussed in his master's house:

I have heard my master read in the Declaration of Independence 'that all men are created free and equal,' and this caused me to inquire for myself why I was a slave. I also heard him talking with some of his visitors about the [revolutionary] war with England, and he said, all wars and fighting for freedom were just and right. If so, in what am I wrong? (CL 190)

George, like Clotel, *universalizes* the basic myth's mytheme. He taps into the historical motives for the American Revolution and applies them to the slaves' uprising, paralleling the American patriots with the slave rebels.[44] He further declares the slaves' *tyrannis* as even more legitimate: "The grievances of which your fathers complained, and which caused the Revolutionary War, were trifling in comparison with the wrongs and suffering of those who were engaged in the late revolt. Your fathers were never slaves, ours are" (ibid.).

Opening his discourse with the principle of equality, Green proceeds to condemn the institution of slavery. He does so by highlighting universal human liberty and gives the discussion a legal as well as a historical turn. The following is an at-

---

44 Brown's *Anti-Slavery Harp* also employs the Revolution myth. In 'I am an Abolitionist' the speaker enlists in the "sacred cause" and becomes "a soldier for the war" (ASH 19). 'We're coming! We're coming!' sings of "sons of brave sires who battled of yore" against England, and are again resolved to "do battle for freedom" against the "slavery which fled from [the] fathers of yore" (32). 'On to Victory' – tellingly set to the melody of 'Scots wha hae' – celebrates the "glorious dead / who for freedom fought and bled" (34). 'Jefferson's Daughter' critiques America's hypocrisy and derogates the "blasphemers in liberty's name" whose "forefathers" spilt their blood for freedom (24). Finally, 'Freedom's Banner' presents a poetical oath in the name of the Revolutionary Fathers: "O, by the virtues of our sires / and by the soil on which they trod / And by the trust their name inspires / and by the hope we have in God / Arouse, my country, and agree / To set thy captive children free" (39).

tempt at re-interpreting Antebellum slave law in the light of the Revolution myth's rewriting. The basic myth ignores the idea that the slaves' modern struggle should be read in the context of its own historical struggle for freedom, and Green rejects a narrow interpretation of the myth and calls for an opening of categories. He allocates the fact that his revolt is not seen in the genealogy of the American Revolution within the discourse of victory and defeat. But for Green, the struggle's outcome does not touch the nature of the struggle itself.

What right has one man to the bones, sinews, blood, and nerves of another? Did not one God make us all? You say your fathers fought for freedom – so did we. You tell me that I am to be put to death for violating the laws of the land. Did not the American revolutionists violate the laws when they struck for liberty? They were revolters, but their success made them patriots – we were revolters, and our failure makes us rebels. Had we succeeded, we would have been patriots too. Success makes all the difference. (CL 191)

The argument clearly champions the Freedom-through-Resistance mytheme, the core aspect of the civic myth that legitimizes revolution. For Green, it is the failure to read (or recognize) Abolitionist rebellions as genealogical to the American Revolution which effects the court's condemnation of modern insurrections.

Simultaneously, Green articulates one of the novel's many jeremiads. A "traditionary freedom," he warns, will not "save" the nation. A narrow interpretation of the Revolution myth "will not do to praise" the revolutionary fathers but shall in fact "build their sepulchers." The American "inheritance" shall be wasted, and the "genius of true humanity" will mourn the demise of the nation (CL 191). Levine notes that his speech refers to a biblical source, namely Christ's admonition of the Jewish people, who rejected the council of the prophets (213).[45] The American errand and promise of a New Jerusalem are taken up by Green as he adopts the role of prophet and castigates the American people: "'O land of Washington, how often would I have gathered thy children together, as a hen doth gather her brood under her wings, and ye would not; behold your house is left unto you desolate'" (CL 191).

George's jeremiad and his judgment of the nation's inability to correctly read its own civic myth differs from Morton's apocalyptic warnings. Morton cautions against a national demise if slavery is not abolished. George's jeremiad, however, intents something different: It attempts to parallel the revolutionary slave and the revolutionary patriot. He aims to mythologically *Americanize* the slave rebels.

---

45 cf. KJV Matthew 23:37f: "Jerusalem, Jerusalem, you who kill the prophets and stone those sent to you, how often I have longed to gather your children together, as a hen gathers her chicks under her wings, and you were not willing."

Bercovitch states that the American jeremiad rationalizes and channels revolutionary and individualistic impulses; it thus reconciles revolutionary violence with the myth of America as god's chosen people (Jeremiad 160). Thus, two types of dissenters emerge, and Hawthorne describes them in *The Scarlet Letter*: The individualistic American revolutionaries and the radical, Un-American "terrorists of France" (SL 42). In Europe, "revolution bared the dialectics of historical change," while in the U.S., calls for dissent occurred in a "grounded" and "ritual form" which "preempted the threat of radical alternatives." Yet Un-American others – may that be a French revolutionary, an Indian fighter, or a slave rebel – could "learn to be True Americans" when in the "fullness of time" they adopt (and adapt to) truly American tenets. These tenets (capitalism and democracy) are embodied by the Revolutionary fathers. Indeed, following Bercovitch, anyone could join "the pantheon of Revolutionary heroes when it was understood that [they want] to fulfill (rather than undermine) the American dream." Thus, the Un-American could "eventually become sons and daughters of the American Revolution" (Jeremiad 160).

Indeed, George Green's speech attempts such an "enlargement of consensus" (Jeremiad 160). The act of rebellion, he argues, should be read as homologous to the rebellious but legitimate actions of the patriots. Green seeks to prove the Americanness of the slave rebels, seeks to partake of the civic ritual of inclusion by calling on the Revolution myth. Wilson notes that George, the son of a congressman, stands before court as the "unacknowledged prodigal son" come to redeem the sins of the novel's father figures (51). While he may be successful in convincing the reader, he fails in convincing the judges. Bercovitch's enlargement of consensus, although attempted by Green, falls flat.

Ultimately, Mary helps George escape his execution; but he finally decides to leave America. After Mary is sold out of state, he escapes to Canada and then, "resolved to quit the American continent," to England (CL 197). Again, the Puritan voyage and the revolutionary battle against oppression are reversed. Green takes up arms not against British taxation but against American slavery; unsuccessful in his attempt to convince the court of the legitimacy of the enslaved branch of the American family, he turns his back on U.S. despotism and seeks freedom in England. Here, he is reunited with Mary, enjoys personal freedom, and is able to marry the woman he loves (CL 201).

This happy ending echoes the nexus between freedom and marriage presented in the novel's first chapter. The Antebellum polity denies both liberty and marriage to the slave; but the U.K., now the primary destination left to Puritan and Revolutionary heirs, not only welcomes them but grants these rights. Of course, Brown played on European sentiment when he concluded the novel's plot with the following:

We can but blush for our country's shame when we recall to mind the fact, that while George and Mary Green, and numbers of other fugitives from American slavery, can receive protection from any of the governments of Europe, they cannot return to their native land without becoming slaved. (CL 207)

He thus enlists British as well as European support for abolition and shames the American polity by revealing the paradox that is the peculiar institution. Just as *The Scarlet Letter* transports Pearl – the novel's first true American – back to Europe, *Clotel* has Jefferson's heirs leave the country to realize the errand on the other side of the Atlantic. Again, Bercovitch comes to mind: The "American was not (like the Frenchman or the Latin American) a member of the 'people.' He stood for a mission that was limitless in effect" (Assent 43). George and Mary, both extralegal heirs to Jefferson, may be denied civil rights in the U.S.; they nevertheless follow the cultural script to not only yearn for freedom but to realize it by means of resistance and voyage.

Brown closes *Clotel* by another jeremiad, again in a transnational setting. He calls for British support in the question of abolition and simultaneously situates the Atlantic as the sphere of activity.

Finally, let the voice of the whole British nation be heard across the Atlantic, and throughout the length and breadth of the land of the Pilgrim Fathers, beseeching their descendants, as they value the common salvation, which knows no distinction between the bond and the free, to proclaim the Year of Jubilee. (CL 209)

It is the perspective that knows no distinction which the novel seeks to produce in the reader. Brown believes that this perspective should be an American one, and he mourns the fact that it is not. But the Puritan as well as the Revolution myth has been re-worked in order to unfold this perspective.

The variant Ongoing Revolution myth in George Green describes an enslaved subject whose love for freedom and hatred of oppression situate him in the genealogy of the American Revolution. Moreover, his active resistance to the oppression of slavery produces a black Revolutionary, homologous to the *tyrannis*-driven founding fathers. By tapping into the Freedom-through-Resistance mytheme, mythological resignification produces a character whose person and dissent present a direct descendant of the American patriots. Antebellum America, however, is depicted as a space that no longer follows revolutionary tenets. Just as in the Puritan variant in Clotel, the Revolution variant in George reverses original structures: The oppressed now needs to journey east, back to Europe, where freedom and liberty await the enslaved children of the American Revolution. Indeed, that these individuals remain Americans is also discussed in Brown's novel. I shall close this chapter with a short discussion of how the mythological resignification in *Clotel* effects a naturalization of blacks into American national identity.

4.4 THE NATURALIZATION OF NATIONAL IDENTITY

Bercovitch notes that the label 'American' is not one that describes a strict belonging to a people but rather presents carriers of an ideological mission (Assent 43). The subjective adherence to American values produce a national identity based on the two civic mythologies discussed so far. I hold that in *Clotel*, American national identity is thought of in terms of a mythological mindset that produces a distinct political agency. The American people are depicted as a community united under the banner of the Puritan errand and the Enlightenment promises codified by the Declaration; a *Schicksalsgemeinschaft* [destined community] rather than a *Volk* [ethnic people]. Jefferson's heirs are distinguished by conduct and a form of American idealism based on Puritan and revolutionary values, rather than by biological genealogy. Regarding belonging and citizenship, legal discourses such as *jus sanguinis* or *jus terrae* are insufficient to capture national naturalization.[46]

Brown's mythological resignification attempts to naturalize the black subject. I have already shown how the novel constructs variant myths that incorporate fugitive individuals. This last section will be devoted to the larger debate of black belonging and analyze relevant passages that elaborate the question of the black subject as American.

The notion of America as an ideological space that rejects distinctions between North and South is elaborated in Georgina Peck. The daughter of John Peck, slaveholder and Currer's master, dissolves the North/South binary which informs Clotel and William's journey. The Southern mindset is represented by her father, who defends slavery in the name of the bible. The North, on the other hand, finds a representative in Carlton, who opposes both slavery and religion in the name of the Enlightenment. John Peck disregards all "talk about rights as mere humbug" and insists upon biblical dogma (CL 73); Carlton, a "disciple of Rousseau," is "no great admirer of either the Bible or slavery" and upholds the rights of man as codified in

---

46 In nationality law, the term *jus sanguinis* [right of blood] describes the attainment of citizenship by right of birth to parents who already hold citizenship. In contrast, *jus terrae* or *jus soli* [right of the soil] grants citizenship to anyone who is born on national territory. The U.S., as most nations in the Americas, follows *jus terrae*, while European nations generally defer to *jus sanguinis*. For more see Vincent: *Nationalism and Particularity* (2002); Dynneson: *Civism. Cultivating Citizenship in European History* (2001); Weil: *How to be French* (2008).

the Declaration (74). Both arguments, the novel suggests, are tinged with dogmatism. Peck views all other opinions on this matter as "fanaticism" (75), and Carlton "had drunk too deeply of the bitter waters of infidelity" (74). Here, the reader is offered characters that represent the radical views of their time: Peck[47] the Southern slaver backed by Christian dogma, and Carlton, the Northern intellectual backed by Enlightenment philosophy.

The narrator introduces Georgina as a middle ground, one who will argue for the bible as both "the bulwark of Christianity and liberty." Her argument, in contrast to Peck and Carlton's theoretical elaborations, is pragmatic: She claims that in order to "judge justly the character of anything, we must know what it does." Her pragmatic stance culminates in the rejection of all that "destroys, abridges, or renders insecure, human welfare" (CL 74f). Georgina arrives at an almost Kantian postulation that describes what Brown may have defined as the American spirit: "True Christian love is of an enlarged, disinterested nature" (75). Georgina presents an advocate of the kind of Christian humanism that Brown attributes to the "great and good men" of the Mayflower (154). Georgina – although "a native of the South" – is "by education and sympathy a Northerner" (74). Her argument illuminates the novel's desire to balance the two major competing forces in the slavery debate. Instead of partisan politics, she councils balance and compromise without sacrificing her fundamental convictions. Georgina's marrying of religion, philosophy, and pragmatism not only echoes Brown's conception of the Puritan genesis; she also offers a balanced, universalized perspective, one that "knows no distinction between the bond and the free" (209).

It is significant that Brown devises Georgina as the "Young Christian." She navigates a middle ground and continuously tries to reconcile partisan viewpoints. The result of such reconciliation is, of course, imagined as the Abolitionist perspective. She opposes her father's proslavery arguments and becomes Carlton's missionary, converting the "thoughtless man" by interpreting the bible in its "true light." She labors to "vindicate the Bible from sustaining the monstrous institution of slavery" and dwells on this issue for quite some time (CL 94f). Acts of interpretation are of central importance here: Before Georgina is introduced, we hear Snyder's sermon on slavery, whose reading clearly distorts biblical meaning. In Georgina's elaborations, Brown elucidates on the fact that a text *requires* an interpreter but that methods of interpretation (Georgina's argumentation and Snyder's distortions) can differ greatly.

---

47 Fabi notes that John Peck is based on Peck of Rochester, a reverend and preacher, famous for his stand against natural rights. Brown attended one of his lectures in Farmington, New York in 1846 (CL 260).

Indeed, Georgina Peck is imagined as a representative of a Christian Humanism in the Puritan myth's vein. Her stand is one of universal love for humanity, and she uses both the secular and the sacred as her vanguard. It is in this spirit that she argues for the 'American-ness' of the slaves in a discussion with Carlton. Again, we are offered a lesson in interpretation. This lesson further effects the naturalization (IIc) of the black subject into the nation's civic myths.

After her father's death, Georgina resolves to free her slaves. This act of emancipation is performed out of a subjective motivation, which separates individual agency and societal circumstances. Georgina liberates out of a desire to do justice: "I will not be unjust because the state is" (CL 128). Slavery's despotism is depicted as statist/national despotism, against which personal resistance is necessary. It is, however, not only the Freedom-through-Resistance mytheme that guides Georgina's actions; it is also the idea of the enslaved subject's natural belonging.

After John Peck's death and Georgina's marriage to Carton, the latter proposes to send the emancipated slaves to Liberia. There, he argues, would be their "native land." The following exchange presents a critique of colonization in general and of the American Colonization Society in particular.[48] Importantly, it naturalizes the black subject as *American* subject by inserting them in the imagery of civic narratives. Georgina's argument, like the Declaration, is heavily Lockean in tone.[49] Chapter XVIII, entitled 'The Liberator,' opens with the first lines of the Declaration, and its argument unfolds along the same Lockean lines. First, the U.S. is proclaimed the native land of any black subject, free or enslaved: "Is not this their native land? What right have we, more than the Negro, to the soil here, or to style ourselves native Americans? Indeed it is as much their home as ours, and I have sometimes thought it was more theirs" (CL 134).

The justification for this latter claim is clearly derived from Locke's labor theory of property.[50] I have stated that the legal discourse of *jus terrae* is insufficient for

---

[48] I have argued in a similar vein before. For a related argument and a detailed discussion of colonization see Drescher: *A Home in a Native Land* in Gabrowski and Kozak (eds): *The United States as a Divided Nation* (2014).

[49] See Jayne: *Jefferson's Declaration of Independence* (1998); Marshall: *John Locke: Resistance, Religion and Responsibility* (1994); Stephens: *Locke, Jefferson and the Justices* (2002).

[50] Gould notes that liberty itself can be regarded as a form of property. Thus, the property discourse is used to derogate racist ideology and affirm black humanity (114f). The property discourse in *Clotel* refers directly to Lockean thought when it contests the unjust conversion of man into chattel. Enlightenment ideas of labor, human value, and property rights inform Georgina's speech, and her elaborations stage the virtue of black labor and

American national belonging. Nevertheless, Georgina taps into this discourse and discusses ownership of American soil to further her claim. Here, she relies on Locke, whose *Second Treatise on Government* discusses the notion of land ownership. If a subject seeks to own ground, that ground needs to be changed in its natural state by the labor of the claimant. Thus, human labor *transforms* the ground into something that can be owned: Those who *work* the soil can *own* the soil. Clearly, Georgina has this notion in mind when she states: "The Negro has cleared up the lands, built towns, and enriched the soil with his blood and his tears; and in return, he is to be sent to a country of which he knows nothing" (CL 134). The black subject is thus justified by right of his labor. They are further naturalized by right of their historical contributions in the second American genesis.

Georgina reminds the reader that blacks, too, fought against the British in the American Revolution. Modern black revolutionaries like George Green are but a second generation; there were those who fought for freedom before and who where then denied their share in the victory over Britain. Here, her speech evokes images of the Revolution myth:

Who fought more bravely for American Independence than the blacks? A Negro, by the name of Attucks, was the first that fell in Boston at the commencement of the revolutionary war; and, throughout the whole of the struggles for liberty in this country, the Negroes have contributed their share. (CL 134)

Georgina thus highlights the participation of blacks in the Revolution.[51] If Anglo-Americans won citizenship, why should that reward be denied to black soldiers? Now, "that the danger is past," what justification is there to "deny [them] a home in [their] native land?" (135).

The young Christian is motivated not solely by the principles of Christian humanism. Emancipation is presented as a long overdue *re-installation* of the black subject into the citizen category. Her insistence of America as the native land of free and enslaved blacks transcends the birthplace policies of *jus terrae*. It is rather their *active* contribution to the American project that entitles them, just as any other

---

    thereby undermine racist tenets. Likewise, the auction block scene in Chapter I, where Jefferson's daughters are sold, contests property and humanity conceptualizations.

51 Gould notes that early black writing often recurred to a revitalization of the revolution to open up republican discourses on rights and liberty. The Declaration becomes a fundamentally abolitionist document and the source of an enduring cultural legacy of a revolutionary national genesis based on the Enlightenment theory of natural rights. The One Father Argument inherent in the Declaration is used to philosophically and religiously contest the pseudoscientific notion of black inferiority (117).

American, to the right to belong. Their contributions, however, are depicted as a forgotten chapter of the Revolution myth. Here, the mythological resignification salvages historical fact from the processes of mythological naturalization, only to then naturalize the protagonists of said historical fact into a newly created variant myth. The Ongoing Revolution myth now incorporates the black subject, opening the possibility of citizenship and belonging.

Thus, Georgina Peck imagines an American identity which is universal, and I hold that in *Clotel*, Brown argues for such universalism. Instead of pushing partisan politics, or the establishment of a distinctive black American identity, his mythological resignification attempts at naturalizing the black subject into the structures of a renewed civic myth. Later, indeed, Brown will champion different identities. He will turn to the elaboration of African characteristics in the black population, push for an African national identity, and argue for African colonization.[52] Be that as it may, his debut novel presents an attempt at constructing an American national identity by means of returning to the mythological beginnings of Puritans and Revolutionaries.

Although opposed to expatriation and colonization, the novel describes how fugitives gain freedom elsewhere. Mary and George find freedom and happiness in Europe; William escapes to Canada. Clotel and other characters who remain in the U.S. (Currer, Althesa, Ellen, Jane) die in slavery or take their own life. Brown celebrates the North as home of the American spirit while at the same time depicting the entire nation as hostile to black freedom. If we regard the different instances of mythological resignification, we arrive at one conclusion: For Brown, the U.S. has ceased to be America. The nation that was shaped by Puritan and Revolutionary fathers has succumbed to the despotism of slavery. Brown suggests that a return to the Northern values of universal freedom, to the "good genius" of the American genesis, may alleviate the nation's modern despotism (CL 155). But in the Antebellum moment, no true refuge is found for the fugitive slave. Thus, the Puritan voyage is reversed and freedom is found on Europe's shores; the Revolution now battles tyrants on Capitol Hill; the oppressed still cross the Atlantic, but they journey east.

Yes, Brown seeks to enlist British support for abolition, and he naturally flatters his European audience. But the depiction of 'Europa the Free' and 'America the Despotic' functions as jeremiad and urges to *continue* the heritage of Puritan and

---

52 Levine notes that Brown, interested in black revolutions in the Americas, will actively support emigration shortly before the Civil War. By 1862, Brown embraces the conflict as a war against slavery and ultimately abandons schemes of expatriation. Throughout his career, he will be torn between American nationalism and colonization for black Americans (Monuments 158).

Revolutionary fathers. Thus, Brown's mythological resignification presents an *affirmative treatment* of civic myths. He marries the jeremiad with acts of prophetic revelation: "The great aim of the true friend of the slave would be to lay bare the institution, so that the gaze of the world may be upon it" (CL 3f). He calls upon the "British Crown" and "British public opinion" to influence U.S. policies. That this shames the American audience is clear: The Land of the Free has evolved to the "land of bondage," and the stories in *Clotel* are to be read as factual testimonies. Despite the novel's fictionality, Brown insists that the incidents related are "founded in truth." He numbers his "sources" in the novel's conclusion and hopes that these "facts" may be pondered by his European audiences. Moreover, he enlists their "influence" and their feeling to be "publicly manifested" in the transatlantic fight against the horrors of slavery (208).

"My narrative," Brown writes as he calls for Atlantic support, "has come to a close" (CL 208). Throughout this narrative, an aesthetics of the personal has helped the reader to identify with the characters, to produce sympathy, and, importantly, to engage in lessons of interpretation. Brown resignifies the Puritan and the Revolution myth but also "provide[s] his intended audience with adequate tools to interpret" and re-interpret their meaning (Fabi xv).

In the character of Clotel, Brown resignifies the Puritan myth by focusing on the Freedom-through-Voyage mytheme. The variant Newer Shores myth depicts Clotel as a black Puritan, a character who flees the oppressive spaces of the South in order to gain freedom in the North. Thus, she re-enacts the Puritan voyage, crosses water, and attains freedom by means of a transformative journey. The variant myth produced in Clotel, however, is pessimistic. Returning to the South to rescue her daughter, Clotel is captured and finally driven to suicide. Her death, like Wally's, is imagined as symptomatic of a despotic polity, which makes black freedom impossible. Clotel's reversal of the Puritan voyage ultimately fails, while the Puritan voyage reversed is successful in William.

In the character of George Green, the novel works on the Revolution myth by focusing on the Freedom-trough-Resistance mytheme. George is imagined as a revolutionary culture-hero homologous to the Revolutionary fathers. He embodies the values of the founders: love of freedom, hatred of oppression, and a willingness to enact the right to resist. The variant Ongoing Revolution myth in George produces a black Revolutionary who universalizes the revolutionary situation and adapts it to the Antebellum. Thus, the fight against slavery is depicted as a continuation of the American Revolution. America, however, has turned into a despotic space, so that George cannot find freedom in the U.S. He, too, reverses the Puritan voyage but unlike Clotel finds freedom and happiness in Europe.

Brown's mythological resignification works on two civic myths. As such, his narration is mythologically and historically broader then Hawthorne and Gutzkow's, who focused on one particular mythological moment. Yet Brown's variant myths, his production of black Puritans and Revolutionaries, are *affirmative* of traditional basic myths and attempt to recognize and naturalize the black subject as a true member of the American family. His creation and subsequent naturalization of black Puritans and Revolutionaries seek to open the basic myths to modern, more democratic possibilities for the Antebellum polity. In fact, however, his narratives are conservative: Only a *return* to the original values of the fathers can save the nation. Brown's variant myths are myths of aboriginality, narratives that celebrate Enlightenment values and allocate them through myth (and sometimes against history) in the images of the Puritan and Revolutionary founders. His outlook, however, is universally humanist.

5. Heinrich Heine's *Wintermärchen* and the Laughter of the Age

> Deutscher Boden duldet keine Knechtschaft.
> GRIMM/APPLICATION FOR THE DRAFT OF THE
> PAULSKIRCHEN CONSTITUTION

In 1849, when members of the Frankfurt Parliament discussed the future constitution of Germany, the first democratic revolution had just swept over German soil, and the dreams of democratic authors like Heine and Gutzkow seemed to be materializing. Those dreams, we know, were short-lived indeed. Yet before reactionary forces dissolved Germany's first parliament, Jacob Grimm presented his draft for the first constitutional article: "The German people are a people of freemen, and German soil does not suffer serfdom. Foreign unfree, who dwell on it, are made free by it" (in Deutsche Freiheit 53). The process of national identity building, which scholars like Grimm initiated, centered on this one key aspect of the Germanic myth: *libertas germaniae*. Yet the notion that German *soil* makes free is remarkable; it was a liberal and deeply anti-feudal statement.

Heinrich Heine's *Deutschland. Ein Wintermärchen* (1844) will denaturalize the basis of such high-minded claims; his poem reveals the civic myths in Vormärz identity building and renders them ridiculous. For German soil, Heine knew, did not make free. His poetry was the literary attempt to recognize the German polity for what it was and to suggest what it should be. For in this, Heine concurred with Grimm: The German people *should* be free. Therefore, *Wintermärchen* exorcizes the mythological spirits of the Germanic past and displaces civic gods, making room for the imagination of a new deity. The narrator preparing this *Götterdämmerung* is, of course, a poet: He walks the reader towards individual deification, the attainment of material bliss, and the renunciation of the god(s) of yore. It is his songs that refute medieval myths to focus on the demands of the present. These new songs smirk and thunder: They are the music of a democratic, humanist, and materialistic epoch. Above all, Heine's mythological resignification designs them to be songs of (and for) a new age. And the music of that age is laughter.

5.1. A NEW SONG AND THE SILENCING OF DEATH-KNELLS

The aesthetics of the personal that infused *Clotel* is continued in *Wintermärchen*. Whereas Brown's narration is personalized, Heine's is almost personal. *Wintermärchen* is narrated by an authorial alter ego (a *narrator-poet*) who closely approaches the author without being identical with him. This definition is significant, as the author's personal life and literary work are intimately connected (Kiermeier-Debre 138). Kruse notes that Heine believed his existence to be attuned to history, and a parallelism of the personal and the historical was to haunt him all his life (Leben 16). But as the narrator describes his way back to his native land, he does not present himself as a victim oppressed by historical circumstance. On the contrary: He takes the reader on a journey which reveals the poet's ability to shatter the mythological and political institutions of the German Confederation. This poem is very much a text about an individual. But the narrator's subjective journey is informed by ideas that seek to make the world anew.

The Exiled Poet

Born in the French occupied Rhineland in 1797, Heine's childhood in Düsseldorf was relatively sheltered. Jewish emancipation under the Napoleonic *Code Civil* freed his family from the confines of the ghetto and guaranteed legal equality. But the *Befreiungskriege* [German Campaign] (1813-1815) soon changed Heine's legal status. After Napoleon's defeat, Prussia gained control over the Rhineland, and in 1815, monarchic power was restored in Europe. Heine relocated to the Free City of Frankfurt am Main (Leben 11-31).[1]

In 1831, Heine moved to Paris, high in hopes for democratic change; but to the disappointment of the author, the July Revolution of 1830 ultimately gave way to a

---

1   As mentioned, there is a remarkable parallelism of politically significant dates and private events throughout Heine's biography. In 1815, Heine moved to Frankfurt and later Hamburg to make it as a businessman. While in Hamburg, he fell in love with his cousin Amalie. But in 1821, two years after he left the North to study law at Bonn, Berlin, and Göttingen, his uncle announced Amalie's engagement to a tradesman. In the same year, his childhood hero Napoleon Bonaparte died, and Heine was doubly devastated (Leben 11-31).

bourgeois monarchy. Shortly after, in 1835, the Bundestag prohibition against Heine, Börne, and the Young Germans restricted his literary production in Germany and transformed his Parisian residence into permanent exile. Finally, as France and Germany rose in 1848, Heine suffered a fatal collapse. From the confines of his bedchamber he witnessed the revolutionary failures west and east of the Rhine. He would not leave his sick-chamber, his *Matratzengruft*, until his death in Paris in 1856 (Leben 39-71). At this point, Germany was well on its way to achieve national unity (but not freedom) in the establishment of the German Empire.

The failure to join German aspirations of unity with democratic freedom in the March Revolution was to haunt Heine for the rest of his life. In the 1840s, however, the poet was all but resigned when it came to the establishment of democracy in his native land. He eventually undertook two trips to Germany: the first in October 1843, the second in July 1844. His destination was Hamburg, where his family had taken up permanent residence. But while the Free City tolerated him and allowed his publications, Prussia was eager to lay hands on the dissident writer.[2] Aware of the danger, he undertook the second voyage by sea. The first trip, however, took him through Confederate German (and Prussian) territory. It is the poetic documentation of this particular voyage that produced *Wintermärchen* (Leben 56f).

Wintermärchen is a return poem. It is inspired by the journey of a poet who, for the first time in over a decade, dares to set foot on German soil once more. Reed comments that as Heine comes home in 1843, he returns to "a country held in Metternich's wintry grip." After the Congress of Vienna (1815), the Austrian chancellor Metternich reunited the numerous German states into the loose and ineffective German Confederation. His goal was not national unity but the prolongation of the monarchic principle. Metternich was rather successful in his restorative aspirations: He "put back the clock, put back thirty-six German princes on their thrones, put back the revolutionary jack-in-the-box and sat on the lid." Indeed, the winter landscape of Heine's poem reflects Germany's state of inertia. *Wintermärchen* seeks to combat this inertia, to enlighten, reveal, and bring "warmth and light by means of a little friction" (Reed 10).

Reed notes that *Wintermärchen* has three main objectives. First, it presents a satirical attack on German societal backwardness, on monarchic modes of governance, and on a cultural obsession with the Middle Ages. In this context, it uses irony and satire to make its point. Second, the poem offers a push of ideology, a declaration of age-adequate principles with which to order German society. This ideology is liberal, materialistic to the point of hedonism, and based on an enlightened secularism rooted in the humanist tradition. Lastly, "the poem's third and equally im-

---

2   A Prussian warrant threatened arrest due to his connection to *Vorwärts!*, a journal co-edited by the young Karl Marx (Leben 57).

portant aim is not to get bogged down under the earnestness of the other two" (10). More to the point, the text aims at Heiterkeit: By not taking itself too seriously, it expresses a cheerfulness that aides in ridiculizing (and thus resisting) "those grim but never wholly serious things, the powers that be and ought not to be" (20). The poem's light treatment of serious powers produces laughter: And laughter, Laude notes, is the very best exorcism (126).

Heine began working on the text during his 1843 journey.[3] In a letter to his publisher Campe, he states: "I have also produced some verses on my journey, which come to me quite easily, as I breathe German air" (in Kiermeier-Debre 135f).[4] The poem traces Heine's return journey to Paris and inverses the individual stops.[5] Also, the journey's start was moved to "the dismal month of November" (GWT 29),[6] so as to achieve the dark and sad atmosphere of a winter month (Kiermeier-Debre 136). Kruse and colleagues note that Heine finally produces a poem which stands in the epic tradition. Like Dante's *Inferno*, Goethe's *Hermann und Doda*, and Byron's *Don Juan*, the poem marries narration and verse form. Also, it places particular focus on the wanderer and the events that accompany his journey (105). *Wintermärchen* consists of 27 chapters (capita), follows the traditional German folk ballad, and alternates an iambic metre[7] (Kiermeier-Debre 140). The simplicity of the four-liner is mirrored in the simplicity of the text's poetic ductus: The stanzas' rhythmic structure is dynamic, effecting a "wonderfully spring-heeled rhythm" (Reed 22). This form is a variation of the *Vargantenstrophe*, which is of medieval origin and most famously employed in the song collection *Carmina Burana*. A *vargant* was a travelling singer, someone who wandered from town to town and offered his services. Heine's narrator becomes such a poetic wanderer, always on the move, never static in his belonging (Kruse et al. 109). Wintermärchen is an epic

---

3 The poem was originally published in two editions: the first in September 1844 as a section of *Neue Gedichte*, the second as a separate chapbook in October 1844 (Kruse et al 108).

4 [Hab auch auf meiner Reise mancherley Verse gemacht, die mir mit größerer Leichtigkeit gelingen, wenn ich deutsche Luft athme].

5 The correct order of the journey back to France was: Hamburg, Celle, Hannover, Bückenburg, Minden, Teutoburger Wald, Unna, Hagen, Köln, Aachen, Brüssel, Paris.

6 For quotation purposes in German (marked DWM), I use a modern reprint of Heine's original 1844 edition: *Heinrich Heine: Deutschland. Ein Wintermährchen* (2008). For the English translation (GWT), I rely on Reed: *Deutschland. A Winter's Tale* (1986). All unmarked translations of primary texts are my own.

7 Generally, lines I and III follow an iambic tetrametre, lines II and IV an iambic trimetre, the latter creating female endings which can act as long lines (Kiermeier-Debre 140).

journey featuring a narrating hero who "bring[s] a whole new body of possibilities into the field of experience for other people to experience" (Campbell 49).

But the poem's form also supports its mythological resignification, especially in terms of ideological input. The folk ballad structure and the dynamic simplicity of its metre are reinforced by the narrator's reader-friendly voice: Heine treats the reader to "companionable talk" (Reed 15). This heightens the narrator's persuasiveness, which is crucial for the political intentions of *Wintermärchen*. Kruse notes that like "Martin Luther, Heine considered the people's vernacular and therefore chose a form capable of modulation: the folk song"[8] (Leben 87).

Heine's mythological resignification is also enforced by his use of rhyme. He generally uses the simple end-rhymes of the folk song ballad (rhyming lines II and IV) to structure the stanzas and thus gives his text a lyrical dimension. Simple rhyme, Reed reminds us, is a "powerful ally." By using a lyrical form ingrained in the collective consciousness, the lines' ongoing flow creates the repeating expectation of phonetic coincidence. The argument made in a stanza (or sequence of stanzas) can be reinforced by syntactical and discursive means but also by the phonetic phenomenon we call rhyme. The sense of conclusiveness thereby attained goes beyond rational authority and reinforces the poem's political communication with the reader (22). Rhyme reinforces the message, makes it accessible, and memorable; Kruse notes that here, the reader becomes a face-to-face partner in communication. As mentioned, poetry and autobiography are entangled in Heine: His writing is personal in such a way that the reader becomes the recipient of a personalized sender (Leben 74). This kind of communication humanizes both narrator and reader. Instead of assuming an authoritative or didactical position, Heine's narrator shows, explains, and ridicules. He assumes that the reader is reasonable, sensible, and thus elevates them to a position of individual dignity. Of course, the text aims at the pushing of ideology but it does not indoctrinate. It rather aims at conviction through reason. Yet if it is reason that is relied on, why would Heine recur to myth?

Wintermärchen is an attack on Germany's obsession with medieval and romantic narratives. One could argue that Heine's use of myth only aims at denaturalization by means of ridicule, and certainly, *Wintermärchen* is a text that aims at denaturalizing the veil of medieval nostalgia. But the mythological resignification employed in this poem goes beyond the necessary denaturalization of civic myths. Mythological resignification is a narrative strategy with political intention, the *re*writing of civic myths, not a mere *un*writing. The analysis will show instances of revelation and denaturalization but also the elaboration a variant mythology.

---

8   [Wie Martin Luther hatte Heine dem Volks auf Maul geschaut und darum die modulationsfähige Volksliedstrophe gewählt].

As for his usage of romantic and medieval narratives, I hold that mere refutation would in fact be insufficient. Heine's understanding of history is, in a way, deeply attuned to Germanic notions of time and fate. I have already elaborated on the concept of *wyrd* while discussing *The Scarlet Letter*.[9] It is this notion – the idea that the past (and the future) are not separate entities but inherent parts of the present moment – that informs Heine's treatment of myth. He rejects overcome myths due to their inapplicability to the Vormärz situation but uses their mythemes and imagery to construct a narrative that makes room for contemporary realities.

Wintermärchen, like *Wally*, offers no distinct political instructions (Reed 20). But it would be wrong to state that it only offers criticism. Indeed, Heine constructs a variant myth on which a free polity may rest; that myth is materialistic and centered on the individual to a degree that effects human deification. But the process that leads to the production of the variant includes the treatment of romantic-mediaeval material. Reed has found a telling metaphor for this fact: "Insofar as Romantic attitudes (false medievalism, excessive attachment to the past) were part of [Heine's] target, he is turning the enemy's guns round on him. Insofar as he was half a Romantic himself, they were always his guns too" (15).

Heine's relation to romanticism was complicated. In Geständnisse, he describes himself as a romantic gone astray, a "romantique défroqué" (in Kruse et al. 117). But to be sure, he detested many of the sentimental songs produced by his contemporaries. In this context, *Wintermärchen* is not just a political poem but an aesthetic response to Vormärz poetics. The present, Heine believed, was in need for new melodies.

The Song of Abstinence and the Song of Joy

The narrator-poet begins his journey in the "dismal month of November" and arrives at the French-German border. As he nears German soil, a well of emotion makes his "heart beat quicker" and his eyes "trickle" (GWT 29). The effect that the *Vaterland* has on the exile reaches its climax as he hears his native tongue:

Und als ich die deutsche Sprache vernahm,
Da war mir sehr seltsam zu Muthe;
Ich meinte nicht anders, als ob das Herz
Recht angenehm verblute. (DWM 7)

---

9   cf. Chapter 1.3.

It did strange things to me when I heard
the German language spoken –
like nothing so much as if my heart
was pleasantly being broken. (GWT 29)

Indeed, Heine never stopped thinking of Germany as home. He suffered from homesickness constantly and awaited the day when he would be able to return (Hermand 270). Yet although the German language breaks the narrator's heart, it is a pleasant breaking, a tension between pain and pleasure which is continued in a song that follows the border crossing. The first thing the narrator hears is a melody of "genuine feeling" sung by a girl playing the harp. Indeed, the music is "out of tune" but nevertheless "most appealing" (GWT 29).

Sie sang von Liebe und Liebesgram,
Aufopferung und Widerfinden
Dort oben, in jener besseren Welt,
Wo alle Leiden schwinden. (DWM 7)

She sang of love and sacrifice,
of pain and a tomorrow
when all shall meet in a better world
beyond this vale of sorrow. (GWT 29)

Caput I offers the first of many dialectical pairs in the poem. The girl's song is the *Entsagungslied* [song of abstinence], the "ancient lullaby" of religious asceticism, entailing the deferral of happiness to a heavenly future where "all sufferings will be past" and the soul shall have "joys eternal." The text immediately comments on its therapeutic function: The song of abstinence works towards soothing the people (the "great oaf") in times of sadness. Yet instead of decrying the song, the poet is rather generous in its assessment: Understanding is expressed for those who seek consolation in religious melodies, for these songs are based on "genuine feeling" (GWT 29).[10] However, the song is presented as discordant and escapist. The narrator is quite familiar with it ("I know the tune, I know the words / I know every single author") and offers a first installment of critique when he adds: "I know they tippled wine on the quiet / while publicly drinking water" (30). Indeed, criticism is not so much aimed at the harpist but rather reserved for the song's ideological content. Clerical corruption and critique of religion will occupy this analysis later; for

---

10 In contrast to the English "oaf" the German original "Lümmel" evokes the image of a naughty but not unintelligent person (DWM 8; GWT 29).

now, suffice it to say that the *Entsagungslied* prepares (Ia) for one of the basic myths (the *Three Magi myth*) which *Wintermärchen* will resignify.

Caput I presents a dialectic between the *Entsagungslied* and a new song. Early on, the text also prepares for the variant myth (IIa) and offers, in the mode of poetic prophecy, an oppositional melody. This new song is best described as *Freudenlied* [song of joy]:

Ein neues Lied, ein besseres Lied,
O Freunde, will ich euch dichten!
Wir wollen hier auf Erden schon
Das Himmelreich errichten. (DWM 8)

A different song, a better song,
will get the subject straighter:
let's make a heaven on earth, my friends,
instead of waiting till later. (GWT 30)

The song of joy contains the ideological aspects the text wishes to install; it entails materialistic needs, a celebration of subjective dignity, and, finally, a deification of the individual. Consequently, concepts such as religious abstinence, feudal hierarchy, and serfdom are refuted. The *Freudenlied* postulates happiness "on earth" and resistance to a feudalistic-economic structure where the "idle belly" consumes "what working hands have wrought." Physical sustenance (i.e. food) is of central concern: Again and again, the narrator will use traditional cuisine (and of course, regional wines) to further his arguments. "[B]read enough grows here on earth," he claims, and joins physical sustenance with aesthetic pleasures: "[R]oses and myrtles, beauty and joy" need to be savored on the mortal plain (GWT 30).

Despite the Utopianism of his prophetic elaborations, the narrator remains dedicated to a folk-targeted tone, avoids romantic idealizations, and anchors his discourse on solid ground. He sings of *peas*.

Ja, Zuckererbsen für Jedermann,
Sobald die Schooten platzen!
Den Himmel überlassen wir
Den Engeln und den Spatzen. (DWM 9)

Yes, fresh green peas for everyone
as soon as the pods have burst.
Heaven we'll leave to the angels, and
the sparrows, who had it first. (GWT 30)

Reed notes that the narrator thus grounds his prophetic claims in the everyday. He avoids romantic hyperbole and ensures comprehension. The recurrence to popular language is "a means to keep it real, credible" (17).

The *Freudenlied* is concerned with social justice, and Heine's elaborations are indeed connected to an evolving Marxist criticism. Heine and Marx met in Paris and collaborated in the publication of the journal *Vorwärts!* (Leben 57). Schmitter notes that while the young Marx revered the older poet, Heine remained suspicious of the socialist project. He feared an "egalitarian delirium"[11] just as much as he rejected the radical elements in socialist policy. Although fighting for 'the people,' the bourgeois Heine never idealized the masses (262). Yes, Heine and Marx focused on equality in a materialistic and economic sense. But a proletarian revolution went against the convictions of a writer who believed in gradual progress and pushed for a constitutional monarchy as the next step in Germany's democratic development (Hermand 264).

Moreover, Werner notes that the materialistic character of Heine's ideology derives from the philosophical influence of Saint-Simonianism (20). This French social movement proposed universal human emancipation and focused on materialistic rather than idealistic notions. This approach tried to unite a belief in teleological progress with the political and technological development of modern society.[12] In the spirit of universal emancipation, the *Freudenlied* must be read universally. Indeed, it is sung in the context of Germany, and Germany is its main concern. But if the new song is successful in silencing the old song's "Miserere" and the "death-knells" of an overcome religious myth, Heine imagines that the melody will have European consequences (GWT 30):

Die Jungfrau Europa ist verlobt
Mit dem schönen Geniusse
Der Freiheit, sie liegen einander im Arm,
Sie schwelgen im ersten Kusse. (DWM 9)

The maiden Europa is betrothed
to that handsome Genius, Freedom.
They lie in each other's arms embraced,
it warms my heart to see them. (GWT 30)

---

11 [Gleichheitstaumel].
12 For more on Saint-Simonianism see Carlise: *The Poffered Crown* (1987); Gille (ed.): *Literaturkritiken* (1977); Drukheim: *Socialism and Saint Simon* (2011); Crossley: *French Historians and Romanticism* (1993).

The allegorical union of Europa and Freedom is paramount. The *Freudenlied* is a wedding song ("ein Hochzeitskarmen ist mein Lied") for the newly-wed's "future children" (DWM 9, GWT 31). A song of materialistic freedom thus attains the character of prophesy, and indeed, Heine defined the poet's societal function as a prophetic endeavor. So, as the narrator sets foot on German soil, the exile is transformed. His aim is twofold: prophecy and creation. This narrator presents himself as traveler, prophet, and, ultimately, as a god.[13]

Progress and the Deification of Humanity

The replacement of the old song by a new song prepares for the basic and the variant myth (Ia & IIa). In order to understand this replacement and Heine's general perspective on myth, we have to regard his view of history, and his essay *Verschiedenartige Geschichtsauffassungen* [Different Views on History] (1833) is helpful at this point. Here, the poet discusses two historical philosophies which aim at the explication of world history: organicism and the idea of progress. The first, the idea of cyclic history, sets development analogous to nature; it imagines a "growing, blooming, decaying and dying"14 in the historical process. We may remember that Hawthorne is one of the many proponents of this romantic position. But in contrast to Hawthorne, Heine rejects the vegetative stance. He criticizes its "sentimental indifference"15 and accuses its supporters of relativism and apathy. If all is to return, why invest in humanity's improvement? He complains that organicists "shrug their shoulders at our civilization, which will give way to barbarism in the end."16 Organicism, a "bleak circulation"17 in Heine's view, carries little hope for the betterment of humanity (in Oheler 27).

Heine therefore champions the Hegelian idea of progress. Here, he claims, is an optimistic perspective on history, a position related to the idea of fate. Progress offers a history "in which all earthly things strife towards a beauteous perfection, and the great heroes and heroic ages are but steps towards a higher, god-like state of

---

13 For a similar position on the poet as travelling, foretelling, and creating entity, see Riccobono: *Dante: Poeta, Profeta, Pellegrino, Autore* (2013).
14 [Wachsen, Blühen, Welken und Sterben].
15 [sentimentalen Indifferentismus].
16 [Sie zucken die Achseln über unsere Zivilisation, die doch endlich wieder Barbarei weichen werde].
17 [trostloser Kreislauf].

humanity."[18] This state is one of eternal bliss and will enable the construction of an "ideal polity based exclusively on reason, which will ultimately refine and bless humanity to the highest degree"[19] (in Oheler 28). Heine aligns organicism with a romantic world view and imagines teleological progress as the modern, more adequate, humanist perspective on history.

Still, Heine is conscious of the scholarly nature of both concepts. Neither organicism nor teleology can satisfactorily attune to actual human existence: The past is rendered useless, and the present becomes the future's function. Yet functionality and instrumentality, he claims, are conventional terms, humanly constructed, not naturally given. By insisting that creation intents itself, Heine separates life's dignity from historical considerations: "Life is neither function nor instrument; life is a right. Life wants to assert that right against the solidification of death, against the past; and this assertion is the revolution"[20] (in Oheler 29). The revolutionary assertion of life against all other considerations explains Heine's focus on material values, especially in his promise of a new song.

Höhn notes that Heine in fact presupposed a union of time, a relation in which past, present, and future are one and stand in reciprocal elucidation (178). This *unio tempora*, I hold, is deeply informed by the concept of *wyrd*. Any revolution is therefore rooted (and legitimized) only in life's ongoing and ever-present assertion of itself.[21] Historical particularities fade into the background, and the political revolu-

---

18 [wonach alle irdischen Dinge einer schönen Vollkommenheit entgegeneifern, und die großen Helden und Heldenzeiten nur Staffeln sind zu eine höheren gottähnlichen Zustande des Menschengeschlechts].

19 [idealische Staatsform, die, ganz basiert auf Vernunftgründen, die Menschheit in letzter Instanz veredeln und beglücken soll].

20 [Das Leben ist weder Zweck noch Mittel; das Leben ist ein Recht. Das Leben will dieses Recht geltend machen gegen den erstarrenden Tod, gegen die Vergangenheit, und dieses Geltendmachen ist die Revolution].

21 Revolution thus becomes a concept inherent to societal and individual development. Indeed, Heine and the Young German's view of history entails a revolutionary concept almost identical with Bercovitch's idea of the ongoing American Revolution. In Germany, too, revolution was understood as a natural phenomenon, a natural, necessary, and perpetual element in teleological time. From a Hegelian perspective, Heine's definition of revolution as centered in life itself is not designed to unnaturally upset or accelerate history but is understood as a normalized instrument in the ongoing development of freedom. Further, it is not an egotistical or "Promethean" act of self-assertion in Bercovitch's sense (Revolution 609). It is rather based on the idea that in the Vormärz situation, revolution needs to stem from the constitutive elements that make the modern nation, i.e. the individuals. Individual emancipation, however, gradually leads to societal, and lastly, to uni-

tion is joined (and trumped) by a social revolution. Here, Heine espouses a teleological, progress-centered perspective and recurs to Hegel's philosophy of history.[22] Hegel held that world history is defined by a teleological progress of the consciousness of freedom, a perspective that deeply impressed Heine, who studied with him during his time in Berlin (Leben 26). Indeed, Habermas notes that the young student saw an undercover revolutionary in his professor of philosophy (23). Hegelian history further explains Heine's need to reject traditional civic myths and his endeavor to construct a variant myth able to express the present moment.

If we follow Hegel, history is the ongoing development of revolutions of freedom. Heine connects this teleological process with his Saint-Simonian belief in technological progress and the possibility to reconcile historical antagonisms. These antagonisms and their tension constitute the Hegelian dialectic: The ongoing conflict between the forces of *reaction* and *progress* in the course of history. Hermand notes that this perspective will become Heine's "dialectic optic" (261).[23] Concerning historical development, the poet generally champions progress, a fact evident in his rejection of overcome myths in *Wintermärchen*.[24]

At the end of progress, Heine envisions a universal human brotherhood. The peoples, the new "heroes of the age," are to unite so as to overcome the feudal and monarchic constraints of the past (in Mende 88). As he rejects the idea of the mass-as-individual, he focuses on the subject: "For every single human being is a world in himself, which is born with him and dies with him; beneath every tombstone lies

---

    versal emancipation. In Heine, Bercovitch's "transatlantic contrast" fails to establish a significant difference between America and Germany in this regard (Office 35).

22 For an overview on Hegel's philosophy of history, see Hegel: *Vorlesungen über die Philosophie der Geschichte* (1986); Winter: *Hegels formale Geschichtsphilosphie* (2015); Nuzzo: *Memory, History, Justice in Hegel* (2012); Hodgson: *Shapes of Freedom* (2012); Pöggeler: *Hegel: Einführung in seine Philosophie* (1977).

23 [dialektisierende Optik].

24 Still, Höhn is correct in reminding us that Heine does not claim an absolute linearity of history (179). He sometimes merges progress and organicism, and holds that, due to the obvious irrationality in the world, historical development can recur to cyclic forms in times of crisis, i.e. in post-revolutionary ages. "Not only reason and the history of salvation dictate the world's course but equally unreason and folly" [Nicht allein Vernunft und Heilsplan bestimmen den Lauf der Welt, sondern ebenso Unvernunft und Narrheit]. Interestingly, it is this proto-Nietzschean idea that "the world, as a rule, makes fun of itself" [daß die Welt grundsätzlich sich selbst spottet] which may transform historiography to a *Weltbühne* where irony and satire may play at will (in Höhn 180).

a world history"[25] (in Mende 89). Thus, Heine promotes democratization in the form of a *universal revolution* which overcomes traditional disparities. Mende holds that the lynchpin here is the people's material welfare (90). Consequently, Heine opposed a purely bourgeois transformation but hoped for the elevation of the "King in rags"[26] (in Mende 91).Very much like Hawthorne, he mistrusted spontaneous revolutionary action and opted for a constitutional monarchy as the first step on the road towards democratic emancipation. Understood in a Hegelian context, Mende notes that Heine pushed for the victory of the democratic *principle* before considering policy particulars (91). True to his belief in democratic progress, he rejects kings and Kaiser (and their mythologies) as things of the past. The people, he holds, are the heroes of the age, and universal freedom becomes the new religion of the West (Höhn 186).[27] The individual subject is thereby deified in Heine's thinking, and his mythological resignification will build on this deification.

The deification of the individual is palpable in *Wintermärchen*. Not only does the poet's song silence the death-knells of Christian religiosity, it promotes the edification of an earthly paradise that is to fulfill subjective material needs. At the same time, the narrator himself is deified by his poetic mission. He enters a realm that is stuck in the flow of history: Germany looks backwards and fashions the state according to medieval or romantic myths. But the exile who postulates the universal emancipation and deification of humankind arrives to set Germany onto the right course again. He becomes a heroic demigod; and as his foot touches "German soil," the narrator feels his "powers" (GWT 31):

Seit ich auf deutsche Erde trat
Druchströmen mich Zaubersäfte –
Der Riese hat wieder die Mutter berührt,
Und es wuchsen ihm neu die Kräfte. (DWM 10)

Since I set foot on German soil
the magic juices are flowing –
the giant has touched his mother again,
and he feels his powers growing. (GWT 31)

---

25 [Denn jeder einzelne Mensch ist schon eine Welt, die mit ihm geboren wird und mit ihm stirbt, unter jedem Grabstein liegt eine Weltgeschichte].
26 [Königs in Lumpen].
27 Kortländer notes that this new religion carries all the characteristics of a religious institution: It has priest, saints and gospels, martyrs and prayers, and ultimately, the right to condemn heretics (32).

Caput I ends by conflating the narrator-poet with a figure of Greek mythology, a conflation which further prepares for the variant myth (IIa). The famous Titan Antaeus, son of Earth mother Gaia, was feared for his strength. Ultimately, he would be defeated by another demigod, Hercules, son of Zeus. Antaeus, however, proved a problematic adversary, as his powers were fully restored the moment he touched the ground (i.e. his mother Gaia). Hercules was only able to defeat his enemy by holding him up in the air and there crush him to death (Hamilton 229). Heine taps into this myth in order to describe the imaginative power that may be attained by returning to one's native land. Simultaneously, the identification with Antaeus carries additional meaning. Reed notes that in Schiller's *Die Worte des Wahns* (1799), the battle between Antaeus and Hercules is recast as the battle between idealism and materialism (101). Antaeus, the earth-bound, is locked in eternal combat with the airy realm of ideas represented by Hercules. Schiller designs his poem as a celebration of idealism's ongoing (yet fruitless) battle against earthly concerns and at the same time warns against materialism's resilience:

So lang er glaubt an die Goldene Zeit,
Wo das Rechte, das Gute wird siegen,
Das Rechte, das Gute führt ewig Streit,
Nie wird der Feind ihm erliegen,
Und erstickst du ihn nicht in den Lüften frei,
Stets wächst ihm die Kraft auf der Erde neu. (Schiller 131)

As long as he trusts in the Golden Time
Where the good, the righteous shall triumph
The righteous, the good forever fights
But the enemy's ever defiant
And if you don't choke him in the heavenly blue
He touches the earth and his strength is renewed.

For Schiller, truth and beauty are found in inner-subjective depths, and Antaeus, who derives his powers from the earth, is cast in the role of enemy, one who can only be vanquished by severing earthly ties.[28] Heine, of course, disagrees. He casts Antaeus as hero, who by re-connecting with the earth (materialism) regains his strength. This is in line with the poem's aesthetic and political intentions: The vari-

---

28 Schiller's poem elaborates on the idealist's futile quest against the powers of materialism. Simultaneously, his is an obstinate call to resist the temptation of despair and retain one's faith in idealist values. It offers a (romantic) reminder that beauty and truth are not found in material reality, where only the "fool" thinks them existent (131).

ant myth, the *New Generation myth*, promotes earthly values and material bliss against the idealism of religion and romanticism. Heine's narrator is therefore cast in the role of a materialistic Titanic demigod, who is strengthened by renewed contact with German soil.

The new song of materiality finds its prophetic voice in the deified narrator-poet. His strength renewed, the wanderer begins to denaturalize (Ic) the old song's ideology. Indeed, the new song is highly critical of religion and focused on human dignity on earth (Kruse et al. 122). But by means of the Antaeus reference, the narrator is able to comment on Vormärz Germany with more than human authority.

Denkler notes that in the culture wars of the time, the poet was assigned the role of prophet and priest, regardless of political persuasion. Liberal writers were seen as utopian prophets, whereas conservative voices saw themselves as temple guards (200f). Kruse further comments that Heine taps into the traditional notion of the poet as prophetic voice: "Indeed, he understands the poet's office as one born out of historical responsibility and targeted at a future, which will secure humanity's position in the world, so that it may shape the world sensibly and not become a victim of circumstance"[29] (Leben 10). But the traditionally dual relationship between prophet (medium) and divine entity (speaker) implodes in this case. The narrator does not speak for a god; he *is* a god and speaks for his fellow gods, the individuals.

Wapnewski has elaborated on the poet as *alter deus*. The idea of a creating god (*deus creator*) in mind, a human deity (*poeta creator*) is vindicated due to the poet's ability of "world-creation"[30] (Dichtergott 37). In the context of Heine's poetry – for which Wapnewski refutes any differentiation between author and narrator– he assigns Heine the status of such a *poeta creator*: "He was the divine creator of his self, he created his own life. And that life was art."[31] Such a position, however, has Luciferian consequences. The relationship between *deus creator* and *poeta creator* can be characterized by partnership, competition, even succession (43).[32]

---

29 [[T]atsächlich versteht er das Amt des Dichters als eines aus historischer Verantwortung zugunsten einer Zukunft, die den Menschen ihren Platz in der Welt sichert, damit sie nicht Opfer der Verhältnisse werden, sondern die Erde sinnvoll gestalten].

30 [Weltschaffung].

31 [Er war der Schöpfergott seiner selbst, hat sich sein eigenes Leben gezeugt. Und dieses Leben war die Kunst].

32 The idea of the artist's deification is, of course, older than the Vormärz. The first German examples are found in Minne poetry, where Walther von der Vogelweide elaborated on the *unio mystica* of human and deity. This union consequently leads to a *deificatio* of humanity itself, a "complete deification of the universe" [Totalvergottung des Universums] (Dichtergott 43). On the road to such universal deification, the poet is the other god (*alter deus*), the human-divine entity that by the power of the word names and creates re-

Now, the narrator in *Wintermärchen* experiences a certain level of deification by means of his identification with the demigod Antaeus, an identification which prepares (IIa) for the variant myth. Indeed, the narrator's deification is a first step leading to universal deification. This is congruent with Heine's hope for the general emancipation of humanity. In his deified narrator, the text offers a utopian foil for the rest of humanity. The readers (the new heroes of the time) are to re-enact what the poet enacts: the creation of a free world. The narrator is both prophet and creator of a polity which is to be based on the new song of individualistic and materialistic happiness.

The Reichsadler and Prussian Veiling

The prophetic voice of the *poeta creator* will return at the end of *Wintermärchen*, when the narrator discusses Germany's future with the goddess Hammonia and naturalizes the variant myth (IIc). The first Caput, however, offers the intention and legitimation of walking the road ahead: The song of joy does not only refute the old *Entsagungslied*, it offers the ideological content to construct a new German polity, one that is in tune with the author's liberal politics and belief in the teleological progress of humanity.

That this narrating *poeta propheta* is a poet who fights his battles with literary weapons becomes evident in Caput II. As the maiden sings the *Entsagungslied*, the poet has to pass border control. Prussian soldiers rummage through his belongings to no avail, for they cannot know that the most dangerous "contraband" travels behind the his "forehead:" sharp, well-crafted "needles"[33] can be found there; also, the crown jewels of the "unknown god" that shall free the land; and books, dangerous volumes that even "Satan's shelves" cannot provide (GWT 31f). It is literary dissent he is smuggling in:

---

ality from a position of independence, autonomy, and responsibility (40f). God becomes the *Urpoet*, whereas poets are, in Heine's words, "little post-creators" [der kleine Nachschöpfer] (in Dichtergott 45).

33 Reed translates German "Spitzen" with 'needles' (DWM 11). In German, the word *Spitze* (point, tip, peak) contains a homonymity which in this case results in the *double entrende* of pointed weapons (such as a spear or a knife) and the climax of a joke (French: pointe), which is also described as a *Spitze* in German. Heine makes clear that his words, especially his jokes, have the same effect as a well-crafted military blade.

Und viele Bücher trag ich im Kopf!
Ich darf es euch versichern,
Mein Kopf ist ein zwitscherndes Vogelnest
Von konfiszirlichen Büchern. (DWM 12)

And books! I'm full of them, like a tree
in spring when the songbirds have nested
and fledglings clamour to take the wing –
any one would get me arrested. (GWT 32)

The narrator proceeds, in Caput III, to the city of Aachen. This caput can be compared to Hawthorne's preparation and exposition of the Puritan myth in *The Scarlet Letter*. The image that is presented here prepares for and simultaneously denaturalizes (Ic) the imperial myth attached to the medieval Kaiser Barbarossa (Ia). Here is what I would like to describe as the *Reichsadler* image. In *The Custom House*, Hawthorne imagines the Federal Eagle as a hostile and greedy animal. Likewise, Heine abuses the imperial bird of the Holy Roman Empire, now transformed and reduced to adorn the sigils of Prussia and Austria. The Reichsadler image, however, does not only represent the kingdom of Prussia but comprises the general recurrence of Confederate Germany to Germanic myths. While the *Entsagungslied* prepares (Ia) for the poem's critique of religion in the Three Magi myth, the Reichsadler functions as a recurring image for political circumstance and prepares the exposition (Ib) of the Barbarossa myth. It critiques the modern adaption of romantic ideas about the German past (monarchy, unity, cultural importance) and the appropriation of medieval imagery (castles, knights, maidens). Here, the denaturalization (Ic) of the Barbarossa myth begins by means of ridicule and critique aimed especially at Prussian representations. In this context, Werner notes that Prussia was engaged in a "contortion of the empire's old glory"[34] which led to a national parody of antiquity (22). In Caput III, the narrator presents (and attacks) this parody in the Prussian eagle.

Indeed, Aachen is the perfect locale to investigate the political circumstance represented by the Reichsadler. Aachen was the capital of Karl I (Karl der Große or Charlemagne), who first united the Holy Roman Empire and was crowned its first Kaiser in 800 A.D. However, it is with the "*bones* of Carolus Magnus"[35] that the reader is introduced to this once imperial city. The narrator immediately contrasts the burial place of the founding Kaiser with the present age: He would not wish to be buried here, despite all its "splendid imperial shining" but would prefer to "be

---

34 [Verdrehungen der alten Reichsherrlichkeit].
35 Italics MRD.

living" in any other city, even in Stuttgart.[36] Indeed, Aachen acts as a synecdoche for Germany: It is a "boring hole" where even the "dogs are so bored" that a voluntary servility is the order of the day. This indoctrinated serfdom is apparent in the dog's (read citizen's) "servile wagging" of their tails. Death, want, and servitude – main themes of the religious *Entsagungslied* – reign supreme in Karl's city. They do so hand in hand with "Prussian soldiers" (GWT 33).

The Prussians, just as Hawthorne's Puritans, are introduced in all but flattering colors. Interestingly, both authors focus on color-coding and garments in their denaturalization (Ic) of political powers.[37] Puritan and Prussian colors converge, and a general tint of grey and black pervades the scene in Aachen. Red (Hester's color) is reserved for Prussia's own witch-hunt victims: the French. Further, both authors use iron and steel as descriptive signifiers for the conservative powers that be. Prussian military representatives wear "grey coats," are "wooden and pedantic," and as graceful as a "right-angled triangle." Puritan discipline (the whip, the scaffold) is similar to Prussian discipline and also remarked upon early. Prussian soldiers are said to have swallowed "the corporal's stick" and repeated beating has indoctrinated a harsh, violent discipline (GWT 33). Its violence and harshness have "never quite been lost," just as the "old iron hand" which hides itself under the "glove of newer ways" is still existent (34).

Here, the narrator begins to elaborate on what can be described as the practice of Prussian *veiling*. It is in the critical revelation of the veiling practice that the basic Barbarossa myth begins to be denaturalized (Ic). Prussia aims at hiding raw power (iron hands) behind cultural images (glove). Heine thus designs an imagerial genealogy (authentic medieval imagery and contemporary pseudo-medieval imagery) and reinterprets the signifiers of a romanticized past by attaching new meanings. The spiked Prussian helmet may be an adequate example. Reminiscent of the armament of medieval knights, modern Prussian cavalry wears a knight's "helmet" with a "spike of steel" added to it (GWT 34). This new "Costum" refers to the imagery that constitutes the Reichsadler (DWM 14): It tells of "knights in times Romantic;" "of the good olde Middle Ages so fine;" of "Crusade and tourney" and an "age of faith without the blessing of print" (GWT 34).

The Reichsadler image – and here we may remember the critique of artificiality in *Wally* – is presented as an artificial veil. While Gutzkow takes the veiling process quite seriously, Heine's narrator is highly amused: The helmet, he states, is an ex-

---

36 This is the first of numerous attacks on the Swabian School, a conservative group of authors whom Heine abhorred both politically and aesthetically. Stuttgart was the capital of the Kingdom of Württemberg and remains the capital of today's State of Baden-Württemberg.

37 cf. Chapter 1.2.

cellent "royal jest" which (like his own verses) is "most delicately pointed." Further, the joke attests to "the wit of the Lord's Anointed" who hide Prussian dominance behind pseudo-medieval images (GWT 34). The only problem lies in how history may react to such romantic drapery:

Nur fürcht' ich, wenn ein Gewitter entsteht,
Zieht leicht so eine Spitze
Herab auf Euer romantisches Haupt
Des Himmels modernste Blitze! (DWM 15)

It's really only the thought of storms
that I find a little fright'ning –
that spike on your Romanic heads
might attract some modern lightning. (GWT 34)

The narrator-poet assures the reader of the incompatibility of such romantic dress-up with the modern age. Prussian usage of medieval drapery may fool some but not modernity itself. This exposé on Prussian recurrence to medieval imagery culminates in the introduction of the Prussian eagle itself, which looks at the wanderer "with an eye / most poisonously malign" (GWT 35) The eagle is stylized as the ultimate enemy; here, Heine certainly meant Prussia but also a general mytho-political reliance on the emblems, ideas, and polity structures of the Holy Roman Empire. If we remember the Falcon myth in *Wally*, we see that the concept of the bird as the wanderer's faithful companion[38] is reversed in *Wintermärchen*. This bird indeed accompanies the narrator on his journey but always as adversary:

Du häßlicher Vogel, wirst du einst
Mir in die Hände fallen,
So rupfe ich dir die Federn aus
Und hacke dir ab die Krallen. (DWM 15)

You ugly devil, just you wait,
if I ever manage to catch you
I'll pluck out your feathers and hack off your claws
and then as follows dispatch you. (GWT 35)

Caput III closes with announcing an attack against Prussian dominance. But it is primarily the skillful proclamation (and menace) of mythological resignification.

---

38 cf. Chapter 3.2, footnote 33.

The narrator-poet describes what he intends to do in the following capita: denaturalize (pluck feathers) and then dethrone (hack off claws) dominant civic myths. The two main instances of critique have now been given mythological garb: critique of religion will focus on the *Entsagungslied*, and political circumstance is enshrined in the *Reichsadler* image. Indeed, the text prepares (Ia) and begins to denaturalize (Ic) both basic myths very early on. In its poetical attack on throne and altar, *Wintermärchen* begins with the latter and takes the reader to the most controversial building site in Vormärz Germany to begin its resignification of the Three Magi myth.

5.2 Dreaming Freedom and the Dethroning of Saints

In *Wally*, Gutzkow's female protagonist is eventually crushed under the paradoxes of theology. Similarly, *Wintermärchen* entails a critique of institutionalized religion. The mythological resignification in Heine's poem works on two basic myths, both of which are paramount to the Vormärz alliance of throne and altar and infused with Christian meaning. The first is the *Three Magi myth*, which will be resignified in the Cologne capita. The story of the magi who foretell the coming of Christ will be denaturalized by working on the *Coming-of-the-King* mytheme.

The Gods in Exile

The work that *Wintermärchen* achieves in denaturalizing religious myth is indebted to Heine's teleological view of human progress. Kortländer notes that Heine saw religion, like political power, as subject to the ongoing progress of history and regarded Christianity as the religious expression of a time past. The now, in his view, required a new religion of freedom (32). The Vormärz, therefore, was in need of a myth that explained the demise of Christianity and legitimized the edification of a new religious regime. Heine produced such a myth in his essay *Die Götter im Exil* [The Gods in Exile] (1854).

As a mythologist, Heine studied not only Greek, Roman, and German myth but developed his own mythological system. The writing of myths as a literary technique was indeed a means of explaining the past, but it also had political significance. Holub notes that as the "creator of a new mytho-political universe,"[39] Heine combined his mythological studies with the writing of new, contemporary mytholo-

---

39 [Schöpfer eines neuen politisierten mythischen Universums].

gies. In this context, *Die Götter im Exil* presents a topos that saturates his oeuvre: the fall and rise of gods (315f).[40]

Die Götter im Exil traces Western religious development, explaining the fall of Hellenism and the rise of Christianity. What is crucial to this narrative is the teleological perspective it encourages the reader to adopt; its function lies in the recognition of a world-process from which no human institution is exempt (Holub 317). Religions are understood as expression of their time; yet the essay reminds the reader that as Pagan deities were dethroned, they were recast as demons,[41] spirits who live on and retain a "real, but cursed existence."[42] Nature cults become Satanic worship, and Pagan gods are now supposed to deal in the seduction of humanity by means of their "lust and beauty," "dances and songs"[43] (GIE 45). Further, the old gods live as exiles: Apollo, for instance, is now a shepherd in the Austrian South (47).

The exiled gods, Holub comments, allow Heine to compare Pagan and Christian religiosity. In doing so, he unfolds a dialectic which informs the mythological resignification in *Wintermärchen*: Christian spiritualism vs. Hellenic sensuality, monotheistic Nazarenes vs. pantheistic Hellenists (319, 324). The essay's Dionysus story illustrates this point. It tells of a fisherman, who is visited by three monks asking for passage to the other side of a lake. On arrival, the fisherman grows curious and follows the monks into the forest. They arrive at a clearing, where a bacchanal is in full progress. Young women and men crowned with wreaths greet the monks, and an orgiastic night of merrymaking begins (GIE 48). The monks finally reveal themselves to be old gods: two acolytes, the first representing lust (he was endowed with a "ridiculously exaggerated gender"),[44] the second a corpulent embodiment of food and drink. The third monk is Dionysus himself, a youthful beau clad in a diamond tunic (49). The progress, however, is a feast of the dead; once a year the old spirits leave their temple-ruins to celebrate a "joyous mass"[45] in honor of Dionysus, the "divine emancipator"[46] and "Messiah of sensual pleasure."[47] The bacchanal fills the

---

40 It may be noted that Neil Gaiman's *American Gods* (2001) takes up Heine's approach and describes the rise and fall of gods in historical time while at the same time discussing the translation of deities from other world regions to the American continent by means of migration.
41 cf. Chapter 2.1.
42 [wirkliche, aber vermaledeite Existenz].
43 [Wollust und Schönheit, besonders durch Tanz und Gesang].
44 [lächerlich übertriebende Geschlechtlichkeit].
45 [fröhlichen Gottesdienst].
46 [Göttlichen Befreiers].
47 [Heiland der Sinneslust].

fisherman with fascination and dread, and the music invades "his spirit like flames" (50).[48] This fire burns too hot for the devout Christian, and he flees the scene. The next day, he comes before the superior of a local Franciscan monastery to give witness. But it turns out that the superior is Dionysus himself, and as superior, he offers counsel: "Indeed, we do not wish to speak ill of this [Dionysus], for he is surely a sometime breaker of sorrows and delights the human heart, but he is very dangerous for those, who cannot hold their own, and you seem to be one of them."[49] Therefore, he presses the fisherman not to overindulge in wine (51).

The Dionysus story works on the same grounds as *Wintermärchen*: It entails a dialectic between spiritualistic and materialistic morality. Dionysus' "ambrosian regiment of joy"[50] contrasts the fisherman's "regiment of the cross, of suffering" (GIE 56).[51] Further, it exposes clerical hypocrisy in casting the god of wine as a Franciscan superior: The Janus-faced practice of preaching water and drinking wine is already present in *Wintermärchen* ("I know they tippled wine on the quiet / while publicly drinking water") and finds a later elaboration in this story (GWT 30). Moreover, the development from joyful pantheism to serious monotheism is explained in entropic terms: The once fiery god and his entourage celebrate a feast of the dead, not of the living; Dionysus himself advises the fisherman to exercise restraint in the drinking of wine; the music of myth ignites a fire the modern Christian cannot stand. The point here is that the modern civilized subject can no longer bare the sensual intensity of antiquity.

Höhn notes that it is in this entropic disenchantment of the world that Heine situates religion. Indeed, he thought of civilization itself as a constant loss of beauty and sensuality but regarded this "continuous sacrifice"[52] to be the motor that allowed for Western rationalization and the realization of freedom (177). Religion is no exception to this process. Heine held that in the warmer days, pantheism and enjoyment of the sensual reigned supreme, but civilization moved on to the spiritual, immaterial, abstinent stance of monotheism. Now, if we follow Heine, the age of monotheism is also coming to a close in the Vormärz, and the West is preparing for the dawn of a religion of individual, materialistic, and secular freedom. Indeed, there is no going back: Entropy will not allow a return to the days of Dionysus. En-

---

48 [weichen, zärtlichen und doch zugleich grausamen Töne der Musik, die [der Fischer] vernahm, drangen in sein Gemüth wie Flammen, lodernd, verzehrend, grauenhaft].
49 [Wir wollen bei Leibe nichts Unliebiges von diesem Gotte sagen, er ist gewiß manchmal ein Sorgenbrecher und erfreut des Menschen Herz, aber er ist sehr gefährlich für diejenigen, die nicht viel vertragen können, und zu diesen scheint Ihr zu gehören].
50 [ambrosisches Freudenregiment].
51 [Regiment des Kreuzes, des Leidens].
52 [Geschichte als kontinuierliches Opfer].

tropy, alienation, and disruption are described as the price of progress, a price Heine was willing to pay, as it was the only way to guarantee a free, autonomous, and individual life (187).[53]

But Heine will insist, despite all entropy, on humanity's "ambrosian right"[54] and remain adamant in his proposal of material enjoyment (Holub 319). It is a new form of joy that the marriage between Freedom and Europa promises: It is less Olympian and certainly more down to earth. Instead of ambrosia for the few, Heine envisions green peas for all. But before the poem constructs a materialistic variant myth, it will denaturalize the old. The resignification begins in the realm of religion and with the Three Magi myth.

The Ghosts of Cologne

The Cologne capita continue motifs used in Caput I. First, German space once more affects the narrator-poet: As his cheeks are "fanned by German air," he feels a deep influence work upon him. Also, the insistence on sustenance is continued, as the air's effect is channeled onto his "appetite," a need which he appeases with a generous helping of local fare and wine (GWT 35). Moreover, medieval imagery is used again: The wine is served in Roman glassware ("im grünen Römerglase"), and the wanderer grows intoxicated (DWM 17). Inebriated by wine and nostalgia, he walks by "ancient houses" which tell the "legends of holy Cologne." Indeed, these legends are without exception tales of clerical abuse: Cologne is represented as the "centre of clerisy" and "Men Obscure," referring to the medieval culture wars between citizenry and clergy. The poem goes on to report of denunciations, inquisi-

---

53 Within the notion of entropy lies another distinction: the opposition between the sacred and the profane. Indeed, the process of ongoing profanization demands an epoch-specific historical critique. From a Vormärz perspective, this means the allocation of the sacred to the times of gods, heroes, and geniuses, which leaves the present as the age of the petty bourgeoisie. Heine, very much like Gutzkow, claimed that the truly sacred died with the French Revolution and Napoleon. The Congress of Vienna, on the other hand, hailed the age of the philistines (Höhn 185). This development has consequences for the arts: Romantic idealism does not fit the age of increasing profanity; the flowery language of heroes needs to be substituted with a language that focuses on the new hero (the people) and befits contemporary technological progress. This holds even (and especially) for myth. In *Die Götter im Exil*, Heine insists on the "magic of the generally comprehensible word" [Zaubermacht des allgemein verständlichen Wortes] and proposes the "black art of a healthy, clear, and popular style" [die Schwarzkunst eines gesunden, klaren, volksthümlichen Stiles] (GIE 47).

54 [ambrosisches Recht].

tion, hypocrisy, and pyres. Monks and nuns danced a medieval "cancan" in the city, and the poet is able to identify their "progeny" by their "theological hatred" (GWT 36).

From these descriptions, the Cathedral of Cologne rises "black as the devilish powers" (GWT 36). The gigantic structure represents the epitome of religious influence and abuse previously described. Consequently, its function is equally suspect: It was meant to be the "mind's Bastille," built to imprison "German reason" in its vaults. This plan was halted by Luther's Reformation, and the poet once again turns prophet and foresees that the cathedral shall one day be used as a horse stable (37). This means that the magi, whose bones rest in the cathedral, would have to be moved. Here, the narrator offers a suggestion: They could be put in the iron cages that hang from a tower in the city of Münster.[55] Indeed, should one of the oriental kings be lost, one could always "hang high" an "occidental" king in his stead (38f).[56]

Caput IV casts the Cathedral of Cologne as a symbol of ecclesial power. What is crucial for the mythological resignification here is how the cathedral is allocated in teleological time, for Heine has the building's ongoing construction mirror the flow of history. The construction process is interrupted by the Reformation, which from a Hegelian point of view constitutes a revolution for the enlargement of freedom. After the Reformation, the cathedral can be no more than the architectural representation of an overcome religious ideology. In terms of form, every stanza drives towards the cathedral image: "It was getting late" when the wanderer arrives

---

55 The iron cages the narrator refers to are three penal constructions. In the 1530s, Anabaptists proclaimed an independent theocracy in the city of Münster. Their rebellion ended in 1535, when prince-bishop Franz von Waldeck retook the city. In 1536, the three leaders were publicly tortured to death and then hung in the iron cages made especially for the occasion. The cages were never taken down. For more, see Albrecht: *Das Königreich der Täufer* (2001); Dülmen: *Das Täuferreich zu Münster* (1974); Arthur: *The Tailor King* (1999).

56 The idea to hang the Three Magi, let alone a modern German king, is highly provocative. Yet there are unpublished stanzas that go further. Here, the reference to the Münster Rebellion is elaborated, and the narrator explains why the three kings should suffer such a gruesome fate. As no one knows "what deeds they perpetrated when living," the magi may have been "the kind of princes who promise a constitution" and then "break their word" (GWT 38f) The suggestion to put a modern prince in the cage makes more sense with these rejected stanzas in mind, because it becomes clear who is meant exactly. During the *Befreiungskriege*, the Prussian King Friedrich Wilhelm III was able to enlist liberal forces by promising a constitution in case of victory. When the time came, however, the king went back on his word.

in Cologne. He walks the streets, medieval legends surround him like ghosts in the now "dusky night" (GWT 36). These ghosts are neither glorious nor heroic: They tell of the scandal of clerical politics. The narrator's path is accompanied by the scenery's darkening; then, in complete darkness, the cathedral rises before his eyes. Here, Caput IV and its critique of institutionalized religion offer a first act of denaturalization (Ic).

Wintermärchen's critical denaturalization in this instance is threefold. First, contemporary religion is described as historically overcome and oppressive to the present moment. Second, the text denounces religious hypocrisy, especially concerning the clergy's supposedly abstinent lifestyle. Third, it rejects theological hatred, a mixture of "malice and stupidity" that caused the inquisition, a culture of denunciation, and the burning of dissenters (GWT 36). Caput IV, however, does not stop at criticism of religion. It attacks the altar first but does not forget that the Cathedral of Cologne, like the Cathedral of Aachen, houses the bones (and thrones) of kings.

The Lictor and the Power of the Word

Before the narrator-poet faces the oriental kings, he elaborates on a rather unique figure. In Caput VI, we are introduced to a "*spiritus familiaris*," an entity that takes the form of a Roman lictor.[57] The lictor appears to the poet when he sits down to write; he shows himself as a cloaked figure, hiding an "executioner's axe" beneath his cloak (GWT 42). The spirit appears again in Cologne, and as the poet confronts the apparition, it replies:

'Ich bin kein Gespenst der Vergangenheit,
Kein grabesentstiegener Strohwisch,
Und von Rhetorik bin ich kein Freund,
Bin auch nicht sehr philosophisch'

---

57 The lictor, a precursor to the Praetorian, was an armed guard that protected Roman potentates. He carried a bundle of wooden rods to which an axe was attached. This symbol of military power was called *fasces*, from which the term fascism derives. The *fasces* is a symbol of authority, both political and military, representing unity, power, and justice (Rabbow 77). The *fasces* is found on the flag of the Italian National Fascist Party but also on many other representative emblems, such as the coat of the Spanish Guardia Civil, the coat of the Swiss canton St Gallen and, notably, on numerous seals of the United States, among them the official seal of the U.S. Senate.

'Ich bin von praktischer Natur,
Und immer schweigsam und ruhig.
Doch wisse: was du ersonnen im Geist',
das führ' ich aus, das thu' ich.' (DWM 27)

'I'm not a phantom from the past,
Nor a wraith whose tombstone has lifted,
I'm not inclined to rhetoric
Nor philosophic'lly gifted.'

'My disposition is practical,
silence and calmness suit it.
But know: what you conceive in your mind,
I do it, I execute it.' (GWT 43)

Habermas notes that Heine has long pondered the relation between thought and action (29). These musings have found its embodiment in the lictor: The spirit transforms "abstraction / into reality." While the poet's realm is "thought," the lictor's sphere is "action" and the execution of the poet's contemplations (GWT 44).

'Ich bin der Lictor, und ich geh'
Beständig mit dem blanken
Richtbeile hinter dir – ich bin
Die That von deinem Gedanken.' (DWM 28)

'I am your lictor, and I march
Behind you, with axe well polished:
Whenever your thought condemns a thing –
I act, and it's demolished.' (GWT 44)

Habermas is correct in claiming that the lictor represents Heine's philosophy of action. In the context of mythological resignification, the lictor embodies the real-life consequences of Heine's mythological work. The poet as intellectual may have been neither a professional politician nor a revolutionary, but Heine insisted on an agency element in his aesthetical work. He opposed a *radical* autonomy of art yet insisted on *general* autonomy so as to efficiently influence politics. The word, so to speak, can be the foundation of action (29f). Therefore, the relation between poet and lictor is best understood as a *Doppelgänger* motif. In a societal context, the lictor enacts thoughts which may develop a polity that is in dire need of action. Indeed, the triggering of such agency is one of the tasks of the political poet (Kruse et al. 126). In opposition to romanticism, Heine hoped for a societal impetus of literary endeavors: "Action is the word's child, and Goethe's beautiful words are childless."[58] (in Habermas 29). As a result, the autonomy of art in Heine's definition needs to carefully negotiate between a position removed from societal concern and a total absorption by politics (Habermas 29f).

This middle ground nevertheless poses problems in the dialectic of thought and action. Heine is concerned that "proud men of action"[59] tend to be no more than henchmen for "men of thought"[60] (in Habermas 29). Thus, men of thought (and the thinking poet) are ultimately accountable. The lictor as the executive branch of poetry is both: a testimony to the power of literature and a reminder of authorial responsibility (Habermas 30). Be that as it may, the lictor raises the poet's societal position: He becomes tribune, a potentate whose thoughts have real-life consequences. Schmitter is correct in stating that in the lictor, the "dreamer" has regained his active shadow without whom art would be renderer powerless (244).

Dreaming and Denaturalizing the Magi

Dreams are paramount for the mythological resignification in *Wintermärchen*, for the work on myth occurs largely in the *dream capita*. In Caput VII, the discussion of the relationship between thought and action is continued as the poet sleeps for the first time. In "German bedding" he escapes to realms where the soul is "free / of any earthly tethers" and "sours to touch / the heights of heaven eternal" (GWT 44). The ongoing stanzas, thick with irony, attest to the German capacity to dream. Germany, the poet claims, reigns "unchallenged" in the sphere of "dreamy abstract notions" (45). These stanzas elaborate on idealism as it was described in the Antaeus image and Schiller's *Die Worte des Wahns*, and the realm of transcendental ideas is described as the central sphere of German thought.

Despite its ironic treatment, a possibility for agency is found in dreaming. Kruse and colleagues note that Heine regarded dreams as fundamental to human nature. Although skeptical of the escapism in dreaming, he held that dreams may uncover and preserve humane values in an inhumane world (126). Dreaming, therefore, becomes an exercise that may lead to the edification of freedom:

---

58 [Die Tat ist das Kind des Wortes, und die Goetheschen schönen Worte sind kinderlos].
59 [stolze Männer der Tat].
60 [Gedankenmänner].

Spottet nicht unserer Träumer, dann und wann, wie Somnambüle sprechen sie Wunderbares im Schlafe, und ihr Wort wird Saat der Freiheit. Keiner kann absehen die Wendung der Dinge. – Wenn einst, was Gott verhüte, in der ganzen Welt die Freiheit verschwunden ist, so wird ein deutscher Träumer sie in seinen Träumen wieder entdecken. (Heine in Hermand 261)

Do not mock our dreamers, now and then, like sleepwalkers they speak of wonderful things while sleeping, and their word becomes the seed of freedom. No one can foresee the final turn of things. – When one day, freedom is gone from the entire world (which god forbid), it shall be a German dreamer who will rediscover it in his dreams.

Indeed, the first basic myth, the Three Magi myth, is resignified in such a dream.

In the case of the basic Three Magi myth, we have the luxury to be able to rely on an original textual source.[61] The Three Magi myth is a biblical mythology and can be found in the gospel according to Matthew. The narrative is situated in the context of Jesus' birth: Magicians from the East come to King Herod on their quest to find the newborn king of Judea and speak of a prophesy according to which a new king is to be born in Bethlehem. The magi, being skilled astronomers, followed a star and came to worship the child. Hearing this, King Herod encourages the magi in their search for the babe and asks to be informed of its whereabouts. The magi find the manger, worship the child, and offer three gifts: gold, frankincense, and myrrh. However, they are warned in a dream not to return to King Herod, because he means to do the child harm (KJV Matthew 2, 1-12). Over time, this biblical narrative has been added to, transforming the magi into kings, defining their number as three (according to the gifts), and fashioning names for the worshippers: Caspar, Melchior and Balthazar (Oepen 11).

Landau notes that there are remarkable gaps in the Matthew story (3). The account lacks basic information, e.g. names, origin, and number of the magi. These gaps have been filled in, and apocrypha, hymns, and sermons added to the narrative throughout time (6). One of the most comprehensive medieval sources is the *Historia Trium Regnum* (1364), a Latin manuscript by the German cleric Johannes von

---

61 For more on the history of the Three Magi myth and the relics in the Cathedral of Cologne see Hofmann: *Die Heiligen Drei Könige* (1972); Lauer: *Der Schrein der Heiligen Drei Könige* (2004); Timmermans: *Das Triptychon von den Heiligen Drei Königen* (2008); Kehrer: *Die Heiligen Drei Könige in Literatur und Kunst* (1976); Schock-Werner et al (eds.): *Bauphasen des Kölner Domes und seiner Vorgängerbauten* (2011); Kemper: *Die Goldschmiedearbeiten am Dreikönigsschrein* Vol.1 (2014).

Hildesheim (Schaer 11).[62] This account appropriates apocryphal material and was quickly translated into numerous languages (17).[63]

For Heine's contemporaries, the Hildesheim account was the most significant. The text was a medieval bestseller: Supported by the enthusiasm with which the magi's relics where greeted in Cologne in 1164, the story became a commonplace narrative in Germany and Europe as Western interest in the myth climaxed with Dassel's translation of the relics from Milan (Schaer 22). This interest was to revive in the 19th century as Goethe re-discovered a Hildesheim manuscript and issued a modern translation in 1818. This edition, entitled *Die Legende von den Heiligen Drei Königen*, re-connected the German public with the myth (Westermann-Angerhausen 11). Importantly, it revived the myth's medieval argument for the legitimation of religious submission and sacralized kingship, an argument which Heine's mythological resignification will contest.

The Three Magi myth focuses on one crucial aspect: adoration.[64] Therefore, one of the myth's core consequences was the demand of venerable submission. Jacobus

---

62 The *Historia Trium Regnum* tells of the Prophecy of Balaam, which foretells the birth of a new king and the coming of a messianic kingdom: "I shall see him, but not now. I shall behold him, but not nigh. There shall come a Star out of Jacob, and a Sceptre shall rise out of Israel, and shall smite the corners of Moab, and destroy all the children of Sheth" (KJV Numbers 24:17f). The *Historia* imagines that this prophecy spreads, so that Persian and Chaldean magi install a watch on Mount Vaus (Mountain of Victory). Finally, the star rises, and a voice commands to seek and adore the new king. The three kings set out and complete their journey miraculously in twelve days without food, drink, or rest. They bring gifts and kneel before the Christ-child and then return to their lands. Later, the apostle Thomas meets the kings in their old age, baptizes them, and makes them archbishops of their domains (Schaer 19f).

63 Centuries of elaboration will continue to mold the myth. At the end of the 2nd century, Tertullian assigns the magi to Tharsis, Arabia, and Saba, and sermons by bishop Caesarius of Arles attests to their kingship. The names Caspar, Melchior, and Balthazar appear as early as the 9th and are agreed upon in the 13th century in Jacobus de Vorgaine's *Legenda Aurea* (Westermann-Angerhausen 7). Another important source is the gospel commentary *Opus Imperfectum in Mattheum*, written by John Chrysostom in the 5th century. The *Opus Imperfectum* places particular focus on the star of Bethlehem and reports on a significantly longer journey (Schaer 21). Finally, work on the anonymous *Revelation of the Magi* has recently expanded the scholarship on the myth. *Revelation* presents a magus' first person narrative reporting on the journey and the adoration of Christ (Landau 6). The originally Syriac text relates to the *Opus Imperfectum* and was later incorporated in an 18th century collection by Guiseppe Assemani (16f).

de Voragine notes in a sermon on the signification of the magi's gifts: A true Christian must "sacrifice spiritually to Christ" as the magi did in Bethlehem (in Westermann-Angerhausen 11).65 The magi were not only prophets of a Christian age but foils for true Christian behavior; they suffered voluntarily so as to follow Christ and submitted without reservation to the new king of kings. The modern Christian subject was to follow these ancient examples. But religious adoration was also tied to the justification of monarchic rule, especially with regard to the divine right of kings. Westermann-Angerhausen notes that in the Three Magi myth, kingship was legitimized and sacralized in the image of the magi. Whereas the adoration of the Christ-child is understood as a religious act, the magi's kingship entails secular significations:

The three oriental kings' adoration of the newborn Christ-child sitting on his mother's lap always remains a sign of the child's divinity and universal power. At the same time, the magi's kingship is in itself ennobled and simultaneously newly established, as it is blessed by god. (7)66

Indeed, the magi are understood as the first Christian kings and become the foil for the Christian subject as well as the Christian ruler. The transformation from magus to king justifies and cements the divine installation of royal authority.

Interestingly, the magi and the narrator-poet in *Wintermärchen* share characteristics. They are wanderers who come to a land that is expecting an era of transformation; they are prophets and foretell the coming of a new age; lastly, paramount events are communicated to them in dreams. However, it is the magi's religious signification which sets them in opposition to the narrator. In the course of Christian history, the magi have become emblematic of adoration and conversion: The once Pagan kings read the course of history and came to hail the dissolution of the Hebrew covenant and its replacement by the new covenant of Christ. Becks and colleagues note that the magi are the first converted Pagans who decide to follow Jesus (57). Indeed, the narrator in *Wintermärchen* fulfills the same prophetic function. Almost two thousand years later, he *succeeds* the magi. He ends the age of

---

64 A significant number of depictions show the kings on their knees presenting their gifts. In one of the largest collections on the matter, 53 of 74 images are depictions of adoration (cf. Becks et al. Katalog II).
65 [also sollen wir geistlich Christo opfern].
66 [Immer bleibt die Huldigung der drei Könige aus dem Morgenland vor dem neugeborenen Jesuskind auf dem Schoß seiner Mutter ein Zeichen für dessen Göttlichkeit und weltumspannende Macht. Zugleich wir das Königtum der Weisen selbst geadelt und gleichsam neu begründet, weil es von Gott gesegnet wird].

Christianity by proclaiming the religion of freedom, just as the magi ended the age of the old covenant. That proclamation, however, comes at a cost.

As mentioned, the work on myth occurs largely in the narrator's dreams. In this case, the poet's dream begins to turn nightmare. His heart is slid open; reminiscent of Caput I, it bleeds from a "gaping wound." In preparation (Ia) of the encounter with the biblical kings, the narrator reverses a biblical image: As he walks the streets, he dips his finger in the wound and coats the "doorpost[s]" of houses. Whenever he does this, a death-knell rings from afar (GWT 45). Here, the caput refers to an image from the Old Testament: Moses marked the Israelites' doorposts with the blood of a lamb; doors that did not bear the mark were visited by the Angle of Death (KJV Exodus 12, 13-17). In *Wintermärchen*, the image is reversed, and the death-knell rings as the poet's blood is applied to the posts. We know that death-knell from Caput I: It is part of the *Entsagungslied*, which in due time will be silenced in the denaturalization of the magi. The fact that the narrator himself will be hurt in the process is also foreshadowed in this reversal of biblical imagery.

The exposition (Ib) and simultaneous denaturalization (Ic) of the basic Three Magi myth occurs in the Cathedral of Cologne. Once again, a gradual darkening accompanies the poet on his way to the cathedral: The moon's "wan light ever receding," he arrives and is greeted by a decaying interior where "[d]eath and night and silence reigned." Finally, he encounters three "skeletons" in royal garments "with crowns upon their pathetic / yellow skulls" (GWT 46). The kings smell of death and incense, and one of them begins to give a long speech, scolding the visitor for his discourteous behavior. The "dead," the skeleton claims, should be respected; further, they are "kings" and "saint[s]" and therefore even more deserving of his deference (47).

Faced with the magi, the poet's answer presents the climax of the ongoing mythological denaturalization (Ic). His answer adheres to structures of exorcism combined with the expression of the age, laughter:

Ich gab ihm zur Antwort lachenden Muths:
Vergebens ist deine Bemühung!
Ich sehe, daß du der Vergangenheit
Gehörst in jeder Beziehung.

Fort! fort von hier! im tiefen Grab
Ist Eure natürliche Stelle.
Das Leben nimmt jetzt in Beschlag
Die Schätze dieser Kapelle. (DWM 33)

I answered him with an easy laugh:
'You might as well stop trying.
I see you belong in all respects
to an age that's dead or dying.

'Take yourself off! The deepest grave
is the place for you and your kin there.
Life lays claim to your chapel now
and the treasures you've hoarded in there. (GWT 47)

As the poet turns away, the lictor steps up and shatters "the old bones of false beliefs." But as the blows reverberate in the halls, the poet himself is wounded: "Blood spurted" from his breast, and he wakes (ibid.).

The lictor shatters what is left of the paragons of the *Entsagungslied*. But when the relics were fist moved to Cologne in 1164 by Rainhald von Dassel, several functions were attached to the bones. Oepen explains that Chancellor Dassel intended to establish the relics as a central imperial sanctum (11, 13). Also, the Three Magi myth was to ignite a new wave of pilgrimage (Schäfke 15). However, the adoration of the magi in Cologne also entailed political dimensions. The relics were war booty from the second sacking of Milan in 1162 and represented imperial power (Oepen 11). Further, the shrine attained a deeply political signification, as it came to represent the ideal of Christian kingship (Becks 173). The kings that bowed to the Christ-child became a role model of the religiously steadfast secular ruler; thus, kingship itself was sacralized, albeit by means of a myth that found its material center in Cologne (Oepen 13).

Caput VII may denaturalize (Ic) a predominantly religious basic myth, but it is crucial to remember the alliance of throne and altar in Vormärz Germany. The Three Magi myth is not only a narrative that promotes religious piety; its medieval history incorporates monarchic hierarchy. After all, it was Kaiser Friedrich Barbarossa who sacked Milan and gave the relics to his friend and chancellor Dassel. Weinfurter reminds us that he was the Kaiser who pushed for the 'holiness' of the Holy Roman Empire (*sanctum imperium*) and was successful in doing so against papal authority (118). The relics undoubtedly helped Friedrich in achieving a degree of independence from papal rule by means of religious myth making.

In the poem, the Three Magi emerge from their shrine as if from a tomb, and the lictor shatters both. Becks notes that this shrine is the most elaborate gold work of the Middle Ages, a masterpiece in European art history. In contrast to every other relic encasement, this one bears a significant difference. A shrine's iconography usually focuses on the saint whose relics it holds; the Cologne shire, however, does not particularly champion the magi in its representations. It is the only relic shrine that presents the *entire* history of salvation (175). As such, it represents not just one set of Christian saints but the history of Christianity from its very beginning. This may explain what the lictor is shattering: the sum of Christian religiosity represented by the Three Magi myth. That myth comes to an end in *Wintermärchen* by means of mythemic elaboration (IIb).

Inherent to the Three Magi myth is what I referred to as the Coming-of-the-King mytheme. It is this mytheme that the narrator uses to denaturalize the myth. The magi are thought of as both kings and prophets, harbingers of the Age of Christ. It makes little difference if one interprets the Coming-of-the-King as a biblical narrative (the magi awaiting the Christ child) or as an eschatological promise of Christ's Second Coming (Christendom awaiting Christ's return). The prophetic stance of the magi functions transhistorically and makes the same demands: ascetic conduct, submission, and adoration of Christ in light of the coming deliverance. The mytheme has behavioral (spiritualization, asceticism, world-denial) as well as perceptional consequences (earth as a valley of suffering, primacy of spirituality). These consequences are undone and redefined as the narrator-poet denaturalizes the magi.

The *poeta propheta* reveals the old prophets as overcome, dead skeletons that have no actual authority to level their claims. The new prophet, however, bears the power to ban the specters of the old religion with laughter and thus enforces their ultimate destruction. His actions are homologous to the magi's when they came to King Herod: The poet displaces an old covenant and hails the coming of something new. He prophesizes the advent of a new king, a new deity: the "unknown god" who will "free" the land from the "old one" (GWT 32). For Heine, this unknown god is the people (the King in rags) and the sovereign individual. As the early Christians smashed Pagan temples, the lictor now smashes the magi's shrine to make room for the future deity. Thus, Heine's first instance of mythemic elaboration (IIb) adheres to the Coming-of-the-King mytheme and keeps its eschatological promise but reworks it in a way that refutes the tenets of abstinence, submission, and adoration. Thus, it steers the narrative in a direction which allows for the imagination of a new deity. Also, he dismisses the messianic undertones of the mytheme (no distinct savior is offered) and focuses on the prophetic stance. A messianic-eschatological promise is replaced by a prophetic-eschatological one. This mythemic elaboration will be continued as the narrator denaturalizes the medieval German messiah in the Barbarossa capita.

Capita I (*Entsagungslied*) and VII (reversed Passover image) prepare (Ia) for the resignification of the Three Magi myth. The process of denaturalization (Ic) begins by describing Cologne's history of religious corruption and delegitimizing claims of medieval glory in Caput IV. The cathedral itself becomes the epitome of what is described as obsolete religiosity. Then, in Caput VII, a dream voyage mirrors the narrator's real-life journey in Cologne, leading to the confrontation with the magi. In line with the assumption that Christianity is decaying, the oriental kings are cast in the role of undead entities, skeletons devoid of actual power and authority, demanding respect on the grounds of tradition, not reality. The image suggests that Christianity as an institution is populated by things of the past, beliefs that are incompatible with the modern age. Consequently, the narrator turns prophet once more: He appropriates biblical imagery (the prophet Moses and the Passover tradition) and reverses its import, becoming the harbinger of death for the kings. The basic myth is declared obsolete and refuted in an act of exorcism, which finds its physical execution by the poet's lictor. Heine's mythemic elaboration (IIb) of the Coming-of-the-King mytheme begins by casting his own narrator as prophet who displaces an old covenant so as to prepare the way for the democratic King is rags. A new meaning is installed: the prophetic-eschatological *Coming-of-Freedom* mytheme. The basic myth has thereby been denaturalized (Ic), its fundamental tenants (piety, abstinence, submission, sacralized kingship) refuted. The cathedral remains empty, ready to be filled with the "future's merry cavalry" (GWT 47).

But as the lictor smashes the magi's bones, blood gushes from the poet's breast. This image seems counterintuitive, as it suggests connectivity, even identification between narrator and the magi. Such a connection, however, can be explained by Heine's adherence to the concept of *wyrd*. Christianity may be historically overcome, but as a religious expression of an earlier age it constitutes a historical reality in the teleological flow of time. If that flow of time is believed to be centered in the present moment, i.e. if the past remains an intricate part of the now, violence against the past is always violence against the present. The narrator, prophet of the age of freedom, feels the lictor's axe as it shatters the prophets of Christianity. This does not mean that the bones should not be shattered; it means that historical transformation comes with a cost: "Bu oh! every inch humanity progresses costs rivers of blood" (Heine in Höhn 188).[67] The representative of modernity may smash the gods of the past; but if the past is ever-present, such actions will wound the heart of a poet who was nurtured by the tenets of older religions. Indeed, the idea that the attainment of a free future includes sacrifice will resurface in the naturalization of the variant (IIc) at the end of the poem.

The denaturalization (Ic) of the Three Magi myth is the first step in the process of mythological resignification in *Wintermärchen*. The central myth of the altar has now been refuted. The construction of a variant, however, will have to wait, for the next step is yet another denaturalization. This time, Heine will attack the throne. He uses a myth that is connected to a number of medieval narratives, which present a familiar protagonist. The Barbarossa myth revolves around the Kaiser who caused the magi's relics to be moved to Cologne. It is a mythology that celebrates Friedrich I as the ultimate German messiah.

---

67 [Aber ach! jeder Zoll, den die Menschheit weiter rückt, kostet Ströme Blutes].

5.3 THE SLEEPING KAISER AND THE SEALING OF GRAVES

The Barbarossa myth was without question one of the central civic myths of Vormärz Germany. While Gutzkow's *Wally* takes a detour and focuses on rituals of love and conquest in order to critique societal circumstance, Heine goes directly against a myth that celebrates medieval forms of governance and societal organization. He connects the Barbarossa narrative with the legend of Tannhäuser and ridicules German hopes for a reinstallation of imperial polity structures. His mythological resignification will denaturalize this myth of Kaiser and Reich and pave the road towards the construction of a variant civic myth.

The Kaiser in the Mountain

In the attempts to construe a German national identity, a politicized version of the medieval Barbarossa myth emerged in the 19th century. Again, cultural elites looked back on history and perused an old legend that was able to articulate the needs and issues of the day.

The myths' protagonist is Kaiser Friedrich I, German King and Holy Roman Emperor of the House of Hohenstaufen (1122-1190). The reign of the Staufer dynasty was interpreted as the empire's golden age, the heyday of cultural, political, and artistic achievement. Friedrich I established a realm that enjoyed overall peace and prosperity; at the same time, he opposed papal authority in matters of secular governance, strengthening German political hegemony. Crowned King of Germany in 1152 and Holy Roman Emperor in 1155, he began consolidating his dominion over Northern Italy, which led to six military campaigns, one of which caused the magi's relics to be moved to Cologne. Ultimately, his expansion politics failed, and he lost his struggle with Rome. Still, Friedrich I, or Barbarossa, as the Italians named him, became a veritable savior figure in the German imagination (Rödger 23f).

Rödger notes that Barbarossa's character and ominous death in 1190 further enabled his legendarization. When his grandson Friedrich II died, the latter's demise left the empire in a state of interregnum, causing internal war and adversity. In this context, popular legends appeared calling for the emperor's return. The people's desire for stability encouraged the legendarization of Friedrich I and II, and the ideas of imperial greatness, unity, and peace were associated with the memory of the Staufer reign (25). At the end of the 12th century, Friedrich I is mentioned in this tradition: He first appears in Heinrich von Veldecke's *Eineid* (1170), Gunther von Pairis *Ligurinius* (1187), and Archipoeta's *Kaiserhymnus* (1159). These narratives find a continuation in popular stories that begin to emerge in the 14th century (Frenzel 278). Legends revolve around Friedrich I and II respectively, until the figures are conflated in the Barbarossa character. Popular legends find their way into collections, the first of which is the anonymous *Volksbuch von Friedrich Barbarossa* (1519), which already allocates the Kaiser in a mountain. That mountain is first identified as the Kyffhäuser in Behrens' *Hercynia Curosia* (1703), a tradition which will be continued in texts such as Büsching's *Volkssagen, Märchen und Legenden* (1815) and significantly in Rückert's poem *Kaiser Friedrich im Kyffhäuser* (1817) (279).

The basic Barbarossa myth experienced little variation throughout the centuries, although its function varied considerably. In *Thüringer Sagenbuch* (1836), Bechstein summarizes it as follows: Friedrich I goes on a crusade, never to return. He is, however, not dead but still alive and lives in the Kyffhäuser Mountain with his court. In the mountain there is a great hall, and he sits at a golden table wearing a crown. His red beard has grown greatly, to such an extent that it already circles the table twice. The day his beard circles the table a third time, Barbarossa shall rise and re-establish the empire. Yet the Kaiser is not fully asleep: In a state of half-sleep, he nods and blinks every once in a while. Every century, he sends a dwarf or child to the surface, to see whether the ravens still circle the mountain. If they do, Barbarossa grows sad and sleeps for yet another hundred years (in Rödger 26).

Indeed, the Barbarossa myth entails an eschatological prophecy of messianic return. The fact that this myth has been read as prophecy from the beginning is evident in the 13th century Italian collection *Sibyla Eritrea*. Here, the legend is understood as commemorating Barbarossa as an immortal entity: "[A]mong the peoples the cry shall arise: he lives and lives not"[68] (in Schneider 124). Moreover, Schneider notes that the fact that Barbarossa repairs to the mountain in the first place must be understood in an apocalyptical context. In the early Middle Ages, the belief that the end of days is nigh was cultural commonplace. In light of these apocalyptic expectations, Friedrich I was seen from two distinct and opposing perspectives. Rome and the Church saw in him a precursor of the Antichrist, and Innozenz IV and Gregor IX proclaimed crusades against the Staufer king. His supporters, however, saw a *novus dux*, a new type of ruler who would fight clerical corruption and renew the Church. Naturally, the conflict between emperor and pope had apocalyptical undertones for the contemporaries. After the death of Friedrich II and the end of the Staufer dynasty, the Friedrichs are conflated, and a belief in the Staufer's survival spreads. Further, Schneider comments that in de Adam's *Cronica* (1280) and in the *Sächsische Weltchronik* (1260), Barbarossa is not just a new but the final type of ruler: an emperor of peace and the latter days. Messianic hope converges with the

---

68 [Verborgenen Todes wird er die Augen schließen und fortleben; tönen wird es unter den Völkern: Er lebt und lebt nicht].

belief in the coming of a golden age which the Staufer king is to realize (125f).[69] Moreover, Frenzel notes that with Rückert's 1817 poem, the myth arrived in Vormärz negotiations of national identity and was introduced to the national political arena. That the myth resonated so strongly with Vormärz needs is due to two medieval notions: *Kaiser* and *Reich* (279).

The medieval Barbarossa myth was the articulation of two societal desires which arose in the interregnum after the Staufer reign. In a state of political transition, the Staufer dynasty experienced as nostalgic coloring, resulting in the legendarization of Friedrich I. This figure was to be the foil onto which societal desires could be projected. The first was a longing for the re-unification and consolidation of an empire on the brink of dissolution. The second notion revolves around the emperor's office itself. As *novo dux* and opponent of clerical abuse, Barbarossa embodied secular imperial governance, which was imagined as superior to the fractured reign of German princes. The ideas of Kaiser and Reich as guarantees for an effective, peaceful, and prosperous state of society infused the image of Barbarossa; in connection with the eschatological promise of a golden era, the myth emerged as a dominant narrative in the medieval collective memory (Röder 25).

Vormärz interpretations of the myth recur to the ideas of a return to imperial glory, unification, and the coming of a golden age for Germany. Kaul states that the wish for freedom and unity is expressed in the aforementioned terms Kaiser and Reich, uniting medieval nostalgia and modern political aspirations (147). The Barbarossa myth, originally a popular, social-utopian legend, becomes increasingly political by highlighting the imperial undertones of the narrative and then incorporating them into a religious-national context (756). Indeed, German nationalism was highly informed by religion. The idea of the nation was grounded on the people, their language, their culture, and everything popular was given the tinge of natural authenticity and aboriginality; but in concert with the messianic-eschatological promise in the Barbarossa myth, the nation itself became sacralized.[70] The liaison

---

69 Indeed, the motif of the king in the mountain is pan-European and not restricted to one specific ruler or region. Friedrich dwelt in German and Italian mountains, and English sources speak of King Arthur's mountainous dwelling and eventual return. Specificity lies in the shared mytheme of these stories, namely the idea of return and societal salvation. This mytheme is significant for the Vormärz interpretations of the myth. Until the 19th century, the Barbarossa myth was primarily used for regional narratives of noble families, especially of the houses Wittelsbach and Welfen (Schneider 132).

70 For an overview on the concept of the nation in Germany including the Middle Ages, see Garber: *Vom universalen zum engogenen Nationalismus. Die Idee der Nation im deutschen Spätmittelalter und in der frühen Neuzeit* in Scheuer (ed.): *Dichter und ihre Nation* (1993); Werner: *Nationen und Imperien. Zur Heines Sicht auf die Konzeptionen und*

between religion and nation not only resulted in the glorification of the imperial Middle Ages but also positioned nationalism as an *Ersatz* religion (757). In contrast to other mythological figures of national identification (e.g. Germania or the German Michel), Barbarossa was the figure that offered both political and religious fulfillment. In the Vormärz situation, this fulfillment was imagined as a restoration of German unity and power[71] (759). The mytheme of this civic myth, the *Return-of-the-King*, was of crucial importance for both progressive and conservative identity politics. Heine's narrator poet will elaborate on this mytheme as he confronts the Kaiser in the mountain.[72]

Old Gods in Old Caves

Heine's treatment of the Barbarossa myth in *Wintermärchen* is not his first working with mythological entities roaming mountainous caves. A short look at his essay *Elementargeister* will give us the necessary contextual knowledge of the Barbarossa myth and its central location: the mountain. *Elementargeister* is Heine's most detailed mythological text. It is a tract on German mythology, an overview of the sprites and spirits that populate Germany's imaginary landscape. Holub notes that here, German myths are presented as part of an anti-spiritualistic, sensualistic tradition which the rise of Christianity could not completely obliterate (320). Heine's

---

Praktiken der politischen Organisationsformen im Europa des 19. Jahrhunderts in Kortländer (ed.): *"was die Zeit fühlt, und denkt und bedarf." Die Welt des 19. Jahrhunderts im Werk Heinrich Heines* (2014).

71 Kaul notes that after 1871 and the establishment of the German Empire, the myth will find its fulfillment in Wilhelm I (*Barbablanca*), in whom the mythological Kaiser receives a modern successor (761). Moreover, an originally universal and cosmopolitan definition of the Reich will be transformed into a nationalism based on ethnicity, and radicalize itself in ideas of *Kulturhöhe*, *Deutsche Sendung*, and imperial aspirations (764). The Barbarossa myth's messianic-eschatological fixation and its further development will then offer parts of the mythological material for Germany's fall from civilization during the NS-regime.

72 Heine was not the only author engaging the Barbarossa myth. Frenzel notes that a vast number of texts appeared in the Vormärz dealing with the Kaiser in the mountain, both on the progressive and conservative side. Friedrich Rückert's poem *Friedrich im Kyffhäuser* (1817) retells the legend, albeit in a descriptive, apolitical manner. Yet political voices followed Rückert's poem: Fallersleben's *Wenn der Kaiser doch erstände* (1840) and Arndt's *Deutsche Kaiserfahrt* (1849) call for Barbarossa's return, whereas rejection is voiced in Herwegh's *Der Schwabenkaiser* (1867) (279).

mythological resignification taps into this sensualistic tradition and aims at reactivating the appreciation of the materialistic dimensions of human existence.

The tract begins with discussing the main types of spirits that can be attributed to the four elements. The reader is introduced to the earthy realm of the gnomes, taken to witness the elves' airy dances, and invited to swim with mermaids and undines. The fire elementals, however, receive a more detailed discussion. Heine claims that in folklore, there is but one spirit of fire: Lucifer. In a fascinating passage, he draws on Dante and recasts the fallen angel as "representative of human reason,"[73] a true advocate for the "rights of materiality."[74] Reminiscent of Milton's devil, Heine's Lucifer is the ultimate rebel, who opposes ascetic spiritualization and celebrates individual reasoning (EG 222).[75] But the Church, the poet claims, has "demonized individual reasoning and thus declared the devil to be the Father of Lies"[76] (222f). In this context, the new religion has not only banned free thought but all that pertains to the world of myth; what remains of myth now belong to the realm of art (232). Still, old mythologies do not have to be resurrected or rejuvenated: What Heine hopes for is to conserve the inner significance of mythological narratives, in order to defend Hellenic joy in the face of Nazarene suffering (240f). Yet as myth pertains to art now, it needs to be furthered in art. It is in this dialectic of exoteric religion and esoteric mythology that Heine elaborates on his work on myth. As an example, he refers to the *Tannhäuser myth* and describes *in nuce* what I have been defining as mythological resignification.

The Tannhäuser myth, like the Barbarossa myth, tells of a mountain. Inside dwells a beautiful goddess (usually Venus), who, pursued by Christianity, fled her temple and retreated with her court of nymphs to the shadows of the caves. A knight (Eckhart) guards the entrance so that no one may enter this realm of sensual pleasure (EG 255). Nevertheless, the knight Tannhäuser is able to slip by the guard

---

73 [Repräsentant der menschlichen Vernunft].

74 [Rechte der Materie].

75 Bercovitch claims that European representations of revolution entail a "Promethean self-assertion" against "paternal gods." Dante, Milton, and Heine's Luciferian characters certainly fall under this category. But Heine's Promethean narrator is also in the process of "affirming order," a notion that Bercovitch restricts to American revolutionary ideology (Revolution 609). Later, Heine will link the narrator-poet to the Titan Prometheus, just as he linked him to the Titan Antaeus. But this Promethean character labors not solely for self-assertion but for the establishment of a new order. Just like Cäsar in *Wally*, Heine's narrator enacts an individual dissent in a time of transition but always for the construction of a societal stability which is yet to come.

76 [das Selbstdenken als Teufeln verdammt und den Teufel, den Repräsentanten der Vernunft, für den Vater der Lüge erklärt].

and enter the Venus Mountain (*Mons Veneris*). He lives in utter bliss with the goddess, until he feels that he needs to atone for his sins. He goes to Rome and begs for forgiveness, but the pope rejects his supplications, claiming that not even God could forgive his trespasses. The bishop of Rome then takes an oath: Tannhäuser's sins will be forgiven the moment his dead wooden staff begins to bloom. The inconsolable knight returns to the mountain and is never heard of again. But three days later, the staff does bloom, and indignation is heaped upon the pope for turning a repentant soul away (257).

Heine takes this basic version of the Tannhäuser myth from Armin and Brentano's *Des Knaben Wunderhorn* (1808), which follows Prätorius' version in *Blockes-Berges Verichtung* (1668). As far as medieval myth goes, this narrative is rather exceptional. It celebrates divine mercy and forgiveness but also entails a critique of the papacy. What is important for this analysis is the fact that the mountain as mythological locus is elaborated as a space of *overcome gods*. Indeed, the Venus Mountain is a place of sensual fulfillment and eventual return for Tannhäuser, but it remains a space divorced from history and reality. Now, Heine makes it clear that he does not wish to resuscitate the old gods. He affirms that the rise of Christianity was part of teleological history and the entropy of ongoing civilization: Hellenism had run its course, and Christianity came as a "flame" which warmed the "igneous bark from the inside" so that "fresh leaves and fragrant flowers" could grow once more (EG 232).[77]

Yet in order to save their signification, not the gods themselves, Heine offers a new myth based on the medieval text, a "reworking of the same song"[78] where the "inner motives"[79] have been changed (EG 265). His poem *Der Tannhäuser* (1836), like *Wintermärchen* first published in *Neue Gedichte* (1844), tells of a knight who leaves the Venus mountain because he misses being miserable: "Ich schmachte nach Bitternissen" (266). Further, and in contrast to the medieval version, the young man is beyond forgiveness due to his absolute love for the goddess; the pope wishes to help but cannot. Most importantly, the hero embarks on a journey through Germany, delivering his own societal critique:

Und als ich auf dem Sanct-Gotthardt stand,
Da hört' ich Deutschland schnarchen,
Es schlief da unten in sanfter Huth
Von sechs und dreißig Monarchen. (276)

---

77 [diese Flamme hat den erstarrten Stamm wieder von innen erwärmt, daß frisches Laub und duftige Blüthen hervorsproßten].
78 [Bearbeitung desselben Liedes].
79 [die inneren Motive jedoch aufs sonderbarste verändert sind].

And as I stood on Sanct Gotthardt's mount
I listened to Germany snore
It slept well kept by thirty-six
monarchs or even more.

Heine's Tannhäuser returns to Venus to lead a blissful life, far removed from German inertia. The goddess, however, stays in her mountain. She does not resurrect, does not rise, does not return to transform Germany into a new Greece.[80]

The Tannhäuser myth illuminates Heine's treatment of old gods in mountains. As myth pertains to art, not to religion, the magic mountain becomes an escapist aesthetic space, a location for myths of the past where the human being can be nostalgically happy. Still, Tannhäuser's desire for pain and misery suggest a conceptualization of human nature that excludes the capability of perfect and eternal bliss (EG 256). The mountain as a space of art/myth is sharply divorced from the sphere of reality/politics represented by the snoring country. In the mountain, the protagonists find joy unknown but only at the price of complete world withdrawal. This is, of course, a romantic stance; and while Heine celebrated the power of myth/art to produce such happiness, it is removed to a separate, autonomous sphere that has no influence on the world and vice versa. We know that Heine, who called for a poetics of life, nevertheless defended art's autonomy. These variants explain what the author intends for myth to do: remind the reader of the basic values of material happiness and the ambrosian rights of humanity. But myth does not (for it cannot) offer a societal blueprint: Its social structures are incompatible with the present. Indeed, the Tannhäuser myth makes no political claims; the Barbarossa myth does. The latter's mytheme is not sensual-materialistic but messianic-eschatological.

---

80 That the old gods need to stay gone is evident in yet another variant of the same myth. *Die Götter im Exil* is followed by an addendum entitled *Die Göttin Diana* [The Goddess Diana]. Written for the stage in five tableaus, the play opens with a knight who falls in love with Diana and shares in her divine lifestyle. Returning to his castle (and a rather dull wife), the knight grows depressed. During a ball, a progress of masks enters the scene, revealing Apollo, Dionysus, and lastly Diana herself. Diana came back for her lover, and the confrontation between goddess and housewife is cast as a battle between sensuality and spiritualism. Later, on returning to the mountain, the knight is slain by Eckart, who functions as a kind of moral police. Diana, heartbroken, transports her lover's body into the mountain, where the reader beholds a Renaissance palace decked in gold and flowers. Inside, another ball is held, Venus and Tannhäuser leading the dance. Diana begs Venus to restore her lover, but the goddess of love is powerless against death. Then, Apollo tries to revive him, but his lyre only makes him stir once. Finally, Dionysus comes forward: A cup of wine revives the knight and all celebrate a feast of resurrection (DGD 65-74).

The Return-of-the-King mytheme is constituted by Barbarossa's messianic-eschatological promise. It imagines a legendary potentate in a mountain, a space that is divorced from contemporary reality but which remains permeable, allowing a resurrection in time. This mytheme effects the actual *return* of an old god and the subsequent re-establishment of old (imperial) *ordo* principles. In the Barbarossa case, this entails a re-unification of Germany, a re-institution of monarchic-imperial governance, and a return to feudal hierarchy. It is not simply the person that returns: Barbarossa brings armies and his court. The re-edification of the Holy Roman Empire means the edification of an imperial kingdom: not a New Jerusalem but certainly a New Aachen.

It may become clear that the Three Magi mytheme and the Barbarossa mytheme stand in a reciprocal relationship. Although the first pertains to religion and the second to politics, they necessitate each other both in function and imagery. The Coming-of-the-King presents the announcement of a new religious regime focused on the spiritualization of human existence. The Return-of-the-King is the latter's logical mytho-political extension: As the reign of Christ on earth has come to a close and Christendom is awaiting a Second Coming, so Germany, on a political level, awaits the return of the Staufer Kaiser who promises a golden age. Christ and Barbarossa converge in the messianic, uniting religion and politics. This union is to come to a fulfillment in the Kaiser's awakening, which entails a return to a state of grace for Germany as a polity. The Tree Magi myth and the Barbarossa myth work together towards the imagination of a Christian-Imperial German future. In contrast to Venus and Tannhäuser, these deities do not remain in their graves. They seek to resurrect.

For a democratic writer who espoused a new religion of freedom, such a return is ahistorical and would constitute a back drift to the Middle Ages. Therefore, Heine's narrator-poet will attack Barbarossa in his mountain and deliver a simple message: Remain in your grave.

The Sealing of the Grave

Wintermärchen gives an abbreviated version of the basic Barbarossa myth in Caput XIV. The narrator remembers his wet-nurse telling him of the "Emperor-in-hiding," a tale which exposes the basic myth (Ib) (GWT 60). In the *Wintermärchen* version, the Kyffhäuser consists of numerous halls, all of which are filled with decay and inertia: The first is a stable full of petrified horses; the second houses soldiers clad in armor but fast asleep; the third is an armory filled with rusting equipment, a black-red-golden flag in its midst. In the fourth hall, the Kaiser sits at his table (DWM 51f). The fact that Heine has the revolutionary flag mounted in the armory attests to his initial desire to democratize the narrative. Barbarossa was appropriated by conservative and progressive forces, and Caput XIV suggests a hope for Barbarossa's democratic return, envisioning a resurrection *qua* vengeance: The Kaiser is to punish those who murdered the "wondrous golden-haired" "Germania," and especially "complacent" princes will not be exempt from Barbarossa's wrath. But the idea of a democratic Kaiser is short-lived indeed. The narrator finally reminds the reader that, despite the idea's appeal, only a "superstitious heart" may indulge in fairy tales (GWT 61f).

In the poem's second dream caput (XV), the narrator meets the legendary Kaiser and begins to denaturalize (Ic) the myth. He falls asleep in a carriage and finds himself inside the Kyffhäuser; as he meets Barbarossa, the poet is disappointed because the Kaiser lacks the "imposing air" he had expected. Indeed, the Kaiser "waddles" through the halls and, like an antiquarian, shows him his memorabilia. Barbarossa takes the narrator through the mountain, repeating the imagery of decay already apparent in the preceding caput: He polishes the swords in the armory, missing the "rust in one or two places." Helmets and armor are "thick with dust," just as the tricolor. In the soldier's hall, the visitor is asked to tread quietly, for Barbarossa does not wish to wake his men. Proceeding to the stables, he takes inventory with pleasure but admits of not havening enough horses. "But when there's enough," he assures the narrator, he shall put his plan to work (GWT 63). The poet grows impatient at this, demanding that he strike now. The Kaiser, however, wishes to wait:

'Wer heute nicht kommt, kommt morgen gewiß,
Nur langsam wächst die Eiche,
Und cha va piano va sano, so heißt
Das Spüchwort im römischen Reiche.' (DWM 58)

'Tomorrow's another day, more haste
less speed, festina lente
and chi va piano va sano – you see
there's wisdom in proverbs aplenty.' (GWT 64)

The first Barbarossa dream entails two crucial aspects of the poem's overall resignification. First, the Kaiser is depicted as at least partially being able to bring freedom, not just unity. The text has the emperor plan to rise under the revolutionary banner, thereby suggesting a democratic revolt ignited by his resurrection. That imagery, however, is revealed as wishful thinking by the omnipresent decay and inertia in all things Barbarossian. Even if the Kaiser were to ride beneath the tricolor: The flag does not necessarily signify *democratic* unification. Second, Barbarossa is depicted as stuck in eternal preparations. His referral to ancient proverbs further proves the emperor's detachment from outside reality. That detachment will be discussed in the second Barbarossa dream, where the narrator will ultimately refute the Kaiser's return.

In the second Barbarossa dream, the narrator brings the emperor up to date. Reporting on the French Revolution, the poet speaks of the guillotine, and the Kaiser, baffled, inquires as to its meaning.

Das Guillotinieren – erklärte ich ihm –
Ist eine neue Methode,
Womit man die Leute jeglichen Stands
Vom Leben bringt zum Tode. (DWM 61)

'The guillotine' – I explained to him –
'Is a recent innovation
for putting human beings to death
regardless of social station. (GWT 66)

Shocked at the news, Barbarossa orders the poet to cease his elaborations. It is especially the report of royals being put to death that terrifies the Kaiser.

'Der König und die Königin!
Geschnallt an einem Brette!
Das ist ja gegen allen Respekt
Und alle Etiquette!' (DWM 61)

'The Sovereign and his Lady Queen!
Strapped down! It's a disgrace, sir!
Against all the rules of etiquette!
People should know their place, sir. (GWT 67).

Here, the emperor betrays his true colors, which further denaturalizes (Ib) his messianic image. The faint democratic hope which flickered in the preceding caput is extinguished by Barbarossa's pulling of feudal rank. In a speech reminiscent of the magi in Cologne, the Kaiser scolds the poet for his lack of respect. Interestingly, after turning in horror from the guillotine ("Lord forbid / that ever I should make use of it"), Barbarossa threatens the poet with decapitation ("I'll take you down / a peg or two"). The narrator is accused of "lèse-majesté" and a breath that reeks of "treason" (GWT 67). Emboldened by the attack, the poet, too, decides to speak his mind:

Herr Rothbart – rief ich laut – du bist
Ein altes Fabelwesen,
Geh', leg dich schlafen, wir werden uns
Auch ohne dich erlösen.

Die Republikaner lachen uns aus,
Sehn sie an unserer Spitze
So ein Gespenst mit Zepter und Kron';
Sie rissen schlechte Witze. (DWM 62)

'Barbarossa' – I cried in return –
'You're only some old fable,
go back to bed, we'll free ourselves
without you, we're quite able.

'If they were to see us led by a ghost
with scepter and crown imperial,
the Republicans would laugh us to scorn,
we'd just be joke-material. (GWT 67)

Similar to the attack on the magi, the poet employs a formula of exorcism, banning the imperial ghost. He further links monarchic and feudal governance structures (scepter and crown) to the past and foresees the modern laughter such outdated notions must evoke. The poet goes on to discard Barbarossa's usefulness for contemporary Germany and thereby refutes the black-red-golden flag the Kaiser flies in his armory. His own experiences in student fraternities made him loose his taste for the germanomanic "fetish" that has been attached to the revolutionary banner[81] (GWT 67).

In Cologne, the poet had his lictor destroy the shrine of the magi; in the Kyffhäuser, the lictor is nowhere to be seen. Still, the narrator refutes the resurrection of imperial spirits:

---

81 As a member of the Allemania fraternity, Heine experienced anti-Semitic and germanomanic tendencies in Bonn and Göttingen. As it was especially the student movement that used the revolutionary banner, Heine's relationship to the flag remained ambivalent. Although the student movement was the earliest and strongest liberal opposition during Heine's youth, he was highly critical of its inherent chauvinism (Hermand 258f). The revolutionary banner came to represent a vast array of oppositional forces, among them democrats but also hyper-nationalists.

Das Beste wäre du bliebest zu Haus,
Hier in dem alten Kiffhäuser –
Bedenk' ich dich Sache ganz genau,
So brauchen wir gar keine Kaiser. (DWM 63)

'Perhaps on reflection you'd better stay
In your cave, a historical oddity;
For our present purposes Emperor's aren't
A necessary commodity. (GWT 68)

The third dream caput closes with this act of exorcism. The imperial ghost is to remain in his mountain, leave modern Germany in peace so that it may free itself. In the notion of Barbarossa as an overcome Kaiser, the office of emperor is refuted generally; further, the rebuttal of the return of *any* king presents another instance of mythemic elaboration (IIb). The fact that Germany has no need of kings and Kaiser molds the Return-of-the-King and leaves it open for the negotiation of a new meaning in the variant myth (the Coming-of-Freedom mytheme).

However, no lictor leaves Barbarossa or his halls in ruins, and no blood gushes from the poet's breast this time. The narrator bans the Kaiser to the mountain but allows him to live. In the subsequent caput, he will even apologize. In this caput (XVII), the narrator notes that, after all, it is only in the "Utopia of dreams / that a German dare fling" their "German opinion" into royal faces. So the poet, on waking, realizes how impertinent he was with the old Kaiser and asks him to forgive his "hasty words" (GWT 68). Interestingly, he once more urges the Kaiser to rise soon and begins to bargain. If the guillotine is not to his liking, he may resort to medieval tradition: the sword for the noble, the cord for the lowly. The only thing the poet asks is that Barbarossa may "hang a nobleman now and then" and sometimes "behead a burgher or peasant" so as to accommodate modern change. In an ironic *tour de force*, the narrator urges the Kaiser to come back, and if he must, reinstall the Holy Roman Empire with all its "musky junk." The re-institution of feudalism ("divide the people into estates") and the return to pre-Reformation religiosity ("bring back the Lawcourts of Charles the Fifth") are grudgingly accepted by the poet, as they would offer a historically "genuine article" (69). In the end, the poet prefers a return to an authentic age than to suffer through the Vormärz parody:

Das Mittelalter, immerhin,
Das wahre, wie es gewesen,
Ich will es ertragen – erlöse uns nur
Von jenem Zwitterwesen,

Von jenem Kamaschenritterthum,
das ekelhaft ein Gemisch ist
Von gothischem Wahn und modernem Lug,
Das weder Fleisch noch Fisch ist. (DWM 65)

'The Middle Ages, well, I suppose
if you give us the genuine article,
I'll put up with that. Just rescue us
from all this hybrid, farcical,

'revolting, pseudo-knightliness
which, under its Gothic cover,
is just a lot of modern deceit,
neither one thing or the other. (GWT 69)

Barbarossa is ironically accepted as the bringer of medieval culture and politics, as long as he does away with the inauthenticity the author discerns in modern German pretentions of medieval greatness. The Kaiser becomes an anti-savior who shall propel the country back a few centuries yet deliver the land from modern hypocrisy. Indeed, the narrator awaits the day that Barbarossa expels "that pack of comedians / who parody times long gone" (ibid.). He would rather suffer the oppression of the Dark Ages than remain in this state of farce, veiling, and nostalgia.

Heine's treatment of Friedrich Barbarossa is truly ambivalent. Yes, his apology and invocation of the Kaiser's rise must be read ironically; nevertheless, the figure regains a certain degree of seriousness in the last caput. Be that as it may, the mythological resignification in the Barbarossa capita denaturalizes (Ic) the appeal of the Kaiser figure for democratic purposes. The ironic apology in Caput XVII actually reinforces the point made in the dream capita: Friedrich Barbarossa is a ghost who needs to remain in his mountain, for the rise of the Kaiser would bring a return of the Middle Ages. These are, despite their nostalgic glorification, everything but glorious. There can be no union of modern (democratic) needs with an overcome and outdated ruler. Heine insists on the notion that any hope in the Kaiser's return is a fool's hope, for the Vormärz needs no emperors.

The basic Barbarossa myth has thus been denaturalized (Ic). The Return-of-the-King mytheme, just as its reciprocal twin, the Coming-of-the-King mytheme, have been elaborated (IIb). What follows is the next step in mythological resignification, the construction of a variant. If the magi can no longer foretell the coming of a spiritual king, and the Kaiser is not to return, who or what will deliver Vormärz Germany from its cultural inertia and pave the road to a better future? The variant myth in *Wintermärchen* has been prepared (IIa) by the *Freudenlied* in Caput I, and it will come to fruition at the end of the road: in the Free City of Hamburg.

5.4 The Song of Joy and Germany's Future

In this last subchapter, I will elaborate on the variant myth in Heine's *Wintermärchen*. The variant promotes a human existence focusing on material values and offers a new civic myth for the imagination and formation of a free German polity. It employs food imagery to effect its mythological import and the *Hammonia myth* to discuss and refute a Biedermeier escapism in questions of political and artistic political agency.

Turning Towards Food

Passing through Minden and Hannover, the narrator-poet finally arrives in Hamburg, where his mother welcomes him with a meal. At home, he sits down to enjoy what has been of central significance to the poem throughout: good food. But his mother interrupts his enjoyment by turning to "distinctly awkward" topics, and he evades her questions and prefers to discuss the meal in front of him. As she inquires as to his marital life, he praises the fish, hoping that he might not "swallow a bone" due to her questioning. She proceeds to ask about his situation in Paris; here, the poet praises the "German goose" and goes on to tell of the culinary excellence of "French stuffing" (GWT 74). Finally, as "juicy and sweet" oranges are served, she asks about the most delicate matter: how he judges affairs in Germany, and if he still suffers from an "addiction to politics" (75). The poet's answer is telling:

Die Apfelsinen, lieb Mütterlein,
Sind gut, und mit wahrem Vergnügen
Verschlucke ich den süßen Saft
Und ich lasse die Schalen liegen. (DWM 75)

'These oranges, mother dear, are good
so rich in tasty juices.
But I'm not inclined to swallow the peel,
The wrapping they come in is useless.' (GWT 75)

Kruse and colleagues read this dialogue as a private communication made impossible by freedom of speech restrictions (132). While this reading has value, it does not quite hit the point, for Caput XX in fact continues the narrator's discussion of human enjoyment. Throughout the text, the narrator uses food imagery to direct attention away from political concern onto subjective matters of enjoyment and sustenance. These motifs are linked to the materialistic *Freudenlied* in Caput I, where we first encounter food in the form of peas (GWT 30). The imagery continues in

Cologne (IV), where the poet enjoys a "ham omelet" and later Rhineland wine (35). The narrator praises, not without irony, "the real old Germanic food" in Caput IX and expands on sauerkraut, sausages, cod in butter, and apple sauce (50f).

Food and drink are used to support the materialistic outlook of the variant myth. Food consumption goes beyond mere functionality and is cast as an active aesthetic experience and political activity. That these are conscious acts is palpable in the first Hamburg caput. The communication between mother and son is not hindered by the public realm but diverted from it: The narrator consciously evades political inquires because he did not come to discuss politics but to enjoy his mother's company (and cooking). Indeed, "food is part of the grand doctrine" of the poem (Reed 17). The crux of the scene is the elevation of nourishment and enjoyment which can trump the crude affairs of the public realm. Politics has been given an image in the Reichsadler, and Heine designs opposing ornithological images to counter it.

Kruse and colleagues note that in Caput IX, the poem adheres to the epic tradition of depicting regional cuisine (127). As the narrator finds roasted "fieldfares" on his plate, the little birds scold their "countryman" for preferring "foreign birds" (GWT 51). Then, he perceives a goose on the table. That bird will represent the poet's personal history, his private enjoyments paired with his nostalgia for a long lost innocence:

Es stand auf dem Tisch eine Gans,
Ein stilles, gemüthliches Wesen.
Sie hat vielleicht mich einst geliebt,
Als wir beide noch jung gewesen. (DWM 38)

A quiet homely German goose
was waiting to still my hunger.
Perhaps she loved me long ago
when both of us were younger. (GWT 51)

In contrast to the Reichsadler, the *German goose* becomes the image for a more regional, small-scale, and private German existence, a simple and innocent life, sheltered from political chaos. The poet's homesickness is mirrored in the bird's doleful eyes, a glance that reminds him of his youth. However, the Biedermeier[82] possibil-

---

82 Eke notes that the term *Biedermeier* describes both an historical age and a socio-political attitude. A parallel and more conservative term for the Vormärz, it refers the socio-political and literary culture between 1815 and 1848. It expresses a restricted, apolitical form of bourgeoisie, a way of life focused on the private, on ordered social hierarchies, a

ity to reject the public world is immediately discarded: A "pig's head" is put on the table, representing the "old custom" to crown German swine with laurels (GWT 51). The Biedermeier goose in Hagen cannot capture the poet's love, for the crowned pig's head is also part of the German menu. However, in its focus on individual sustenance and enjoyment, the German goose image serves to prepare (IIa) for the variant under construction.

The German goose image will return in Hamburg, where the narrator can enjoy the meal and contemplate a retreat into the private. But its antithesis, the Reichsadler, will return as well. In Minden (XVIII), right after the Barbarossa capita, the eagle delivers a mythological punishment. The poet, asleep once more, is plagued by varying visions of a tassel that hangs from the roof of his bed. That tassel transforms itself into the Prussian eagle, which holds him down and begins to eat his liver (GWT 71).

This referential treatment of the Prometheus myth is significant, as it again attests to the narrator's divinity and the emancipatory nature of his dissent.[83] Prometheus, whose name translates into the 'the one who thinks ahead,' was the Titan who rebelled against the Olympian gods and brought fire to humanity. He is held as the founder of human culture and, in some versions of the myth, as the creator of the human race. But as punishment for his theft, Zeus has Prometheus bound to a rock, where an eagle (Zeus' animal) devours his liver on a daily basis. The liver grows back over night so that the torture can resume (Hamilton 84-91). Interestingly, *Wintermärchen* clearly champions the Titans over the Olympian powers that be: The narrator assumed the role of the Titan Antaeus in Caput I; now, he is identified with the Titan Prometheus. Indeed, Prometheus' dissent may have been exemplary for the rebellious Vormärz poet:

There is no force which can compel my speech.
So let Zeus hurl his blazing bolts,
And with the white wings of the snow,
With thunder and with earthquake,
Confound the reeling world.
None of all this will bend my will. (90)

The reference to this Greek myth identifies the narrator-poet as a benefactor of humanity; again, he becomes an *alter deus*. Moreover, the battle between the Olympian gods and the dissenting Titans is recast on a Vormärz level: The narrator, the

---

Protestant morality, and a love for the small things in life. The Biedermeier is a world of conscious restrictions which entails a retreat from public affairs (15f).

83 cf. footnote 75.

modern Prometheus, seeks the advancement of the people, whereas Prussia, the modern Zeus, punishes the poet for his bringing of fire. That punishment and the fire metaphor further parallel Heine's Luciferian concept elaborated in *Elementargeister*, where fire and light are understood as the elements of reason. Just as Prometheus, Lucifer (the Light-Bringer) is cast from heaven and punished in hell. Thus, Heine positions his narrator in this tradition of exiled and penalized bringers of light. The Reichsadler becomes the executioner of Prussian punishment for a poet who dares to enlighten the people.

The Reichsadler returns in Hamburg. Apparently, Prussian influence in the Free City is increasing, and the narrator warns of the "vile bird" that has "laid an egg in the Lord Mayor's wig." The antithetical relation between goose and eagle is again made apparent in Caput XXI: The poet had just enjoyed his mother's meal but thinking of the Prussian eagle sets his "stomach heaving" (GWT 77). As pseudo-medieval imagery is attached to the Reichsadler, food and material enjoyment are attached to the German goose; apparently, they do not go together well. Yet if the German goose is of regional character, and the Reichsadler strives towards national unity, it must be asked how the poem imagines the future of Germany as a nation.

Cosmopolitan Nationalism and German Manifest Destiny

In the Vormärz, national unification was certainly a major concern, but the question of which political characteristics a unified Germany would have was equally important. Unification could be attained in a number of ways, not all of them democratic. Indeed, 18th century forms of nationalism were universal and cosmopolitan in character, but during the German campaign against Napoleon (1813-1815), they experienced a dogmatization and gradually shifted towards an integral nationalism. Humanist ideals gave way to a narrow definition of nationhood, and unification started to emerge as the dominant factor before and after the March Revolution (Scheuer 13).

Werner notes that Heine viewed the loss of humanism in the national idea as deeply problematic. While he conceded that the nation was the adequate form of societal organization, he was critical of all forms of chauvinism (12). He clung to the humanist conception of the nation and pushed for a cosmopolitan form. In a preface to the separate print of *Wintermärchen*, he comments on what kind of national future he envisions for Germany.

The preface to *Wintermärchen* is one of the most controversial texts in Heine scholarship, because it entails a form of German Manifest Destiny. The poet begins by refuting the "Pharisees of nationalism,"[84] who accuse him of being a "despiser of

---

84 [Pharisäer der Nazionalität].

the Fatherland."[85] The debate was caused by Heine's disrespect regarding the black-red-golden banner in the Barbarossa capita. Turning to these "heroic lackeys in black-red-golden livery,"[86] he elaborates on his own form of nationalism and describes a patriotism rooted in humanist cosmopolitism (VWM v).

> Beruhigt euch. Ich werde eure Farben achten und ehren, wenn sie es verdienen, wenn sie nicht mehr eine müßige und knechtische Spielerei sind. Pflanzt die schwarz-roth-goldne Fahne auf die Höhe des deutschen Gedankens, macht sie zur Standarte des freien Menschenthums, und ich will mein bestes Herzblut für sie hingeben. Beruhigt euch, ich liebe das Vaterland eben so sehr wie ihr. (vf)

> Calm down. I shall respect and honor your colors as soon as they deserve it, as soon as they cease to be an idle and menial shenanigan. Plant your flag on the height of German thought, elevate it to be the banner of a free humanity, and I shall give my heart's blood for it. Calm down, for I love the Fatherland just as much as you.

Here, Heine defines the goal of such an ideology: to make universal emancipation Germany's mission. Only then, the author contends, will Germany be able to abolish feudal hierarchies, return the population to a state of dignity, and redeem the "god that lives on earth in the human being."[87] In this way, Germans shall become the "saviors of god,"[88] and all other nations may join it (VWM vi). Universal emancipation is cast as a German mission legitimizing cultural and geographical expansion: The coming together of nations, indeed, is imagined in imperialist terms. If Germany succeeds in flying the banner of universal emancipation, not only

> Lothringen, sondern ganz Frankreich wird uns alsdann zufallen, ganz Europa, die ganze Welt – die ganze Welt wird deutsch werden! Von dieser Sendung und Universalherrschaft Deutschlands träume ich oft wenn ich unter Eichen wandle. Das ist m e i n Patriotismus. (ibid.)

> Lorraine, but all of France will be ours, all of Europe, the whole world – the whole world will become German! I often dream of this mission and of Germany's universal rule whenever I walk beneath oaks. That is m y patriotism.

---

85 [Verächter des Vaterlandes].
86 [heldenmüthigen Lakaien in schwarz-roth-goldner Livree].
87 [wenn wir den Gott, der auf Erden im Menschen wohnt, aus seiner Erniedrigung retten, wenn wir die Erlöser Gottes werden, wenn wir das arme, glückenterbte Volk und den verhöhnten Genius und die geschändete Schönheit wieder in ihre Würde einsetzten].
88 [Erlöser Gottes].

In Heine's view, this mission and universal hegemony is a humanist, cosmopolitan rule based on the values of freedom, equality, and emancipation. It is nonetheless imperial and highly reminiscent of the Antebellum notion of Manifest Destiny. Indeed, Heine's preface elaborates on a global and missionary mandate to emancipate Germany, Europe, and, gradually, the world. Here, a German exceptionalism is articulated on the basis of humanist and civilizatory notions which entail a clear imperial element.

Kruse notes that in this preface, Heine proposes a form of cosmopolitan nationalism (Leben 58). Narrow nationalism is rejected, while patriotism based on the values of a cosmopolitan humanism remains recommendable. However, Werner adds that the author deems an imperial power structure to be necessary for the attainment of such humanist goals (23). This definition of patriotism takes a middle position: A patriot for Heine is a *Weltbürger*, a universal citizen (Mende 94). In this aspect, Heine's nationalism approaches the notion of nationality-as-ideology which Lipset and Bercovitch deem restricted to the U.S. In contrast, Habermas notes that Heine promoted an open form of national belonging and opposed all narrow and bigoted types (23). Heine's is, indeed, an open, humanist, albeit imperial national ideology. The Hammonia capita will elaborate on Heine's private and patriotic national alternative and situate Germany's future in the development of the variant myth.

Dining and Wining in Hamburg

The Hammonia capita (XXIII-XXVI) begin apologetically. Hamburg, the reader is informed, has never been as great as republic as Venice or Florence, even if it has the "better oysters" (GWT 80). Again divorcing political from private concerns, the narrator-poet dines with his publisher Julius Campe. Instead of discussing censorship or the exile's publications, he praises Campe's hospitable generosity: While he "ate and drank most heartily," he gushes over a man with whom "there's wining as well as dining." He thanks god for giving him Campe as publisher and for the creation of oysters and Rhineland wine (81). This short scene continues the food imagery that has accompanied the Hamburg section. Again, it focuses on individual enjoyment in spite of adverse political circumstance. The latter does echo in the background (the poet had just admitted Hamburg's political failure as a true republic), and the hyperbolic description regarding Campe (he is compared to Amphytrion and the Madonna) suggest a certain irony being at work here.[89]

---

89 Julius Campe was known for his thrift. At the same time, the dinners he gave in honor of his authors were legendary (Kruse et al. 133f).

One may be tempted to regard the use of food imagery as an evasive technique to avoid political issues. Indeed, the tension between political concern and the mundane nature of regional cuisine offers much of the satiric material at work. But the focus on private enjoyment must not be misread as a Biedermeier retreat. Instead of retreating from politics to the private, the private becomes political: The focus on food makes food a weapon to further the materialistic ideology of the *Freudenlied*. The narrator's insistence on enjoying the culinary exploits of Hamburg is a form of dissent, and his enjoyment opposes the spiritualistic-ascetic demands of the *Entsagungslied*. For the narrator, the mundane world of food trumps the world of religion and politics because it is in the mundane that the ambrosian rights of the individual are met and fulfilled. For instance, in a stanza bearing an obvious double-entendre, the poet attests to the effect of Rhineland wine: It awakens his love for humanity.

Der Rheinwein stimmt mich immer weich,
Und löst jedwedes Zerwürfniß
In meiner Brust, entzündet darin
Der Menschenliebe Bedürfniß. (DWM 85)

Hock always gets me going, a mood
of benevolence and urbanity
comes over me, I feel the need
to express my love for humanity. (GWT 81)

Granted, the following stanzas attest to the fact that the poet also wishes to express his love for beautiful Hamburg women ("Die Katzen scheinen mir alle grau, / die Weiber alle Helenen") (DWM 85). Nevertheless, food and drink (and sex) are offered as alternatives to political concerns, not because they offer an escape, but because they fulfill human needs. In Hamburg, the narrator celebrates the material foundations of humanity, the subjective desires and requirements of the free human being. Yes, these are not fundamental *to* politics; but the text suggests them to be the fundament *for* politics. The text insists on its claims that politics should be based on the material needs of the population. Therefore, in his endeavor to find a "soul" with whom to share his "love of humanity," the narrator meets a being that offers both political and sexual fulfillment (GWT 82). In one of the most humorous passages of the poem, he meets Hammonia, the goddess of Hamburg.

Wintermärchen employs the Hammonia myth to give the last capita a mythological frame and offer a representation of Hamburg with which the narrator can converse. This myth is not utilized as a basic myth for mythological resignification; like the Greek myths used in the course of the poem, it presents a mythological reference. It is, however, used to discuss the city's grappling with the question of nationalism in the Vormärz.[90]

The image of Hammonia, a female allegory of the city, has been used since the Middle Ages.[91] Jaacks notes that her depiction draws on the Greek Athena and adorns maps, official documents, medallions, and buildings. She is represented as a young, proud, and beautiful woman, who wears a mural crown and holds a Mercurian wand[92] (62). This goddess receives a more material and less venerable description in Heine's poem.

The narrator beholds a "wondrously large-breasted" woman, her face round and healthy. Her "cheeks were like roses, like cherries her lips / and her nose was reddish too." In contrast to other goddesses, this one possesses a "naturalness quite of this world" but has "superhuman hinderparts" which betray her divine being. Hammonia welcomes the poet, laments his long absence, and notices that his tastes have not changed: He still looks for the "Beautiful Souls" who would once upon a time meet him by the Elbe River (GWT 82). But the maidens of old are no more, just as everything else has changed in the city of Hamburg.

Everything the poet once treasured is gone: The flowers disappeared, their "petals blown down by the stormwind." All past beauty has been "trod down" "by Fate with its brutal feet," and the "monster Life" shall not give back "those good old times." It seems that the entropy of civilization has not stopped at Hamburg's gates, and a new, albeit colder world unfolds before the poet's eyes: "What's left of the

---

90 For more on Hammonia and Hamburg's history and position in the German Confederation see: Jaacks (ed.): *Hamburgs Geschichte – Mythos und Wirklichkeit* (2008); Stephan and Winter (eds): *"Heil über dir, Hammonia:" Hamburg im 19. Jahrhundert* (1992); Schambach: *Stadt und Zivilgesellschaft* (2015); Schilling: *Stadtrepublik und Selbstbehauptung* (2012).

91 Reinecke begins the goddess' development in the medieval connection between Hamburg and Jupiter (Hammon). In unison with an ancient Marian cult in the city, Hamburg receives a second name: Hammonia (urbis Hammoniae). This identification, however, does not ascribe a personality but presents a simple nomination. Hammonia is the product of the commonplace tradition of allegorizing a city and using a (female) counterfeit for representative purposes (14). With time, Hammonia begins to wear a mural crown and a Mercurian wand; later, she will be identified as a nymph of the Elbe River (16). In 1828, Hammonia's role as city patroness is solidified in the Hamburg hymn *Heil über dir, Hammonia* by Georg Nikolaus Bärmann (16)

92 The Greek Hermes and his Roman equivalent Mercury were gods of commerce and communication and notably patrons of salesmen (and thieves).

Germany we knew / has been left to wither and weather"[93] (GWT 83). Intrigued, the poet offers to escort the goddess home, and she invites him to her chamber.

The first Hammonia caput continues the dialectic between past and present that has suffused the Hamburg capita. Since his arrival in the Free City, the narrator sought out old places and acquaintances, yearning for the pleasures of his youth. Hammonia, however, shatters his hopes of regaining his personal history and explains that Hamburg, just as Germany, is a very different place now. The impossibility to resuscitate the past, which up till now has been discussed in religious and political matters, is now elaborated in the private. Just as the Three Magi are but bones and Barbarossa naught but a ghost in a mountain, the poet's personal history is a thing of the past. The Hammonia capita will discuss the poet's nostalgia, the present state of German affairs, and the possibilities of the future.

Private Patriotism and the Future in a Chamber Pot

As the narrator arrives in Hammonia's chamber, the goddess confesses her affection. She used to prefer bards who told "the story of the Messiah," but now the narrator's portrait hangs "at the head of [her] bed" (GWT 85). Then, the poet elaborates on his homesickness and confesses a true love for his fatherland. Their dialogue continues the discussion of misguided patriotism: The narrator expresses patriotic feelings heightened by exile. He felt suffocated in France, yearned to "breathe German air again" and have "German soil" under his feet. These rather abstract notions, well known from Caput I and IV, are given a personal dimension for the first time. The poet relates what he misses precisely: his mother, his sister, old lovers, friends and patrons, and the places where he felt joy and sadness in his youth (86f). He admits that this "kind of patriotism" may be no more than a "disease" which he is ashamed of revealing in public (87).

What is significant in the poet's confession is that patriotism is cast as a *private* emotion. The memories causing homesickness are removed from any pretensions of national greatness or nostalgia. Here is a personal patriotism based on the poet's life history: love of *Vaterland* is distinguished from love of *Heimat*. Consequently, the poet is reluctant to confess these intimate feelings and vents his anger at those who cloak personal emotions as political expression:

Fatal ist mir das Lumpenpack,
Das, um die Herzen zu rühren,
Den Patriotismus trägt zur Schau
Mit allen seinen Geschwüren. (DWM 91)

---

93 This line taken from a stanza cut from the first edition.

There's nothing I hate like that villainous pack
who, to stir up easy emotions,
flaunt their patriotism about
and lay bare their ulcerous notions. (GWT 87)

The poet decries the national hyperbole employed by poets like Menzel and the Swabian School; at the same time, he hopes to be soon relieved of this emotional disease. The cure for his illness could be a permanent return to Germany, an act that would have (negative) political and private consequences. Therefore, he prefers another cure, which is food, or in this case, drink: "Yes, I am sick – a cup of tea / I would take as a friendly favour; [...] Just add a little rum for flavour" (ibid.).

Thus, Hammonia offers him tea with rum and enjoys her own cup without tea. Emboldened, the goddess criticizes the Vormärz as an age of "doubters" and "scoffers" and presses the narrator to remain in Germany, a country that shows "signs of progress" (GWT 88). This progress, however, is cast as an entropic and unwelcome development: "This practical outward freedom, you'll see, / will kill the ideal we cherish." The "dream of Germany lily-pure" – just as the poet's memories of his youth in Hamburg – belongs to the past, and the goddess fears that Germany is espousing a primacy of materiality (89):

'Der Enkel wird essen und trinken genug,
Doch nicht in beschaulicher Stille;
Es poltert heran ein Spektakelstück,
Zu Ende geht die Idylle.' (DWM 94)

'Our children will eat and drink their fill,
but it won't be our old-world idyll;
a Big Spectacular's on the way
which will cut it off short in the middle.' (GWT 90)

The goddess may mourn the old idyll, but her words must be taken positively considering the food imagery that preceded her speech: The future will ensure material sustenance for coming generations, even if it shall be bought at the price of entropy and the loss of old ideals. Indeed, we are not informed how the narrator reacts to this statement, but it seems safe to state that Heine would have sacrificed sentimentality to the establishment of material security. Be that as it may, the goddess images the coming of an age of artificiality and inauthenticity.

Indeed, Hammonia's elaborations do not paint a concise picture of Germany's future, but she offers a vision that appears all but optimistic. She informs the poet that while the throne of Germany's first Kaiser rests in Aachen, his chamber pot is in her keeping. It is an "old chair," its seat decaying and "moth-eaten," but the met-al pot is still intact. Indeed, this pot is a "magic pot" which allows the poet to see the future (GWT 92):

'Die Zukunft Deutschlands erblickst du hier,
Gleich wogenden Phantasmen,
Doch schaudre nicht, wenn aus dem Wust
Aufsteigen die Miasmen!' (DWM 98)

'The future of Germany you will see
down there like a shifting phantasma,
but do not shudder if the filth
sends up a foul miasma!' (GWT 92)

The narrator looks into the pot, but an oath of silence forbids him to relate his vision. He nevertheless reports on his olfactory experience:

Entsetzlich waren die Düfte, o Gott!
Die sich nachher erhuben;
Es war als fegte man den Mist
Aus sechs und dreißig Gruben. (DWM 99)

But the scents that followed this prelude, God!
were anything but respites;
it smelt as if they were sweeping the dung
from six-and-thirty cesspits. (GWT 92)

Germany's future is never specifically reported on, but what is given is the stench that accompanies it. One may be tempted to read this as a pessimistic outlook, but the report is more optimistic at a second glance. The text refers to Greek myth once more: One of Hercules tasks was to clean King Augeas' stables (Hamilton 226). Preparing Germany for the future is presented as equally exhausting work. I concur with Reed who notes that the chamber pot's stench must not necessarily mean a dystopian future for the country; it rather makes the reader conscious of the work at hand, the need of cleaning the thirty-six cesspits of the German Confederation (110). Naturally, the possibility of failure cannot be argued away. The future of Germany may indeed be akin to the contents of a chamber pot, especially if one adheres to Hammonia's fear of the rise of an inauthentic age. The narrator, however, disagrees with her divine opinion.

The Joys of the New Generation

Throughout *Wintermärchen*, laughter dominated the discourse. Laughter exorcised the ghosts of religion as well as the imperial spirit in the Kyffhäuser. Equally dominant, however, is the poem's insistence on material joy. Laughter not only characterizes the narrative point of view in relation to the past but also to the future. The present, however, demands the active enjoyment of humanity's ambrosian rights.

The variant myth in Heine's poem rests on this sensualistic-materialistic ideology. Hinderer notes that as a political poem, *Wintermärchen* entails an intention: to humorously relate facts, the reflection of which may trigger agency and produce attunement to the proposed set of ideas (15). How that set of ideas is related is significant, for political literature knows several ways with which to transfer a message. Heine's mythological resignification in *Wintermärchen* aims at information, persuasion, and revelation. As such, his technique is to be differentiated from strategies of agitation and propaganda (27). In a rhetorical context, the latter are categorized as emotional speech, which intents the description of strong passions. In contrast, Heine employs rational speech intending the description and reflection of given facts and circumstances. Rational speech is argumentative and explicative; it aims at enabling the reader to take a critical position and individually reflect an issue. Whereas political literature as propaganda aims at the production of enthusiasm, Heine's poem is both critical of and constitutive to a set of values and norms (29).

Thus, the variant myth, the *New Generation myth*, is constructed as a counter-ideological narrative to the denaturalized basic myths. The mythological resignification at work here is a transformation of ideas: Its method is rational and indebted to the principles of debate and discussion rather than propagandistic in the production of affirmative emotions. In this sense, the narrator-poet converses with Hammonia, who does not wish to face new realities and seeks consolation in the denial of the present age.

"Put back the lid!" the goddess commands as the narrator is finished with the chamber pot. Then, she begs him to stay with her; they could "attend to the eating and drinking / of oysters and wine" and simply forget "the dark German future." Hammonia confesses her love for the "handsome German poet:" His kiss is "poetic inspiration" and intoxicates her senses, and outside, the watchmen are already singing "marriage songs" (GWT 93). Reminiscent of the wedding song in Caput I, Hammonia proposes a marriage between the poet of freedom and Hamburg. But while the union between Europa and Freedom is consecrated by the "stars" themselves, this particular liaison has a different outcome (31). One after the other, city senators, diplomats, priests, and rabbis appear to congratulate the couple. But these representatives of political and religious circumstance ultimately preclude a happy ending: Freedom and Hamburg, it seems, cannot unite without certain alterations to freedom itself. Unfortunately for the poet, the censor appears, brings his scissors, and it takes but a "snip" and the poet's "best piece is missing" (94).

Thus, the last Hammonia caput ends with castration. The marriage between narrator and goddess is found lacking and ends with the poet's impotence. The wedding song in Caput I sings the ideal union between the continent and the principle of freedom; the union between Hammonia and the narrator, however, is a union that *exaggerates* materiality. Kruse and colleagues note that Hammonia wishes to give herself up to material enjoyment and let Germany be; this Biedermeier retreat from the world, however, will not do (135). Their union is crushed by public forces, precisely *because* the couple would espouse a Biedermeier philosophy: A complete retreat from politics is equivalent to the loss of individual political power represented in the castration motif. Freedom, it seems, cannot be achieved by the "eating and drinking / of oysters and wine" (GWT 93). Despite the inherent dissent in material enjoyment, the poem suggests that a certain degree of idealism is necessary to bring about a free German future. The castration scene further reveals which ideal is not to be forsaken: freedom itself. Thus, the text refrains from rejecting idealism completely, despite the dominance of materialistic thought throughout. This dominance, however, informs the variant myth, which is constructed in several instances, beginning with the *Freudenlied* in Caput I.

The variant myth in *Wintermärchen* is developed parallel to the basic myths. It does not evolve from the basic myths *per se* but stems from a reworking of the messianic-eschatological promise of their mythemes. The variant New Generation myth is a narrative that describes the coming of a new, materialistic age based on universal emancipation and the claiming of humanity's ambrosian rights. It begins in Caput I, appears again and again throughout the poem, and is naturalized (IIc) in the last caput.

The New Generation myth begins with the *Freudenlied*. It is in the promise of a "different song" that the text commences to develop the variant. Its core meanings are given here already: happiness on earth ("heaven on earth"), bodily nourishment ("green peas for everyone"), and sensualistic-aesthetic enjoyment ("beauty and joy") (GWT 30). These notions elaborate a new mytheme (IIb) and cumulate in the wedding song which sings the union between Europa and Freedom. Universal human emancipation is the core value of the new song, and the coming of an age of freedom presents the mytheme of the narrative: *Coming-of-Freedom*. The Coming-of-Freedom mytheme develops against and with the Coming-of-the-King and the Return-of-the-King mytheme. In its mythemic elaboration (IIb), it rejects spiritualistic and imperial connotations but retains the prophetic promise of a new beginning. It is as prophetic as the mythemes enshrined in the Three Magi and Barbarossa myth but claims material joy in the present rather than dislocating joy to a heavenly or imperial future. The New Generation myth and the Coming-of-Freedom mytheme repeat the teleology and eschatological promise inherent in the basic myths, while at the same time rejecting the traditional civic myths as overcome and outdated.

After promising a variant in the first caput, the poem adds to the myth throughout. The New Generation myth is built in the very act of walking the road: First, it occurs by means of food imagery in Caput IV (food and wine in Cologne), IX (German cuisine), XX (mother's meal), XXI (stomach ache), XXIII (dinner with Campe), and XXVI (Hammonia's oysters). The poem politicizes the enjoyment of food as a conscious enactment (and expression) of the new primacy of the material. Second, the variant is furthered in musical terms: The ideology of the new age is encompassed in a wedding song (I), in a new Rhine song (V), and lastly, in the song of a newly tuned lyre (XXVII). Still, the new songs in the poem are never fully elaborated. They offer a promise, not a blueprint.

Why is the variant myth given in the form of promise, rather than in a more cohesive narrative? The reason for this lies with the impossibility of defining a future without simultaneously restricting it. The concept of *wyrd* and the Young German Poetics of Life have to be remembered in this context. The present is thought of as the crucial moment in the flow of time. Work on the future is decisively the work of the moment, and all predictions of events that shall come to pass can be no more than forebodings. This is evident in Caput II: the prophet who carries the "temple jewels" of the future does so in the name of an "unknown god" (GWT 32). He prepares for a new age of freedom, but the distinct features of that age remain unknown. What is known, however, is the progressive teleology of history, which rejects the old gods (spiritualistic religion and imperial governance) as overcome.

The New Generation myth experiences a final naturalization (IIc) in the poem's last caput. In contradiction to Hammonia's fears, the poet foretells the rise of a new, authentic era:

Es wächst heran ein neues Geschlecht,
Ganz ohne Schminke und Sünden.
Mit freien Gedanken, mit freier Lust –
Dem werde ich alles verkünden. (DWM 102)

A new generation is rising that has
no hang-ups or pretences;
it thinks what it likes, enjoys what it likes –
I will help it keep its senses. (GWT 95)

It is evident how the abhorrence of pretense and the desire for authenticity inform both Heine and Gutzkow's texts. Artificiality is presented as the Vormärz way; the new age, however, is to attain the status of a historically valid (because authentic) generation.

Again, the narrator is cast as the lyrical prophet of the coming generation, and the new song will be sung on a lyre tuned by the "noblest of graces." Moreover, the poet attains a final characterization: In his prophetic role, he becomes as "loving as the light" and as "chaste as fire." The usage of light and fire imagery here reminds us of the dialectic between the darkness of overcome spirituality (the magi's chapel, the Kyffhäuser) and a new Luciferian materiality of reason. Indeed, the new song is imagined as a song of reason, not of idealism or superstition. Therefore, in a final *tour de force*, the narrator allocates himself and the new song in the tradition of Aristophanes.[94] He is described as Aristophanes' "offspring," a progeny who uses the same "lyre [his] father struck" (GWT 95).

However, the narrator is certain that should Aristophanes ever come to Germany, he would be arrested immediately. Consequently, he utters a warning for the King of Prussia:

O König! Ich meine es gut mit dir,
Und will einen Rath dir geben:
Die todten Dichter, verehre sie nur,
Doch schone die da leben.

Beleid'ge lebendige Dichter nicht,
Sie haben Flammen und Waffen,
Die furchtbarer sind als Jovis Blitz,
Den ja der Poet erschaffen. (DWM 104)

O King! I have your welfare at heart,
this is good advice I'm giving:
by all means honour the poets of yore –
but watch your step with the living.

Don't rub live poets up the wrong way;
they have weapons that make Jove's lightning
(a poet invented that) look tame.
If you cross them, your prospects are frightening. (GWT 96)

In this final passage, the *alter deus* ascends to new heights: He becomes the creator of gods. Indeed, the term Luciferian is not out of place here, for the king may safely offend "Zeus" and "Jehovah" but offending a poet would result in a fiercer punish-

---

94 Aristophanes (445-385 B.C.), a Greek poet celebrated for his political satires.

ment (ibid.): The king may be locked in "Dante's Hell," in the "terrible *terza rima*" (97). In short, the king is threatened to be locked in a poem.

Kein Gott, kein Heiland, erlöst ihn je
Aus diesen singenden Flammen!
Nimm dich in Acht, das wir dich nicht
Zu solcher Hölle verdammen. (DWM 105)

The poet's flames have got him for good,
they scorch and scourge and scorn him.
Take care: we might roast you in just such a hell
as an everlasting warning. (GWT 97)

The poem's naturalization of the variant myth (IIc) ends by making two significant points. First, the new song of materiality is to be realized by the coming generation. This generation will be able to shed the pretensions of medieval nostalgia and return to the teleological flow of time by establishing an authentic existence. Second, the narrator-poet reveals himself (and poets like him) as divine constructors of that era. Poetry is cast as the creator of social reality: It is poets who write the gods, as it is poets who deliver the final judgment on historical actors.

In Caput XXVII, the narrator brings two major narrative threads to a close. He concludes the mythological resignification by defining the New Generation myth as civic myth for the future. He designs this myth as a work in progress, refrains from giving specifics, but offers the ideological fundament for its establishment. At the same time, he cautions contemporary political powers to be mindful (and fearful) of the inherent power of art to articulate the future tenets of German society. Poetry and the poet are celebrated as creators of gods and therefore as the essential cultural institutions for the creation of social reality.

The narrator's journey ends in Hamburg, a road that has witnessed the denaturalization and naturalization of civic myths. Indeed, the road is not at its end, but in the development of the New Generation myth, the poem offers the ideological groundwork from which to continue the edification of a new age. The narrator's path has been accompanied by satire, irony, and a fair amount of laughter. This attitude has effected the formulation of ideas which may be able to realize human happiness. Indeed, laughter proved a powerful weapon, and with a final nod to Aristophanes and the ancient tradition to confront the powers that be with a smile, *Wintermärchen* ends with the insistence on the political power of literature.

6. Conclusion
The Rewriting of Foundations

> It eluded us then, but that's no matter—
> tomorrow we will run faster,
> stretch our arms farther.
> FITZGERALD/THE GREAT GATSBY

After Gatsby's death, Nick Caraway celebrates his friend's "extraordinary gift for hope" (TGG 6). Looking over the bay that separates East and West Egg, he reminds the reader of the "green light" which inspired the American upstart all his life (20). At the same time, Caraway remembers the first "Dutch sailors" who beheld a "new world" from the deck of their ships dreaming of a new beginning, this "last and greatest of all human dreams" (140). This dream is redeemed at the end of *The Great Gatsby* (1925), and the failure of Gatsby's "romantic readiness" is attributed to the "rotten crowd" that inhabits the age (6, 120).

By evoking the Dutch settlers who first beheld the island of Manhattan, Fitzgerald ties the hopes and dreams of his 20th century generation to the beginnings of the nation. This study has examined the recurrence of 19th century authors to foundational myths, and the authors' mythological resignifications share one significant aspect with Fitzgerald's celebrated novel: They end their narratives by directing the nation towards hope. Heine foresees the rise of an "authentic generation" and warns political powers to be heedful of the *Zeitgeist* (GWT 95); Brown levers an Atlantic call for abolition and sees the "Year of jubilee" approaching (CL 208); Gutzkow puts his faith in humanity and its ability to always know "the best course" (WTS 112); and finally, Hawthorne ends *The Scarlet Letter* with "one ever-glowing point of light" (SL 166).

Indeed, these authors share Gatsby's "extraordinary gift for hope" (TGG 6). They hope that the transformation and adaptation of myth will result in democratic change. Yes, mythological resignification is a strategy which seeks to influence the present, but in doing so it is always concerned with the future also. I will conclude this study by contrasting the resignifications, comment on similarities and differences regarding ideas of time and revolution, and elucidate on political literature and its construction of nationality through myth.

American and German Resignifications

The mythological resignification in *The Scarlet Letter* attempts to bring the Puritan myth into the 19th century. Hawthorne was aware that a civic myth based on a theocratic polity would never suffice to inspire compromise and balance in the fractured Antebellum. Thus, a more pluralistically minded set of forefathers needed to be positioned next to the "black flower" of Puritan civilization (SL 36). Hawthorne denaturalizes the basic Puritan myth by means of historical critique, refutes its inherent Sin-as-Sign mytheme, and designs an alternative set of ancestors. These ancestors are dissenters, women and men who champion the values of sympathy, mercy, and pluralism in a theocratic system. By focusing on those who resisted Puritanism, Hawthorne is able to adapt the basic myth to the 19th century in form a variant.

The Order of Roses myth still champions Puritans; but it tells of the sacrifices entailed in the balancing of societal and private concerns and of the possibilities that accompany the breaking of law. The new Sin-as-Possibility mytheme amends the radical justice of the Puritan settlers and achieves an equilibrium which allows for democratic development. By casting Ann Hutchinson, William Blackstone, and Hester Prynne as dissenting ancestors, the novel offers an alternative history which changes the foundations of the nation and repositions its identity towards a more democratic outlook.

Simultaneously, Pearl Prynne becomes the Sin-as-Possibility mytheme made flesh, an American Eve representative of a nation made of the elements of justice and mercy, law and nature. Thus, *The Scarlet Letter* suggests a national identity which Bercovitch has correctly summarized as the "both/and" perspective, an "identity built on fragmentation and dissent" (Office 9, Assent 29f). The Order of Roses myth describes an identity constituted by dissent, self-reliance, individual authenticity, and the possibility to include diversity. Puritan forefathers *and* those who resisted them are imagined as the founders of the American nation.

Like Hawthorne, Brown turns to the Puritan myth to reinterpret the American genesis. Indeed, he imagines the settlers as the epitome of Christian humanism: The Puritan fathers become unconquerable rebels, divinely sanctioned harbingers of god's kingdom. The mythological resignification in Brown's novel strictly adheres to one of the basic meanings of the Puritan myth: Freedom-through-Voyage. It constructs the North as the space of freedom, while the South is cast as the realm of despotism. His denaturalization of the basic myth, however, is different from Hawthorne. *Clotel* does not denaturalize the Puritan myth *per se* but rather denaturalizes its Antebellum interpretation. Brown's resignification opts for a *return* to the myth's original signification. The stories in *Clotel* tell of a nation that has turned from its foundational principles.

Thus, Brown's characters re-enact the Puritan voyage, flee spaces of slavery, and seek liberty on new shores. While William is able to find freedom in Canada, Clotel's journey ends in suicide. Her death is a jeremiad, an apocalyptic call to abolish slavery and return to the tenets of the Puritan errand. The Newer Shores myth tells of black Puritans, who reverse the original voyage, are forced to flee the U.S., and find freedom in Canada and Europe. At the same time, the variant adds a new hero-protagonist to the basic myth: The fugitives are cast as American heroes homologous to the Puritan fathers, rebels motivated by a sense of inherent liberty who seek to realize their freedom by resistance and voyage. Brown's resignification works towards the inclusion of the black subject into the structures of the Puritan myth; it does not elaborate a new mytheme but casts the fugitive as heir to the errand.

The same holds for his resignification of the Revolution myth. Again, it does not elaborate a new mytheme but stays true to the idea of Freedom-through-Resistance. In George, another slave character is naturalized into civic identity structures: He parallels the struggles of insurgent slaves with the rise of American revolutionary forces. Resistance to slavery is thus imagined as the continuation of the Revolutionary fathers' struggle, and by extension, as a result of the original dissent of the Puritan settlers. The Ongoing Revolution myth assents to the basic myth but once again refutes its Antebellum interpretation. The novel criticizes the inability to read resistance against slavery in the light of revolutionary values; this inability causes the black subject to reverse the Puritan voyage. Nevertheless, the resignification adds a black Revolutionary to the basic myth and thus broadens American identity.

Clotel's mythological resignification effects an opening of identity categories and the subsequent inclusion of the enslaved subject. By identifying fugitive and insurgent slaves as Puritans and Revolutionaries, the black subject becomes heir to the founding fathers. Both variant myths effect a universalization of identity categories and include the enslaved individual. In doing so, the novel celebrates love of freedom, self-reliance, dissent, and resistance as constitutive to American identity.

Gutzkow does not share Brown's conservative approach. Instead of treating his basic myth affirmatively, he denaturalizes it completely. *Wally, die Zweiflerin* employs a resignification that transcends even Hawthorne's critical treatment of the Puritan myth. *Wally* denaturalizes the Sigune myth, produces a new mytheme, and constructs a variant which refutes the myth's medieval tenets in their entirety. Here, Gutzkow's main concern is to reveal the incompatibility of medieval values with the Vormärz. He unfolds his critical treatment of myth by preparing the resignification with a detailed elaboration of the Falcon myth, a narrative concerned with courtly love and romantic possession. Then, a scene from the Sigune myth is re-enacted by the main protagonist, whose performance clashes with the realities of the time. Indeed, the romance between Wally and Cäsar is central to the resignification process: Their inability to form a happy relationship is rooted in their reliance on overcome love rituals. This inability calls for an age-adequate myth, for the novel suggests that the protagonists' enactment of medieval norms results in an artificial, inauthentic life.

Especially Wally is unable to establish a free identity because of her dependence on the Love-is-Consolation mytheme. She is equated with Sigune, and by extension, with the function of the prophetic valkyrie. The text designs Wally as prophetess, and her despair and suicide function as jeremiad: It is in Wally that Gutzkow exemplifies the consequences of relying on the past to construct a modern identity. Cäsar, on the other hand, functions as the protagonist of the variant. In his marriage to Delphine, the skeptic elaborates the Love-is-Choice mytheme, thus separating the tenets of love from societal concern and pushing for a primacy of individuality. The variant, the Inner Poems myth, relies on the construction of political, cultural, and subjective reality by means of the elaboration of inner and personal motivations.

The variant myth in *Wally* rejects medieval values, societal restrictions, and champions the subjective creation of social and personal categories. Thus, Gutzkow suggests a primacy of individuality and experimentation for the construction of German nationality. Instead of recurring to Germanic myths, the novel urges the adoption of a creative strategy to construct reality. The edification of personal and societal freedom is to be achieved by relying on inner, subjective truth.

Like Brown, Heine employs two basic myths to effect his mythological resignification. *Deutschland. Ein Wintermärchen* denaturalizes civic myths which concern religious and political salvation. His poem is exceptional in the fact that its resignification is intimately connected to the narrator, whose journey produces the variant. In Cologne, the narrator denaturalizes the ascetic tenets of Christianity in the Three Magi myth. By destroying the bones of the prophets of Epiphany, the narrator adopts his own prophetic function. Indeed, he is imagined as the prophet who, like the magi, foretells the rise of a new religion of freedom. The Coming-of-the-King mytheme is thus superseded by a new meaning: Coming-of-Freedom.

This new meaning is also employed in the poem's resignification of the Barbarossa myth. While the Three Magi myth tells of the coming of a religious messiah, the Barbarossa myth envisions the return of a political savior. Its Return-of-the-King mytheme imagines the rise of Kaiser Friedrich I, whose return would entail the reunification of Germany under imperial conditions. The prophetic narrator, however, denaturalizes Barbarossa's claim by revealing his incompatibility with Vormärz realities. Thus, the rise of a political messiah for Germany is rendered mute, and the narrator proceeds to Hamburg, where he will articulate a new prophecy.

In his dialogues with the goddess Hammonia, the narrator replaces the messianic-eschatological element of the basic myths with a prophetic-eschatological perspective on the future of Germany. By insisting on a new materialistic and individualistic religion of freedom, he foretells the coming of the King-in-rags, the rise of popular sovereignty. The New Generation myth tells of a new age of material bliss and individual primacy. In this manner, the narrator supersedes the basic myths' religious and political prophecies and offers his own: the rise of individuality and material-subjective enjoyment. Germany is to refute monarchic modes of government, attain popular sovereignty in the democratic King-in-rags, and develop a national identity based on individual freedom, subjective enjoyment, and a historically authentic existence.

Mythological Resignifications Contrasted

The authors' resignifications of myth are diverse. Hawthorne and Gutzkow employ one basic myth, while Heine and Brown recur to two; the texts in Part II focus on personal, individual sovereignty (which may free the nation), while the works analyzed in Part I rather situate the free individual in a national context (which disallows or allows for individual freedom); all except Brown treat myth critically, whereas *Clotel* entails an affirmative treatment of myth; while the American texts use the same myth (the Puritan myth), the German texts are more heterogeneous in their choice of basic mythologies. However, all texts share one endeavor: the transformation of mythological meaning.

Indeed, it is the use of the resignification strategy itself which constitutes an element of transatlantic literary connectivity, a connectivity which may be read as an instance of transculturation, i.e. the "Americanization of European culture and, vice versa, the Europeanization of American culture" (Fluck 1). However, this specific transculturation lacks moments of directional influence: The recurrence to and resignification of myth in the 19th century was not only a European phenomenon but simultaneously an American.

If we regard the theoretical concept of mythological resignification, it becomes clear that all texts employ the resignification strategy while differing in its execution. *The Scarlet Letter* and *Wintermärchen*, for instance, construct images which foreshadow both basic and variant myths (Ia & IIa). *Wally*, on the other hand, does not prepare for its variant. It prepares only for its basic myth in an extensive preparation phase. *Clotel*, similarly, prepares for the Puritan and Revolution myth but does not prepare for the variants. Be that as it may, differences in preparation do not entail significant consequences for the quality of the resignification; they are stylistic choices. Yet style does not account for other differences, especially differences in the process of denaturalization.

While the texts concur in their expositions of the basic myths (Ib), they differ in their form of denaturalization (Ic). Indeed, it is always the insistence on the basic myth's *contemporary inadequacy* which pervades and legitimizes the denaturalization processes. All except *Clotel* use historical critique to denaturalize the basic myth.

Brown's novel is the only text which employs an affirmative treatment of myth. Instead of criticizing the myths themselves, he criticizes their Antebellum interpretation. In fact, his exposition and denaturalization heightens the mythological legitimacy of the Puritan and Revolution myth; especially the Puritan settlers undergo an increased sacralization and are elevated to divine emissaries and founders of god's kingdom. Brown therefore advocates a return to what is imagined as the true foundation of the American polity. In *Clotel*, moments of historical critique are levered against Antebellum misinterpretations of foundational values, misinterpretations that render the U.S. a despotic polity *despite* its Puritan beginnings. Thus, a return to Puritan values is imagined as the cure for the national *status quo*.

It is this affirmative treatment of basic myths which precludes a mythemic elaboration in the novel. The reason for this deviation lies in Brown's political intention: *Clotel* does not work towards a denaturalization of the basic myths *per se* but attempts the inclusion of the black subject into the myths' existent identity structures. He seeks to broaden – not refute – the myths and thus mutes the process of mythemic elaboration.

Mythemic elaboration (IIb) is the core element of mythological resignification. The appropriation, transformation, and reinstallation of myth functions primarily by molding the myth's core meaning; this process renders a new mytheme which nevertheless stands in an organic relationship to the old one. All texts, except *Clotel*, evidence this process: The *Scarlet Letter* produces the Sin-as-Possibility mytheme by reinterpreting Sin-as-Sign; *Wally* renders Love-is-Choice on the basis of the Love-is-Consolation mytheme; *Wintermärchen* transforms the Coming-of-the-King and the Return-of-the-King and constructs the Coming-of-Freedom mytheme. But with or without mythemic elaboration, all four works produce variant myths so as to renegotiate the tenets of national identity.

While authors differ regarding mythemic elaboration, the naturalization of a variant (IIc) occurs in all four works. At the same time, there is a significant difference in the *extent* of naturalization, and it is the first difference which appears to be conditioned along national lines. It is here, in the assessment of underlying conceptualizations and ideologies, where I wish to elaborate on the comparative results of this analysis. German and American authors used mythological resignification; but there exist significant differences in the resignification process, which are rooted in diverging conceptual stances with regard to time and revolution. These differences are most evident in the processes of variant naturalization (IIc). American texts offer a detailed naturalization of their variants, whereas German works remain vague in their naturalization effort. All texts produce a variant myth, and all texts suggest tenets for the construction of national identity. But the nature of their construction differs: *The Scarlet Letter* and *Clotel* are more detailed and therefore more restricted in their variants, whereas *Wintermärchen* and *Wally* offer a more open and unrestricted perspective.

Ideas of Time

This difference can be explained by examining the underlying presuppositions regarding time and history in the texts. I have mentioned that constructions of nationality in the U.S. and Germany adhere to Hegelian notions:[1] The nation is imagined as a spiritual phenomenon (*Volksgeist*), and history is understood as a progressive and linear process of development. However, organicist elements are found especially in Hawthorne, Brown, and Heine's resignification of myth. The American texts, indeed, espouse a much stronger organic perspective, while the German texts rely more strongly on the idea of historical progress.[2]

In a national context, historical organicism is constituted by two elements: vegetative growth and chronological circularity. The first imagines history to grow naturally and gradually, a deterministic development conditioned by the nation's foundational moment. In organic terms, this means that a nation's development is restricted to its genesis: It grows like a plant from its seeds. The second element, on the other hand, is concerned with the cyclic recurrence of history: Time progresses in repetitive cycles of birth and decay. This progression is also deterministic and precludes intervention in the natural advance of time.

---

1   cf. Chapter 1.
2   While this is true for the present texts, the separation of linear and cyclic time is complicated when comparing Heine and Hawthorne, especially with regard to *The House of the Seven Gables* (1851). In this novel, Hawthorne unifies teleological and organic time, a *unio tempora* which approaches Heine's general time conceptualization. For Heine, past, present, and future come together in the present moment (*wyrd*); yet while generally supporting progress, Heine imagines that cyclic time can occur in moments of transition. Heine thus combines teleology and organicism to explain historical development and revolutions. In a similar way, linear and cyclic time are synthesized into an "ascending spiral curve" by Hawthorne (HSG 183). Organicism and progress are combined to represent the course of human history as well as history as actually lived by individuals. Heine constructs a similar combination when he situates revolution in the context of life itself. For more see Al-Shalabi: *Nathaniel Hawthorne's Conception of Time in* The House of the Seven Gables in *Cross-Cultural Communications* Vol.7.4 (2011).

Teleology, in contrast, presupposes a linear development. It entails the ever-ongoing progress of time which allows for intervention and change. In a Hegelian sense, it also includes a dialectic of reaction and progress which influences the chronological flow of history. The latter is imagined as the continuous progress and enlargement of freedom, a perspective which enables human agency and revolutionary intervention.

Myth in *The Scarlet Letter* is deeply informed by an organic perspective. Hawthorne was unable to conceive the development of a democratic polity from theocratic foundations; his novel therefore examines the *roots* of Antebellum democracy and designs an alternative line of descend which can better explain (and sustain) a modern democratic nation. Hester's prophecy is one of *gradual* development towards freedom and equality, a "brighter period, when the world should have grown ripe for it, in Heaven's own time" (SL 166). But in fact, Hawthorne complicates the clear-cut distinction between teleology and organicism and combines the teleological progress of freedom with organic elements; he imagines the progression of freedom in organic, vegetative terms. However, the novel dominantly adheres to an organic perspective, especially to the element of natural growth.

Brown also recurs to organicism in *Clotel* but focuses more on the cyclic element. Instead of critically examining Puritan foundations, he designs his characters as re-emerging representatives of the values, voyages, and revolutions of the American past. In constructing black Puritans and Revolutionaries, the novel imagines the re-establishment of the American idea, a cyclic repetition of the revolutionary impetus in the Antebellum. Indeed, the Ongoing Revolution myth and the New Shores myth adhere to the idea of a cyclic, repetitive emergence of the original Puritan dissent which re-establishes the idea of America, a notion which Bercovitch describes as a "continuing revolution" and the very "condition of progress" (Revolution 609). This progress is imagined as a cyclic recurrence of the revolutionary impulse inside American culture itself.

Interestingly, Heine's poem also includes organic elements despite the fact that it is generally devoted to teleology. *Wintermärchen* refutes its basic myths because they are imagined as mythological baggage of times past; in a teleological flow of history, these overcome elements have no significance for the present moment. At the same time, the narrator-poet is situated in cyclic time: On the one hand, he is the teleological prophet of a new age of freedom who comes to end the era of Christianity and monarchy; on the other, he supersedes the prophetic function of the Three Magi, thus representing the beginning of a new cycle of repetitive history. In organic terms, he ends Germany's 'winter' by foretelling the coming of 'spring.' Indeed, Heine generally opposed organicism, but he did not presuppose an absolute teleology of history: Historical development could recur to cyclic forms in times of crisis such as the Vormärz (Höhn 179). For Heine and Hawthorne, a progressive perspective does not exclude the organic and *vice versa*.

Gutzkow is the only author who completely rejects organicism (Kaiser 197). In line with his Young German colleagues, this author decried organic determinism and championed the potential of human agency in the course of historical development. Indeed, it is not in a simplistic, reciprocal exclusion, but in the complex *tension* between teleological and organic history that we may account for the difference between American and German constructions of variant myths. The detailed and consequently restricted character of the Order of Roses myth, the New Shores myth, and the Ongoing Revolution myth is the result of the belief in recurring cycles of historical development. Hawthorne's perspective can foretell America's future in a much more detailed way because the nation's development is imagined to function organically: Mercy and justice, the black flower and the rose-bush, the Puritan fathers and the Puritan dissenters offer the constitutive elements that necessitate a specific (democratic) future. Hester's free sphere at Boston's margins presents the 'seed' of civil society which enforces the 'growth' of a pluralistic, balanced, and finally democratic polity. Similarly, the trajectory of Brown's characters is 'rooted' in the original Puritan voyage and Revolutionary resistance. As organic re-enactors of historical events, the modern dissenters repeat history yet simultaneously enlarge the nation's freedom in a teleological sense. The nation's future is therefore restricted to two possibilities: Either a return to Northern (read Puritan) freedom or a despotic development under Southern slavery. Organicism narrows the imagination of future possibilities because progress functions in the cyclic repetition of past; but it also allows for a more detailed elaboration of the variant myth, because it repeats already known histories in the present moment.

German variant myths do not follow this dominantly organic logic. Devoted rather to the idea of progress and insisting on the supersession of the past and by the present, the Inner Poems myth and the New Generation myth refrain from exact elaborations of the future. Because of the belief in the teleological enlargement of freedom, no further details for the future can, and indeed, should be elaborated. This is why Gutzkow abstains from giving precise political instructions in *Wally*. The Inner Poems myth simply elaborates a primacy of individuality which functions as the constitution of the future's general direction; but for the details of Germany's national development, Gutzkow counsels experimentation. Similarly, Heine's New Generation myth tells of a German future based on the principles of the new religion of freedom. But the question as to how such a future is to be attained remains unanswered. The German texts construct open and consequently vague variant mythologies; they suggest the ideological foundations of the future German nation without describing specific details. Their teleological perspective does not allow for specificity, because a detailed variant would necessarily restrict developmental possibilities. Indeed, mythological resignification in the American texts is conditioned by a "process of revision, not replacement" (Assent 36), whereas the German variant myths replace more than they revise.

Concepts of Revolution

But while American and German resignifications differ in their perspectives on time and history, they largely concur in their approach to revolution. Bercovitch is correct in claiming that Hawthorne adopts a "Romantic organicism," rejects interventionism, and hopes for a gradual (because organically natural) historical development (Office 41). *Clotel*'s George, similarly, organically incorporates the American Revolution in the Antebellum situation. In this context, Bercovitch grounds his claim of American exceptionalism in the idea that the American notion of revolution constitutes a "controlling metaphor" which enables each generation to continue the Puritan errand in a "continuing revolution." The American people become a "people in transition" who celebrate revolution as an "indefinitely self-renewing rite of passage." This impetus never creates an actual violent uprising yet functions as an affirmation of order (Revolution 608f). But Europe, Bercovitch claims, enacts revolution as a "Promethean self-assertion," an individualistic and egotistical revolt against "paternal gods" (609) which bears the "dialectic of historical change" (Jeremiad 160). Indeed, this study's results contest Bercovitch's "transatlantic contrast" in matters of revolution (Office 35).

Yes, Heine and Gutzkow's dissenting characters work in the dialectic of historical change: They promote becoming revolutionary "agents of Necessity" and bear Promethean elements of individual self-assertion (Office 41). Cäsar is a self-centered conqueror who elaborates a variant myth which celebrates individual primacy; Heine's narrator-poet is explicitly identified with the Titan Prometheus and furthers a materialistic ideology centered on the individual. Additionally, the German authors supported forms of interventionism which assumed a Hegelian dialectic of past and present, reaction and progress. But the contrast between American and German conceptualizations is not as clear-cut as Bercovitch would have it. The German authors' teleological perspective is nevertheless informed by organicist elements which suggest a revolutionary ideology very similar to Hawthorne and Brown's.

Heine and Gutzkow *included* organicism in their teleological perspective, but they did so with a specific turn on its deterministic elements. This turn is rooted in the imagination of Germany's historical backwardness: Here, intervention and revolution do not present an unnatural interference in historical development but are a *Naturgesetz*, a principle of nature in times of transition. Eke notes that the Vormärz *status quo* was imagined as an unnatural and historically inauthentic era; so as to return the nation to an age-adequate state, revolution was regarded as natural and necessary, as the realization of a "historical process identified with the *Weltgeist*" (22). Heine and Gutzkow, and their works, become agents of such a natural and necessary revolution.

Indeed, the German revolution is conceptualized as an instrument of *re-affirming order*, albeit a new order. Along these lines, Kaiser notes that Gutzkow supported intervention and held that literature needed to be revolutionary so as to construct a *stable* state of society (197). This author opted for a creative approach towards reality and history, an approach which needed to be understood as a "revolutionary" endeavor (WTS 111). Heine's elaborations on the matter also define revolution as a natural phenomenon, an inherent principle of life itself: Life is a "right" which seeks to "assert itself" against death and the past. This "assertion," Heine claims, "is the revolution" (in Oheler 29). Revolution is imagined as a natural necessity rooted and legitimized in life's ongoing self-assertion, both on an individual and societal level.

Indeed, Heine and Gutzkow's idea of revolution is universal and defined as the furthering of emancipation (Mende 90). Like Hawthorne, Heine mistrusted violent uprisings and believed in gradual development; but this development required *agency*. This may be the crux in contrasting American and German ideas of revolution: Heine and Gutzkow insist that natural, gradual development requires proactive human intervention. While *The Scarlet Letter* trusts in heavens own time, *Wintermärchen* and *Wally* call for individual agency, because nature and life requires the activity of the living. Heine's poem exemplifies this agency in the wandering narrator, who refutes myths of the past so as to foretell an age of individuality. Similarly, *Wally*'s Cäsar actively creates his own reality by dissenting from societal norms and thereby offers an exemplification of individual sovereignty. Their dissent is subjective – even Promethean and Luciferian – but it is a dissent which has societal consequences and aims at the re-establishment of order and stability.

Here, Vormärz Germans, like Antebellum Americans, become a "people in transition" who celebrate revolution as a "self-renewing rite of passage" (Revolution 608f). The only difference is that the German revolution is not indefinite; its transitional (organic) moment is embedded in a normalized (teleological) flow of time and informed by the dialectic of reaction and progress. But Heine and Gutzkow's revolution is not disruptive, but understood as inherent to historical development. Yes, Heine's teleological time concept allowed for organicism in moments of transitional crisis; but these cyclic instances were imagined as times of historical acceleration, were time and space move faster than in normalized time (Eke 21). Indeed, this acceleration legitimizes revolution organically: It compresses vegetative development in the historical moment.

In this context, the German revolution approaches Bercovitch's idea of the on-going American Revolution. In Germany, too, revolution was understood as a natural phenomenon, a necessary and perpetual historical element for the creation of order. Revolution does not unnaturally upset history but presents a normalized instrument in historical moments of transition. Indeed, it is not a Promethean act of self-assertion in Bercovitch's sense. It is rather based on the idea that in the

Vormärz situation, revolution needs to stem from the constitutive elements that make the nation: the individuals. Individual emancipation thus gradually leads to societal, and lastly, to universal emancipation.

Further, Bercovitch errs in his claim the Hawthorne's approach to revolution denies agency (Office 41). *The Scarlet Letter*, while trusting in heaven's own time, does not do so blindly or passively. Yes, Hester adopts a seasoned dissent in her eventual return to Boston, but Colacurcio is correct when he states that her dissent remains active. She is still a "visionary" motivated by individual agency and self-affirmation (310f). Hawthorne certainly calls for a reasonable approach towards revolutionary impulses, but he does not suggest that "our best recourse is to let it be" (Office 41).

In Hawthorne, Heine, and Gutzkow, Bercovitch's historical "laissez-faire" and "transatlantic contrast" fail to establish a clear-cut difference between America and Germany (Office 41, 35). While differing in their dominants and legitimations, American and German conceptualizations of revolution find themselves at diverging but complementary positions in the tension between teleology and organismic. The German revolution, too, is a constructive and order-affirming event and perfectly embedded in the teleological (and organic) progression of history. Simultaneously, Hawthorne and Brown's revolutionary characters are also represented as "agents of Necessity," albeit less radical ones (41).

National Naturalization and Belonging

As a result of this study's comparative analysis, an idea which heavily informs American exceptionalism needs to be reconsidered: the possibility of national naturalization by means of ideological assent. Bercovitch holds that American identity – in contrast to European identities – is not restricted by ethnic or genealogical concerns but presents an ideology. One can "learn" to be an American: The "Un-American" can be naturalized into national belonging by assenting to the fundamental values of the nation (democracy and capitalism). The moment they "fulfill (rather than undermine) the American dream," aspirant citizens would "become sons and daughters of the American Revolution," thereby effecting an "enlargement of consensus" over time (Jeremiad 160) Indeed, Brown and Hawthorne's novels contest this idea, and they do so in characters who reverse the Puritan voyage and return to Europe.

In *Clotel*, George attempts an enlargement of consensus and fails. His insurgent actions seek to fulfill the conditions of the American idea; he thus joins, in theory, the ranks of the Revolutionary fathers because of his adherence to the Freedom-through-Resistance mytheme. He is nevertheless refused access to the "pantheon of Revolutionary heroes" (Jeremiad 160). Indeed, George fulfills the ideological prerequisites of American identity but is denied naturalization because of an ethnic (read racist) bias. He even adheres to the Freedom-through-Voyage mytheme but is forced to reverse the Puritan voyage and find freedom in Europe. In the case of George, American nationality seems to betray the fact that it is not only an ideology, at least not one that grants inclusion without ethnic discrimination. This circumstance motivates George's reversal of the Puritan voyage, a reversal which is also evident in *The Scarlet Letter*.

Pearl leaves Boston, reverses the Puritan voyage, and chooses a life in Europe. Like George, she is imagined as an American, even more so, as the *first* American. Boston, however, does not seem to be ready for the "elf-child" (SL 115), just as Washington D.C. is not ready for George, the "unacknowledged prodigal son" (Wilson 51). Yes, Hawthorne and Brown imagine American identity as divorced from geography and ethnicity; it is presented as a set of values which make the American individual. Further, the universalization of the errand in both novels suggests American identity to be ideological rather than ethnical or genealogical. But *The Scarlet Letter* reminds us that, paradoxically, the U.S. does not always suffer the American to remain in America. Similarly, *Clotel* reveals the fact that assenting to American values is not sufficient for belonging, and that genealogical and ethnic considerations are in fact relevant. Whether or not Bercovitch's enlargement of consensus holds for the 20th and 21st century is a question I cannot answer in this context. However, it is safe to say that it does not hold for the tenets of American identity as elaborated in Hawthorne and Brown's texts. Yes, American identity is primarily an ideological construct, but it includes ethnical and genealogical elements.

The same holds for Heine and Gutzkow: They negotiate a German identity which is largely ideological. I do not seek to contest the idea that European nations based their categories of belonging on ancestry; but I must highlight the fact that Heine and Gutzkow completely disregard elements of ethnicity and genealogy and define a *cosmopolitan* identity for the German Vormärz. Eke notes that these early forms of nationalism present an "emancipatory ideology," and the authors' identity negotiations occur in this ideological context (24). In *Wally*, Cäsar represents a new German who rejects the cultural restrictions of the past and embraces individual primacy and sovereignty. Gutzkow holds that the tenets of national identity are to be negotiated by means of experimentation, not by tradition or ancestry. Also, Delphine's Jewish background is never discussed in ethnical but exclusively in religious terms. Indeed, her religious neutrality, her parent's liberality, and Cäsar's indifference to her ethnicity further highlight the centrality of values and beliefs – rather than the importance of a family tree – for German belonging. Finally, Cäsar's insistence on self-reliance, dissent, and individuality, as well as Gutzkow's elaborations in *Wahrheit und Wirklichkeit*, describe a German identity that is almost Emersonian.

Gutzkow's male protagonist evokes the imperial individual Emerson describes in *Self-Reliance*: Cäsar is the "center of all things" and "measures you, and all things, and all events" (Emerson 126). This German nonconformist believes in his "own thought" (121), and his arguments have the "edge" which for Emerson defines an American's subjective and true relation to society (123). Even in his inconsistency of opinion he evokes the "great soul" who has "simply nothing to do" with consistency (125). Cäsar foreshadows Gutzkow's elaborations in *Wahrheit und Wirklichkeit*, where the Young German author, like Emerson, will celebrate the reliance on the inner, subjective self. Here, the novel offers the foil for a German identity which concurs with the Emersonian idea of the American.

Heine's elaborations in this context also inform on the ideological nature of German nationality. Not only is any discussion of ethnicity or genealogy completely absent from *Wintermärchen*; belonging is represented as intimately connected to the narrator's private history. He belongs because he was born in Germany, not because he is of German descent, and he remains German despite his exile. Further, the poet misses his *Heimat* [Home] rather than his *Vaterland* [Fatherland], an emotion which is conceptualized as deeply private. National identity is separated from political and geographical circumstance and imagined as a subjective category based on lived experience. The most crucial instance, however, is given in the poem's preface: German identity is defined as a cosmopolitan, humanist, and emancipatory construct. Heine's "patriotism" is constituted by "the height of German thought" and the dream of a "free humanity" (VWM vf).

Indeed, German identity in *Wintermärchen* and *Wally* is as much an ideological construct as its American counterpart. Yes, Kaul is correct in noting that an originally ideological definition of German identity would be superseded by a focus on ethnicity at the end of the 19th century (764). Indeed, this turn is in the making during the Vormärz, but it has not yet ultimately restricted the categories of German belonging, especially not in Heine and Gutzkow's works. However, the preface to *Wintermärchen* elaborates on another aspect of German identity negotiations which parallels one of the most central notions of Antebellum America: Manifest Destiny.

Manifest Destinies

The idea of America's Manifest Destiny finds a parallel in Heine's elaboration of a German mission. Osterhammel notes that the while "the civilizing mission of the United States used to come under the label of a 'manifest destiny,'" Germany, too, knew its very own *"Zivilisierungsmission."* Generally, such a civilizing mission is based on "a firm conviction of the inherent superiority and higher legitimacy of one's own collective way of life." This conviction is expressed in a "comprehensive *Sendungsbewusstsein*, a general propensity to universalize the Self" (7f).

In the preface to *Wintermärchen*, Heine describes such a German Manifest Destiny. He defines the global enlargement of freedom as a distinctly German assignment and bases it on the qualities of German philosophy. Heine constructs a cosmopolitan identity for Germany, one which defies the narrow categorizations of ethnical belonging; it rather subsumes German identity under the tenets of idealism and humanism. This approach credits German culture with the elaboration and subsequent realization of German, European, and ultimately global freedom. Indeed, an ideological imperialism is at work here, one which other Vormärz authors employed in a similar manner. In *Briefwechsel zweier Deutschen* (1831), Pfizer describes the "rather exceptional nation"[3] that is the German. This nation, he claims, conquered Rome, developed the root of all representational systems, and began the battle for "spiritual freedom"[4] with the Reformation (BZD 161f). Pfizer, like Heine, recurs to the "will of fate"[5] and imagines German unification as the beginning of a new era of freedom (233). He holds that Germans are "consecrated to be cosmopolitans" and destined to preach the "evangelism of humanism"[6] to the entire world (163).

In fact, Heine's Manifest Destiny follows the same lines. Hohendahl notes that Heine seeks to adapt Germany's "idealistic heritage"[7] to the Vormärz situation. As a result, *Wintermärchen* endeavors to transform a traditional "cosmopolitan humanism"[8] into a new "patriotic sense of citizenship[9]" (227). Its mythological resignification celebrates the "utopia of an ideal Germany,"[10] a nation dedicated to the principles of freedom: "For Heine, the real Germany was […] a country of the Enlightenment, of cosmopolitanism, of human brotherhood, a country which was to be an example of philosophical and cultural progress" (Scheuer 271).[11] This perspective on nation and national identity eschews ethnicity and genealogy but is indeed deeply ideological.

Thus, Heine and Gutzkow's variant myths contest the notion that German identity was imagined solely as an aboriginal, organic, and historical category (Plessner

---

3   [ganz außerordentliche Nation].
4   [geistige Freiheit].
5   [Wille des Schicksals].
6   [zu Kosmopoliten geweiht; Evangelium der Humanität].
7   [Das idealistische Erbe].
8   [der kosmopolitische Humanismus].
9   [patriotische Bürgerlichkeit].
10 [Utopie eines idealen Deutschland].
11 [Das wahre Deutschland war für Heine […] ein Land der Aufklärung, des Kosmopolitismus, der Menschenverbrüderung, das anderen Ländern ein Vorbild an philosophischer und kultureller Fortschrittlichkeit sein sollte].

48). Yes, at the end of the century, an ethno-genealogical would have trumped an ideological definition of nationality; but the Vormärz was still in the process of negotiation, and Heine and Gutzkow's texts evidence the fact that an ideological German identity was an intricate part of this process. However, the imperialist idea of a *Deutsche Sendung*[12] [German Mission] is as evident in *Wintermärchen* as is the idea of Manifest Destiny in the American novels. American and German conceptualizations of national identity in the present texts, however distinct and different they may be, entail the idea of an emancipatory, democratizing, and humanist mission, whether it be granted by a divine errand or necessitated by philosophical avant-gardism. America and Germany both claim the role of civilizatory (and imperialist) leadership in an age of the universal enlargement of freedom and thus, indeed, seek to "universalize the [national] Self" (Osterhammel 8).

Only Gutzkow refrains from elaborating a Manifest Destiny. He allocates his primacy of political experimentation in a general humanist belief in mankind. This author claims that mankind has "inner resources" which enable it to know "the best course to take" (WTS 112). He positions Germany *inside* the general development of humanity rather than assigning it an exemplary or exceptional role. Only Gutzkow does not offer a national exceptionalism in his mythological resignification.

All other texts, however, imagine their respective nation as both: exceptional and destined. The American variants concur with Lipset's notions of the American Creed and the U.S. as the first new nation (19); they engage in the discourses of the divine errand, the American way, and the imperial spread of democracy by god's newly chosen people. Similarly, Heine's resignification elaborates on Germany's cosmopolitan nature, its philosophical and cultural uniqueness, and a specifically German errand: the emancipation of humanity. As a consequence, these texts offer the construction of national exceptionalisms and imperial Manifest Destinies.

Political Literature and National Identity Building

To be sure, the reason for this is not found in mythological resignification *per se* but in the nature of its ultimate product: national identity. A national identity needs to set itself apart from other identities, is always exclusivist, and must perforce aim at a contrastive exceptionalism.[13] Hawthorne contrasts the U.S. with Europe; Brown

---

12 For an overview on the idea of civilizatory missions in Europe, see Osterhammel: *Europe, the 'West' and the Civilizing Mission* (2006).

13 It does not, however, need to be hierarchical in its identity constructions. The elaboration of difference and the claim of superiority present two notions which need to be thought separately in order to avoid terminological and analytical confusion. Osterhammel notes that the notion of civilization can present an "asymmetric counterconcept," i.e. "a concept

constructs a despotic Southern identity so as to successfully elaborate on what he deems to be the true (Northern) character of America. Heine, similarly, attacks Prussian and religious representations so as to elucidate on a humanist, material, and secular German identity; lastly, Gutzkow decries German social and religious institutions which adhere to medieval values. We may like it or not, but contrastive discrimination is a *sine qua non* for the elaboration of national identity.

Hegel notes that *nation* exists in peoples who are conscious of themselves (Perperzak 513). But this consciousness is not so much produced by introspection but by the *conscious-making* of difference. Indeed, the production of nationality in the 19th century relies on the imagination of natural characteristics, but this imagination rarely occurs in a self-restricted manner. The nation requires an *Other* to be self-conscious. This cognitive process, however, is influenced by the manner in which identity is negotiated. One way is the recurrence to emotion and affect, the imagination of identity governed by the affirmative treatment of constructed notions. Hinderer notes that this strategy, generally, is propagandistic: It relies on texts that agitate, shock, and move the reader emotionally (20). Indeed, political literature which aims at the construction of national identity can follow one of two strategies: It can manipulate and agitate, or it can inform and convince (27). Mythological resignification as presented in this study follows the second strategy. In a rhetorical context, all four texts employ an explicative and argumentative approach to install their ideological content.

Despite the fact that the variant myths once again "distort" history (Barthes 121), the process of mythological resignification champions a rational rhetoric. This is due to the fact that the very act of denaturalizing myth needs to be legitimized; this legitimization is offered by means of historical critique. A new, age-adequate myth is based on the denaturalization of the traditional narrative, yet instead of simply refuting a basic myth on emotional grounds, the texts critically examine it, employ critique, and encourage reflection and re-assessment of its meaning. If we follow Hinderer's definition of political rhetoric, mythological resignification adheres to the tenets of explicative-argumentative speech: It aims at creating the pos-

---

in need of a less-valued opposite" (Koselleck in Osterhammel 7). But national identity, in contrast to the term civilization, belongs to a more "universal" category, a concept which is "specific and culture-bound" but at the same time "translatable and suited to mutual recognition" (6). Indeed, national identity can become an asymmetrical counterconcept, but its construction must not necessarily be restricted to this one result. Heine's idea of the German mission employs an asymmetrical approach, while Gutzkow is decisively universal in his construction of national identity. The categories of exceptionality and asymmetry must indeed be treated separately.

sibility of reader-reflection and discourages (or decreases) an emotional response (29).

The fact that mythological resignification follows a rational rhetoric allows for the construction of a democratic (because reader-centered) variant myth. The variant is constructed in such a way that the reader is included in the resignification process; the ultimate power to decide between a basic and a variant myth lies with the reader. Therefore, if the text seeks to disseminate ideas, the reader must be presented with the necessary interpretative tools. The adoption of the proposed ideological content is based on the didactical and critical endeavor to convince. Hawthorne, Heine, Brown, and Gutzkow employ historical critique, rational conviction, and argumentative input so as to further their political intentions.

Even Brown's affirmative treatment of myth follows a rational approach. Yes, many passages in *Clotel* aim at the creation of sympathy on the basis of affective identification. However, its mythological resignification seeks to convince the reader of the inclusion of the black subject into American identity categories. Here is a didactical approach which rests on the homology between Puritan/Revolutionary fathers and fugitive/insurgent slaves. Brown follows the logic of the myths themselves and argues rationally for the broadening of American national identity. The lack of historical critique[14] with regard to the Puritan myth does not change the fact that the novel's overall rhetoric is argumentative and explicative. It explains the mythological tenets of the myths and argues for a more democratic, inclusive reading of traditional narratives.

Yes, national identity building through myth generally aims at the construction of exceptionalism, and it does so by means of contrast and discrimination. But in the case of mythological resignification, the function of political literature to produce nationality is accompanied by a communication process based on a pragmatic and argumentative rhetoric. In contrast to propaganda, mythological resignification is a rational strategy which includes the reader and is ultimately depended on them for the acceptance and dissemination of ideological content. Myth, indeed, is neither historical nor democratic, but for the sake of democratization, the authors' resignification processes endeavor to be as rational as possible.

I have used the term democratization in its most general sense throughout this study. Indeed, we cannot and should not apply 21st century standards to 19th century situations. However, the mythological resignification in all four texts aims at the expansion, improvement, and/or installation of democratic values by means of literature. Brown's variant myths call for the inclusion of a vast part of the American

---

14 Also, we should not forget that while the Puritan fathers are not treated critically, Jefferson and the Revolutionary fathers undergo a process of critical denaturalization which functions as an argument for a whole-hearted enactment of foundational principles.

population into identity categories, and Hawthorne opts for mercy, sympathy, and pluralism as fundamental values for the appeasing of conflict. Heine champions the ambrosian rights of the population in calling for a materialistic outlook on societal organization, and Gutzkow refutes feudalistic norms and pushes for the primacy of the individual. Indeed, the socio-political interest which pervades all four works does not necessarily result in exact policies; these authors were neither politicians nor policy consultants. They rather elaborate and expand the democratic *principle*, open restricted categories for participation, value the dignity of the individual, and elevate dissent as the driving force for the edification of a democratic future.

It is the idea of futures which informs mythological resignification in the American and German works. Mythological resignification must necessarily look to the past, but the resignification process occurs for the sake of the present. Regardless of whether we adopt a teleological or organic view on time, none of these authors are fatalistic in their perspective on the future. Gutzkow's Poetics of Life, Heine's recurrence to the notion of *wyrd*, Hawthorne's insistence on agency, and Brown's Atlantic calls for intervention all suggest that the future can be changed in the work on the present. Indeed, any attempt to transform civic myths would be rendered mute if it were not motivated by the belief that the present moment offers the possibility for improvement—not only for this but for the generations to come.

Myth Today

If we consider the literary endeavors of 19th century authors to consolidate their polities by means of myth, we must attest that mythological resignification failed to peacefully consolidate Germany and the U.S. But the cultural effects of such literature must not be underestimated. The Puritan and Revolution myth continue to inform American national identity, especially, I would argue, in their variant forms. Hawthorne's critical perspective on the Puritan myth has prevailed, and Brown's call for the incorporation of the black subject into American belonging certainly furthered the Abolitionist movement. Similarly, Heine and Gutzkow's works are part of a body of literature which provides Germany with a democratic tradition preceding the Weimar Republic. The events of 1848/49 were indispensable for the country's democratic development, and I hold that the literature that accompanied and supported these events likewise remains indispensable for a democratic German identity. However, one should not be misled to believe that literary dissent is sufficient: Political literature is but one form of the complex sphere of public communication we call civil society, a sphere which is the very center of "normative integration" and the "primary locus for the potential expansion of democracy" (Cohen and Arato ix, viii). Literature is an active and necessary agent in that civil locus, but it takes more than novels and poems to establish and safeguard democracy. They are nevertheless an intricate and significant part of the process.

Moreover, if we follow Hornung and aim at "Transcultural learning" (in this case, transhistorical transcultural learning), we may remember the fact that both American and German authors primarily seek to establish, promote, and expand the democratic principle itself (in Fluck et al. 2). In a modern context, expanding the democratic principle means re-positioning political institutions and political culture towards democratic values. Like the authors in this study, I argue that solving America and Europe's problems requires more, not less, democracy. A new American, German, or European novel may be helpful to reconstruct a democratic identity under contemporary circumstances, especially in the long run. But the U.S. and the E.U. will not be able to overcome their inner divisions if their political cultures do not adopt what Heine, Gutzkow, Brown, and Hawthorne championed throughout their works: constructive hope.

For when Wienbarg and Choate called on literature to elaborate the tenets of the nation, they did so from a position of hope. Hawthorne, Gutzkow, Brown, and Heine took that hope seriously. They let themselves be borne into the past, appropriated, transformed, and re-installed civic myths so as to democratize the very foundations of the nation. These writers were aware that the past must be considered in the imagination of the future, and they adopted an optimistic perspective which allowed them to construct variant myths to re-position their communities towards hope.

Fitzgerald was right when he ended *The Great Gatsby* by claiming that whenever we steer towards the future, we are "borne back ceaselessly into the past." Ancient and modern myth is able to make sense of the chaos that is time and history: It can emancipate from the powers that be, realize human sovereignty, and finally help us to overcome the temptation of despair and continuously set our "boats against the currents" (TGG 141). Myth can make us more hopeful persons and enable us to comprehend that, in the end, the horizon will not swallow us after all.

Works Cited

Anderson, Benedict. *Imagined Communities: Reflections on the Origin and Spread of Nationalism*. Revised edition. London: Verso, 2006.
Andrews, William L. *To Tell a Free Story: The First Century of Afro-American Autobiography, 1760-1865*. Urbana: University of Illinois Press, 1986.
Archer, Jermaine O. *Antebellum Slave Narratives: Cultural and Political Expressions of Africa*. New York: Routledge, 2009.
Baisch, Martin. "Der 'Jüngere Titurel' zwischen Didaxe und Verwilderung: Neue Beiträge zu einem schwierigen Werk." *Aventiuren* Vol. 6. Göttingen: V&R Unipress, 2010.
Barthes, Roland. *Mythologies*. New York: Hill and Wang, 1972.
Baum, L. Frank, and W. W. Denslow. *The Wonderful Wizard of Oz*. New York: Signet Classics, 2006.
Becks, Leonie. "Der Schrein der Heiligen Drei Könige im Kölner Dom. Nikolaus von Verdun und die Goldschmiedekunst des frühen 13. Jahrhunderts." *Caspar - Melchior - Balthasar: 850 Jahre Verehrung der Heiligen Drei Könige im Kölner Dom*. Matthias Deml, Leonie Becks, Klaus Hardering, eds. Köln: Kölner Dom Verlag, 2014.
Becks, Leonie, Matthias Deml, Klaus Hardering, eds. *Caspar - Melchior - Balthasar: 850 Jahre Verehrung der Heiligen Drei Könige im Kölner Dom*. Köln: Kölner Dom Verlag, 2014.
Bercovitch, Sacvan. *American Jeremiad*. Madison: U of Wisconsin Press, 2012.
---. "How the Puritans won the American Revolution." *The Massachusetts Review* 17.4 (1976).
---. *The Office of the Scarlet Letter*. London: John Hopkins UP, 1991.
Blumenberg, Hans. *Arbeit Am Mythos*. Frankfurt am Main: Suhrkamp, 1979.
---. *Work on Myth*. Cambridge: MIT Press, 1988.
Boudreau, Kristin. "Hawthorne's Model of Christian Charity." *Nathaniel Hawthorne: The Scarlet Letter and Other Writings*. Leland S. Person, ed. New York: Norton, 2005.

Boyer, Paul S., ed. *The Oxford Companion to United States History*. Oxford: Oxford UP, 2001.

Braunagel, Robert. *Wolframs Sigune: Eine vergleichende Betrachtung der Sigune-Figur und ihrer Ausarbeitung im 'Parzival' und 'Titurel' des Wolfram von Eschenbach*. Göppingen: Kümmerle, 1999.

Brown, William Wells. *Clotel or, the President's Daughter*. 10th edition. New York: Penguin Books, 2004.

---. *The Anti-Slavery Harp: A Collection of Songs for Anti-Slavery Meetings*. Boston: B. Marsh, 1848.

---. *Clotel, or, the President's Daughter: A Narrative of Slave Life in the United States*. Robert S. Levine, ed. Second edition. Boston: Bedford/St. Martin's, 2011.

Bunyan, John. *The Pilgrim's Progress: An Authoritative Text, Contexts, Criticism*. Cynthia Wall, ed. New York: Norton, 2009.

Campbell, Joseph, Bill D. Moyers, and Betty S. Flowers. *The Power of Myth*. First Anchor Books Edition. New York: Anchor Books, 1991.

Choate, Rufus. *Adresses and Orations of Rufus Choate*. Sixth edition. Boston: Little, Brown, and Company, 1891.

Cohen, Jean, and Andrew Arato. *Civil Society and Political Theory*. London: MIT Press, 1992.

Colacurcio, Michael J. "Footsteps of Ann Hutchinson: The Context of The Scarlet Letter." *Nathaniel Hawthorne: The Scarlet Letter and Other Writings*. Leland S. Person, ed. New York: Norton, 2005.

Denkler, Horst. "Zwischen Julirevolution (1830) und Märzrevolution (1848/49)." *Geschichte der politischen Lyrik in Deutschland*. Walter Hinderer, ed. Würzburg: Königshausen & Neumann, 2007.

Eke, Norbert. *Einführung in die Literatur des Vormärz*. Darmstadt: Wissenschaftliche Buchgesellschaft, 2005.

Elias, Norbert and John L. Scotson. *Etablierte und Außenseiter*. München: Suhrkamp, 1990.

Emerson, Ralph Waldo. *Emerson's Prose and Poetry: Authoritative Texts, Contexts, Criticsm*. Joel Porte and Saundra Morris, eds. New York: Norton, 2001.

---. *Poems*. New York: Alfred A. Knopf, 2004.

Farrison, William Edward. *William Wells Brown: Author and Reformer*. Chicago: U of Chicago Press, 1969.

Fitzgerald, Francis Scott. *The Great Gatsby*. The Cambridge Edition of the Works of F. Scott Fitzgerald. Matthew Joseph Bruccoli, ed. Cambridge: Cambridge UP, 1991.

Flavell, M. Kay. "Women and Individualism: A Re-Examination of Schlegel's Lucinde and Gutzkow's Wally, die Zweiflerin." *The Modern Language Review* Vol. 70.3 (1975).

Fluck, Winfried, ed. *Transnational American Studies*. Tübingen: Narr, 2007.
Fludernik, Monika. *An Introduction to Narratology*. London: Routledge, 2009.
Frenzel, Elisabeth, and Sybille Grammetbauer. *Stoffe der Weltliteratur: Ein Lexikon dichtungsgeschichtlicher Längsschnitte*. Stuttgart: Kröner, 2005.
George, Andrew, ed. *The Epic of Gilgamesh: The Babylonian Epic Poem and Other Texts in Akkadian and Sumerian*. New York: Penguin Books, 2003.
Gould, Philip. "Early Black Atlantic Writing and the Cultures of Enlightement." *Beyond Douglass: New Perspectives on Early African-American Literature*. Michael J. Drexler and Ed White, eds. Lewisburg: Bucknell UP, 2008.
Grimm, Jacob. *Deutsche Mythologie*. Second edition. Göttingen: Dieterich, 1844.
Guerber, Helene A. *Myths of the Norsemen from the Eddas and Sagas*. London: George G. Harrap, 1909.
Gutzkow, Karl. "Die Beigaben der Ausgabe von 1852." *Karl Gutzkow: Wally, die Zweiflerin. Studienausgabe mit Dokumenten zum zeitgenössichen Literaturstreit*. Günter Heintz, ed. Stuttgart: Philipp Reclam, 1983.
---. *Wally, die Zweiflerin. Studienausgabe mit Dokumenten zum zeitgenössichen Literaturstreit*. Günter Heintz, ed. Stuttgart: Philipp Reclam, 1983.
---. *Wally, die Zweiflerin/Wally the Sceptic*. Ruth-Ellen Boetcher-Joeres, ed. and trans. Bern: Herbert Lang, 1974.
Habermas, Jürgen. "Geist und Macht: Ein deutsches Thema. Heinrich Heine und die Rolle des Intellektuellen in Deutschland." *Das Junge Deutschland: Kolloquium zum 150. Jahrestags des Verbots vom 10. Dezember 1835*. Joseph A. Kurse and Bernd Kortländer, eds. Hamburg: Hoffmann und Campe, 1987.
Hamilton, Edith. *Mythology*. New York: Back Bay Books, 2013.
Hartnett, Stephen John. *Democratic Dissent and the Cultural Fictions of Antebellum America*. Chicago: U of Illinois Press, 2002.
Hawthorne, Nathaniel. *The House of the Seven Gables: Authoritative Text, Contexts, Criticism*. Robert S. Levine, ed. New York: Norton, 2006.
---. "Mrs. Hutchinson." *Nathaniel Hawthorne: The Scarlet Letter and Other Writings*. Leland S. Person, ed. New York: Norton, 2005.
---. "Young Goodman Brown." *Nathaniel Hawthorne: The Scarlet Letter and Other Writings*. Leland S. Person, ed. New York: Norton, 2005.
---. *The Scarlet Letter and Other Writings: Authoritative Texts, Contexts, Criticism*. Leland S. Person, ed. New York: Norton, 2005.
Hegel, G.W.F. *Vorlesungen über die Philosophie der Geschichte*. Frankfurt am Main: Suhrkamp, 2015.
Heine, Heinrich. *Deutschland. A Winter's Tale*. T. J. Reed, ed and trans. London: Angel Books, 1986.
---. *Deutschland. Ein Wintermährchen*. Joseph Kiermeier-Debre, ed. Bibliothek der Erstausgaben. München: DTV, 2008
---. "Die Göttin Diana." *Heinrich Heine's Sämtliche Werke*. Vol. V. Philadelphia: Schäfer & Koradi, 1867.

---. "Elementargeister." *Heinrich Heine's Sämtliche Werke.* Vol. V. Philadelphia: Schäfer & Koradi, 1867.

---. "Vorwort zur Separatausgabe des Wintermärchens." *Heinrich Heine's Sämtliche Werke.* Vol. IV. Philadelphia: John Weick, 1855.

Heintz, Günter, ed. *Karl Gutzkow: Wally, die Zweiflerin. Roman. Studienausgabe mit Dokumenten zum zeitgenössischen Literaturstreit.* Stuttgart: Reclam, 1979.

Hermand, Jost. "Der 'Deutsche' Jude H. Heine." *Dichter und ihre Nation.* Helmut Scheuer, ed. Frankfurt am Main: Suhrkamp, 1993.

Hesiod. *Homeric Hymns and Homerica.* Trans. Hugh G. Evelyn-White. Loeb Classical Library. [Greek Authors, 57]. London: MacMillan, 1914.

Hinderer, Walter. "Versuch über Begriff und Theorie politischer Lyrik." *Geschichte der Politischen Lyrik in Deutschland.* Walter Hinderer, ed. Würzburg: Königshausen & Neumann, 2007.

Hohendahl, Peter Uwe. "Vom Nachmärz bis zur Reichsgründung." *Geschichte der Politischen Lyrik in Deutschland.* Walter Hinderer, ed. Würzburg: Königshausen & Neumann, 2007..

Höhn, Gerhard. "Blutrosen der Freiheit: Heinrich Heines Geschichtsdenken." *Heinrich Heine: Ästhetisch-Politische Profile.* Gerhard Höhn, ed. Frankfurt am Main: Suhrkamp, 1991.

Holub, Robert C. "Heine als Mythologe." *Heinrich Heine: Ästhetisch-Politische Profile.* Gerhard Höhn, ed. Frankfurt am Main: Suhrkamp, 1991.

Horrocks, David. "Maskulines Erzählen und feminine Furcht: Gutzkows Wally, die Zweiflerin." *Karl Gutzkow: Liberalismus, Europäertum, Modernität.* Roger Jones and Martina Lauster, eds. Bielefeld: Aithesis, 2000.

Jaacks, Gisela. "Hermann, Barbarossa, Germania und Hammonia: Nationalsymbole in Hamburger Festzügen des Kaiserreichs." *Beiträge zur deutschen Volks- und Altertumskunde* Vol. 18 (1979).

Jay, Paul. *Global Matters: The Transnational Turn in Literary Studies.* Cornell Paperbacks. Ithaca, NY: Cornell UP, 2010.

Jones, Roger and Martina Lauster. *Karl Gutzkow: Liberalismus, Europäertum, Modernität.* Vormärz-Studien Vol. 6. Bielefeld: Aisthesis, 2000.

Kaiser, Herbert. "Karl Gutzkow: Wally, die Zweiflerin (1835)." *Romane und Erzählungen zwischen Romantik und Realismus: Neue Interpretationen.* Paul M. Lützeler, ed. Stuttgart: Reclam, 1983.

Karlsen, Carol F. *The Devil in the Shape of a Woman: Witchcraft in Colonial New England.* New York: Norton, 1998.

Kaul, Camilla G. *Friedrich Barbarossa im Kyffhäuser (Textband).* Köln: Böhlau, 2007.

Kavanagh, Richard. "Gutzkow und die Schauerromantik." *Karl Gutzkow: Liberalismus, Europäertum, Modernität.* Vormärz-Studien Vol. 6. Roger Jones and Martina Lauster, eds. Bielefeld: Aisthesis Verlag, 2000.

Kieckhefer, Richard. *Magic in the Middle Ages.* New York: Cambridge UP, 2000.

Kiermeier-Debre, Joseph. "Nachwort zu Deutschland. Ein Wintermährchen." *Heinrich Heine: Deutschland. Ein Wintermährchen*. Joseph Kiermeier-Debre, ed. München: DTV, 2008.

KJV. *The KJV Study Bible*. Red Letter Edition. Urichsville, OH: Barbour Publishing, 2011.

Klaits, Joseph. *Servants of Satan: The Age of the Witch Hunts*. Bloomington: Indiana UP, 1985.

Kortländer, Bernd. "'... als wollte die Zeit sich selbst vernichten:' Zum Begriff der Zeit bei Heine." *Was die Zeit fühlt und denkt und bedarf: Die Welt des 19. Jahrhunderts im Werk Heinrich Heines*. Bernd Kortländer, ed. Vormärz-Studien Vol. 32. Bielefeld: Aisthesis Verlag, 2014.

Koschorreck, Walter, ed. *Codex Manesse: Die Grosse Heidelberger Liederhandschrift. Vollständiges Faksimile des Codex Palatinus Germanicus 848 der Universitätsbibliothek Heidelberg*. Frankfurt am Main: Insel, 1979.

Kragl, Florian. "Klarifunkel. Oder: Warum beim Jüngeren Titurel der Teufel nicht im Detail steckt." *Der 'Jüngere Titurel' zwischen Didaxe und Verwilderung: Neue Beiträge zu einem schwierigen Werk*. Johannes Keller, Martin Baisch, Florian Kragl, Matthias Meyer, eds. Göttingen: V&A Unipress, 2010.

Krüger, Bruno. *Die Germanen: Mythos, Geschichte, Kultur, Archäologie*. Beiträge zur Ur- und Frühgeschichte Mitteleuropas Vol. 29. Weissbach: Beier & Beran, 2003.

Kruse, Joseph A. *Heinrich Heine: Leben Werk Wirkung*. Frankfurt am Main: Suhrkamp, 2005.

Kruse, Joseph A., and Bernd Kortländer, eds. *Das Junge Deutschland: Kolloquium zum 150. Jahrestag des Verbots vom 10. Dezember 1835*. Hamburg: Hoffmann und Campe, 1987.

Kruse, Jospeh A., Christian Liedtke, Marianne Tilch, eds. *Heinrich Heine: Deutschland. Ein Wintermährchen. Text und Kommentar*. Berlin: Suhrkamp, 2010.

Kurscheidt, Georg, ed. *Friedrich Schiller: Sämtliche Gedichte und Balladen*. Berlin: Insel, 2013.

Landau, Brent. *Revelation of the Magi: The Lost Tale of the Wise Men's Journey to Bethlehem*. New York: HarperOne, 2010.

Laude, Patrick. *Divine Play, Sacred Laughter, and Spiritual Understanding*. New York: Palgrave Macmillan, 2005.

Lauster, Martina. "Gutzkows Modernebegriff als Grundlage seines institutionskritischen Liberalismus." *Karl Gutzkow - Liberalismus - Europäertum - Modernität*. Martina Lauster and Roger Jones, eds. Bielefeld: Aisthesis Verlag, 2000.

Leitzmann, Albert. "Untersuchungen über Wolframs Titurel." *Beiträge zur Geschichte der deutschen Sprache und Literatur* Vol. 26. Eduard Sievers, ed. Halle: M. Niemeyer, 1901.

Lévi-Strauss, Claude. "The Structural Study of Myth." *The Journal of American Folklore* Vol. 68 (1955).

Levine, Robert S. "Monuments and Careers: Teaching William Wells Brown, Martin Delany, and their Contemporaries." *Beyond Douglass: New Perspectives on Early African American Literature*. Michael J Drexler and Ed White, eds. Lewisburg: Bucknell UP, 2008.

Lind, Louise. *William Blackstone: Sage of the Wilderness*. Bowie, MD.: Heritage Books, 1993.

Lipset, Seymour Martin. *American Exceptionalism: A Double-Edged Sword*. New York: Norton, 1997.

Male, Roy R., Jr. "From the Innermost Germ: The Organic Principle in Hawthorne's Fiction." *ELH* Vol. 20.3 (1953).

Mende, Fritz. "Heinrich Heine, Sohn der Revolution." *Heinrich Heine: Ästhetisch-Politische Profile*. Gehard Höhn, ed. Frankfurt am Main: Suhrkamp, 1991.

Meyer, Elard Hugo. *Germanische Mythologie*. Mayer & Müller, 1891.

Milton, John. *Paradise Lost*. John Leonard, ed. New York: Penguin Books, 2011.

Morford, Mark and Robert Lenardon. *Classical Mythology*. 7th edition. New York: Oxford UP, 2003.

Müller, Willhem. *Die Winterreise und Die Schöne Müllerin*. Zürich: Diogenes, 1991.

Newberry, Frederick. "A Red-Hot A and a Lusting Divine: Sources for the Scarlet Letter." *Nathaniel Hawthorne: The Scarlet Letter and Other Writings*. Leland S. Person, ed. New York: Norton, 2005.

O'Brien, Susie and Imre Szeman. *Popular Cullture: A User's Guide*. Scarborough: Thomson Nelson, 2004.

Oepen, Joachim. "Die Translation der Heiligen Drei Könige." *Caspar - Melchior - Balthasar: 850 Jahre Verehrung der Heiligen Drei Könige im Kölner Dom*. Matthias Deml Leonie Becks, Klaus Hardering, eds. Köln: Kölner Dom Verlag, 2014.

Oheler, Dolf. "Die Prosa nimmt mich auf in ihre weiten Arme." *Heinrich Heine: Poesie und Politik*. Jospeh A. Kruse, ed. München: Carl Hanser, 1997.

Osterhammel, Jürgen. *Europe, the 'West' and the Civilizing Mission*. Annual Lecture / German Historical Institute. London: German Historical Institute, 2006.

Pennington, James W.C. *The Fugitive Blacksmith, or Events in the History of James W.C. Pennington*. London: Charles Gilpin, 1849.

Peperzak, Adriaan Theodoor. *Modern Freedom: Hegel's Legal, Moral, and Political Philosophy*. Dordrecht: Kluwer, 2001.

Pfizer, Paul Alasius. *Briefwechsel zweier Deutschen*. Stuttgart: Gottasche Buchhandlung, 1831.

Plessner, Helmuth. *Die verspätete Nation: Über die politische Verführbarkeit bürgerlichen Geistes*. Second edition. Stuttgart: Kohlhammer, 1959.

Pooley, Roger. "The Pilgrim's Progress and the Line of Allegory." *The Cambridge Companion to Bunyan*. Anne Dunan-Page, ed. Cambridge: Cambridge UP, 2010.

Rabbow, Arnold. *DTV Lexikon der Politischen Symbole*. München: DTV, 1970.

Reed, T.J. "Introduction and Notes." *Heinrich Heine: Deutschland. A Winter's Tale*. T.J. Reed, trans. London: Angel Books, 1986.

Reinecke, Heinrich. "Die Schutzpatrone der Stadt Hamburg." *Hamburger Geschichtliche Beiträge: Festschrift Hans Nirrnheim*. Heinrich Reinecke, ed. Hamburg: Boysen & Maasch, 1935.

Rödger, Ralf, ed. *Der Kyffhäuser: Ein Gebirge, ein Berg, eine Burg, ein Denkmal*. Regensburg: Schnell & Steiner, 2013.

Ryskamp, Charles. "The New England Sources of the Scarlet Letter." *Nathaniel Hawthorne: The Scarlet Letter and Other Writings*. Leland S. Person, ed. New York: Norton, 2005.

Sanford, Ezekiel. *The Humours of Eutopia: A Tale of Colonial Times*. Philadelphia: Carey, Lea & Carey, 1828.

Schachner, Nathan. *The Founding Fathers*. New York: Putnam, 1954.

Schaer, Frank, ed. *The Three Kings of Cologne: Edited from London, Lambeth Palace Ms 491*. Heidelberg: Winter, 2000.

Schäfke, Werner. "Angerührt. Angerührtzettel und Pilgerzeichen: Sehen, Begreifen und Bezeugen." *Caspar - Melchior - Balthasar: 850 Jahre Verehrung der Heiligen Drei Könige im Kölner Dom*. Matthias Deml Leonie Becks, Klaus Hardering, eds. Köln: Kölner Dom Verlag, 2014.

Scheuer, Helmut, ed. *Dichter und Ihre Nation*. Frankfurt am Main: Suhrkamp, 1993.

Schmidt, Hans Jörg. *Die Deutsche Freiheit: Geschichte eines kollektiven semantischen Sonderbewusstseins*. Frankfurt am Main: Humanities Online, 2010.

Schmidt, Manfred G. *Wörterbuch zur Politik*. Third Edition. Stuttgart: Alfred Kröner, 2010.

Schmitt, Carl and G. L. Ulmen. *The Nomos of the Earth in the International Law of the Jus Publicum Europaeum*. New York: Telos Press, 2003.

Schmitter, Elke. "Und Grüß mich nicht unter den Linden." *Heinrich Heine: Poesie und Politik*. Jospeh A. Kruse, ed. München: Carl Hanser, 1997.

Schneider, Christian. "Historie und Reichsmystik: Kyffhäuser und Trifels." *Erinnerungsorte - Erinnerungsbrüche*. Frank Meier and Ralf H. Schneider, eds.. Ostfildern: Jan Thorbecke Verlag, 2013.

Schocket, Andrew M. *Fighting over the Founders: How we remember the American Revolution*. New York: New York UP, 2015.

Simpson, J. A., E. S. C. Weiner, and Donna Lee. *The Compact Oxford English Dictionary: Complete Text Reproduced Micrographically*. Second Edition. New York: Oxford UP, 1991.

Spalding, Johann. "200 Jahre Reden über die Religion." *Akten des 1. Internationalen Kongresses der Schleiermacher-Gesellschaft*. Ulrich Barth und Claus-Dieter Osthövener, eds. Boston: de Gruyter, 2011.

Speller, John R.W. *Bourdieu and Literature*. Cambridge: Open Books Publishers, 2011.

Steinecke, Hartmut. "Romantheorien der Restaurationsperiode." *Romane und Erzählungen zwischen Romantik und Realismus*. Paul M. Lützeler, ed. Stuttgart: Reclam, 1983.

Stowe, Harriet Beecher. *Uncle Tom's Cabin*. Elizabeth Ammons, ed. Second Edition. New York: Norton, 2010.

Taylor, William Robert. *Cavalier and Yankee: The Old South and American National Character*. Cambridge, MA: Harvard UP, 1979.

Thiele, Ulrich. *Die politischen Ideen: Von der Antike bis zur Gegenwart*. Wiesbaden: Marix Verlag, 2008.

Thomas, Brook. "Citizen Hester: The Scarlet Letter as Civic Myth." *American Literary History* Vol. 13.2 (2001).

Trier, Jost. "Zaun und Mannring." *bgsl* Vol. 66 (1942).

Tuleja, Tad, ed. *Usable Pasts: Traditions and Group Expressions in North America*. Logan: Utah State UP, 1997.

Vries, Eric De. *Hedge Rider*. Sunland, CA: Pendraig Publishing, 2008.

Wabnegger, Erwin. *Literaturskandal: Studien zur Reaktion des öffentlichen Systems auf Karl Gutzkows Wally, die Zweiflerin (1835-1848)*. Würzburg: Königshausen und Neumann, 1987.

Wall, Robert Emmet. *Massachusetts Bay: The Crucial Decade, 1640-1650*. New Haven: Yale UP, 1972.

Wapnewski, Peter. "Dichtergott: Heinrich Heine und die Tradition seiner Schöpfungsgedichte." *Wirkendes Wort: Deutsche Sprache und Literatur in der Forschung* Vol. 53 (2003).

---. *Waz ist Minne: Studien zur mittelhochdeutschen Lyrik*. München: Beck, 1975.

Wapnewski, Peter, and Ewald M. Vetter. *Minnesänger: Codex Manesse (Palatinus Germanicus 848): Eine Auswahl aus der Grossen Heidelberger Liederhandschrift*. Genf: Ricci & Weber, 1982.

Wehler, Hans-Ulrich. *Das deutsche Kaiserreich: 1871-1918*. Göttingen: Vandenhoeck & Ruprecht, 1973.

---. "Gegen die Dynastien." *Die Erfindung der Deutschen*. Klaus Wiegrefe and Dietmar Pieper, eds. München: Deutsche Verlags-Anstalt, 2007.

Wehrli, Max. *Geschichte der deutschen Literatur im Mittelalter: Von den Anfängen bis zum Ende des 16. Jahrhunderts*. Third edition. Stuttgart: Reclam, 1997.

Weil, Bernd. *Das Falkenlied des Kürenbergers: Interpretationsmethoden am Beispiel eines mittelhochdeutschen Textes*. Frankfurt am Main: R.G. Fischer, 1985.

Weinauer, Ellen. "Considering Posession in The Scarlet Letter." *Nathaniel Hawthorne: The Scarlet Letter and Other Writings*. Leland S. Person, ed. New York: Norton, 2005.

Weinfurter, Stefan. *Das Reich im Mittelalter: Kleine deutsche Geschichte von 500 bis 1500*. Second edition. München: Beck, 2011.

Werner, Michael. "Nationen und Imperien: Zu Heines Sicht auf die Konzeptionen und Praktiken der politischen Organisationsformen im Europa des 19. Jahrhunderts." *Was die Zeit fühlt und denkt und bedarf: Die Welt des 19. Jahrhunderts im Werk Heinrich Heines*. Bernd Kortländer, ed. Bielefeld: Aisthesis Verlag, 2014.

Westermann-Angerhausen, Hiltrud, ed. *Die Heiligen Drei Könige*. Köln: Greven, 1996.

Whaley, Joachim. *Germany and the Holy Roman Empire*. Oxford: Oxford UP, 2012.

Wienbarg, Ludolf. *Aesthetische Feldzüge*. Hamburg: Hoffmann & Campe, 1834.

Wilson, Ivy G. *Specters of Democracy: Blackness and the Aesthetics of Politics in the Antebellum U.S*. New York: Oxford UP, 2011.

Wilson, Peter H. *The Holy Roman Empire, 1495-1806*. New York: Macmillan Press, 1999.

Winkler, Heinrich August. *Deutsche Geschichte vom Ende des alten Reiches bis zum Untergang der Weimarer Republik*. München: Beck, 2000.

Winship, Michael. "Hawthorne and the 'Scribling Women:' Publishing the Scarlet Letter in the Nineteenth-Century United States." *Nathaniel Hawthorne: The Scarlet Letter and Other Writings*. Leland S. Person, ed. New York: Norton, 2005.

Wiwjorra, Ingo. *Der Germanenmythos: Konstruktion einer Weltanschauung in der Altertumsforschung des 19. Jahrhunderts*. Darmstadt: Wissenschaftliche Buchgesellschaft, 2006.

Zeller, Rosemarie. "'Diese Verhüllung ist das reizende Gegenteil dessen, was sie scheint.' Verhülltes und Enthülltes in Gutzkows Wally, die Zweiflerin." *Verbergendes Enthüllen: Zu Theorie und Kunst dichterischen Verkleidens*. Wolfram M. Fues and Wolfram Mauser, eds. Würzburg: Königshausen und Neumann, 1995.